GPU Pro 360

Guide to GPGPU

GPU Pro 360

Guide to GPGPU

Edited by Wolfgang Engel

CRC Press
Taylor & Francis Group
Boca Raton London New York

CRC Press is an imprint of the
Taylor & Francis Group, an **informa** business

AN A K PETERS BOOK

CRC Press
Taylor & Francis Group
6000 Broken Sound Parkway NW, Suite 300
Boca Raton, FL 33487-2742

International Standard Book Number-13: 978-1-138-48439-9 (Paperback)
International Standard Book Number-13: 978-1-138-48441-2 (Hardback)

Library of Congress Cataloging-in-Publication Data

Names: Engel, Wolfgang F., editor.
Title: GPU pro 360 guide to GPGPU / [edited by] Wolfgang Engel.
Description: First edition. | Boca Raton, FL : CRC Press/Taylor & Francis Group, 2018. | Includes bibliographical references and index.
Identifiers: LCCN 2018020469| ISBN 9781138484399 (pbk. : acid-free paper) |
   ISBN 9781138484412 (hardback : acid-free paper)
Subjects: LCSH: Computer graphics. | Graphics processing units--Programming.
Classification: LCC T385 .G68878 2018 | DDC 006.6--dc23
LC record available at https://lccn.loc.gov/2018020469

Visit the eResources: www.crcpress.com/9781138484399

Visit the Taylor & Francis Web site at
http://www.taylorandfrancis.com

and the CRC Press Web site at
http://www.crcpress.com

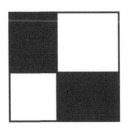

Contents

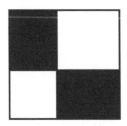

Introduction

Today, the use of GPGPU is prevalent in most modern architectures. With the parallel nature of the GPU, any algorithm that can process data in parallel can generally run orders of magnitudes faster than their CPU counterparts. Therefore it makes sense to take advantage of this power, considering that suitable hardware can now be found on most common hardware configurations. This book will cover chapters that present techniques that go beyond the normal pixel and triangle scope of GPUs and take advantage of the parallelism of modern graphic processors to accomplish such tasks.

In the first chapter, "2D Distance Field Generation with the GPU," Philip Rideout presents a simple and effective technique to generate distance fields from an image using the OpenCL API. Distance fields have many applications in image processing, real-time rendering, and path-finding algorithms. A distance field is a grayscale bitmap in which each pixel's intensity represents the distance to the nearest contour line in a source image. Rideout explains how such distance fields can be efficiently generated on the GPU and also provides a few examples of how the resulting distance fields can be used in practical applications.

In the next chapter, "Order-Independent Transparency Using Per-Pixel Linked Lists" by Nicolas Thibieroz, a technique is presented that takes advantage of unordered access views to generate a dynamic link list, which can in turn be used to render order-independent translucency. By storing translucent pixels in such a list, they can be sorted as an after process and therefore properly render translucencies regardless of their order.

The third chapter, "Simple and Fast Fluids" by Martin Guay, Fabrice Colin, and Richard Egli, presents a new algorithm that can be used to solve fluid simulations efficiently using compute APIs on the GPU. The chapter details how the fluid solver works, discusses boundary conditions for single phase flows, and provides a few examples of how such solvers can be used in practical scenarios.

In "A Fast Poisson Solver for OpenCL Using Multigrid Methods" by Sebastien Noury, Samuel Boivin, and Olivier Le Maître, a novel technique is presented to allow the solving of Poisson partial differential equations using OpenCL. The resolution of Poisson partial differential equations is often needed to solve many techniques in computer graphics, such as fluid dynamics or the merging and deformation of complex meshes. This chapter focuses on the presentation of an algorithm that allows for the efficient implementation of a Poisson solver using the GPU.

"Volumetric Transparency with Per-Pixel Fragment Lists" by László Szécsi, Pál Barta, and Balázs Kovács, presents an efficient approach to rendering multiple layers of translucency by harnessing the power of compute shaders. By implementing a simple ray-tracing approach in a computational shader, they can determine the appropriate color intensity for simple particles. The approach can then be taken further and extended to even account for visual effects such as refraction and volumetric shadows.

In the next chapter, "Practical Binary Surface and Solid Voxelization with Direct3D 11" by Michael Schwarz, a new real-time voxelization technique is presented. This technique is efficient and tackles some of the problems, such as voxel holes, that occur in rasterization-based voxelization algorithms. The resulting voxels can then be used in the application of a variety of techniques such as collision detection, ambient occlusion, and even real-time global illumination.

In "Interactive Ray Tracing Using the Compute Shader in DirectX 11" by Arturo García, Francisco Ávila, Sergio Murguía, and Leo Reyes, a novel technique is presented to allow for real-time interactive ray tracing using a combination of the GPU and CPU processing power. This implementation properly handles glossy reflections as global illumination. An efficient bounding volume hierarchy is also offered to accelerate the discovery of ray intersections.

"Bit-Trail Traversal for Stackless LBVH on DirectCompute," by Sergio Murguía, Francisco Àvila, Leo Reyes, and Arturo García, describes an improvement to existing stackless bounding volume hierarchy (BVH) methods that enables the fast construction of the structure while maintaining traversal performance sufficient for real-time ray tracing. The algorithm can be used for basic ray tracing but can also be extended for use in global illumination and other algorithms that can depend on rapid BVH traversal on the GPU. The chapter covers an implementation of the stackless linear BVH running solely on the GPU as well as the various traversal algorithms that may be needed.

In "Real-Time JPEG Compression Using DirectCompute," Stefan Petersson describes a complete JPEG encoder implementation on the GPU using Direct-Compute. This allows for the real-time storage and encoding of not only image data but also video sequences. With the close integration of the encoder with the application, the latency and compression cost is reduced, making real-time video streaming from 3D applications more feasible. In the chapter, he covers all aspects from color quantization to color-space conversions and entropy coding—and how each of the different elements can be implemented on the GPU.

The chapter by Dongsoo Han, "Hair Simulation in TressFX," describes the simulation algorithms used in the game *Tomb Raider* to animate Lara Croft's hair and in the AMD demo *Ruby*. TressFX can simulate 19,000 strands of hair, consisting of 0.22 million vertices in less than a millisecond on a high-end GPU.

The next chapter, "Object-Order Ray Tracing for Fully Dynamic Scenes" by Tobias Zirr, Hauke Rehfeld, and Carsten Dachsbacher, describes the implementation of a ray tracer that is capable of utilizing the same art assets as a rasterizer-based engine, which is one of the major obstacles in using ray tracers in games.

The chapter "Quadtrees on the GPU" by Jonathan Dupuy, Jean-Claude Iehl, and Pierre Poulin describes a quadtree implementation that is implemented with linear trees on the GPU. The chapter explains how to update linear trees, which are a pointer-free alternative to recursive trees on the GPU, and how to render multiresolution, crack-free surfaces with frustum culling using hardware tessellation and a distance-based LOD selection criterion.

A key feature for simulating rigid bodies on the GPU is the performance of the constraint solver. Takahiro Harada shows in his chapter "Two-Level Constraint Solver and Pipelined Local Batching for Rigid Body Simulation on GPUs" an implementation that uses pipelined batching to run the entire solver on the GPU. This constraint solver is also implemented in the Bullet Physics Engine.

The next chapter, "Non-separable 2D, 3D, and 4D Filtering with CUDA" by Anders Eklund and Paul Dufort, covers the efficient implementation of filtering algorithms tailored to deal with 3D and 4D datasets, which commonly occur in medical imaging, and 2D datasets.

"Compute-Based Tiled Culling," Jason Stewart's chapter, focuses on one challenge in modern real-time rendering engines: they need to support many dynamic light sources in a scene. Both forward and deferred rendering can struggle with problems such as efficient culling, batch sizes, state switching, or bandwidth consumption, in this case. Compute-based (tiled) culling of lights reduces state switching and avoids culling on the CPU (beneficial for forward rendering), and computes lighting in a single pass that fits deferred renderers well. Stewart details his technique, provides a thorough performance analysis, and deduces various optimizations, all documented with example code.

In "Rendering Vector Displacement-Mapped Surfaces in a GPU Ray Tracer," Takahiro Harada's work targets the rendering of vector displacement-mapped surfaces using ray-tracing–based methods. Vector displacement is a popular and powerful means to model complex objects from simple base geometry. However, ray tracing such geometry on a GPU is nontrivial: pre-tessellation is not an option due to the high (and possibly unnecessary) memory consumption, and thus efficient, GPU-friendly algorithms for the construction and traversal of acceleration structures and intersection computation with on-the-fly tessellation are required. Harada fills this gap and presents his method and implementation of an OpenCL ray tracer supporting dynamic tessellation of vector displacement-mapped surfaces.

"Smooth Probablistic Ambient Occlusion for Volume Rendering" by Thomas Kroes, Dirk Schut, and Elmar Eisemann covers a novel and easy-to-implement solution for ambient occlusion for direct volume rendering (DVR). Instead of applying costly ray casting to determine the accessibility of a voxel, this technique employs a probabilistic heuristic in concert with 3D image filtering. This way, ambient occlusion can be efficiently approximated and it is possible to interactively modify the transfer function, which is critical in many applications, such as medical and scientific DVR.

The chapter, "Octree Mapping from a Depth Camera," shows how to render artificial objects with consistent shading from arbitrary perspectives in a real-world scene. This chapter uses CUDA to reconstruct 3D scenes from depth cameras at near real-time speeds. The scene is represented by a sparse voxel octree (SVO) structure that scales to large volumes.

The last chapter, "Interactive Sparse Eulerian Fluid," describes a method for computing and rendering smoke-like fluid in real time on the GPU using DirectX 11+ with a key focus on the advantages of simulating and storing these simulations in a sparse domain. This technique was used with impressive results in the NVIDIA *Mech Ti* demo.

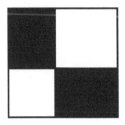

Web Materials

Example programs and source code to accompany some of the chapters are available on the CRC Press website: go to https://www.crcpress.com/9781138484399 and click on the "Downloads" tab.

The directory structure follows the book structure by using the chapter numbers as the name of the subdirectory.

General System Requirements

The material presented in this book was originally published between 2010 and 2016, and the most recent developments have the following system requirements:

- The DirectX June 2010 SDK (the latest SDK is installed with Visual Studio 2012).

- DirectX 11 or DirectX 12 capable GPUs are required to run the examples. The chapter will mention the exact requirement.

- The OS should be Microsoft Windows 10, following the requirement of DirectX 11 or 12 capable GPUs.

- Visual Studio C++ 2012 (some examples might require older versions).

- 2GB RAM or more.

- The latest GPU driver.

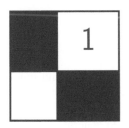

2D Distance Field Generation with the GPU

Philip Rideout

Distance fields have many applications in image processing, real-time rendering, and path-finding algorithms. Loosely speaking, a distance field is a grayscale bitmap in which each pixel's intensity represents the distance to the nearest contour line in a source image (see Figure 1.1). The source image often consists of monochrome vector art or text. Distance fields can also be defined in higher dimensions—in the 3D case, the value at each voxel represents distance to the nearest surface. When extended to 3D, many more applications come into play, including facilitation of ray casting and collision detection.

In this chapter we focus on the 2D case. The flat world is much less daunting than 3D, and serves as a good starting point for learning about distance fields. We will focus on the generation of distance fields rather than their application, but will conclude with a brief overview of some rendering techniques that leverage distance fields, including one that enables cheap, high-quality antialiasing.

Perhaps the most classic and commonly-used technique for generating distance fields stems from Per-Erik Danielsson [Danielsson 80]. He describes a method by which pairs of distances are "swept" through an image using a small grid of

Figure 1.1. Fleur-de-lis seed image (left) and its resulting distance field (right).

weights (which he calls a *skeleton*). Danielsson's method is ingenious and much faster than a brute-force technique; however, his algorithm cannot be conveyed succinctly, and is difficult to parallelize on present-day GPU architectures.

Some fascinating and efficient methods for 2D distance field generation on the GPU have been proposed recently [Cao et al. 10] but many of these methods are complex, requiring cunning tricks such as embedding doubly-linked lists within a texture. Here, we give an overview of techniques that are GPU-amenable while still being relatively easy to follow, starting with the simplest (and least accurate) method, which we're calling *Manhattan grassfire*. Although intuitive and easy to implement with OpenGL, this algorithm does not produce accurate results.

After reviewing Manhattan grassfire, we'll introduce a new, more accurate, technique called *horizontal-vertical erosion*, which is also easy to implement using OpenGL. Finally, we'll cover an efficient algorithm proposed by Saito-Toriwaki [Saito and Toriwaki 94]. The nature of their algorithm is amenable to the GPU only when using a compute API rather than a graphics-oriented API. We'll show how we implemented their method using OpenCL.

1.1   Vocabulary

In the context of distance fields, the definition of distance (also known as the *metric*) need not be "distance" in the physical sense that we're all accustomed to.

- *Euclidean metric.* This is the classic definition of distance and corresponds to the physical world.

- *Manhattan metric.* The sum of the axis-aligned horizontal and vertical distances between two points. As Pythagoras taught us, city block distance is not equivalent to Euclidean distance. However, it tends to be much easier to compute.

- *Chessboard metric.* Rather than summing the horizontal and vertical distances, take their maximum. This is the minimum number of moves a king needs when traveling between two points on a chessboard. Much like the Manhattan metric, chessboard distance tends to be easier to compute than true Euclidean distance.

- *Squared Euclidean metric.* This is a distance field where each value is squared distance rather than true distance. This is good enough for many applications, and easier to compute. It also serves as a convenient intermediary step when computing true Euclidean distance.

- *Seed image.* Ordinarily this isn't thought of as a distance metric; it's a binary classification consisting of *object pixels* and *background pixels*. In this chapter, object pixels are depicted in black and background pixels are white.

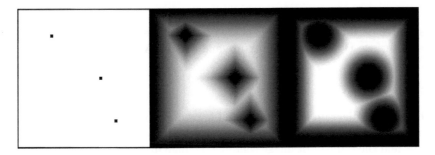

Figure 1.2. Seed image (left), Manhattan distance (middle), Euclidean distance (right).

See Figure 1.2 for an example of a seed image and a comparison of Manhattan and Euclidean metrics.

It also helps to classify the generation algorithms that are amenable to the GPU:

- *Grassfire.* These types of algorithms incrementally flood the boundaries of the vector art outward, increasing the distance values along the way. Once a pixel has been set, it never changes. The algorithm's termination condition is that all background pixels have been set.

- *Erosion.* Much like grassfire methods, erosion algorithms iteratively manipulate the entire image. Unlike grassfire, pixel values are constantly readjusting until an equilibrium state has been reached.

- *Scanning.* Instead of generating a succession of new images, scanning methods "sweep" through the seed image, propagating values horizontally or vertically. Scanning techniques are less amenable to OpenGL, but are often parallelizable using OpenCL or CUDA.

- *Voronoi.* Distance fields are closely related to Voronoi maps, which are classically generated on the GPU by drawing z-aligned cones into the depth buffer. Alternatively, cone tessellation can be avoided by splatting soft particles with a blending equation of `min(source, dest)`. Voronoi-based techniques tend to be raster-heavy, and are more amenable to source images that contain clouds of discrete points (much like Figure 1.2) rather than source images that have continuous outlines (like the Fleur-de-Lis shape). *Jump flooding* is an interesting Voronoi-based technique presented in [Rong and Tan 06].

Grassfire and erosion techniques are typically implemented with a graphics API using an image-processing technique called *ping-ponging*. The fragment shader cannot read values back from the render target, so two image surfaces are created: surface **A** and surface **B**. On even-numbered passes, surface **A** is used as a source texture and surface **B** is used as the render target. On odd-numbered passes, surface **B** is the source texture and surface **A** is the render target.

1.2 Manhattan Grassfire

The following diagram illustrates a well-known method for computing the Manhattan metric using a 4 bits-per-pixel surface. The left-most image is the seed image, and the right-most image contains the final distance field. Blue cells represent background pixels and contain a value of 0xF. Note that the last two images are identical; the last pass is intentionally redundant to allow an occlusion query to signal termination (more on this later).

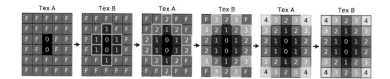

The fragment shader (for OpenGL 3.0 and above) used in each rendering pass is shown in Listing 1.1. This shader assumes that the render target and source texture have formats that are single-component, 8-bit unsigned integers.

```
out uint FragColor;
uniform usampler2D Sampler;

void main()
{
    ivec2 coord = ivec2(gl_FragCoord.xy);

    uint color = texelFetch(Sampler,coord,0).r;
    if (color != 255u)
        discard;

    uint n = texelFetchOffset(Sampler,coord,0,ivec2(0,-1)).r;
    uint s = texelFetchOffset(Sampler,coord,0,ivec2(0,+1)).r;
    uint e = texelFetchOffset(Sampler,coord,0,ivec2(+1,0)).r;
    uint w = texelFetchOffset(Sampler,coord,0,ivec2(-1,0)).r;

    FragColor = min(n,min(s,min(e,w)));
    if (FragColor < 254u)
        FragColor++;
}
```

Listing 1.1. Grassfire fragment shader.

To summarize the shader: if the current pixel is not a background pixel, it can be skipped because it has already been filled. Otherwise, find the minimum value from the neighboring pixels in the four cardinal directions (n, s, e, w). To enhance this shader to compute a chessboard metric, simply add four new texture lookups for the diagonal neighbors (ne, nw, se, sw).

The grassfire algorithm is easy to implement, but it's not obvious how to detect when a sufficient number of passes has been completed. In the worst case, the number of passes is max(width, height). In practice, the number of passes is much fewer.

The occlusion query capabilities in modern graphics hardware can help. In Listing 1.1, we issue a discard statement for non-background pixels. You might wonder why we didn't do this instead:

```
if (color != 255u) {
    FragColor = color;
    return;
}
```

Using discard instead of return is crucial; it allows us to leverage an occlusion query to terminate the image processing loop. If all pixels are discarded, then no change occurs, and the algorithm is complete.

One consequence of using discard in this way is that some pixels in destination surface are left uninitialized. To fix this, we need to blit the entire source texture before running the erosion shader. Luckily this is a fast operation on modern GPUs. See Listing 1.2 for the complete image processing loop.

```
bool done = false;
int pass = 0;
while (!done) {

    // Swap the source & destination surfaces and bind them
    Swap(Source,Dest);
    glBindFramebuffer(GL_FRAMEBUFFER, Dest.RenderTarget);
    glBindTexture(GL_TEXTURE_2D, Source.TextureHandle);

    // Copy the entire source image to the target
    glUseProgram(BlitProgram);
    glDrawArrays(GL_TRIANGLE_FAN,0,4);

    // Execute the grassfire shader and measure the pixel count
    glUseProgram(GrassfireProgram);
    glBeginQuery(GL_SAMPLES_PASSED,QueryObject);
    glDrawArrays(GL_TRIANGLE_FAN,0,4);
    glEndQuery(GL_SAMPLES_PASSED);

    // If all pixels were discarded, we're done
    GLuint count = 0;
```

```
        glGetQueryObjectuiv(QueryObject,GL_QUERY_RESULT,&count);
        done = (count == 0) || (pass++ > MaxPassCount);
  }
```

Listing 1.2. C algorithm for Manhattan grassfire.

Note that Listing 1.2 also checks against the `MaxPassCount` constant for loop termination. This protects against an infinite loop in case an error occurs in the fragment shader or occlusion query.

1.3 Horizontal-Vertical Erosion

Although intuitive, the method presented in the previous section is only marginally useful, because it computes distance according to a city block metric. In this section, we present a new technique that generates distance according to a squared Euclidean metric. The algorithm consists of two separate image-processing loops. The first loop makes a succession of horizontal transformations and the second loop makes a succession of vertical transformations. At each pass, an odd integer offset is applied to the propagated distance values (β in Figures 1.3 and 1.4, which illustrate the process on a 4-bit surface). This is similar to a parallel method proposed by [Lotufo and Zampirolli 01].

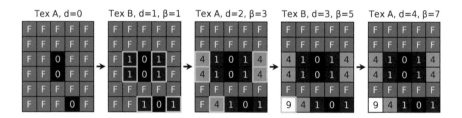

Figure 1.3. Horizontal erosion.

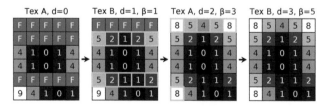

Figure 1.4. Vertical erosion.

You might be wondering why this is erosion rather than grassfire, according to our terminology. In Figure 1.4, notice that a **9** changes into an **8** during the second pass. Since a nonbackground pixel changes its value, this is an erosion-based method.

The fragment shader for the horizontal stage of processing is shown next.

```
out uint FragColor;
uniform usampler2D Sampler;
uniform uint Beta;
uniform uint MaxDistance;

void main()
{
    ivec2 coord = ivec2(gl_FragCoord.xy);

    uint A = texelFetch(Sampler,coord,0).r;
    uint e = texelFetchOffset(Sampler,coord,0,ivec2(+1,0)).r;
    uint w = texelFetchOffset(Sampler,coord,0,ivec2(-1,0)).r;
    uint B = min(min(A,e+Beta),w+Beta);

    if (A == B || B > MaxDistance)
        discard;

    FragColor = B;
}
```

Listing 1.3. Erosion fragment shader.

Background pixels are initially set to "infinity," (i.e., the largest possible value allowed by the bit depth). Since the shader discards pixels greater than the application-defined `MaxDistance` constant, it effectively clamps the distance values. We'll discuss the implications of clamping later in this chapter.

To create the shader for the vertical pass, simply replace the two East-West offsets (+1,0) and (-1,0) in Listing 1.3 with North-South offsets (0,+1) and (0,-1).

To give the erosion shaders some context, the C code is shown next.

```
GLuint program = HorizontalProgram;
for (int d = 1; d < MaxPassCount; d++) {

    // Swap the source & destination surfaces and bind them
    Swap(Source,Dest);
    glBindFramebuffer(GL_FRAMEBUFFER,Dest.RenderTarget);
    glBindTexture(GL_TEXTURE_2D,Source.TextureHandle);

    // Copy the entire source image to the destination surface
    glUseProgram(BlitProgram);
```

```
    glDrawArrays(GL_TRIANGLE_FAN,0,4);

    // Execute the erosion shader and measure the pixel count
    glUseProgram(program);
    glUniform1ui(Uniforms.Beta, 2*d-1);
    glUniform1ui(Uniforms.MaxDistance, 65535);
    glBeginQuery(GL_SAMPLES_PASSED,QueryObject);
    glDrawArrays(GL_TRIANGLE_FAN,0,4);
    glEndQuery(GL_SAMPLES_PASSED);

    // If all pixels were discarded, we're done with this stage
    GLuint count = 0;
    glGetQueryObjectuiv(QueryObject,GL_QUERY_RESULT,&count);
    if (count == 0) {
        if (program == HorizontalProgram) {
            program = VerticalProgram;
            d = 0;
        } else {
            break;
        }
    }
}
```

Listing 1.4. C algorithm for horizontal-vertical erosion.

Applying odd-numbered offsets at each pass might seem less intuitive than the Manhattan technique, but the mathematical explanation is simple. Recall that the image contains squared distance, d^2. At every iteration, the algorithm fills in new distance values by adding an offset value β to the previous distance. Expressing this in the form of an equation, we have

$$d^2 = (d-1)^2 + \beta.$$

Solving for β is simple algebra:

$$\beta = 2 * d - 1;$$

therefore, β iterates through the odd integers.

1.4   Saito-Toriwaki Scanning with OpenCL

Saito and Toriwaki developed another technique that consists of a horizontal stage of processing followed by a vertical stage [Saito and Toriwaki 94]. Interestingly, the horizontal stage of processing is not erosion-based and is actually $O(n)$. Their method is perhaps one of the best ways to generate squared Euclidean distance on the CPU, because it's fast and simple to implement. Their algorithm is also fairly amenable to the GPU, but only when using a compute API such as OpenCL rather than a purely graphics-oriented API.

Several researchers have improved the worst-case efficiency of the Saito-Toriwaki algorithm, but their methods often require additional data structures, such as a stack, and their complexity makes them less amenable to the GPU. (For an excellent survey of techniques, see [Fabbri et al. 08].) We found the original Saito-Toriwaki algorithm to be easy to implement and parallelize. At a high level, their method can be summarized in two steps:

1. Find the one-dimensional distance field of each row. This can be performed efficiently in two passes as follows:

   - First, crawl rightward and increment a counter along the way, resetting the counter every time you cross a contour line. Write the counter's value into the destination image along the way. After the entire row is processed, the seed image can be discarded.

   - Next, crawl leftward, similarly incrementing a counter along the way and writing the values into the destination image. When encountering an existing value in the destination image that's less than the current counter, reset the counter to that value.

   In code, the operations performed on a single row can be expressed as follows:

```
// Rightward Pass
d = 0;
for (x = 0; x < Width; x++) {
    d = seed[x] ? 0 : d+1;
    destination[x] = d;
}

// Leftward Pass
d = 0;
for (x = Width-1; x >= 0; x--) {
    d = min(d+1, destination[x]);
    destination[x] = d;
}
```

2. In each vertical column, find the minimum squared distance of each pixel, using only the values computed in Step 1 as input. A brute-force way of doing this would be as follows:

```
for (y1 = 0; y1 < height; y1++) {
    minDist = INFINITY;
    for (y2 = 0; y2 < height; y2++) {
        d = destination[y2];
        d = (y1 - y2) * (y1 - y2) + d*d;
        minDist = min(minDist, d);
    }
```

```
                destination[y1] = minDist;
        }
```

Note the expensive multiplications in the vertical pass. They can be optimized in several ways:

- The $d * d$ operation can be pulled out and performed as a separate pass on the entire image, potentially making better use of GPU parallelization.

- The $d * d$ operation can be eliminated completely by leveraging the β trick that we described in our erosion-based method. In this way, the horizontal pass would track squared distance from the very beginning.

- The $(y1 - y2)^2$ operation can be replaced with a lookup table because $|y1 - y2|$ is a member of a relatively small set of integers.

In practice, we found that these multiplications were not very damaging since GPUs tend to be extremely fast at multiplication.

For us, the most fruitful optimization to the vertical pass was splitting it into downward and upward passes. Saito and Toriwaki describe this in detail, showing how it limits the range of the inner loop to a small region of interest. This optimization doesn't help much in worst-case scenarios, but it provides a

Figure 1.5. Seed image, rightward, leftward, downward, upward (top to bottom).

substantial boost for most images. To see how to split up the vertical pass, see the accompanying sample code. The step-by-step process of the Saito-Toriwaki transformation is depicted in Figure 1.5.

In reviewing the OpenCL implementation of the Saito-Toriwaki algorithm, we first present a naive but straightforward approach. We then optimize our implementation by reducing the number of global memory accesses and changing the topology of the OpenCL kernels.

1.4.1 OpenCL Setup Code

Before going over the kernel source, let's first show how the CPU-side code sets up the OpenCL work items and launches them. For the sake of brevity, we've omitted much of the error-checking that would be expected in production code (see Listing 1.5).

```
void RunKernels(cl_uchar* inputImage, cl_ushort* outputImage,
                cl_platform_id platformId, const char* source)
{
    size_t horizWorkSize[] = {IMAGE_HEIGHT};
    size_t vertWorkSize[] = {IMAGE_WIDTH};
    cl_context context;
    cl_mem inBuffer, outBuffer, scratchBuffer;
    cl_program program;
    cl_kernel horizKernel, vertKernel;
    cl_command_queue commandQueue;
    cl_device_id deviceId;

    // Create the OpenCL context
    clGetDeviceIDs(platformId, CL_DEVICE_TYPE_GPU, 1,
        &deviceId, 0);
    context = clCreateContext(0, 1, &deviceId, 0, 0, 0);

    // Create memory objects
    inBuffer = clCreateBuffer(context,
                CL_MEM_READ_ONLY | CL_MEM_COPY_HOST_PTR,
                IMAGE_WIDTH * IMAGE_HEIGHT, inputImage, 0);
    outBuffer = clCreateBuffer(context, CL_MEM_READ_WRITE,
                IMAGE_WIDTH * IMAGE_HEIGHT * 2, 0, 0);

    // Load and compile the kernel source
    program = clCreateProgramWithSource(context, 1,
                                        &source, 0, 0);
    clBuildProgram(program, 0, 0, "-cl-fast-relaxed-math", 0, 0);

    // Set up the kernel object for the horizontal pass
    horizKernel = clCreateKernel(program, "horizontal", 0);
    clSetKernelArg(horizKernel, 0, sizeof(cl_mem), &inBuffer);
    clSetKernelArg(horizKernel, 1, sizeof(cl_mem), &outBuffer);
```

```
// Set up the kernel object for the vertical pass
vertKernel = clCreateKernel(program, "vertical", 0);
clSetKernelArg(vertKernel, 0, sizeof(cl_mem), &outBuffer);

// Execute the kernels and read back the results
commandQueue = clCreateCommandQueue(context, deviceId, 0, 0);
clEnqueueNDRangeKernel(commandQueue, horizKernel, 1, 0,
                    horizWorkSize, 0, 0, 0, 0);
clEnqueueNDRangeKernel(commandQueue, vertKernel, 1, 0,
                    vertWorkSize, 0, 0, 0, 0);
clEnqueueReadBuffer(commandQueue, outBuffer, CL_TRUE, 0,
                    IMAGE_WIDTH * IMAGE_HEIGHT * 2,
                    outputImage, 0, 0, 0);
}
```

Listing 1.5. OpenCL Saito -Toriwaki algorithm.

Listing 1.5 uses OpenCL memory buffers rather than OpenCL image objects. This makes the kernel code a bit easier to follow for someone coming from a CPU background. Since we're not leveraging the texture filtering capabilities of GPUs anyway, this is probably fine in practice.

Also note that we're using a seed image that consists of 8-bit unsigned integers, but our target image is 16 bits. Since we're generating *squared* distance, using only 8 bits would result in very poor precision. If desired, a final pass could be tacked on that takes the square root of each pixel and generates an 8-bit image from that.

1.4.2 Distance Clamping

The finite bit depth of the target surface leads to an important detail in our implementation of the Saito-Toriwaki algorithm: distance clamping. Rather than blindly incrementing the internal distance counter as it marches horizontally, our implementation keeps the distance clamped to a maximum value like this:

```
ushort nextDistance = min(254u, distance) + 1u
```

Even though the target is 16 bit, we clamp it to 255 during the horizontal scan because it gets squared in a later step. Note that distance clamping results in an interesting property:

> If distances are clamped to a maximum value of x, then any two seed pixels further apart than x have no effect on each other in the final distance field.

We'll leverage this property later. For some applications, it's perfectly fine to clamp distances to a very small value. This can dramatically speed up the generation algorithm, as we'll see later.

1.4.3 OpenCL Kernels: Naïve and Optimized Approaches

Listing 1.6 is the complete listing of the horizontal kernel used in our naïve implementation. For simplicity, this kernel operates on a fixed-width image. In practice, you'll want to pass in the width as an argument to the kernel.

```
kernel void horizontal(global const uchar* indata,
   global ushort* outdata)
{
    const int y = get_global_id(0);
    global const uchar* source = indata + y * IMAGE_WIDTH;
    global ushort* target = outdata + y * IMAGE_WIDTH;
    uint d;

    // Rightward pass
    d = 0;
    for (int x = 0; x < IMAGE_WIDTH; x++) {
        ushort next = min(254u, d) + 1u;
        d = source[x] ? 0u : next;
        target[x] = d;
    }

    // Leftward pass
    d = 0;
    for (int x = IMAGE_WIDTH - 1; x >= 0; x--) {
        ushort next = min(254u, d) + 1u;
        d = min(next, target[x]);
        target[x] = d;
    }

    // Square the distances
    for (int x = 0; x < IMAGE_WIDTH; x++) {
        target[x] = target[x]  * target[x];
    }
}
```

Listing 1.6. Naïve horizontal kernel.

The biggest issue with the code in Listing 1.6 is the numerous accesses to shared memory. Specifically, the number of reads and writes to the target pointer should be reduced. On present-day GPU architectures, each access to global memory incurs a huge performance hit.

The obvious way to reduce these high-latency accesses is to change the kernel so that it copies the entire row into local memory and performs all the necessary processing locally. As a final step, the kernel copies the results back out to the shared memory. This strategy would require enough local memory to accommodate an entire row in the image, which in our case exceeds the hardware cache size.

Figure 1.6. OpenCL work item for the horizontal pass (blue), with two overlapping neighbors (yellow).

To reduce the need for generous amounts of local storage, we can break up each row into multiple sections, thus shrinking the size of each OpenCL work item. Unfortunately, operating on a narrow section of the image can produce incorrect results, since contour lines outside the section are ignored.

This is where we leverage the fact that far-apart pixels have no effect on each other when clamping the distance field. The middle part of each work item will produce correct results since it's far away from neighboring work items. We'll use the term *margin* to label the incorrect regions of each work item. By overlapping the work items and skipping writes for the values in the margin, the incorrect regions of each work item are effectively ignored (see Figures 1.6 and 1.7). Note that tighter distance clamping allows for smaller margin size, resulting in better parallelization.

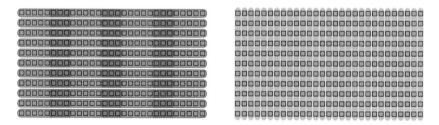

Figure 1.7. OpenCL topology for the horizontal and vertical kernels.

We now need to set up the work groups for the horizontal pass using a two-dimensional arrangement (see Listing 1.7); changed lines are highlighted. The SPAN constant refers to the length of each work item, not including the throw-away margins.

```
void RunKernels(cl_uchar* inputImage, cl_ushort* outputImage,
                cl_platform_id platformId,
                const char* kernelSource)
{
    size_t horizWorkSize[] = {IMAGE_WIDTH / SPAN, IMAGE_HEIGHT};
    size_t vertWorkSize[] = {IMAGE_WIDTH};
```

```
      // function body is same as before -- see Listing 1.5

      // Execute the kernels and read back the results
      commandQueue = clCreateCommandQueue(context, deviceId, 0, 0);
      clEnqueueNDRangeKernel(commandQueue, horizKernel, 2, 0,}
                             horizWorkSize, 0, 0, 0, 0);}
      clEnqueueNDRangeKernel(commandQueue, vertKernel, 1, 0,
                             vertWorkSize, 0, 0, 0, 0);
      clEnqueueReadBuffer(commandQueue, outBuffer, CL_TRUE, 0,
                          IMAGE_WIDTH * IMAGE_HEIGHT * 2,
                          outputImage, 0, 0, 0);
}
```

Listing 1.7. Optimized Saito-Toriwaki algorithm.

Listing 1.8 is the listing for the new kernel code. Instead of looping between 0 and WIDTH, we now perform processing between Left and Right, which are determined from the value returned by get_global_id(0). You'll also notice the InnerLeft and InnerRight constants; these mark the portion of the work item that actually gets written out.

```
kernel void horizontal(global const uchar* indata,
                       global ushort* outdata)
{
    const int y = get_global_id(1);
    global const uchar* source = indata + y * IMAGE_WIDTH;
    global ushort* target = outdata + y * IMAGE_WIDTH;
    uchar scratch[MARGIN + SPAN + MARGIN];
    uint d;

    const int InnerLeft = SPAN * get_global_id(0);
    const int InnerRight = min(IMAGE_WIDTH, InnerLeft + SPAN);
    const int Left = max(0, InnerLeft - MARGIN);
    const int Right = min(IMAGE_WIDTH, InnerRight + MARGIN);

    // Rightward pass
    d = 0;
    for (int x = Left; x < Right; x++) {
        ushort next = min(254u, d) + 1u;
        d = source[x] ? 0u : next;
        scratch[x - Left] = d;
    }

    // Leftward pass
    d = 0;
    for (int x = Right - 1; x >= Left; x--) {
        ushort next = min(254u, d) + 1u;
        d = min(next, (ushort) scratch[x - Left]);
        scratch[x - Left] = d;
```

```
    }

    // Square the distances and write them out to shared memory
    for (int x = InnerLeft; x < InnerRight; x++) {
        target[x] = scratch[x - Left] * scratch[x - Left];
    }
}
```

Listing 1.8. Optimized horizontal kernel.

The only remaining piece is the kernel for the vertical pass. Recall the code snippet we presented earlier that described an $O(n^2)$ algorithm to find the minimum distances in a column. By splitting the algorithm into downward and upward passes, Saito and Toriwaki show that the search area of the inner loop can be narrowed to a small region of interest, thus greatly improving the best-case efficiency. See this book's companion source code for the full listing of the vertical kernel.

Due to the high variability from one type of GPU to the next, we recommend that readers experiment to find the optimal OpenCL kernel code and topology for their particular hardware.

Readers may also want to experiment with the image's data type (floats versus integers). We chose integers for this chapter because squared distance in a grid is, intuitively speaking, never fractional. However, keep in mind that GPUs are floating-point monsters! Floats and half-floats may provide better results with certain architectures. It suffices to say that the implementation presented in this chapter is by no means the best approach in every circumstance.

1.5 Signed Distance with Two Color Channels

Regardless of which generation algorithm is used, or which distance metric is employed, a choice exists of generating *signed distance* or *unsigned distance*. The

Figure 1.8. Signed distance in two color channels.

former generates distances for object pixels in addition to background pixels. Object pixels have negative distance while background pixels have positive distance.

It's easy to extend any technique to account for signed distance by simply inverting the seed image and applying the algorithm a second time. We found it convenient to use an unsigned, integer-based texture format, and added a second color channel to the image for the negative values. In Figure 1.8, we depict a signed distance field where the red channel contains positive distance and the green channel contains negative distance.

In the case of the horizontal-vertical erosion technique presented earlier, we can modify the fragment shader to operate on two color channels simultaneously, thus avoiding a second set of passes through the image for negative distance. Listing 1.9 shows the new fragment shader.

```
out uvec2 FragColor;
uniform usampler2D Sampler;
uniform uint Beta;

void main()
{
    ivec2 coord = ivec2(gl_FragCoord.xy);

    uvec2 A = texelFetch(Sampler,coord,0).rg;
    uvec2 e = texelFetchOffset(Sampler,coord,0,ivec2(+1,0)).rg;
    uvec2 w = texelFetchOffset(Sampler,coord,0,ivec2(-1,0)).rg;
    uvec2 B = min(min(A,e+Beta),w+Beta);

    if (A == B)
        discard;

    FragColor = B;
}
```

Listing 1.9. Erosion fragment shader for signed distance.

For most applications it's desirable to make a final transformation that normalizes the two-channel distance into a simple grayscale image. The final square-root transformation can also be performed at this time. The following fragment shader makes this final pass:

```
varying vec2 TexCoord;
uniform sampler2D Sampler;
uniform float Scale;

void main()
{
    vec2 D = sqrt(texture2D(Sampler, TexCoord).rg);
```

```
          float L = 0.5 + Scale * (D.r - D.g);
          gl_FragColor = vec4(L);
     }
```

If a distance field is normalized in this way, a value of 0.5 indicates the center of a contour in the seed image.

1.6   Distance Field Applications

Several interesting uses of distance fields for 2D rendering have been popularized by Chris Green of Valve software [Green 07], who builds on work by [Qin et al. 06]. Leveraging alpha testing (as opposed to alpha *blending*) in conjunction with distance fields enables high-quality magnification of vector art. This is useful on low-end hardware that doesn't support shaders, or when using a fixed-function graphics API like OpenGL ES 1.1.

If shaders are supported, then high-quality anisotropic antialiasing can be achieved using inexpensive bilinear filtering against a low-resolution distance field. (This assumes that the shading language supports derivatives.) Additionally, special effects are easily rendered, including outlines, drop shadows, and glow effects. We'll briefly cover some of these effects in the following sections, using fragment shaders written for OpenGL 3.0.

1.6.1   Antialiasing

Both of the source textures in Figure 1.9 are only 128×32; it's obvious that rendering with the aid of a distance field can provide much better results.

Because the gradient vector at a certain pixel in the distance field gives the direction of maximum change, it can be used as the basis for antialiasing. The `fwidth` function in GLSL provides a convenient way to obtain the rate of change of the input value at the current pixel. In our case, large values returned from `fwidth` indicate a far-off camera, while small values indicate large magnification.

Recall that a lookup value of 0.5 represents the location of the contour line. We compute the best alpha value for smoothing by testing how far the current pixel is from the contour line. See Listing 1.10 for our antialiasing shader.

Figure 1.9. Bilinear filtering (left). Magnification using a distance field (right).

```
in vec2 TexCoord;
out vec4 FragColor;
uniform sampler2D Sampler;
void main()
{
    float D = texture(Sampler, TexCoord).x;
    float width = fwidth(D);
    float A = 1.0 - smoothstep(0.5 - width, 0.5 + width, D);
    FragColor = vec4(0, 0, 0, A);
}
```

Listing 1.10. Fragment shader for antialiasing with a distance field.

Figure 1.10. Outline effect.

1.6.2 Outlining

Creating an outline effect such as the one depicted in Figure 1.10 is quite simple when using a signed distance field for input. Note that there are *two* color transitions that we now wish to antialias: the transition from the fill color to the outline color, and the transition from the outline color to the background color. The following fragment shader shows how to achieve this; the `Thickness` uniform is the desired width of the outline.

```
in vec2 TexCoord;
out vec4 FragColor;
uniform sampler2D Sampler;
uniform float Thickness;

void main()
{
    float D = texture(Sampler, TexCoord).x;
    float W = fwidth(D);
    float T0 = 0.5 - Thickness;
    float T1 = 0.5 + Thickness;
```

```
        if (D < T0) {
            float A = 1.0 - smoothstep(T0-W,T0, D);
            FragColor = vec4(A, A, A, 1);
        } else if (D < T1) {
            FragColor = vec4(0, 0, 0, 1);
        } else {
            float A = 1.0 - smoothstep(T1,T1+W, D);
            FragColor = vec4(0, 0, 0, A);
        }
    }
```

1.6.3 Psychedelic Effect

We conclude the chapter with a fun (but less practical) two-dimensional effect
(see Figure 1.11). This effect is simple to achieve by mapping distance to hue,
and performing HSV-to-RGB conversion in the fragment shader. Animating an
offset value (the `Animation` uniform) creates a trippy 70's effect.

```
in vec2 TexCoord;
out vec4 FragColor;
uniform sampler2D Sampler;
uniform float Animation;

void main()
{
    float D = texture(Sampler, TexCoord).x;
    float W = fwidth(D);
    float H =  2.0 * float(D - 0.5);
    float A = smoothstep(0.5 - W, 0.5 + W, D);
    hue = fract(H + Animation);
    FragColor = vec4(A * HsvToRgb(H, 1.0, 1.0), 1.0);
}
```

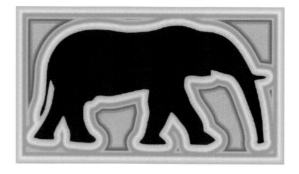

Figure 1.11. Psychedelic effect.

Bibliography

[Cao et al. 10] Thanh-Tung Cao, Ke Tang, Anis Mohamed, and Tiow-Seng Tan. "Parallel Banding Algorithm to Compute Exact Distance Transform with the GPU." In *I3D '10: Proceedings of the 2010 ACM SIGGRAPH Symposium on Interactive 3D Graphics and Games*, pp. 83–90. New York: ACM, 2010.

[Danielsson 80] P. E. Danielsson. "Euclidean Distance Mapping." *Computer Graphics and Image Processing* 14:3 (1980), 227–248.

[Fabbri et al. 08] Ricardo Fabbri, Luciano da F. Costa, Julio C. Torelli, and Odemir M. Bruno. "2D Euclidean Distance Transform Algorithms: A Comparative Survey." *ACM Computing Surveys* 40:1 (2008), 2:1–2:44.

[Green 07] Chris Green. "Improved Alpha-Tested Magnification for Vector Textures and Special Effects." In *SIGGRAPH '07: ACM SIGGRAPH 2007 Courses*, pp. 9–18. New York: ACM, 2007.

[Lotufo and Zampirolli 01] Roberto de Alencar Lotufo and Francisco A. Zampirolli. "Fast Multidimensional Parallel Euclidean Distance Transform Based on Mathematical Morphology." In *SIBGRAPI '01: Proceedings of the 14th Brazilian Symposium on Computer Graphics and Image Processing*, pp. 100–105. Washington, DC: IEEE Computer Society, 2001.

[Qin et al. 06] Zheng Qin, Michael D. McCool, and Craig S. Kaplan. "Real-Time Texturemapped Vector Glyphs." In *Symposium on Interactive 3D Graphics and Games*, pp. 125–132. New York: ACM Press, 2006.

[Rong and Tan 06] Guodong Rong and Tiow-Seng Tan. "Jump Flooding: An Efficient and Effective Communication on GPU." pp. 185–192. Hingham, MA: Charles River Media, 2006.

[Saito and Toriwaki 94] Toyofumi Saito and Jun-Ichiro Toriwaki. "New algorithms for Euclidean Distance Transformation of an *n*-Dimensional Digitized Picture with Applications." *Pattern Recognition* 27:11 (1994), 1551–1565.

2

Order-Independent Transparency Using Per-Pixel Linked Lists
Nicolas Thibieroz

2.1 Introduction

Order-independent transparency (OIT) has been an active area of research in real-time computer graphics for a number of years. The main area of research has focused on how to effect fast and efficient back-to-front sorting and rendering of translucent fragments to ensure visual correctness when order-dependent blending modes are employed. The complexity of the task is such that many real-time applications have chosen to forfeit this step altogether in favor of simpler and faster alternative methods such as sorting per object or per triangle, or simply falling back to order-independent blending modes (e.g., additive blending) that don't require any sorting [Thibieroz 08]. Different OIT techniques have previously been described (e.g., [Everitt 01], [Myers 07]) and although those techniques succeed in achieving correct ordering of translucent fragments, they usually come with performance, complexity, or compatibility shortcomings that make their use difficult for real-time gaming scenarios.

This chapter presents an OIT implementation relying on the new features of the DirectX 11 API from Microsoft.[1] An overview of the algorithm will be presented first, after which each phase of the method will be explained in detail. Sorting, blending, multisampling, anti-aliasing support, and optimizations will be treated in separate sections before concluding with remarks concerning the attractiveness and future of the technique.

2.2 Algorithm Overview

The OIT algorithm presented in this chapter shares some similarities with the A-buffer algorithm [Carpenter 84], whereby translucent fragments are stored in

---

[1] "Microsoft DirectX" is a registered trademark.

buffers for later rendering. Our method uses linked lists [Yang 10] to store a list of translucent fragments for each pixel. Therefore, every screen coordinate in the render viewport will contain an entry to a unique per-pixel linked list containing all translucent fragments at that particular location.

Prior to rendering translucent geometry, all opaque and transparent (alpha-tested) models are rendered onto the render target viewport as desired. Then the OIT algorithm can be invoked to render corrected-ordered translucent fragments.

The algorithm relies on a two-step process.

1. The first step is the creation of per-pixel linked lists whereby the translucent contribution to the scene is entirely captured into a pair of buffers containing the head pointers and linked lists nodes for all translucent pixels.

2. The second step is the traversal of per-pixel linked lists to fetch, sort, blend and finally render all pixels in the correct order onto the destination render viewport.

2.3   DirectX 11 Features Requisites

DirectX 11 has introduced new features that finally make it possible to create and parse concurrent linked lists on the GPU.

2.3.1   Unordered Access Views

Unordered access view (UAV) is a special type of resource view that can be bound as output to a pixel or compute shader to allow the programmer to write data at arbitrary locations. The algorithm uses a pair of UAVs to store per-pixel linked lists nodes and head pointers.

2.3.2   Atomic Operations

The creation of per-pixel linked lists also requires a way to avoid any contention when multiple pixel shader invocations perform memory operations into a buffer. Indeed such read/modify/write operations must be guaranteed to occur atomically for the algorithm to work as intended. DirectX 11 supports a set of `Interlocked*()` Shader Model 5.0 instructions that fulfill this purpose. Such atomic operation will be used to keep track of the head pointer address when creating the per-pixel linked lists.

2.3.3   Hardware Counter Support on UAV

A less well-known feature of DirectX 11 allows the creation of a built-in hardware counter on buffer UAVs. This counter is declared by specifying the `D3D11_BUFFER_UAV_FLAG_COUNTER` flag when generating a UAV for the intended buffer. The programmer is given control of the counter via the following two Shader Model 5.0 methods:

```
uint <Buffer>.IncrementCounter();
uint <Buffer>.DecrementCounter();
```

Hardware counter support is used to keep track of the offset at which to store the next linked list node.

While hardware counter support is not strictly required for the algorithm to work, it enables considerable performance improvement compared to manually keeping track of a counter via a single-element buffer UAV.

2.3.4   Early Depth/Stencil Rejection

Graphics APIs like OpenGL and Direct3D specify that the depth/stencil test be executed *after* the pixel shader stage in the graphics pipeline. A problem arises when the pixel shader outputs to UAVs because UAVs may be written into the shader even though the subsequent depth/stencil test actually discards the pixel, which may not be the intended behavior of the algorithm. Shader Model 5.0 allows the [earlydepthstencil] keyword to be declared in front of a pixel shader function to indicate that the depth/stencil test is to be explicitly performed *before* the pixel shader stage, allowing UAV writes to be carried out only *if the depth/ stencil test succeeds first*. This functionality is important for the algorithm presented in this chapter, since only *visible* translucent fragments need storing into the per-pixel linked lists.

2.3.5   SV_COVERAGE Pixel Shader Input

DirectX 11 allows SV_COVERAGE to be declared as an input to the pixel shader stage. SV_COVERAGE contains a bit mask of all samples that are covered by the current primitive. This information is used by this OIT technique when multi-sampling antialiasing (MSAA) is enabled.

2.3.6   Per-sample Pixel Shader Execution

DirectX 11 allows the pixel shader stage to execute *per sample* (as opposed to *per pixel*) when MSAA is enabled. This functionality will be exploited to allow MSAA support with our OIT technique.

2.4   Head Pointer and Nodes Buffers

The algorithm builds a reverse linked list for each pixel location in the target viewport. The linked list *head pointer* is the address of the first element in the linked list. The linked list *nodes* are the individual elements of the linked list that contain fragment data as well as the address of the next node.

2.4.1 Head Pointer Buffer

The algorithm allocates a screen-sized buffer of type `DXGI_FORMAT_R32_UINT` that contains the address of the head pointer for every 2D coordinate on the screen.

Despite the resource having the same dimensions as the render viewport, the declaration must employ the buffer type because atomic operations are not supported on Texture2D resources. Therefore an extra step will be required in the shader wherein a 2D screen-coordinate location is converted to a byte-linear address:

```
uint uLinearAddressInBytes = 4 * ( ScreenPos.y*RENDERWIDTH +
    ScreenPos.x );
```

The head pointer buffer is initialized to a "magic" value of 0xFFFFFFFF, indicating that the linked list is empty to start with. In effect, an address of 0xFFFFFFFF indicates that no more nodes are available (i.e., the end of the list has been reached).

The term *reverse* linked list is used because the head pointer is dynamically updated at construction time to receive the address of the latest linked list node written out at each pixel location. Once construction is complete, the head pointer value effectively contains the address of the *last* node written out, with this last node sequentially pointing to the nodes previously stored for the same pixel location.

2.4.2 Nodes Buffer

The nodes buffer stores the nodes of *all* per-pixel linked lists. We cannot allocate individual nodes buffers for every linked list since the render viewport dimensions guarantee that a huge number of them will be required (one for each pixel in the render viewport). Therefore the nodes buffer must be allocated with enough memory to accommodate all possible translucent fragments in the scene. It is the responsibility of the programmer to define this upper limit. A good heuristic to use is to base the allocation size on the render viewport dimensions multiplied by the average translucent overdraw expected. Certainly the size of the nodes buffer is likely to be very large, and may place an unreasonable burden on the video memory requirements of the OIT technique. Section 2.9 introduces a significant optimization to dramatically reduce the memory requirements of this algorithm.

The UAV for the nodes buffer is created with a built-in hardware counter initialized to zero as a way to keep track of how many fragments have been stored in the buffer.

2.4.3 Fragment Data

Each linked list node stores fragment data as well as the address of the next node. The address of the next node is stored as a `uint` while the type and size of the fragment data depends on the needs of the application. Typically the fragment structure includes fragment depth and color but other variables may be stored as needed (e.g., normal, blending mode id, etc.). Fragment depth is an essential component of the fragment structure since it will be required at linked list traversal time to correctly sort fragments prior to rendering.

It is important to point out that any additional structure member will increase the total size of the nodes buffer and therefore the total memory requirement of the OIT solution. It is therefore desirable to economize the size of the fragment structure. The implementation presented in this chapter packs the fragment color into a single `uint` type and uses the following node data structure for a total of 12 bytes per fragment:

```
struct NodeData_STRUCT
{
    uint uColor; // Fragment color packed as RGBA
    uint uDepth; // Fragment depth
    uint uNext;  // Address of next linked list node
};
```

2.5 Per-Pixel Linked List Creation

The algorithm presented does not use `DirectCompute`; instead, the storing of translucent fragments into linked lists is done via a pixel shader writing to the head pointer and nodes buffers UAVs. Earlier shader stages in the pipeline are enabled (vertex shader, but also hull shader, domain shader and geometry shader if needed) in order to turn incoming triangles into fragments that can be stored into per-pixel linked lists.

No color render target is bound at this stage although a depth buffer is still required to ensure that only translucent fragments that pass the depth/stencil test are stored in the per-pixel linked lists. Binding a depth buffer avoids the need to store translucent fragments that would result in being completely hidden by previously-rendered opaque or alpha-tested geometry.

2.5.1 Algorithm Description

A description of the algorithm used to build per-pixel linked lists follows.

- For each frame
    - *Clear head pointer buffer to 0xFFFFFFFF (−1). This indicates that the per-pixel linked lists are all empty to start with.*

○ *For (each translucent fragment)*

  ∗ *Compute and store fragment color and depth into node structure.*
    Calculate the fragment color as normal using lighting, texturing
    etc. and store it in node data structure. Pixel depth can be
    directly obtained from the z member of the SV_POSITION input.

  ∗ *Retrieve current counter value of nodes buffer and increment
    counter.* The current counter value tells us how many nodes have
    been written into the nodes buffer. We will use this value as the
    offset at which to store the new node entry.

  ∗ *Atomically exchange head pointer for this screen location with
    counter value.* The previous head pointer for the current screen
    coordinates is retrieved and set as the "next" member of the node
    structure. The node structure being prepared therefore points to
    the previous node that was written out at this pixel location. The
    new head pointer receives the current value of the counter as it
    will represent the latest node written out.

  ∗ *Store node structure into node buffer at offset specified by counter
    value.* The node structure containing fragment data and next node
    pointer is written out to the nodes buffer at the offset specified by
    the current counter value. This is the latest node to be written
    out to the nodes buffer for these pixel coordinates; this is why the
    counter offset was also set as the new head pointer in the previous
    step.

Figure 2.1 illustrates the contents of the head pointer and nodes buffers after
three translucent triangles go through the per-pixel linked list creation step.

The single pixel occupied by the orange triangle stores the current nodes
buffer counter value (0) into location [1, 1] in the Head Pointer Buffer and sets
the previous Head Pointer value (−1) as the "next" node pointer in the node
structure before writing it to the nodes buffer at offset 0.

The two pixels occupied by the green triangle are processed sequentially; they
store the current nodes buffer counter values (1 and 2) into locations [3, 4] and
[4, 4] in the head pointer buffer and set the previous head pointer values (−1 and
−1) as the "next" node pointers in the two node structures before writing them
to the nodes buffer at offset 1 and 2.

The left-most pixel of the yellow triangle is due to be rendered at the same
location as the orange fragment already stored. The current counter value (3)
replaces the previous value (0) in the head pointer buffer at location [1, 1] and
the previous value is now set as the "next" node pointer in the fragment node
before writing it to offset 3 in the nodes buffer.

The second pixel of the yellow triangle stores the current counter value (4)
into location [2, 1] and sets the previous value (−1) as the "next" node pointer
before writing the node to the nodes buffer at offset 4.

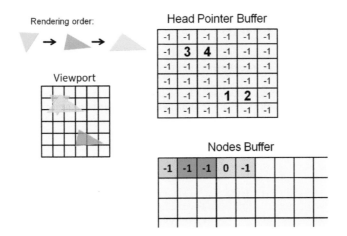

Rendering order:

Viewport

Head Pointer Buffer

Nodes Buffer

Figure 2.1. Head pointer and nodes buffers contents after rendering five translucent pixels (3 triangles) for a 6×6 render target viewport.

2.5.2 Pixel Shader Code

The pixel shader code for creating per-pixel linked lists can be found in Listing 2.1.

```
// Pixel shader input structure
struct PS_INPUT
{
    float3 vNormal : NORMAL;     // Pixel normal
    float2 vTex : TEXCOORD;      // Texture coordinates
    float4 vPos : SV_POSITION;   // Screen coordinates
};

// Node data structure
struct NodeData_STRUCT
{
    uint uColor; // Fragment color packed as RGBA
    uint uDepth; // Fragment depth
    uint uNext;  // Address of next linked list node
};

// UAV declarations
RWByteAddressBuffer HeadPointerBuffer : register(u1);
RWStructuredBuffer<NodeData_STRUCT> NodesBuffer : register(u2);

// Pixel shader for writing per-pixel linked lists
[earlydepthstencil]
float PS_StoreFragments(PS_INPUT input) : SV_Target
{
    NodeData_STRUCT Node;
```

```
// Calculate fragment color from pixel input data
Node.uColor = PackFloat4IntoUint(ComputeFragmentColor(input));

// Store pixel depth in packed format
Node.uDepth = PackDepthIntoUint( input.vPos.z );

// Retrieve current pixel count and increase counter
uint uPixelCount = NodesBuffer.IncrementCounter();

// Convert pixel 2D coordinates to byte linear address
uint2 vScreenPos = uint(input.vPos.xy);
uint uLinearAddressInBytes = 4 * ( vScreenPos.y*RENDERWIDTH +
                                   vScreenPos.x );

// Exchange offsets in Head Pointer buffer
// Node.uNext will receive the previous head pointer
HeadPointerBuffer.InterlockedExchange(
    uLinearAddressInBytes, uPixelCount, Node.uNext);

// Add new fragment entry in Nodes Buffer
NodesBuffer[uPixelCount] = Node;

// No RT bound so this will have no effect
return float4(0,0,0,0);
}
```

Listing 2.1. Pixel shader for creating per-pixel linked lists.

2.6   Per-Pixel Linked Lists Traversal

Once the head pointer and nodes buffers have been filled with data, the second phase of the algorithm can proceed: traversing the per-pixel linked lists and rendering translucent pixels in the correct order.

The traversal code needs to be executed once per pixel; we therefore render a fullscreen quad (or triangle) covering the render viewport with a pixel shader that will parse all stored fragments for every pixel location. Each fragment from the corresponding per-pixel linked list will be fetched and then sorted with other fragments before a manual back-to-front blending operation will take place, starting with the color from the current render target.

2.6.1   Pixel Shader Inputs and Outputs

The head pointer and nodes buffers are now bound as pixel shader inputs, since the traversal step will exclusively be *reading* from them. We will also need a copy of the render target onto which opaque and alpha-tested geometry have previously been rendered. This copy is needed to start the manual blending operation in the pixel shader.

The current render target viewport (onto which opaque and alpha-tested geometry has previously been rendered) is set as output, and the depth buffer that was used to render previous geometry is bound with Z-Writes disabled (the use of the depth buffer for the traversal step is explained in the Optimizations section).

2.6.2 Algorithm Description

A description of the algorithm used to parse per-pixel linked lists and render from them follows.

- For (each frame)

    ○ *Copy current render target contents into a background texture.* This copy is required to perform the manual blending process.

    ○ *For (each pixel)*

        * *Fetch head pointer for corresponding pixel coordinates and set it as current node pointer.* The screen coordinates of the current pixel are converted to a linear address used to fetch the head pointer from the head pointer buffer. The head pointer is therefore the first node address pointing to the list of all translucent fragments occupying this pixel location.

        * *While (end of linked list not reached)*

            · *Fetch current fragment from nodes buffer using current node pointer.* The current node pointer indicates where the next fragment is stored in the nodes buffer for the current pixel location.

            · *Sort fragment with previously collected fragments in front-to-back order.* The current fragment is inserted into the last position of a temporary array. The fragment is then sorted on-the-fly with previous fragments stored in the array.

            · *Set current node pointer to "next" node pointer from current node.* The current fragment has been processed; we therefore proceed to the next fragment in the list by setting the current node pointer to the "next" pointer of the current node. Fragment parsing will stop once the "next" pointer equals 0xFFFFFFFF, as this value indicates the end of the list.

        * *The background color is fetched from the background texture and set as the current color.* Back-to-front blending requires the furthermost color value to be processed first, hence the need to obtain the current value of the render target to start the blending process.

* *For (each fragment fetched from sorted list in reverse order)*
  · Perform manual back-to-front blending of current color with fragment color. The latest entry in the front-to-back sorted array is fetched, unpacked from a uint to a float4, and blended manually with the current color.
* *The final blended color is returned from the pixel shader.* This color is the correctly-ordered translucent contribution for this pixel.

2.6.3 Sorting Fragments

The algorithm used to sort fragments for correct ordering can be arbitrary because it typically has no dependencies with the OIT algorithm described in this chapter.

The implementation presented here declares a temporary array of `uint2` format containing fragment color and depth. At parsing time each fragment extracted from the per-pixel linked list is directly stored as the last entry in the array, and sorted with previous array elements using a standard insertion-sort algorithm. This approach requires an array of a fixed size, which unfortunately limits the maximum number of fragments that can be processed with this technique. The alternative option of parsing and sorting the linked list "in place" resulted in much lower performance due to repeated accesses to memory, and was also subject to limitations of the DirectX Shader Compiler regarding loop terminating conditions being dependent on the result of a UAV fetch. For those reasons, sorting via a temporary array was chosen. In general the smaller the array the better the performance since temporary arrays consume precious general purpose registers (GPRs) that affect the performance of the shader. The programmer should therefore declare the array size as an estimate of the maximum translucent overdraw that can be expected in the scene.

2.6.4 Blending Fragments

The blending process takes place once all fragments for the current pixel coordinates have been parsed and sorted in the temporary array. The blending operation used in this implementation uses the same `SRCALPHA-INVSRCALPHA` blend mode for all translucent fragments. The blending process starts with the background color and then iteratively blends the current color with each fragment color in a back-to-front order. Because the blending is performed "manually" in the pixel shader, actual hardware color/alpha blending is disabled.

A different approach that would avoid the need for copying the render target contents to a texture prior to rendering translucent fragments would be to use underblending [Bavoil 08]. Underblending allows fragments to be blended in a front-to-back order, hence avoiding the need to access the background color as a texture (the background color will be blended with the result of the manually underblended result via actual hardware blending). However, this method imposes restrictions on the variety of per-fragment blend modes that can be used, and did not noticeably affect performance.

It is quite straightforward to modify the algorithm so that per-fragment blend modes are specified instead of adopting a blend mode common to all fragments. This modification allows translucent geometry of different types (particles, windows, smoke etc.) to be stored and processed together. In this case a bit field containing the blend mode id of each fragment is stored in the node structure (along with pixel color and depth) in the per-pixel linked list creation step. Only a few bits are required (this depends on how many different blend modes are specified— typically this shouldn't be more than a handful) and therefore the bit field could be appended to the existing color or depth member of the node structure by modifying the packing function accordingly. When the per-pixel linked lists are parsed for rendering, the blending part of the algorithm is modified so that a different code path (ideally based on pure arithmetic instructions to avoid the need for actual code divergence) is executed based on the fragment's blend mode id.

2.6.5 Pixel Shader Code

The pixel shader code for linked list traversal and rendering is given in in Listing 2.2.

```
// Pixel shader input structure for fullscreen quad rendering
struct PS_SIMPLE_INPUT
  {
    float2 vTex : TEXCOORD;     // Texture coordinates
    float4 vPos : SV_POSITION; // Screen coordinates
  };

// Fragment sorting array
#define MAX_SORTED_FRAGMENTS 18
static uint2 SortedFragments[MAX_SORTED_FRAGMENTS+1];

// SRV declarations
Buffer<uint> HeadPointerBufferSRV : register(t0);
StructuredBuffer<NodeData_STRUCT> NodesBufferSRV : register(t1);
Texture2D BackgroundTexture : register(t3);

// Pixel shader for parsing per-pixel linked lists
float4 PS_RenderFragments( PS_SIMPLE_INPUT input) : SV_Target
{

    // Convert pixel 2D coordinates to linear address
    uint2 vScreenPos = uint(input.vPos.xy);
    uint uLinearAddress = vScreenPos.y*RENDERWIDTH + vScreenPos.x;
```

```
// Fetch offset of first fragment for current pixel
uint uOffset = HeadPointerBufferSRV[uLinearAddress];

// Loop through each node stored for this pixel location
int nNumFragments = 0;
while (uOffset != 0xFFFFFFFF)
{

    // Retrieve fragment at current offset
    NodeData_STRUCT Node = NodesBufferSRV[uOffset];

    // Copy fragment color and depth into sorting array
    SortedFragments[nNumFragments] =
    uint2(Node.uColor, Node.uDepth);

    // Sort fragments front to back using insertion sorting
    int j = nNumFragments;
    [loop]while ( (j>0) &&
        (SortedFragments[max(j-1, 0)].y >
        SortedFragments[j].y) )
    {

        // Swap required
        int jminusone = max(j-1, 0);
        uint2 Tmp = SortedFragments[j];
        SortedFragments[j] = SortedFragments[jminusone];
        SortedFragments[jminusone] = Tmp;
        j--;
    }

    // Increase number of fragment if under the limit
    nNumFragments = min(nNumFragments+1,
    MAX_SORTED_FRAGMENTS);

    // Retrieve next offset
    uOffset = Element.uNext;
}

// Retrieve current color from background color
float4 vCurrentColor =
BackgroundTexture.Load(int3(input.vPos.xy, 0));

// Render sorted fragments using SRCALPHA-INVSRCALPHA
// blending
for (int k=nNumFragments-1; k>=0; k--)
{

    float4 vColor = UnpackUintIntoFloat4
    (SortedFragments[k].x);
    vCurrentColor.xyz = lerp(vCurrentColor.xyz, vColor.xyz,
                            vColor.w);
}
```

```
    // Return manually-blended color
    return vCurrentColor;
}
```

Listing 2.2. Pixel shader for parsing per-pixel linked lists.

2.7 Multisampling Antialiasing Support

Multisampling antialiasing (MSAA) is supported by the OIT algorithm presented in this chapter via a couple of minor modifications to the technique. MSAA works by performing the depth test at multiple pixel sample locations and outputting the result of the pixel shader stage (evaluated at centroid location) to all samples that passed the depth test.

2.7.1 Per-pixel Linked Lists Creation

Directly storing translucent samples into per-pixel linked lists would rapidly become prohibitive from both a memory and performance perspective due to the sheer amount of samples to store. Instead the algorithm adapted to MSAA can simply store fragment data into per-pixel linked nodes as usual, but including *sample coverage* data in the node structure.

Sample coverage is an input provided by the pixel shader stage that specifies whether samples are covered by the input primitive. Sample coverage is a bit field containing as many useful bits as the number of samples, and is passed down to the pixel shader stage via the DirectX 11-specific SV_COVERAGE input (Figure 2.2 illustrates the concept of sample coverage on a single pixel.):

```
// Pixel shader input structure
struct PS_INPUT
{
    float3 vNormal : NORMAL;      // Pixel normal
    float2 vTex : TEXCOORD;       // Texture coordinates
    float4 vPos : SV_POSITION;    // Screen coordinates
    uint uCoverage : SV_COVERAGE; // Pixel coverage
};
```

Only a few bits are required for sample coverage; we therefore pack it onto the depth member of the node structure using a 24:8 bit arrangement (24 bits for depth, 8 bits for sample coverage). This avoids the need for extra storage and leaves enough precision for encoding depth. The node structure thus becomes:

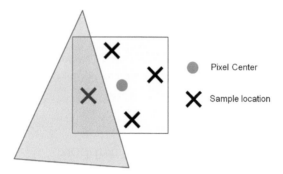

Figure 2.2. Sample coverage example on a single pixel. The blue triangle covers the third sample in a standard MSAA 4x arrangement. The input coverage to the pixel shader will therefore be equal to 0x04 (0100 in binary).

```
struct NodeData_STRUCT
{
    uint uColor;              // Fragment color packed as RGBA
    uint uDepthAndCoverage;   // Fragment depth and coverage
    uint uNext;               // Address of next linked list node
};
```

The pixel shader to create per-pixel linked lists is modified so that depth *and* coverage are now packed together and stored in the node structure:

```
// Store pixel depth and coverage in packed format
Node.uDepthAndCoverage = PackDepthAndCoverageIntoUint(
    input.vPos.z, input.uCoverage );
```

2.7.2 Per-pixel Linked Lists Traversal

The traversal of per-pixel linked lists needs to occur at *sample frequency* when outputting into a multisampled render target. This is because fragments stored in the per-pixel linked lists may affect only some samples at a given pixel location. Therefore both fragment sorting and blending must be performed per sample to ensure that translucent geometry gets correctly antialiased.

As in the non-multisampled case, a fullscreen quad is rendered to ensure that every pixel location in the destination render target is covered; one notable difference is that the pixel shader input for this pass now declares the **SV_SAMPLEINDEX** system value in order to force the pixel shader to execute at sample frequency. This value specifies the index of the sample at which the pixel shader currently executes.

When parsing per-pixel linked lists for rendering, the sample coverage in the current node is compared with the index of the sample being shaded: if the index is included in the sample coverage, then this pixel node contributes to the current sample and is therefore copied to the temporary array for sorting and later blending.

One further modification to the blending portion of the code is that the background texture representing the scene data prior to any translucent contribution is multisampled, thus the declaration and the fetch instruction are modified accordingly.

After the fullscreen quad is rendered, the multisampled render target will contain the sample-accurate translucent contribution to the scene.

2.7.3 Pixel Shader Code

The pixel shader code for parsing and rendering from per-pixel linked lists with MSAA enabled can be found in Listing 2.3. Code specific to MSAA is highlighted. Note that the shader can easily cater to both MSAA and non-MSAA cases by the use of a few well-placed #define statements.

```
// Pixel shader input structure for fullscreen quad rendering
// with MSAA enabled
struct PS_SIMPLE_INPUT
{
    float2 vTex  : TEXCOORD;      // Texture coordinates
    float4 vPos  : SV_POSITION;   // Screen coordinates
     uint uSample :  SV_SAMPLEINDEX;   // Sample index
    };

// Fragment sorting array
#define MAX_SORTED_FRAGMENTS 18
static uint2 SortedFragments[MAX_SORTED_FRAGMENTS+1];

// SRV declarations
Buffer<uint> HeadPointerBufferSRV : register(t0);
StructuredBuffer<NodeData_STRUCT> NodesBufferSRV : register(t1);
 Texture2DMS <float4, NUM_SAMPLES BackgroundTexture :  register(t3);

// Pixel shader for parsing per-pixel linked lists with MSAA
float4 PS_RenderFragments( PS_SIMPLE_INPUT input) : SV_Target
{

    // Convert pixel 2D coordinates to linear address
    uint2 vScreenPos = uint(input.vPos.xy);
    uint uLinearAddress = vScreenPos.y*RENDERWIDTH
                          + vScreenPos.x;

    // Fetch offset of first fragment for current pixel
    uint uOffset = HeadPointerBufferSRV[uLinearAddress];
```

```
// Loop through each node stored for this pixel location
int nNumFragments = 0;
while (uOffset != 0xFFFFFFFF)
{

    // Retrieve fragment at current offset
    NodeData_STRUCT Node = NodesBufferSRV[uOffset];
    // Only include fragment in sorted list if coverage mask
    // includes the sample currently being rendered}
    uintuCoverage =
            UnpackCoverageIntoUint(Node.uDepthAndCoverage);
  if ( uCoverage & (1<<input.uSample) )}
  {
      // Copy fragment color and depth into sorting array
      SortedFragments[nNumFragments] =
          uint2(Node.uColor, Node.uDepth);

      // Sort fragments front to back using
      // insertion sorting
      int j = nNumFragments;
      [loop]while ( (j>0) &&
          (SortedFragments[max(j-1, 0)].y >
              SortedFragments[j].y) )
      {
          // Swap required
          int jminusone = max(j-1, 0);
          uint2 Tmp = SortedFragments[j];
          SortedFragments[j] = SortedFragments[jminusone];
          SortedFragments[jminusone] = Tmp;
          j--;
      }

      // Increase number of fragment if under the limit
      nNumFragments=min(nNumFragments+1,
                        MAX_SORTED_FRAGMENTS);
  }

    // Retrieve next offset
    uOffset = Element.uNext;
}

// Retrieve current sample color from background texture
float4 vCurrentColor =
 BackgroundTexture.Load(int3(input.vPos.xy, 0),
                        input.uSample);}

 // Render sorted fragments using SRCALPHA-INVSRCALPHA
 // blending
 for (int k=nNumFragments-1; k>=0; k--)
 {

     float4 vColor =
             UnpackUintIntoFloat4(SortedFragments[k].x);
```

```
              vCurrentColor.xyz = lerp(vCurrentColor.xyz, vColor.xyz,
                                       vColor.w);
       }

       // Return manually-blended color
       return vCurrentColor;
   }
```

Listing 2.3. Pixel Shader for parsing per-pixel linked lists when MSAA is enabled.

2.8 Optimizations

2.8.1 Node Structure Packing

As previously mentioned in this chapter, the size of the node structure has a direct impact on the amount of memory declared for the nodes buffer. Incidentally, the smaller the size of the node structure, the better the performance, since fewer memory accesses will be performed. It therefore pays to aggressively pack data inside the node structure, even if it adds to the cost of packing/unpacking instructions in the shaders used.

The default node structure presented in previous paragraphs is three `uint` in size whereby one `uint` is used for packed RGBA color, one `uint` is used for depth and coverage, and the last `uint` is used for the next pointer. Some circumstances may allow further reduction of the structure for a performance/memory benefit; for instance, color and depth could be packed into a single `uint` (e.g., by encoding RGB color as 565 and depth as a 16-bit value (such a reduction in depth precision may need some scaling and biasing to avoid precision issues)). The "next" pointer could be encoded with 24 bits, leaving 8 bits for a combination of sample coverage and/or blend id. Such a scheme would reduce the node structure size to two `uint` (8 bytes), which is a desirable goal if the scene circumstances allow it.

2.8.2 Early Stencil Rejection in Parsing Phase

The second pass of the OIT algorithm can be accelerated by ensuring that only screen locations that have received at least one translucent fragment entry are processed. This would avoid the need for "empty" parsing of the per-pixel linked lists, improving performance in the process.

To achieve this goal, the linked lists creation phase is set up so that the stencil buffer is incremented for each fragment that passes the depth test. Once this phase is completed, the stencil buffer will contain translucent overdraw for each pixel in the scene, leaving the stencil clear value at 0 for pixel locations that haven't received any translucent fragment (i.e., for which the head pointer buffer is still 0xFFFFFFFF).

When per-pixel linked lists are parsed for rendering the stencil buffer is set up to pass if the stencil value is above 0. Early stencil rejection ensures that only pixel locations that have been touched by translucent fragments will be processed, saving on performance in the process.

2.8.3 MSAA: Fragment Resolve during Parsing

Executing the pixel shader at sample frequency is a significant performance cost compared to per-pixel execution. It is possible to replace per-sample execution for per-pixel execution for the fragment parsing and rendering pass in MSAA mode if fragments are "resolved" at the same time they are processed. Resolving fragments is a term that refers to the process of converting pixel samples into a single pixel color value that gets written onto a single-sample render target. The most common resolve function is a straight average of all samples belonging to a pixel but some variations exist (e.g., HDR-correct resolves).

To resolve fragments in the OIT rendering phase a *non-multisampled* render target has to be bound as an output. Doing so will prevent any further rendering operation requiring access to multisampled data, so it is important that this optimization is considered only if such access is no longer required. Should this condition be fulfilled, the performance improvements enabled by fragment resolving can be dramatic (up to a 50% increase was observed on a Radeon 5870 at 1024×768 with 4x MSAA) so this is certainly an optimization to consider. Because the render target bound is no longer multisampled the depth stencil buffer that was bound when storing fragments can no longer be used for early stencil rejection in the fragment parsing phase. Still, the performance boost obtained via fragment resolving outweighs the benefit of this previous optimization.

To restore per-pixel shader execution, the pixel shader input structure no longer declares SV_SAMPLEINDEX. Only the blending section of the per-pixel linked list parsing shader needs further code modification to enable fragment resolving. After fragments have been fetched and sorted in the temporary array, the algorithm needs to determine the blending contribution for each sample in the destination pixel. Hence the next node picked from the sorted list will add its blending contribution to a sample only if its pixel coverage includes the sample currently being processed. Once the blending contribution for all samples has been determined, the final average (resolve) operation takes place and the resulting color is output to the destination render target.

The blending portion of the per-pixel linked list parsing shader that implements fragment resolve in MSAA mode can be found in Listing 2.4.

```
// Retrieve color of each sample in the background texture
float3 vCurrentColorSample[NUM_SAMPLES];
[unroll]for (uint uSample=0; uSample<NUM_SAMPLES; uSample++)
{
```

```
        vCurrentColorSample[uSample] =
            BackgroundTexture.Load(int3(input.vPos.xy, 0), uSample);
}

// Render fragments using SRCALPHA-INVSRCALPHA blending
for (int k=nNumFragments-1; k>=0; k--)
{
    // Retrieve fragment color
    float4 vFragmentColor=
                UnpackUintIntoFloat4(SortedFragments[k].x);

    // Retrieve sample coverage
    uint uCoverage =
                UnpackCoverageIntoUint(SortedFragments[k].y);

    // Loop through each sample
    [unroll]for (uint uSample=0; uSample<NUM_SAMPLES; uSample++)
    {
        // Determine if sample is covered by sample coverage
        float fIsSampleCovered= (uCoverage & (1<<uSample)) ?
                                1.0 : 0.0;

        // Blend current color sample with fragment color
        // if covered. If the sample is not covered the color
        // will be unchanged
        vCurrentColorSample[uSample].xyz = lerp(
                vCurrentColorSample[uSample].xyz,
                vFragmentColor.xyz,
                vFragmentColor.w * fIsSampleCovered);
    }
}

// Resolve samples into a single color
float4 vCurrentColor = float4(0,0,0,1);
[unroll]for (uint uSample=0; uSample<NUM_SAMPLES; uSample++)
{
    vCurrentColor.xyz += vCurrentColorSample[uSample];
}
vCurrentColor.xyz *= (1.0/NUM_SAMPLES);

// Return manually-blended color
return vCurrentColor;
```

Listing 2.4. Blending and resolving fragments.

2.9 Tiling

2.9.1 Tiling as a Memory Optimization

Tiling is a pure memory optimization that considerably reduces the amount of video memory required for the nodes buffer (and to a lesser extent the head

Figure 2.3. Opaque contents of render target prior to any OIT contribution.

pointer buffer). Without tiling, the memory occupied by both buffers can rapidly become huge when fullscreen render target resolutions are used. As an example a standard HD resolution of 1280×720 with an estimated average translucent overdraw of eight would occupy a total of $1280 \times 720 \times 8 \times \text{sizeof}$(node structure size) bytes for the nodes buffer only, which equates to more than 168 megabytes with a standard node structure containing 3 units (color, depth and next pointer).

Instead of allocating buffers for the full-size render target, a single, smaller rectangular region (the "tile") is used. This tile represents the extent of the

Figure 2.4. Translucent contribution to the scene is added to the render target via regular tiling. Each rectangular area stores fragments in the tile-sized head pointer and nodes buffers and then parses those buffers to add correctly ordered translucency information to the same rectangle area. In this example the tile size is 1/15 of the render target size, and a total of 15 rectangles are processed.

area being processed for OIT in a given pass. Since the tile is typically smaller than the render size, this means multiple passes are needed to calculate the full-size translucent contributions to the scene. The creation of per-pixel linked lists is therefore performed on a per-tile basis, after which the traversal phase fetches nodes from the tile-sized head pointer and nodes buffers to finally output the resulting color values onto the rectangular region corresponding to the tile being processed in the destination render target. As an example, a standard HD resolution of 1280×720 would take 15 passes with a tile size of 256×240 for the screen to be fully covered. Figure 2.3 shows a scene with translucent contributions yet to be factored in. Figure 2.4 shows the same scene with translucency rendered on top using a set of tile-sized rectangular regions covering the whole render area.

2.9.2   Transformation Overhead

Because multiple passes are required, any objects crossing tile boundaries has to be transformed more than once (once for each tile-sized screen region they contribute to), which can impact performance when objects with higher transformation costs (complex vertex skinning, advanced tessellation algorithms, use of long geometry shaders, etc.) are employed. Ideally, translucent geometry should be decomposed into subobjects to minimize transformation overlap between tile regions. Smaller objects such as particles will particularly benefit from the tiling approach, since overlap between tile regions is likely to be minimal (unless the tiles themselves are small), and boundaries between particles belonging to different rectangle regions are well defined.

2.9.3   Tile Size

Tile size can be arbitrary; it may be a multiple of the render target dimensions, but this is not a strict requirement. Typically tile size will be dictated by the amount of free video memory available for OIT, since larger dimensions will lead once again to significant amounts of memory being consumed. There is also a direct correlation between tile size and performance, since the smaller the tile size, the higher the number of passes required to cover the render area. Thus, it is generally better to allocate a larger tile size if memory can be spared for this purpose.

2.9.4   Minimum Rectangle Optimization

It is not necessary to cover the *full* render target area with multipass tiling. Instead one needs to cover only the *minimum* rectangle area of the render target that will actually receive translucent contributions. This minimum rectangle area can be determined by using bounding volumes transformed to screen space in order to retrieve the 2D screen coordinates extents of all translucent geometry. Once the bounding volumes of all translucent meshes have been transformed,

Figure 2.5. Translucent contribution to the scene is added to the render target via optimized tiling. Only tiles enclosing the bounding geometry of the translucent characters are processed. The bounding boxes of translucent geometry are transformed to screen space and the combined extents of the resulting coordinates define the minimum rectangle area that will be processed. This minimum rectangle area is covered by as many tile-sized rectangular regions as required (six in this example). Each of those regions performs fragment storing and rendering using a single pair of tile-sized head pointers and nodes buffers.

the minimum and maximum dimensions (in X and Y) of the combined set will define the rectangle area of translucent contributions. The minimum rectangle optimization typically allows a reduction in the number of tiles to process when parsing and rendering fragments from linked lists. In order to render a minimum number of tiles, it is desirable to ensure that the bounding geometry used is as tight as possible; for example, axis-aligned bounding boxes are likely to be less effective than arbitrary-aligned bounding boxes or a set of bounding volumes with a close fit to the meshes involved.

Because this optimization covers only a portion of the screen, the previous contents of the render target will need to be copied to the destination render target, at least for those regions that do not include translucent contribution. This copy can be a full-size copy performed before the OIT step, or stencil-based marking can be used to transfer only the rectangle regions that did not contain any translucency.

Figure 2.5 illustrates the optimized covering of tiles to cover only the 2D extents of translucent contributions to the scene.

2.10 Conclusion

The OIT algorithm presented in this chapter allows significant performance savings compared to other existing techniques. The technique is also robust, allowing different types of translucent materials to be used as well as supporting hardware multisampling antialiasing. Although video memory requirements can become unreasonable when larger viewports are employed, the use of tile optimizations allows a trade-off between memory and performance while still retaining the inherent advantages of this technique. The use of per-pixel linked lists can be adapted to techniques other than order-independent transparency, because they can store a variety of per-pixel data for arbitrary purposes: see Part III, Chapter 3 in this volume for an example.

2.11 Acknowledgments

I would like to thank Holger Gruen and Jakub Klarowicz for coming up with the original concept of creating per-pixel linked lists in a DirectX 11-class GPU environment.

Bibliography

[Bavoil 08] Louis Bavoil and Kevin Myers. "Order-Independent Transparency with Dual Depth Peeling." White paper available online at http://developer.download.nvidia.com/SDK/10/opengl/src/dual_depth_peeling/doc/DualDepthPeeling.pdf, 2008.

[Carpenter 84] L. Carpenter. "The A-Buffer, An Antialiased Hidden Surface Method." *Computer Graphics (SIGGRAPH)* 18:3 (1984), 103–108.

[Everitt 01] Cass Everitt. "Interactive Order-Independent Transparency." White paper available online at http://developer.nvidia.com/object/Interactive_Order_Transparency.html, 2001.

[Myers 07] Kevin Myers and Louis Bavoil. "Stencil Routed A-Buffer." *SIGGRAPH '07: ACM SIGGRAPH 2007 Sketches*, Article 21. New York: ACM, 2007.

[Thibieroz 08] Nicolas Thibieroz. "Robust Order-Independent Transparency via Reverse Depth Peeling," In *ShaderX^6*, edited by Wolfgang Engel, pp. 211–226. Hingham, MA; Charles River Media, 2008.

[Thibieroz 10] Nicolas Thibieroz and Holger Gruen. "OIT and Indirect Illumination using DX11 Linked Lists," *GDC 2010 Presentation from the Advanced D3D Day Tutorial.* Available online at http://developer.amd.com/documentation/presentations/Pages/default.aspx, 2010

[Yang 10] Jason Yang, Justin Hensley, Holger Gruen, and Nicolas Thibieroz. "Real-Time Concurrent Linked List Construction on the GPU. *Computer Graphics Forum, Eurographics Symposium on Rendering 2010* 29:4 (2010), 1297–1304.

3

Simple and Fast Fluids
Martin Guay, Fabrice Colin, and Richard Egli

3.1 Introduction

In this chapter, we present a simple and efficient algorithm for the simulation of fluid flow directly on the GPU using a single pixel shader. By temporarily relaxing the incompressibility condition, we are able to solve the full Navier-Stokes equations over the domain in a single pass.

3.1.1 Simplicity and Speed

Solving the equations in an explicit finite difference scheme is extremely simple. We believe that anybody who can write the code for a blur post-process can implement this algorithm and simulate fluid flow efficiently on the GPU. The code holds is less then 40 lines and is so simple we actually had the solver running in FxComposer (see FxComposer demo). Solving every fluid cell (texel) locally in a single pass is not only simple, but also quite fast. In fact, the implementation of

Figure 3.1. 3D simulation with 100k particles visualization.

this algorithm on the GPU is at least 100 times faster than on the CPU.[1] In this chapter, we show how to couple the two equations of the classical Navier-Stokes equations into a single-phase process; a detailed explanation of the algorithm along with example code follows.

3.2 Fluid Modeling

The greatest feature of physics-based modeling in computer graphics is the ability of a model to cope with its environment and produce realistic motion and behavior. Attempting to animate fluids nonphysically is, in our experience, a nontrivial task. In order to physically model the motion of fluids, the simplified classical Navier-Stokes equations for incompressible fluids are a good description of such mechanics, and a solver based on this model is capable of simulating a large class of fluid-like phenomena. Fortunately a deep understanding of the partial differential equations involved is not required in order to implement such a solver.

3.2.1 Navier-Stokes Equations

The Navier-Stokes equations, widely used in numerous areas of fluid dynamics, are derived from two very simple and intuitive principles of mechanics: the conservation of momentum (Equation (3.1)) and the conservation of mass (Equation (3.2)).

$$\rho \left(\frac{\partial \mathbf{u}}{\partial t} + \mathbf{u} \cdot \nabla \mathbf{u} \right) = -\nabla P + \rho \mathbf{g} + \mu \nabla^2 \mathbf{u}, \tag{3.1}$$

where $\mathbf{u}$ is a velocity vector, $\mathbf{g}$ is the gravitational acceleration vector, μ the viscosity, P the pressure and ∇^2 stands for the Laplacian operator $\partial^2/\partial x^2 + \partial^2/\partial y^2 + \partial^2/\partial z^2$.

$$\frac{\partial \rho}{\partial t} + \nabla \cdot (\rho \mathbf{u}) = 0, \tag{3.2}$$

where $\nabla\cdot$ represents the divergence operator. These equations also have to be supplemented with boundary conditions of Dirichlet, Neumann, or even of Robin type. Usually, the incompressibility condition (see Equation (3.3)) is imposed on the fluid by assuming that its density ρ remains constant over time. Using the latter assumption, Equation (3.2) simplifies to

$$\nabla \cdot \mathbf{u} = 0. \tag{3.3}$$

---

[1]The simulation runs on the CPU at 8.5 fps with 4 threads on an Intel Core 2 Quad at 2.66 GHz simulating only the velocity field over a 256 × 256 grid. Keeping the same grid size, the simulation of both velocity and density fields runs at more than 2500 fps on a Geforce 9800 GT using 32-bit floating point render targets. Note that 16-bit floating point is sufficient to represent velocities.

Now one of the main features of the formulation of the Navier-Stokes equations illustrated here, is the possibility, when working with regular grid domains, to use classical finite differences schemes.

3.2.2 Density-Invariance Algorithm

Unfortunately, a direct application of Equation (3.1) results in a nonzero divergence field $\mathbf{u}$ (i.e. (3.3) is no longer satisfied by the vector field $\mathbf{u}$). A lot of popular methods for simulating fluids consist of two main steps. First some temporary compressibility is allowed when Equation (3.1) is solved, and second, a correction is applied to the vector field obtained, in order to fulfill the incompressibility condition. This correction can be done by considering a projection of the resulting vector $\mathbf{w}$ field onto its divergence-free part [Stam 99]. The latter projection can also be performed in the spirit of the smoothed particle hydrodynamics (SPH) method (see for instance [Colin et al. 06]). Another way to deal with this incompressibility problem is to take advantage of the relation between the divergence of the vector field and the local density given by Equation (3.2), by trying to enforce a density invariance (see among others, [Premože et al. 03]). Recently, some techniques combining the two preceding approaches were studied (for an exhaustive study of all the previous techniques in the SPH context, see [Xu et al. 09]).

We choose an approach based on density invariance. It is interesting to note that an algorithm based on the previous approach has proven to be stable for the SPH method [Premože et al. 03]. First, observe that Equation (3.2) can be rewritten as

$$\frac{\partial \rho}{\partial t} = -\nabla \rho \cdot \mathbf{u} - \rho \nabla \cdot \mathbf{u},$$

clearly illustrating the link between the divergence of the vector field and the variation of the local density. After solving the above equation for density, a corrective pressure field could simply be given as

$$P = K(\rho^n - \rho_0), \tag{3.4}$$

where ρ_0 is the rest (initial) density and where the constant K is often chosen according to the gas-state equation (see [Desbrun and Cani 96] or [Muller et al. 03]).

The corrective field P (a density-invariant field) could be interpreted as an internal pressure whose gradient corrects the original velocity field to get a null divergence vector field. Since we are interested only in its derivative, there is no need to retain the P variable and the corresponding correction to be applied is simply given by

$$\nabla P = K \nabla \rho.$$

Now before jumping directly to code, we first need to discretize the formulation.

3.2.3   From Math to Code: Numerical Scheme

One of the main features of the formulation used in this chapter is the ability to use, along a regular grid, simple finite differences. Since the texture is the default data structure on a GPU, a regular grid holding four values per cell is a natural choice for the spatial discretization of the domain. Also, since this is an Eulerian formulation, the spatial discretization stays fixed throughout the simulation and the neighborhood of an element, the elements (in our case, the texels) around it, will always remain the same, greatly simplifying the solver's code.

The simplicity of finite differences along a one-phase coupling of both momentum and mass conservation equations through a density-invariant field enables the elaboration of a very simple algorithm to solve fluid flow in a single step. Note that other grid-based methods on the GPU exist and the interested reader can refer to [Crane et al. 07] for a multistep but unconditionally stable simulation or to [Li et al. 03] (also available in *GPU Gems 2*) for a lattice-based simulation.

3.3   Solver's Algorithm

A solution to the Navier-Stokes equations is a vector-valued function $\mathbf{u}$ and a scalar-valued function ρ which satisfies the momentum and mass conservation equations. These functions are spatially discretized on a texture where quantities $\mathbf{u}$ and ρ are stored at the texel's center. In order to update a solution $\mathbf{u}$ and ρ from time t_n to time t_{n+1}, we traverse the grid once and solve every texel in the following manner:

1. Solve the mass conservation equation for density by computing the differential operators with central finite differences and integrating the solution with the forward euler method.

2. Solve the momentum conservation equation for velocity in two conceptual steps:

   (a) Solve the transport equation using the semi-Lagrangian scheme.

   (b) Solve the rest of the momentum conservation equation using the same framework as in Step 1.

3. Impose Neumann boundary conditions.

3.3.1   Conservation of Mass

In order to compute the right-hand side of the mass conservation equation, we need to evaluate a gradient operator ∇ for a scalar-valued function ρ and a divergence operator $\nabla\cdot$ for a vector-valued function $\mathbf{u}$ both, respectively, expressed using central finite differences as follows:

$$\nabla \rho_{i,j,k}^n = \left(\frac{\rho_{i+1,j,k}^n - \rho_{i-1,j,k}^n}{2\Delta x}, \frac{\rho_{i,j+1,k}^n - \rho_{i,j-1,k}^n}{2\Delta y}, \frac{\rho_{i,j,k+1}^n - \rho_{i,j,k-1}^n}{2\Delta z} \right),$$

$$\nabla \cdot u_{i,j,k}^n = \frac{u_{i+1,j,k}^n - u_{i-1,j,k}^n}{2\Delta x} + \frac{v_{i,j+1,k}^n - v_{i,j-1,k}^n}{2\Delta y} + \frac{w_{i,j,k+1}^n - w_{i,j,k-1}^n}{2\Delta z}.$$

(3.5)

And finally, an integration is performed using forward Euler over a time step Δt:

$$\rho_{i,j,k}^{n+1} = \rho_{i,j,k}^n + \Delta t(-\nabla \rho_{i,j,k}^n \cdot u_{i,j,k}^n - \rho_{i,j,k}^n \nabla \cdot u_{i,j,k}^n).$$

Indeed, there exist other finite difference schemes. For instance, one could use upwinding for the transport term or literally semi-Lagrangian advection. Unfortunately, the latter results in much numerical dissipation; an issue covered in Section 3.3.2.

3.3.2 Conservation of Momentum

We solve the momentum conservation equation for velocity $\mathbf{u}$ in two conceptual steps. The first consists of solving the transport equation $\frac{\partial \mathbf{u}}{\partial t} = -\mathbf{u} \cdot \nabla \mathbf{u}$ with a semi-Lagrangian scheme, then solving the rest of the momentum conservation equation ($\frac{\partial \mathbf{u}}{\partial t} = -\frac{\nabla P}{\rho} + \mathbf{g} + \frac{\mu}{\rho}\nabla^2 \mathbf{u}$) with central finite differences and forward Euler integration.

Semi-Lagrangian scheme. First introduced to computer graphics by Jos Stam in the paper *Stable Fluids* [Stam 99], the following scheme is quite useful for solving the generic transport equation given by

$$\frac{\partial \phi}{\partial t} = -\mathbf{u} \cdot \nabla \phi,$$

(3.6)

at the current texel's position $\mathbf{x}_{i,j,k}$ with

$$\phi_{i,j,k}^{n+1}(\mathbf{x}_{i,j,k}) = \phi^n(\mathbf{x}_{i,j,k} - \Delta t \mathbf{u}_{i,j,k}^n).$$

(3.7)

The idea is to solve the transport equation from a Lagrangian viewpoint where the spatial discretization element holding quantities (e.g., a particle) moves along the flow of the fluid, and answer the following question: where was this element at the previous time step if it has been transported by a field $\mathbf{u}$ and ends up at the current texel's center at the present time? Finally, we use the sampled quantity to set it as the new value of the current texel.

Now when solving the transport equation for velocity, Equation (3.6) becomes $\frac{\partial \mathbf{u}}{\partial t} = -\mathbf{u} \cdot \nabla \mathbf{u}$ and is solved with

$$\mathbf{u}_{i,j,k}^{n+1}(\mathbf{x}_{i,j,k}) = \mathbf{u}^n(\mathbf{x}_{i,j,k} - \Delta t \mathbf{u}_{i,j,k}^n).$$

This method is not only straightforward to implement on the GPU with linear samplers, but is also unconditionally stable. Unfortunately, quantities advected in this fashion suffer from dramatic numerical diffusion and higher-order schemes exist to avoid this issue, such as McCormack schemes discussed in [Selle et al. 08]. These schemes are especially useful when advecting visual densities as mentioned in Section 3.5.

Density invariance and diffusion forces. After solving the transport term, the rest of the momentum conservation equation is solved with central finite differences. Here is a quick reminder of the part of Equation (3.1) which is not yet solved:

$$\frac{\partial \mathbf{u}}{\partial t} = -\frac{\nabla P}{\rho} + \mathbf{g} + \frac{\mu}{\rho}\nabla^2\mathbf{u}.$$

As mentioned earlier, the gradient of the density-invariant field ∇P is equivalent to the density gradient $\nabla\rho$, i.e. $\nabla P \simeq K\nabla\rho$. Since we already computed the density gradient $\nabla\rho^n_{i,j,k}$ when solving the mass conservation equation with Equation (3.5), we need only to scale by K in order to compute the "pressure"" gradient ∇P. As for the diffusion term, a Laplacian ∇^2 must be computed. This operator is now expressed using a second-order central finite difference scheme:

$$\nabla^2\mathbf{u}^n_{i,j,k} = (L(u),\ L(v),\ L(w)),$$

where

$$L(f) = \left(\frac{f^n_{i+1,j,k} - 2f^n_{i,j,k} + f^n_{i-1,j,k}}{(\Delta x)^2} + \frac{f^n_{i,j+1,k} - 2f^n_{i,j,k} + f^n_{i,j-1,k}}{(\Delta y)^2} \right. \\ \left. + \frac{f^n_{i,j,k+1} - 2f^n_{i,j,k} + f^n_{i,j,k-1}}{(\Delta z)^2}\right),$$

for every twice continuously differentiable function f. Finally, an integration is performed using forward Euler over a time step Δt:

$$\mathbf{u}^{n+1}_{i,j,k} = \mathbf{u}^n_{i,j,k} + \Delta t(-S\nabla\rho^n_{i,j,k} + \mathbf{g} + \nu\nabla^2\mathbf{u}^n_{i,j,k}).$$

Since the density ρ value should not vary much from ρ_0, we can interpret the $\frac{1}{\rho}$ scale as a constant held by $\nu := \frac{\mu}{\rho_0}$ and $S := K\frac{(\Delta x)^2}{\Delta t\rho_0}$. One can see how we also scale by $\frac{(\Delta x)^2}{\Delta t}$ which seems to give better results (we found $(\Delta x)^2$ while testing over a 2D simulation) and a sound justification has still to be found and will be the subject of future work.

Up to now we solved the equations without considering boundary conditions (obstacles) or numerical stability. These two topics will be covered in the next two sections.

3.3.3 Boundary Conditions

Boundary conditions are specified at the boundary (surface) of the fluid in order for the fluid to satisfy specific behaviors. They are essential for the interactions between the fluid and the different types of matter such as solids (obstacles) in the domain. Neumann boundary conditions are considered for fluid-solid interactions. Our method does not provide free surface boundaries for fluid-fluid interactions such as liquid and air interactions necessary for water animations. When simulating smoke or fire, for instance, it is possible to consider the air and gas as a single fluid. Therefore, only Neumann boundary conditions are required. Hence in the proposed implementation, computational cells are tagged as either fluid or boundary cells. Note velocities and densities are defined on all cell types. Before discussing in-depth Neumann boundary conditions, it is convenient to first consider the most simple boundary condition: the Dirichlet boundary condition that means "to set directly." Hence, one could set the border cells to null velocities and densities to an initial value and make sure the simulation works well before introducing obstacles.

Neumann boundary conditions. Computational cells are either tagged as fluid or boundary cells. Note velocities and densities are defined on all cell types. The treatment of obstacles requires the use of boundary conditions on the solution **u** and are usually of Neumann type. The simplest boundary condition is the Dirichlet boundary condition, which specifies the value the solution needs to take on the boundary; hence, one could set the border cells to null velocities and densities to an initial value and make sure the simulation works well before considering obstacles.

The Neumann boundary condition is a type of boundary condition that specifies the values of the derivative in the direction of the outward normal vector at the boundary. To keep the fluid from entering obstacles, this condition would result in having the obstacle's corresponding boundary cells fulfill $\frac{\partial f}{\partial n} = 0$ for every component $f \in \{u,\ v,\ w\}$ of the vector function **u**; therefore, the fluid cells around a boundary cell need to be correctly adjusted in order to satisfy this condition. The derivative in the normal direction at such a boundary cell is quite trivial when assuming that the walls of an obstacle are always coincident with the

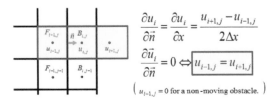

$$\frac{\partial u_i}{\partial \vec{n}} = \frac{\partial u_i}{\partial x} = \frac{u_{i+1,j} - u_{i-1,j}}{2\Delta x}$$

$$\frac{\partial \vec{u}_i}{\partial \vec{n}} = 0 \Leftrightarrow \boxed{u_{i-1,j} = u_{i+1,j}}$$

$$\left(u_{i-1,j} = 0 \text{ for a non-moving obstacle.} \right)$$

Figure 3.2. Neumann boundary conditions.

face of a computational cell (i.e., obstacles would completely fill computational cells). With this assumption, the derivative $\frac{\partial f}{\partial n}$ is either given by $\pm\frac{\partial u}{\partial x}$, $\pm\frac{\partial v}{\partial y}$, or $\pm\frac{\partial w}{\partial z}$ for u, v, and w, respectively. As an example, one can see how the fluid cell $F_{i-1,j}$ is adjusted according to the derivative of the boundary cell $B_{i,j}$ in Figure 3.2.

The true difficulty is the actual tracking of obstacles, specifically when working with dynamic 3D scenes in which objects must first be voxelized in order to be treated by the algorithm. See [Crane et al. 07] for a possible voxelization method.

3.3.4 Stability Conditions

Explicit integration is very simple from both analytical and programmatic points of view, but is only conditionally stable; meaning the time step value Δt has an upper bound defined by a ratio relative to the spatial resolution $\Delta \mathbf{x}$ over the function's range $\mathbf{u}$:

$$\Delta t < \max\left\{\left|\frac{\Delta x}{u}\right|, \left|\frac{\Delta y}{v}\right|, \left|\frac{\Delta z}{w}\right|\right\}.$$

This condition must be satisfied everywhere in the domain.

3.4 Code

Short and simple code for the 2D solver is presented in this section. In two dimensions, the x- and y-components hold velocities and the z-component holds the density. Setting $\Delta x = \Delta y = 1$ greatly simplifies the code. A 3D demo is also available on accompanying web materials ($K \simeq 0.2, \Delta t = 0.15$).

```
///< Central Finite Differences Scale.
float2 CScale = 1.0f/2.0f;

float S=K/dt;

float4 FC = tex2D(FieldSampler,UV);
float3 FR = tex2D(FieldSampler,UV+float2(Step.x,0));
float3 FL = tex2D(FieldSampler,UV-float2(Step.x,0));
float3 FT = tex2D(FieldSampler,UV+float2(0,Step.y));
float3 FD = tex2D(FieldSampler,UV-float2(0,Step.y));

float4x3 FieldMat = {FR,FL,FT,FD};

//du/dx,du/dy
float3 UdX = float3(FieldMat[0]-FieldMat[1])*CScale;
float3 UdY = float3(FieldMat[2]-FieldMat[3])*CScale;

float Udiv = UdX.x+UdY.y;
```

```
float2 DdX = float2(UdX.z,UdY.z);

///<
///< Solve for density.
///<
FC.z -=  dt*dot(float3(DdX,Udiv),FC.xyz);
///< Related to stability
FC.z = clamp(FC.z,0.5f,3.0f);

///<
///< Solve for velocity.
///<
float2 PdX = S*DdX;
float2 Laplacian = mul((float4)1,(float4x2)FieldMat)-4.0f*FC.xy;
float2 ViscosityForce = v*Laplacian;

///< Semi-Lagrangian advection.
float2 Was  = UV - dt*FC.xy*Step;
FC.xy = tex2D(FieldLinearSampler,Was).xy;

FC.xy += dt*(ViscosityForce - PdX + ExternalForces);

///< Boundary conditions.
for (int i=0; i<4; ++i)
{
if (IsBoundary(UV+Step*Directions[i]))
{
float2 SetToZero = (1-abs(Directions[i]));
FC.xy *= SetToZero;
}
}
return FC;
```

Listing 3.1. 2D solver, Shader model 2_a.

3.5 Visualization

One of the disadvantages of the Eulerian formulation is the lack of geometric
information about the fluid. So far, we have captured its motion with the velocity
field, but we still don't know its shape. Nevertheless, there are many ways to
visualize a fluid. In this section we briefly discuss two simple techniques. The first
consists of advecting particles under the computed velocity field and the second,
of advecting a scalar density field.

3.5.1 Particles

Using particles in a one-way interaction with the fluid is by far the most simple
and efficient technique for visualizing a fluid. Since the velocity field is computed

on the GPU, the whole system can run independently with very few interactions with the CPU. Once the particles are initialized, we sample only the velocity field in order to update their positions as illustrated in the following code:

```
v = Field.SampleLevel(LinearSampler,PosToUV(Particle.Pos),0);
Particle.Pos   += dt*v.xyz;
```

3.5.2   Smoke-Fire Density Field

It is possible to simulate smoke and fire by iteratively solving the convection-diffusion equation for a scalar density field (see Figures 3.3 and 3.4). Rendering such a scalar field in 2D is quite simple since only a texture holding the density field needs to be rendered. As for 3D fields, a volume rendering technique is required. Here are the governing equations for both smoke (Equation (3.7)) and fire (Equation (3.8)), respectively:

$$\frac{\partial \phi}{\partial t} = \mathbf{u} \cdot \nabla \phi + \mathbf{k} \nabla^2 \phi, \tag{3.7}$$

$$\frac{\partial \phi}{\partial t} = \mathbf{u} \cdot \nabla \phi + \mathbf{k} \nabla^2 \phi - \mathbf{c}, \tag{3.8}$$

where ϕ is a scalar density, k a diffusion coefficient and c a reaction constant for fire.

Numerical schemes to solve this equation are abundant, and the one which maps best to the GPU is the semi-Lagrangian method (see Equation (3.6)) but unfortunately, the solution loses much detail as dissipation occurs from this numerical scheme—which in turn enables the omission of the diffusion term from the equation. To address this problem and achieve more compelling visual results, we strongly suggest using the three-pass MacCormack method described in [Selle et al. 08]. This scheme has second-order precision both in space and time, therefore keeping the density from losing its small scale features and numerically dissipating its quantity as drastically as with the first-order semi-Lagrangian method. To add more detail to the simulation, one could also amplify the vorticity of the flow (the velocity field) with vorticity confinement, a method discussed in the context of visual smoke simulation in [Fedkiw et al. 01].

3.6   Conclusion

Many algorithms could be generated from this one-phase coupling of both equations through a density-invariant field. We hope the one illustrated here serves as a good basis for developers seeking to make use of interactive fluids in their applications.

Figure 3.3. Smoke density over a 512×512 density and 256×256 fluid simulation grid.

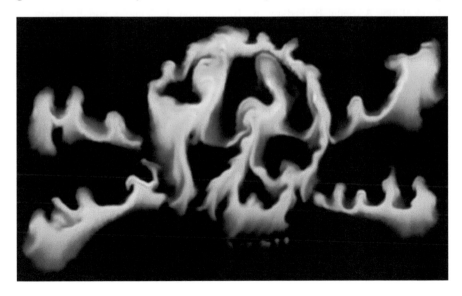

Figure 3.4. Fire density over a 512×512 density and 256×256 fluid simulation grid.

Bibliography

[Colin et al. 06] F. Colin, R. Egli, and F.Y. Lin. "Computing a Null Divergence Velocity Field using Smoothed Particle Hydrodynamics." *Journal of Computational Physics* 217:2 (2006), 680–692.

[Crane et al. 07] K. Crane, I. Llamas, and S. Tariq. "Real-Time Simulation and Rendering of 3D Fluids." In *GPU Gems 3*, pp. 633–675. Reading, MA: Addison-Wesley, 2007.

[Desbrun and Cani 96] M. Desbrun and M.P. Cani. "Smoothed Particles: A New Paradigm for Animating Highly Deformable Bodies." In *Proceedings of EG Workshop on Animation and Simulation*, pp. 61–76. Berlin-Heidelberg: Springer-Verlag, 1996.

[Fedkiw et al. 01] R. Fedkiw, J. Stam, and H. W. Jensen. "Visual Simulation of Smoke." *Proceedings of the 28th Annual Conference on Computer Graphics and Interactive Techniques*, pp. 15–22.

[Li et al. 03] W. Li, X. Wei, and A. Kaufman. "Implementing Lattice Boltzmann Computation on Graphics Hardware." *The Visual Computer* 19:7–8 (2003), 444–456.

[Muller et al. 03] M. Muller, D. Charypar, and M. Gross. "Particle-Based Fluid Simulation for Interactive Applications." pp. 154–159. New York: ACM, 2003.

[Premože et al. 03] S. Premože, T. Tasdizen, J. Bigler, A. Lefohn, and R.T. Whitaker. "Particle-Based Simulation of Fluids." *Computer Graphics Forum (Proceedings of Eurographics)* 22:3 (2003), 401–410.

[Selle et al. 08] A. Selle, R. Fedkiw, K. Byungmoon, L. Yingjie, and R. Jarek. "An Unconditionally Stable MacCormack Method." *Journal of Scientific Computing* 35:2–3 (2008), 350–371.

[Stam 99] J. Stam. "Stable Fluids." In *Proceedings of the 26th Annual Conference on Computer Graphics and Interactive Techniques*, pp. 121–128. New York: ACM, 1999.

[Xu et al. 09] R. Xu, P. Stansby, and D. Laurence. "Accuracy and Stability in Incompressible SPH (ISPH) Based on the Projection Method and a New Approach." *Journal of Computational Physics* 228:18 (2009), 6703–6725.

4

A Fast Poisson Solver for OpenCL Using Multigrid Methods
Sebastien Noury, Samuel Boivin, and Olivier Le Maître

4.1 Introduction

Many techniques in computer graphics are based on mathematical models to realistically simulate physical phenomena, such as fluid dynamics [Stam 99], or to deform and merge complex object meshes together [Yu et al. 04].

Many of these mathematical models involve the solution of Poisson partial differential equations, or more general elliptic equations, making the availability of efficient Poisson solvers crucial, particularly for real-time simulation. For example, the simulation of incompressible fluid flows often relies on projection-correction techniques where the pressure fields are solutions of a Poisson equation. Solving this equation is important, not only to obtain realistic flow dynamics, but also for the stability of the simulation. In fact, many efforts have been dedicated to the development of fast and stable fluid solvers [Stam 99]; the solution of the Poisson pressure equation constitutes the most time-consuming part of these algorithms.

This chapter presents an implementation of various iterative methods for the resolution of Poisson equations on heterogeneous parallel computers. Currently, most fast Poisson solvers implement the simple Jacobi method. After reviewing Jacobi iterative methods and variants in Section 4.3, we introduce more advanced iterative techniques based on multiscale iterations on a set of embedded grids, namely the so-called multigrid methods in Section 4.4. For all of these methods, we provide some theoretical background and discuss their efficiency and complexity with regard to their implementation. We particularly detail the multigrid method which involves several operators whose implementation is critical to efficiency. In Section 4.5, we provide a tutorial for the OpenCL implementation of the various algorithms, which are subsequently tested and compared in

Section 4.6. We end the chapter with a discussion of the efficiency of the methods in Section 4.7. Specifically, we show that although more complex to implement, the multigrid method allows for a significant reduction of both the number of iterations and the length of computation time compared with the simpler fixed-grid iterative methods. Hasty developers can skip directly to the implementation in (Section 4.5) and refer later to the theoretical background in Section 4.2.

4.2   Poisson Equation and Finite Volume Method

In this section, we introduce the Poisson equation, the resolution of which is the focus of the present chapter. We then describe the finite volume discretization of the Poisson equation and, finally, discuss the boundary conditions. These materials are introduced to ease the understanding of the iterative techniques and implementation constraints encountered in the sections that follow.

4.2.1   The Poisson Equation

We wish to solve the Poisson equation on a d-dimensional domain Ω with boundary $\partial\Omega$. Denoting u as the solution of the Poisson equation, it satisfies

$$\boldsymbol{\nabla} \cdot (\boldsymbol{\nabla} u) = \nabla^2 u = -f \quad \text{on} \quad \Omega \subset \mathbb{R}^d, \tag{4.1}$$

where ∇^2 is the Laplacian operator and f is given. The Laplacian operator applied to u is defined as the divergence $(\boldsymbol{\nabla} \cdot)$ of the gradient of u $(\boldsymbol{\nabla} u)$. It can be expressed as the sum of the second partial derivatives of u along each dimension d:

$$\nabla^2 = \sum_{i=1}^{d} \frac{\partial^2}{\partial x_i^2}, \quad \text{with} \quad \mathbf{x} = (x_1, x_2, ..., x_d)^T \in \Omega. \tag{4.2}$$

The elliptic equation (Equation (4.1)) calls for boundary conditions which can be of Neumann type:

$$\frac{\partial u}{\partial n} = g(\mathbf{x}), \quad \mathbf{x} \in \partial\Omega_N, \tag{4.3}$$

where $\partial u/\partial n := \boldsymbol{\nabla} u \cdot \mathbf{n}$ is the normal derivative at the boundary $\partial\Omega_N$ with $\mathbf{n}$ pointing outside of the domain, or of Dirichlet type:

$$u = u_D(\mathbf{x}), \quad \mathbf{x} \in \partial\Omega_D, \tag{4.4}$$

where $\partial\Omega_N$ and $\partial\Omega_D$ are distinct portions of $\partial\Omega$ such that $\partial\Omega = \partial\Omega_N \cup \partial\Omega_D$. This problem is represented schematically in Figure 4.1. In this chapter, we focus on Neumann-type boundary conditions. Other types of boundary conditions are discussed in Section 4.7.

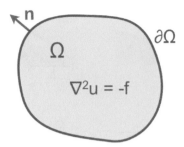

Figure 4.1. Poisson problem (Equation (4.1)) on a 2D domain Ω with a boundary $\partial\Omega$. The vector $\mathbf{n}$ is normal to the boundary and points outside of the domain.

Note that for well-posed problems, when $\delta\Omega_D = \emptyset$, the data f needs to satisfy the compatibility condition

$$\int_\Omega f(\mathbf{x})d\mathbf{x} = \int_{\delta\Omega} g(\mathbf{x})d\mathbf{x}.$$

4.2.2 Finite Volume Discretization

In practice, Equation (4.1) has no close-form solution for general right-hand-sides f and domains Ω. In these cases, one has to rely on a numerical technique where an approximation of the solution u is sought in a finite-dimensional approximation space, by means of a discretization method, leading to a finite—although eventually large—set of equations. Classically, this discretization proceeds from a partition of the computational domain Ω into a finite number of control nodes, volumes, or elements. While several methods exist for the discretization of the Poisson equation, we select here the finite-volume (FV) method. Indeed, beside their intuitive nature and easy physical interpretation, the FV method is widely used in both computational fluid dynamics (CFD) and computer graphics communities, where correspondence between voxels and averages over FV cells is immediate. The popularity of the FV method also makes the availability of efficient solvers important, since the resolution of Poisson-like equations is a key ingredient of many CFD codes.

Roughly speaking, FV relies on the approximation of the average of the function u over the mesh cells (Figure 4.2). Specifically, the FV mesh is made of a set $\mathcal{T}$ of non-overlapping cells C_i covering Ω:

$$\Omega = \bigcup_{i \in \mathcal{T}} C_i, \quad C_i \cap C_j = \emptyset, \quad \forall i \neq j \in \mathcal{T}, \tag{4.5}$$

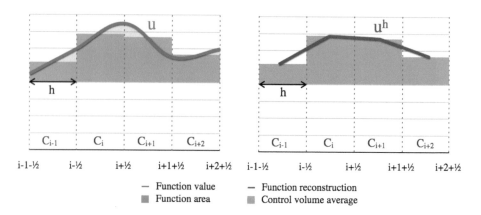

Figure 4.2. Cell values are computed by averaging the 1D function u with a FV method (left). The reconstruction of u^h by linear interpolation over the cell averages (right).

and we denote by u_i^h the computed average of u over the cell with index i:

$$u_i^h \approx \frac{1}{|C_i|} \int_{C_i} u \, dV. \tag{4.6}$$

The superscript h refers here to the discretized nature of the solution, h being related to the size of the cells.

Different types of meshes can be considered; we restrict ourselves to structured Cartesian grids made of cells with equal edge size h in all directions (the cell volume is h^d). For a sufficiently refined grid (i.e., small enough h), u_i^h can be identified with the value of u at the center $\mathbf{x}_i$ of cell C_i. In addition, such structured grids greatly simplify the reconstruction of the smooth approximate u^h from the averages arising from the multilinear interpolation between the cell centers. This reconstruction is schematically illustrated in Figure 4.2 (right).

Once the computational domain has been discretized into finite volumes, the objective is to derive a system of equations relating the values u_i^h for $i \in \mathcal{T}$. This is achieved by making use of Stokes' theorem [Spivak 71], which consists in replacing the integral of the Poisson equation over a cell by the integral of the normal flux $(\partial u / \partial n)$ over the cell's boundaries. Specifically,

$$\int_{C_i} \boldsymbol{\nabla} \cdot (\boldsymbol{\nabla} u) \, d\mathbf{x} = \int_{\partial C_i} \boldsymbol{\nabla} u \cdot \mathbf{n} \, d\mathbf{x} = -\int_{C_i} f \, d\mathbf{x} \simeq -f(\mathbf{x}_i) \, |C_i| \,. \tag{4.7}$$

Since $\boldsymbol{\nabla} u \cdot \mathbf{n}$ is the projection of the gradient of u in the normal direction $\mathbf{n}$ at a cell boundary, it reduces to the normal derivative $\partial u / \partial n$, where n takes value in $\{\pm x_i; \ i = 1, \ldots, d\}$, owing to the Cartesian structure of the mesh. Therefore, in one dimension, for instance, Equation (4.7) reduces to

$$\frac{\partial u}{\partial x}\Big|_{x_i-h/2} - \frac{\partial u}{\partial x}\Big|_{x_i+h/2} = h f_i^h, \tag{4.8}$$

where $x_i \pm h/2$ are the locations of the cell interfaces and we have denoted $f_i^h = f(x_i)$. The FV system is finally obtained by substituting the fluxes $\nabla u \cdot \mathbf{n}$ by their reconstructions from the set of averaged values $\{u_i^h; i \in \mathcal{T}\}$. Again, different reconstruction strategies can be used, and we adopt the second-order reconstruction, where the normal flux is based on the difference between the averages at the two cells C_i and C_j having in common an interface ∂C_{ij}:

$$\frac{\partial u}{\partial n}\Big|_{\partial C_{ij}} \approx \frac{u_i^h - u_j^h}{|\mathbf{x}_i - \mathbf{x}_j|}. \tag{4.9}$$

Inserting this approximation in the one-dimensional case of Equation (4.8), it becomes

$$\frac{u_i^h - u_{i-1}^h}{h} - \frac{u_{i+1}^h - u_i^h}{h} = \frac{2u_i^h - u_{i-1}^h - u_{i+1}^h}{h} \approx h f_i^h. \tag{4.10}$$

Similar expression can be immediately derived for higher-dimensional problems through tensorization, owing to the Cartesian nature of the grid. We only provide the case for $d = 3$, which corresponds to the discretization used in all subsequent development. In 3D, the cells are indexed by 3 subscripts (i, j, k) referring to the location of $C_{i,j,k}$ in the Cartesian grid ($C_{i,j,k}$ and $C_{i,j,k+1}$ are thus two neighboring cells in the third spatial direction). With this notation, the FV approximation of the Poisson equation over cell $C_{i,j,k}$ can be expressed as

$$
\begin{aligned}
6u_{i,j,k}^h - u_{i-1,j,k}^h - u_{i+1,j,k}^h \quad \cdots & \\
\cdots - u_{i,j-1,k}^h - u_{i,j+1,k}^h \quad \cdots & \\
\cdots - u_{i,j,k-1}^h - u_{i,j,k+1}^h &= -h^2 f_{i,j,k}^h
\end{aligned}
\tag{4.11}
$$

The discrete equation for cell $C_{i,j,k}$ involves the (unknown) averages over the cell and its six neighbors having a face in common (see Figure 4.3).

Writing this equation for all cells of the mesh, eventually using modified reconstructions of the flux for the cells neighboring $\partial\Omega$ (see discussion below), one ends with a system of $N = N_x \times N_y \times N_z$ equations for the cell averages $u_{i,j,k}^h$, $1 \le i \le N_x$, $1 \le j \le N_y$ and $1 \le k \le N_z$. This system can be rewritten in a matrix form as

$$A\mathbf{u} = \mathbf{f}, \tag{4.12}$$

where $A \in \mathbb{R}^{N \times N}$ is a sparse matrix, $\mathbf{u} \in \mathbb{R}^N$ is the vector containing the cell averages and $\mathbf{f}$ gathers the corresponding right-hand sides of Equation (4.11).

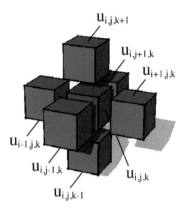

Figure 4.3. Enlarged view of the 3D Laplace stencil, the left-hand-side in Equation (4.11).

The sparsity of A arises from the fact that the fluxes are reconstructed from the immediate neighboring cells, such that each row of A has only seven nonzero entries as seen from Equation (4.11). As a result, the memory allocation for A is less than $7N$ (due to the treatment of the boundary conditions). An example of matrix A is shown in Figure 4.4 for $N_x = N_y = N_z = 3$, before reduction, due to boundary conditions.

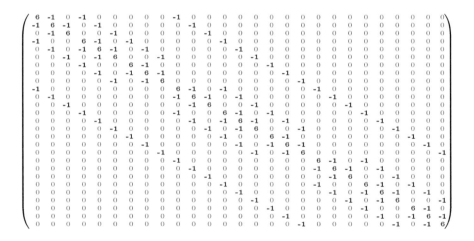

Figure 4.4. Example matrix A for a $3 \times 3 \times 3$ discretization grid ($N = 27$) composed of 27^2 elements, where less than 7×27 of them are nonzero. This matrix results from the Laplace equation (Equation (4.11)), instantiated for each cell of $\mathcal{T}$.

4.2.3 Boundary Conditions (BC)

We choose for simplicity, the homogeneous Neumann condition (Equation (4.3)) on u along the domain boundary $\partial\Omega$,

$$\frac{\partial u}{\partial n} = 0, \quad \text{for } \mathbf{x} \in \partial\Omega. \tag{4.13}$$

This condition states that the flux (or normal derivative) of u is zero everywhere on $\partial\Omega$. In the context of potential flows, where u is the flow potential, this corresponds to no-through flow BC. For instance, in the classical projection-correction methods for solving the incompressible Navier-Stokes equations (see [Chorin 68]), such potential flow is used to enforce the divergence-free constraint on the velocity field.

In practice, ghost-cell techniques are commonly used to implement the homogeneous Neumann BC. It consists of creating a virtual layer of cells along the boundary, with values that mirror the inside domain. One of the interesting features of this ghost-cell approach is that it immediately extends to other types of BC (nonhomogeneous, Dirichlet, Fourier, periodic domains, etc.) making them very attractive in terms of general code implementation. Indeed, after defining the ghost-cells values (eventually updated at each iteration), the same stencil can be used for all the inner cells of the computational domain. In the case of the homogeneous Neumann BC, a ghost cell is taken equal to the inner domain cell sharing a face with it. Therefore, the flux between the two cells is zero (see Equation (4.9)). Other types of BC follow a similar procedure whereby the ghost-cell values are defined from their respective (inner domain) neighboring cell value (see discussion in [Patankar 80]).

4.3 Iterative Methods

Unless otherwise specified, the edge size of a cell is h. We also drop the cell index to alleviate the notation when representing the iteration number α as a subscript.

The sparse matrix A has important properties that can be exploited. First, A is *symmetric*, due to the symmetric definition of the fluxes between two neighboring cells (the flux going from a cell i to its neighbor j is the same as the flux from j to i); this symmetry also implies the conservative nature of the FV scheme. Second, A is *positive definite*. These properties make A invertible with a unique solution

$$\mathbf{u} = A^{-1}\mathbf{f}. \tag{4.14}$$

For small N, the matrix A can be inverted using a direct method, for example, Gaussian elimination or LU decomposition [Cormen et al. 01]. These classical methods are common but not very efficient because of their $O(N^3)$ complexity (recall that N is the number of unknowns to be solved in the system). In addition, direct inversion methods consume a good deal of memory, because even if A is sparse, its inverse is usually full. As an example, the amount of memory required to compute and store A^{-1} for a medium-sized domain discretization, $N = 64^3$, in IEEE 754 single-precision floats would be superior to the capacity of current hardware: $(64^3)^2 \times$ `sizeof(float)` $= 256$ GB.

Iterative methods have been developed to address this issue, because they can work with a matrix-free representation of the linear system. In these techniques, an approximation of the solution $\mathbf{u}$ is iteratively constructed through a sequence of vectors $\{\mathbf{v}_\alpha, \alpha = 0, 1, \ldots\}$ that converges to $A^{-1}\mathbf{f}$,

$$\lim_{\alpha \to \infty} \mathbf{v}_\alpha = \mathbf{u} = A^{-1}\mathbf{f}. \tag{4.15}$$

4.3.1   Simple Preconditioned Iterations

An immediate way to construct a convergent series of approximations is to rely on simple preconditioned iterations. Let P be an appropriate preconditioner of A (see examples below), such that $P^{-1}A$ has a lower condition number (stability to numerical operations) than A.

Let P be a preconditioner in the linear system $A\mathbf{u} = \mathbf{f}$, we can write

$$P\mathbf{u} = (P - A)\mathbf{u} + \mathbf{f} \quad \Leftrightarrow \quad \mathbf{u} = (I - P^{-1}A)\mathbf{u} + P^{-1}\mathbf{f}. \tag{4.16}$$

The smoothing iteration, derived from Equation (4.16), is the core of iterative methods and computes a new approximation $\mathbf{v}_{\alpha+1}$ from $\mathbf{v}_\alpha$ at iteration α,

$$\mathbf{v}_{\alpha+1} = (I - P^{-1}A)\mathbf{v}_\alpha + P^{-1}\mathbf{f}. \tag{4.17}$$

Let $\mathbf{e}_\alpha = \mathbf{u} - \mathbf{v}_\alpha$ be the error. We can subtract Equation (4.17) from (4.16) to obtain the error reduction at iteration α:

$$\mathbf{e}_{\alpha+1} = (I - P^{-1}A)\mathbf{e}_\alpha = M\mathbf{e}_\alpha \quad \text{thus} \quad \mathbf{e}^k = M^k\mathbf{e}_0, \tag{4.18}$$

where the iteration matrix M is multiplied with $\mathbf{e}_\alpha$ until a convergence condition $|\mathbf{e}_\alpha| < \epsilon$ is met (typical values for a $L2$ norm are taken below 10^{-3}).

A wide range of preconditioners is available. Equation (4.18) shows that a good preconditioner should be such that $P^{-1}A \simeq I$. On the other hand, Equation (4.17) shows that, to be applied, the iteration needs the calculation of the effect of P^{-1} on vectors: P should be easily inverted. These two concurrent features lead to the extreme preconditioners, $P = A$, which results in an exact error reduction in just one iteration, and $P = I$, which allows for trivial inversion, but may result in poor error reduction with the iterations (if converging at all).

To construct classical preconditioners, it is convenient to split the square matrix A into three parts:

$$A = L + D + U, \tag{4.19}$$

where L is the lower-triangular part of A, D its diagonal, and U the upper-triangular part of A, as illustrated in Figure 4.5.

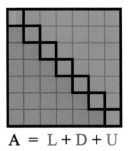

$$A = L + D + U$$

Figure 4.5. Decomposition of the matrix A into its lower-triangular part L, diagonal D, and upper-triangular part U, used in the construction of the preconditioners.

4.3.2 Jacobi Method

The first preconditioner P_J that we introduce is used in the pure iterative Jacobi method. It is defined as the diagonal part of A with $P_J = D$. Introducing P_J into Equation (4.17) gives the following Jacobi iteration:

$$\mathbf{v}_{\alpha+1} = (I - D^{-1}A)\mathbf{v}_\alpha + D^{-1}\mathbf{f}. \qquad (4.20)$$

In the case of the 3D Laplace matrix (Figure 4.4), we observe that the diagonal is equal to 6 for the inner domain, therefore we can write $D = 6I$. Using this simplified form $D^{-1} = 1/6\,I$, the Jacobi iteration (4.20) becomes

$$\mathbf{v}_{\alpha+1} = (I - \frac{1}{6}A)\mathbf{v}_\alpha + \frac{1}{6}\mathbf{f}. \qquad (4.21)$$

This method is also called the *method of simultaneous displacements*. As observed in the visual representation of the Jacobi iteration in Figure 4.6, all

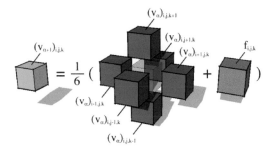

Figure 4.6. Visual representation of the Jacobi iteration. Note that the central cell of the stencil on $\mathbf{v}_\alpha$ is provided only as a visual cue and does not intervene in this equation because the diagonal of M is nullified $(I - 1/6D = 0I)$.

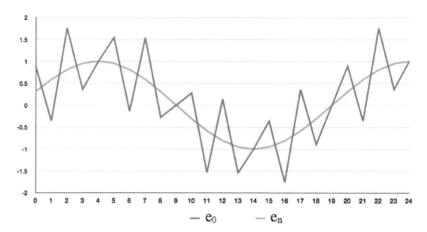

Figure 4.7. Result of several Jacobi iterations on a 1D error function. The high spatial frequency components, sharp edges of e_0, are efficiently smoothed out after a few iterations while the low frequency components remain almost unchanged.

unknowns of $\mathbf{v}_{\alpha+1}$ can be simultaneously computed as each equation is independent and requires knowledge of only $\mathbf{v}_\alpha$ and $\mathbf{f}$.

The computational cost of one iteration is low, and the Jacobi method is straightforward to implement using two separate *ping-pong* buffers for $\mathbf{v}_\alpha$ and $\mathbf{v}_{\alpha+1}$. This method quickly suppresses the local components of $\mathbf{e}$ (with high spatial frequency) after a small number of iterations. Unfortunately, it does a poor job at suppressing the low-frequency components (global features of $\mathbf{e}$ spread across a distance wider than two consecutive cells) as illustrated on a 1D example in Figure 4.7.

The Jacobi method is widely used in the computer graphics community [Stam 99, Crane et al. 07] as it is easy to understand and implement. Despite its popularity, its cost of $O(N^2)$ iterations to reduce the error by a constant factor makes it impractical for problems requiring a good accuracy.

Section 4.5.2 covers the implementation of the Jacobi method using OpenCL.

4.3.3 Gauss-Seidel Method

Instead of considering only the diagonal of A, the Gauss-Seidel preconditioner P_{GS} is composed of its diagonal and lower-triangular part, $P_{GS} = L + D$. This makes P_{GS} closer to A than Jacobi's P_J, yet still easy to work with numerically. Introducing P_{GS} into Equation (4.17) gives the Gauss-Seidel iteration:

$$\mathbf{v}_{\alpha+1} = (I - (L + D)^{-1}A)\mathbf{v}_\alpha + (L + D)^{-1}\mathbf{f}. \qquad (4.22)$$

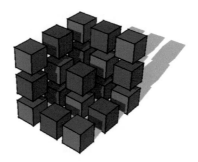

Figure 4.8. Red-black labeling of the grid cells for the Gauss-Seidel method. We observe that all neighbors of a red cell are painted in black and vice-versa, in order to prevent concurrent read and write access by two threads on the same cell.

The inclusion of the lower-triangular part L results in a dependency relation between unknowns in the linear system. The values for grid index (i, j, k) are thus being updated with new values coming from $\mathbf{v}_{\alpha+1}$ instead of $\mathbf{v}_\alpha$, for their neighbors numbered with lower indices $(i-1, j, k)$, $(i, j-1, k)$ and $(i, j, k-1)$. This intuitively leads to an improvement in the error reduction with the iteration. In practice, about half the number of Jacobi iterations is needed for a given reduction of the error.

This method is also called *method of successive displacements* because of the dependency between the updated neighbor cells. From an implementation point of view, the Gauss-Seidel method requires a single buffer to represent old and new values of $\mathbf{v}$ during an iteration, which leads to a concurrency problem when neighbor cells are read and written at the same time by different threads. A simple solution is to use a *red-black* ordering of the cells where each cell is affected by a color just like on a 3D checkerboard [Strang 07], as illustrated in Figure 4.8.

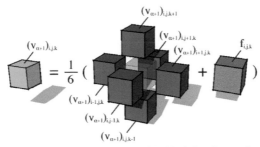

Figure 4.9. Visual representation of the second half of the Gauss-Seidel iteration. Please note that the black neighbors of the red cell have already been computed during the first half iteration on black cells.

The Gauss-Seidel iteration is then split into two steps where the black cells are updated first because they do not have any face in common, and the red cells are updated using the newly computed values of the black cells, as illustrated in Figure 4.9.

Section 4.5.3 covers the implementation of the Gauss-Seidel method using *red-black* ordering with OpenCL.

4.3.4 Successive Over-Relaxation (SOR)

Observing the limitations of the two previous preconditioners and their $O(N^2)$ computational complexity, one wonders if it is possible to over-correct the error and reduce the low-frequency features by extrapolating the local correction provided by each iteration.

We introduce the weighting factor ω to control the amount of overshooting applied to the previous preconditioners. When combined with the Gauss-Seidel preconditioner, this method is called SOR and can be written as

$$\mathbf{v}_{\alpha+1} = (D + \omega L)^{-1}(\omega \mathbf{f} - (\omega U + (\omega - 1)D)\mathbf{v}_\alpha). \tag{4.23}$$

This preconditioner is proven to converge when ω takes value between 0 and 2, but we are more interested in a fast convergence rather than just convergence. Using a weight factor of 1 is equivalent to the standard Gauss-Seidel method, while factors greater than 1 lead to an over-relaxation of the smoothing correction, which results in a faster propagation of low-frequency error components on the grid. The optimal factor ω_{opt}, for which the convergence speed is the fastest, depends on the spectral radius ρ of the iteration matrix M, or the maximum absolute of the eigenvalues λ of this matrix,

$$\rho(M) = \max |\lambda(M)|, \qquad \omega_{opt} = \frac{2}{1 + \sqrt{(1 - \rho^2(M))}}.$$

Finding the maximal eigenvalue of M has the same complexity as computing A^{-1}, which is why good values of ω are often empirically determined. The value $2/3$ is a safe estimation for ω on small domains, while optimal values tend to asymptotically get closer to 2 when the solution domain grows (see Chapter 6.2 of [Strang 07]). Taking a value higher than ω_{opt} usually results in bad performance, because the approximation convergence tends to oscillate.

Section 4.5.4 covers the implementation of the SOR method based on forward Gauss-Seidel with OpenCL.

Other preconditioners do exist and become more efficient as they grow in numerical and understanding complexity. In the next section, instead of an exhaustive review of preconditioners, we address the inherent problem of iterative methods, which is the reduction of the low spatial frequency components. A comprehensive review with a deeper mathematical analysis of preconditioners is available in Saad's and Strang's reference books [Saad 03, Strang 07].

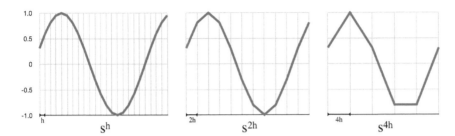

Figure 4.10. Sampling of a smooth function at different resolution levels h (left), $2h$ (center), and $4h$ (right). We observe that the low-frequency component represented on the finest level (h) becomes rougher as the grid gets coarser ($2h$, $4h$).

4.4   Multigrid Methods (MG)

We have observed the good performance of pure iterative methods to smooth out high-frequency components, where error features are spread over a $1h$ distance. Unfortunately, after few iterations, the error reduction per iteration decreases because the remaining error now contains only low frequencies that cannot be efficiently smoothed out.

Southwell [Southwell 35] introduced a method where a second grid helps to maintain a fast convergence: the problem is discretized a second time on a grid with cells of $2h$ edge size in order to smooth out the high frequencies (now spread over a $2h$ distance) using existing preconditioners, as illustrated in Figure 4.10. This concept was later generalized to a new class of multiscale iterative methods where the initial problem is solved on grids of different resolutions.

4.4.1   Multigrid Correction Scheme

The MG correction scheme (CS) method is the most appropriate MG method available to solve partial differential equations with linear coefficients as in the Poisson equation discretized with FV on a uniform grid. Like most MG methods, the smoothing iterations reduce the high-frequency error. The CS accelerates the reduction of the lower frequencies by rescaling the error on a coarser grid.

A typical CS iteration is shaped into a recursive V-cycle, illustrated in Figure 4.11, which can be divided into substeps relying on five different operators:

> (S) smoothing iteration,
> (R) residual computation,
> (P) fine to coarse projection,
> (I) coarse to fine interpolation,
> (C) approximation correction.

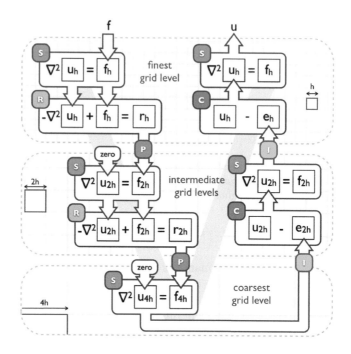

Figure 4.11. Three-level CS MG V-cycle illustrating the connection between the smoothing, residual, projection, interpolation, and correction operators.

Let us illustrate this process by walking through the different steps of a CS iteration.

Any smoothing iteration $\boxed{S}$ from pure iterative methods can be used and is consecutively applied μ_{pre} times to begin the V-cycle. Its role is not to solve the problem, but to smooth the error until its high-frequency components are almost suppressed. This leads to an error $\mathbf{e}_\alpha^h$ composed only of features spread across more than two consecutive cells of size h. Computing the correction term to remove all the remaining components for the error would require the knowledge of the unknown solution $\mathbf{e}_\alpha^h = \mathbf{u}^h - \mathbf{v}_\alpha^h$. Instead, we can compute the residual of $\mathbf{v}_\alpha^h$ using $\boxed{R}$:

$$\mathbf{r}_\alpha^h = \mathbf{f}^h - A^h \mathbf{v}_\alpha^h \qquad (4.24)$$

Reorganizing Equation (4.24) leads to the residual Poisson problem,

$$A^h \mathbf{e}_\alpha^h = \mathbf{r}_\alpha^h. \qquad (4.25)$$

Knowing that we almost suppressed all the high frequencies from $\mathbf{r}_\alpha^h$, we observe that the remaining smooth function can be represented on a coarser grid (where the edge size becomes $2h$) without losing important information. The projection operator $\boxed{\text{P}}$ transfers $\mathbf{r}_\alpha^h$ from a fine -h-spaced- grid to a coarser—$2h$-spaced—grid producing a rougher function $\mathbf{f}_\alpha^{2h}$. This projection actually leads to a new Poisson problem defined on a coarser grid, where all remaining frequencies are a bit higher. The approximated solution to this problem $\mathbf{v}_\alpha^{2h}$ is *not* a projection of $\mathbf{v}_\alpha^h$, but the correction term required to reduce higher error frequencies on $\mathbf{v}_\alpha^h$:

$$A^{2h}\mathbf{v}_\alpha^{2h} = \mathbf{f}_\alpha^{2h}. \tag{4.26}$$

The smoothing-residual-projection step is then repeated to transfer the problem to coarser grids and reduce lowest frequency components. The descent is stopped when the resulting domain grid is coarse enough for the problem to be directly solved, using, for example, a standard elimination method. As the grid is particularly coarse and small at this point, we later choose to apply $\boxed{\text{S}}$ several times to reduce the remaining (fairly high) frequencies.

Once Equation (4.25) has been solved on the coarsest grid, the resulting solution $\mathbf{e}_\alpha^{2^z h}$ is the complement to the correction term required to suppress the lowest spatial frequency error components. It can then be added to the approximation of the finer resolution $\mathbf{v}_\alpha^{2^{z-1}h}$, in order to correct both the lowest and second-lowest frequency errors. This ascending step of the V-cycle is then recursively applied until the approximation $\mathbf{v}_\alpha^h$ is reached on the finest grid. The interpolation operator $\boxed{\text{I}}$ is used to transport this correction term from a coarse grid to a finer one. This operator is coupled with the correction operator $\boxed{\text{C}}$, a simple vector subtraction on the finer level:

$$\mathbf{v}_{\alpha+1}^{2^{z-1}h} = \mathbf{v}_\alpha^{2^{z-1}h} - I_{2^z h}^{2^{z-1}h}\mathbf{v}_\alpha^{2^z h}, \tag{4.27}$$

where $I_{2^z h}^{2^{z-1}h}$ is the matrix of $\boxed{\text{I}}$, interpolating a vector of $2^z h$-width cells to a vector of $2^{z-1}h$-width cells.

By solving the residual Poisson equation on the coarsest grid, we obtain the error correction term that we need to apply to the $\mathbf{v}_\alpha^h$ approximation in order to minimize the lowest frequency of the residual on the finer grid. In order to reduce the residual on the finer grids, we recursively interpolate and correct these terms by chaining $\boxed{\text{I}}$ and $\boxed{\text{C}}$ on finer grids. This process corrects the current approximation for the finer grid, but also adds higher-frequency components due to small information loss during the projection. In order to reduce these, we apply $\boxed{\text{S}}$ μ_{post} times.

While many projection and interpolation schemes exist to transport discretized functions between grids of different resolution, we choose trilinear interpolation as it remains consistent with FV methods (see Figure 4.12). As we later observe during the implementation, it is also one of the most computationally efficient schemes using OpenCL's hardware-accelerated multilinear filtering.

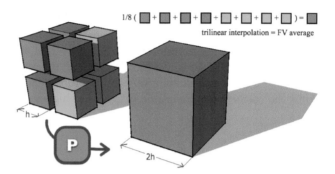

Figure 4.12. Trilinear interpolation process approximating the FV average, used in the OpenCL projection kernel.

Smoothing iterations at coarser grid levels (where N is recursively divided by eight for each projection) are computationally cheaper than iterations on the finest grid. In our implementation, we decide not to use a simple V-cycle but a multi-W-cycle. In that case, the first interpolation ascent is stopped before reaching the finest level and descends again toward the coarsest level to further reduce low-frequency errors with minimal computational cost. After a few of these intermediate cycles, the correction is finally interpolated to the finest level. In fact, we increase up to four subcycles to take advantage of this property, to achieve a faster convergence rate without increasing the computational cost too significantly. Finally, CS MG iterations are repeated until a convergence criterion $(|\mathbf{e}_\alpha| < \epsilon)$ is met.

An extended overview of other MG methods and their applications can be found in McCormick's and Briggs' reference books [McCormick 88, Briggs et al. 00].

4.5   OpenCL Implementation

4.5.1   Overview

OpenCL is an open standard framework for programming heterogeneous parallel computers like multicore CPUs and GPUs. Like OpenGL, its specification is managed by the Khronos Group, which is composed of hardware and software industry leaders. The last revision of the OpenCL 1.0 specification [Khronos Group 09] is available online on the OpenCL registry website (http://www.khronos.org/registry/cl), along with C++ host bindings (`cl.hpp`) which greatly simplify the host API setup and communication calls.

The OpenCL framework is split into two parts. First, a host API, running on the CPU to initializes the devices and memory buffers, controls the execution of compute kernels and enqueues buffer exchanges between the host and devices, in the same way as the traditional OpenGL/GLSL shader and texture setup. Second, *compute kernels* written in the OpenCL C language, are programs executed in parallel on the devices in the same way as traditional vertex or pixel shaders but with greater flexibility to address broader problems.

The OpenCL API specifies two kinds of memory objects: *buffers* and *images*. Buffers are contiguous arrays of memory indexed by 1D coordinates and composed of any available type (`int`, `float`, `half`, `double`, `int2`, `int3`, `int4`, `float2`, ...). These can either be allocated in *global*, *local* or *constant* memory. Global memory can be shared between the host and the devices by enqueuing read or write commands to exchange these data; it is abundant but it has a high latency and must be used with caution, while local memory is faster but has a very limited size. Coalesced memory accesses can reduce the latency, but when memory read and write patterns are random, images can be used to mitigate this latency. Images share many similarities with textures: they support an automatic caching mechanism, their access can be filtered through a *sampler* with multilinear interpolation, and out of bounds access behavior can be configured.

We make use of *images* whenever possible because of two reasons. First, our memory access patterns are mostly random. Second, the sampler filtering can greatly reduce the computational costs of certain operations such as multilinear interpolation in the projection operator, or automatic clamping of image coordinates to handle ghost cells with a homogeneous boundary condition.

Finally, parallelization is achieved by enqueueing the execution of compute kernels over *work-groups* or ranges of threads organized in 1, 2, or 3D. Each work-group is composed of *work-items*, or threads indexed by a unique 1, 2, or 3D identifier inside the global *work-group* range.

Initializing the compute devices is straightforward using the C++ host bindings. We first initialize the platform to access the underlying compute devices and select either CPU devices, GPU devices, or both types. Then we create a context and a command queue in order to execute compute kernels and enqueue memory transfers.

```
// fetch all GPU devices on the first OpenCL platform
std::vector<cl::Platform> platforms;
std::vector<cl::Device> devices;
cl::Platform::get(&platforms);
platforms.at(0).getDevices(CL_DEVICE_TYPE_GPU, &devices);

// setup a context and a command queue for the first device
cl::Context context(devices);
cl::CommandQueue queue(context, devices.at(0));
```

Finally, compute kernels are loaded and compiled from OpenCL source:

```
// load an OpenCL source file into a std::string
std::ifstream srcfile("kernels.cl");
```

```
std::string src(std::istreambuf_iterator<char>(srcfile),
                std::istreambuf_iterator<char>(0));

// compile the device program and load the "zero" kernel
cl::Program program(context, cl::Program::Sources(1,
            std::make_pair(src.c_str(), src.size())));
program.build(devices, "-Werror");
cl::Kernel kzero = cl::Kernel(program, "zero");
```

This *zero* compute kernel is later used to clear global memory buffers on the device. With OpenCL's C language, it is written as follow:

```
kernel void zero(global float *vh)
{
  // id contains the 3D index of the current cell
  const float4 id = (float4)(get_global_id(0),
      get_global_id(1), get_global_id(2), 0);

  // sz contains the buffer stride along each 3D axis
  const float4 sz = (float4)(1, get_global_size(0),
    get_global_size(0) * get_global_size(1), 0); // strides

  // vh is a global buffer used to write the zero output
  vh[(int)dot(id, sz)] = 0; // vh[id.x+id.y*sz.y+id.z*sz.z]
}
```

This kernel must be launched with a global *work-size* equal to the number of elements in the input buffer `vh` so that each element is written by exactly one *work-item* (or thread). The `id` and `sz` variables are initialized with the 3D work-item identifier and work-size stride so that their dot product directly gives the corresponding memory location in the 1D buffer (i.e., `id.x + id.y*sz.y + id.z*sz.z`).

In order to run this compute kernel, we need to allocate a memory buffer on the device and create the global (computational domain) and local (concurrent work-items) work-size ranges:

```
// initialize a read-only buffer for 64^3 4-bytes floats,
// this buffer can not be update by the host, only read from
cl::Buffer buffer(context, CL_MEM_READ_ONLY, 64*64*64 * 4);

// prepare the work-size ranges and kernel arguments
cl::NDRange gndr(64, 64, 64), lndr(8, 8, 8);
zero.setArg(0, buffer); // bind the buffer to vh

// enqueue the kernel and wait for it to finish its task
queue.enqueueNDRangeKernel(zero, cl::NullRange, gndr, lndr);
queue.enqueueBarrier();
```

Finally, data can be retrieved on the host by enqueueing a read command to the command queue,

```
float data[64 * 64 * 64];

// blocking read of the buffer from 0 to 64*64*64 into data
queue.enqueueReadBuffer(buffer, CL_TRUE, 0, 64*64*64, data);
```

Three-dimensional images are allocated in almost the same way as buffers. They require additional knowledge of the data type (`int`, `float`, ...) for interpolation and x-, y-, and z-extents for spatial caching,

```
// one-component float image format
cl::ImageFormat fmt(CL_R, CL_FLOAT);
cl::Image3D img(context, CL_MEM_READ_ONLY, fmt, 64, 64, 64);
```

Before implementing iterative solvers with OpenCL, we define a structure to contain the required elements of a Poisson problem (size, input function f, approximation v, and residual r):

```
typedef struct {
  cl::size_t<3> size; // 3D size of the problem
  cl::Image3D fh  // discretized f function
  cl::Image3D vh; // solution approximation
  cl::Image3D rh; // residual
} Problem;
```

4.5.2 Jacobi Method

In the Jacobi method, each line of the linear system is computed independently from the others. This results in an easy parallelization of the code. In theory, the cost of this advantage is the need to allocate two buffers to store $\mathbf{v}$: one is used as an input for the smoothing iteration Equation (4.20), $\mathbf{v}_\alpha$, and the other to write the result $\mathbf{v}_{\alpha+1}$. In practice, we use a scratch buffer for all kernel outputs leading to no overhead, compared with other methods.

Because we have to access the neighbors of each cell (Figure 4.3), coalescent memory access is not achievable using the device's global memory. In order to overcome this limitation, we use OpenCL *images* which are in many ways similar to textures in classical GPU programming. Furthermore, 3D images have an automatic caching mechanism which greatly accelerates the memory access pattern encountered in smoothing iterations.

In order to satisfy homogeneous conditions on the boundary of the solution domain, access to the value of neighbors located on ghost cells outside of the domain is clamped to the edge of the boundary (and therefore of the *image*) in order to automatically copy the corresponding value on the inside.

First, we define offsets in each dimension to access the cells' neighbors,

```
#define dx (float4)(1, 0, 0, 0)
#define dy (float4)(0, 1, 0, 0)
#define dz (float4)(0, 0, 1, 0)
```

The fourth dimension of the `float4` struct is never used here but is required to specify image sampling coordinates. The Jacobi compute kernel for the device is then implemented as follows:

```
// fh and vh are input images containing the f and v values,
// vvh is an output buffer where the new value of v is
// written and h2 is the cell width h squared
kernel void jacobi(read_only image3d_t fh,
                    read_only image3d_t vh,
                    global float *vvh, float h2)
{
  const float4 id = (float4)(get_global_id(0),
          get_global_id(1), get_global_id(2), 0);
  const float4 sz = (float4)(1, get_global_size(0),
      get_global_size(0) * get_global_size(1), 0);

  // sampler for accessing the vh and fh images,
  // out of bounds accesses are clamped to the domain edges
  const sampler_t sampler = CLK_ADDRESS_CLAMP_TO_EDGE;

  const float s =
    (read_imagef(vh, sampler, id-dx).x +
    read_imagef(vh, sampler, id+dx).x +
    read_imagef(vh, sampler, id-dy).x +
    read_imagef(vh, sampler, id+dy).x +
    read_imagef(vh, sampler, id-dz).x +
    read_imagef(vh, sampler, id+dz).x -
    h2 * read_imagef(fh, sampler, id).x) / 6.0f;

  vvh[(int)dot(id, sz)] = s;
}
```

The function `read_imagef` is a built-in function which accesses a `read_only` image through a sampler at a specific coordinate, passed as a `float4` vector, and returns a `float4` vector containing the result. Since we initialize `fh` and `vh` as one component image, only the first component (x) of the result is meaningful.

This kernel is launched with a global work size equal to the 3D extents of the domain grid. The local work size depends on the capabilities of the OpenCL compute device and must be a divider of the global work-group size along each dimension. Experience shows that a cubic size (and in particular (8, 8, 8) for current GPUs) is an optimal work-group configuration because it leads to a minimal spatial scattering of memory accesses, thus fully exploiting the images cache. After each iteration, the output buffer is copied back to the `vh` image to be reused, using the host API:

```
// offset and sz are size_t[3], offset contains zeros
// and sz contains the Problem size or 3D image extents
queue.enqueueCopyBufferToImage(buffer, image, 0, offset, sz);
queue.enqueueBarrier();
```

Once every few iterations, the approximation error of $\mathbf{v}_\alpha$ is tested on the host to decide wether to continue refining or not by computing the L^2 norm of the residual on the host and comparing it against an ϵ value:

```
// compute the residual for the current Problem p
residual(p.fh, p.vh, p.rh, p.size, h2);
queue.enqueueReadImage(p.rh, CL_TRUE, nullsz,
                       p.size, 0, 0, &r[0]);
float rnorm = L2Norm(r, fine.size); // sqrt(sum(r*r))

// break the solver loop
if(rnorm < epsilon) break;
```

4.5.3   Red-Black Gauss-Seidel Method

This kernel is very similar to the Jacobi kernel, the only remarkable difference in this implementation being the red-black ordering, which accelerates the theoretical convergence rate by a factor of two, where **red** is set to either one or zero, respectively with the current red-black pass type.

```
kernel void rbgs(read_only image3d_t fh,
                 read_only image3d_t vh,
                 global float *vvh,
                 float h2, int red)
{
  // the x cell identifier is multiplied by two
  // only work on either red or black cells
  float4 id = (float4) (get_global_id(0) << 1,
      get_global_id(1), get_global_id(2), 0);
  const float4 sz = (float4)(1, get_global_size(0),
      get_global_size(0)*get_global_size(1), 0);
  const sampler_t sampler = CLK_ADDRESS_CLAMP_TO_EDGE;

  // the initial x cell identifier offset depends on the
  // parity of id.y+id.z and on the current pass color
  id.x += ((int)(id.y + id.z + red) & 1);

  ... // compute s (see Jacobi)

  vvh[(int)dot(id, sz)] = s;
}
```

This kernel is launched twice to perform a full Gauss-Seidel iteration, each time with a global work size equal to the solution domain grid extents but halved on the first dimension to account for the red-black interleaving computed in `id` so that only half of the cells are accessed. As in the Jacobi implementation, the output buffer is copied to the image after each kernel call or half-iteration.

4.5.4 Successive Over-Relaxation

Implementation of SOR is a trivial addition to the Gauss-Seidel kernel, the only difference being the specification of ω, used as a weight factor for error over-correction to accelerate the convergence rate by reducing lower frequency error components faster than the two previous methods.

```
kernel void rbsor(..., float w) // weighting factor w
{
  ... // compute id and sz (see Red-Black Gauss-Seidel)

  vvh[(int)dot(id, sz)] =
    (1 - w) * read_imagef(vh, sampler, id).x + w * s;
}
```

4.5.5 Multigrid Correction Scheme

The host part of the MG CS method exactly mirrors the V-cycle presented in Figure 4.11. It is split into three steps. First, we have a descending step: high frequencies are reduced with iterations of Ⓢ, then the residual is computed using Ⓡ and projected to the next coarser grid using Ⓟ until the coarsest grid is reached. Second, the coarsest grid is solved by applying multiple iterations during Ⓢ until the coarsest problem (8^3) is almost solved. Finally, during the ascending step, the correction is interpolated back (Ⓒ + Ⓘ) and smoothed on the finer grids using Ⓢ until the finest level is reached again. Actual calls to the respective compute kernels are encapsulated into helper functions, which take care of buffer and range initializations for simplicity purposes.

```
std::vector<Problem> p; // allocate a Problem for each level
init_problems(); // and reduce its size accordingly until
                 // the coarsest level is reached

// V-cycle descending step, from finest to coarsest level
for(k = 0; k < int(p.size()-1); ++k)
{
  rbsor(p[k].fh, p[k].vh, p[k].size, h2, 0.75f, preSteps);
  residual(p[k].fh, p[k].vh, p[k].rh, p[k].size, h2);
  project(p[k].rh, p[k+1].fh, p[k+1].size);
  zero(p[k+1].vh, p[k+1].size);
}
```

```
// "Direct" solving on the coarsest level
rbsor(p[k].fh, p[k].vh, p[k].size, h2, 1.5f, directSteps);

// V-cycle ascending step, from coarsest to finest level
for(--k; k >= 0; --k)
{
  interpolate_correct(p[k+1].vh, p[k].vh, p[k].size);
  rbsor(p[k].fh, p[k].vh, p[k].size, h2, 1.25f, postSteps);
}
```

The W-cycle is a direct extension of this code, adding an inner loop for $k_{\max} > k > 0$ in order to repeat the subcycle several times before finally reaching the finest level. Experimentations show that choosing two pre-smoothing passes, four post-smoothing at each level, and 32 direct-smoothing iterations for the coarsest level leads to the best measured convergence rate. Additionally, using four subcycles greatly reduces the overall computation time and seems to be the best configuration for medium to large grid sizes ($\geq 64^3$).

4.5.6   Residual, Projection and Interpolation Operators

In the same fashion as the smoothing operator, the residual operator [R] is a direct translation of the residual equation (Equation (4.24)) into parallel code. Input images are $\mathbf{f}^h$ and $\mathbf{u}^h$, and $\mathbf{r}^h$ is an output buffer to be later copied into an image in order to be projected using multilinear interpolation.

```
void kernel residual(read_only image3d_t fh,
                     read_only image3d_t vh,
                     global float *rh)
{
  ... // compute id and sz (see Jacobi)
  const sampler_t sampler = CLK_ADDRESS_CLAMP_TO_EDGE;

  rh[(int)dot(id, sz)] =
      - read_imagef(fh, sampler, id).x -
    (6 * read_imagef(vh, sampler, id).x -
        (read_imagef(vh, sampler, id-dx).x +
         read_imagef(vh, sampler, id+dx).x +
         read_imagef(vh, sampler, id-dy).x +
         read_imagef(vh, sampler, id+dy).x +
         read_imagef(vh, sampler, id-dz).x +
         read_imagef(vh, sampler, id+dz).x)) / h2;
}
```

To implement the projection operator, [P], we take advantage of the image-filtering capabilities offered by OpenCL, resulting in a tremendous computation acceleration when dedicated hardware is present, like texture units on GPUs. We use trilinear interpolation (Figure 4.12) to average eight cells on the fine level into one cell on the coarser level by enabling linear filtering and taking a sample at the center of the eight fine cells:

```
kernel void project(read_only image3d_t rh,
                    global float *f2h)
{
  ... // compute id and sz (see Jacobi)

  // filter images with trilinear interpolation:
  // cell centers indexing begins at 0.5 so that
  // integer values are automatically interpolated
  const sampler_t sampler = CLK_FILTER_LINEAR;

  // make the image coordinate at the vertex shared
  // between the eight finer grid (see fig. 1.11)
  // then multiply by 4 for coarsening: (2h)^2 = 4 h^2
  f2h[(int)dot(id, sz)] =
    read_imagef(rh, sampler, id * 2 + dx+dy+dz).x * 4;

}
```

In order to avoid redundant copying of buffers to images, we decide to combine the interpolation ⬜ and correction ⬜ operators into one kernel, where the interpolated correction is directly added to the finer grid level in one pass:

```
// interpolate v2h and correct vh to reduce low freqs.
kernel void interpolate_correct(read_only image3d_t v2h,
                                read_only image3d_t vh,
                                global float *vh)
{
  ... // compute id and sz (see Jacobi)
  const sampler_t sampler = 0;

  vh[(int)dot(id, sz)] = read_imagef(vh, sampler, id).x -
                         read_imagef(v2h, sampler, id/2).x;
}
```

4.6 Benchmarks

As expected, we can observe in Figure 4.13 an exponential number of iterations required for the Jacobi as its complexity reaches $O(N^3)$. The Gauss-Seidel method has the same complexity but requires fewer iterations as the constant complexity factor is halved.

The SOR method dramatically reduces this factor by over correcting the local error, but its complexity is still exponential. Fortunately, the CSMG method is confirmed to have a linear complexity of $O(N)$, where N is the number of unknowns or cells.

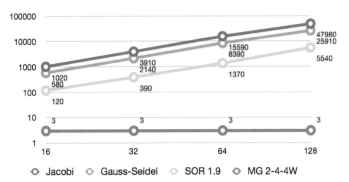

Figure 4.13. Iterations per method for cubic domains until $|e_\alpha| < 10^{-3}$. The X-axis represents the domain size (cubed) and the Y-axis shows the number of iterations required to converge to $\epsilon = 10^{-3}$.

Although its iterations have a higher computational cost, the multigrid correction scheme method shows a clear advantage over the pure iterative methods in terms of computation time per unknown in Figure 4.14. The setup cost of the CSMG method makes it more efficient for large problems than smaller ones ($< 32^3$) where the SOR method should be preferred.

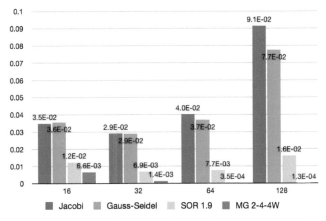

Figure 4.14. Computation time (μs) per cell for cubic domains on a GPU. The X-axis represents the domain size (cubed) and the y-axis shows the computation time per cell to converge to $\epsilon = 10^{-3}$.

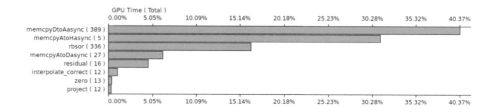

Figure 4.15. Time profiling of the execution of four CSMG 4W-cycles for a 128^3 computational domain, running on a Nvidia GTX-285 GPU. More than half of the time is spent either copying buffers into images (`memcpyDtoAasync`) or transfering the residual to the host (`memcpyAtoHasync`) to test the convergence.

4.7 Discussion

We introduced the theoretical background and implementation framework for a fast OpenCL solver for the 3D Poisson equation with Neumann external boundary condition. This is by no means a generic solver, but it can be extended to address other problems such as different boundary conditions or the discretization method.

In particular, writing to OpenCL images results in a significant computation-time decrease; for the current implementation, half of the time is spent copying output buffers back into images (see Figure 4.15). Unfortunately, this extension would alienate most of the current OpenCL hardware because writing to 3D images is an extension supported by very few devices as of the writing of this book.

Finally, using a parallel reduction on the OpenCL device to compute the residual norm would also result in a significant performance boost. Indeed, it would require transfering only one float value instead of the whole residual grid to test convergence on the host and decide whether or not to continue refining the solution approximation.

Bibliography

[Briggs et al. 00] William L. Briggs, Van Emden Henson, and Stephen F. McCormick. *A Multigrid Tutorial*, Second edition. Philadelphia: SIAM Books, 2000.

[Chorin 68] Alexandre J. Chorin. "Numerical Solution of the Navier-Stokes Equations." *Mathematics of Computation* 22:104 (1968), 745–762.

[Cormen et al. 01] Thomas H. Cormen, Clifford Stein, Ronald L. Rivest, and Charles E. Leiserson. *Introduction to Algorithms.* New York: McGraw-Hill Higher Education, 2001.

[Crane et al. 07] Keenan Crane, Ignacio Llamas, and Sarah Tariq. "Real-Time Simulation and Rendering of 3D Fluids." In *GPU Gems 3*, edited by Hubert Nguyen,
Chapter 30. Reading, MA: Addison Wesley Professional, 2007.

[Khronos Group 09] Khronos Group. *The OpenCL Specification,* version 1.0.48.
Khronos OpenCL Working Group, 2009. Available online (http://khronos.org/
registry/cl/specs/opencl-1.0.48.pdf).

[McCormick 88] Stephen F. McCormick. *Multigrid Methods: Theory, Applications, and
Supercomputing.* New York: Marcel Dekker, 1988.

[Patankar 80] Suhas V. Patankar. *Numerical Heat Transfer and Fluid Flow.* New York:
Hemisphere Publishing Corporation, 1980.

[Saad 03] Youssef Saad. *Iterative Methods for Sparse Linear Systems*, Second edition.
Philadelphia: Society for Industrial and Applied Mathematics, 2003.

[Southwell 35] Richard V. Southwell. "Stress-Calculation in Frameworks by the Method
of Systematic Relaxation of Constraints. I and II." In *Proceedings of the Royal Society of London. Series A, Mathematical and Physical Sciences*, pp. 56–96. London,
1935.

[Spivak 71] Michael Spivak. *Calculus on Manifolds: A Modern Approach to Classical
Theorems of Advanced Calculus.* New York: HarperCollins Publishers, 1971.

[Stam 99] Jos Stam. "Stable Fluids." In *SIGGRAPH '99: Proceedings of the 26th
Annual Conference on Computer Graphics and Interactive Techniques*, pp. 121–
128. New York: ACM Press/Addison-Wesley Publishing Co., 1999.

[Strang 07] Gilbert Strang. *Computational Science and Engineering.* Wellesley, MA:
Wellesley-Cambridge Press, 2007.

[Yu et al. 04] Yizhou Yu, Kun Zhou, Dong Xu, Xiaohan Shi, Hujun Bao, Baining Guo,
and Heung-Yeung Shum. "Mesh Editing with Poisson-Based Gradient Field Ma-
nipulation." *ACM Transactions on Graphics* 23:3 (2004), 644–651.

Volumetric Transparency with Per-Pixel Fragment Lists

László Szécsi, Pál Barta, and Balázs Kovács

In this chapter we describe the *volumetric transparency* method for rendering transparent objects that departs from classic alpha blending. Instead, it builds per-pixel lists of surface fragments and evaluates illumination analytically between neighboring pairs. This new approach allows object transparency and color to depend on material thickness, and transparent objects are allowed to intersect. Thus, the method is geared at the most prevalent application of transparency: particle system rendering, where it avoids all popping and clipping artifacts characteristic of alpha-blended billboard clouds. We also show how texturing, shadows, or light shafts can be added.

5.1 Introduction

In transparent objects and media, light interactions do not happen only on object surfaces but also within its volume. Accurate computation of these, under general conditions, requires costly *ray-marching* [Bunyk et al. 97, Szirmay-Kalos et al. 11] or *slicing* [Ikits et al. 04] algorithms. These use, directly or indirectly, a large number of point samples to find the color of each pixel. Thus, they can be implemented most straightforwardly for voxel grid data; other representations are usually converted to this.

A much more lightweight technique, *alpha blending* allows us to add transparency to regular surface rasterization. However, it requires surface elements to be rendered in a back-to-front order, does not instantly allow for transparency to depend on object thickness, and works poorly with Z-testing. In the case of particle systems rendered with transparent particle billboards, the most distressing problems are addressed by *spherical billboards* [Umenhoffer et al. 06], also called *soft particles*. This method uses pixel shaders to actually compute visible thickness, clipped by opaque surfaces, and to adjust transparency and color accordingly. However, ordering of billboards is still required, and when the order of the billboards changes between two animation frames, visible popping still occurs. This is less pronounced if there are more particles, or if they appear similar. However, in certain circumstances—for example, in fire-and-smoke scenarios, or when shadows are cast onto the medium—particle colors and saturations may be varied, and popping becomes more visible.

The *megaparticles* technique [Bahnassi and Bahnassi 06] eliminates billboard artifacts, rendering actual spheres instead of billboards. This allows particles to be shaded and depth-tested the same way as solid geometry. Their volumetric nature is lost, but the effect can be reintroduced in an image-space distortion and blurring pass. The technique can render stunningly shaded dense smoke, and, with some sorting required, even solid objects are allowed to intersect. However, mixing of low-opacity particles and proper depth-dependent transparency are not addressed. Megaparticles and our volumetric transparency method share the concept of using a few complex volumetric particles rather than thousands of billboards.

The method of this chapter can be grasped both as a special case of ray casting and a generalized case of alpha blending. From the ray-casting point of view, what we do is assume a piecewise homogeneous medium and thus replace costly point sampling with the evaluation of an analytic formula. Compared to spherical billboards, our volumetric transparency method does not only clip the volume thickness against opaque objects, but also accurately handles intersection between particles. Mixing the two media together, it completely eliminates the possibility of popping artifacts.

5.2 Light Transport Model

In rendering algorithms, we need to find *radiance* incoming at the eye along rays through every pixel. Transparent objects and participating media exhibit volumetric lighting effects (see Figure 5.1): they let through some of the background

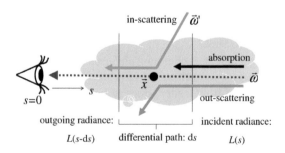

Figure 5.1. Volumetric lighting effects in participating media.

light toward the eye, *absorb* or *scatter out* another part, and *scatter in* light from light sources toward the eye. Emissive media also *emit* light. The chance that a photon gets absorbed or scattered while traveling a small distance ds is $\tau \cdot ds$, where τ is called the *extinction coefficient* or *optical density*. If the incoming radiance is L, then $\tau L \cdot ds$ is the amount lost over distance ds.

How much light is emitted or scattered toward the eye depends on the medium emissivity, on the lighting conditions, and on the scattering properties of the medium. We are going to assume that this contribution is constant over every object volume. For this to be true, lighting must be uniform and the medium must be homogeneous. These, and more, are also assumed in classic alpha-blended transparency. In practice, this means that we use ambient or unattenuated directional lighting, discarding multiple scattering and volumetric self-shadowing effects.

The contribution of the medium to eye-directional radiance over a small distance ds is $g \cdot ds$, where g is called the *source term*. This contribution includes emission and in-scattering due to ambient or directional lighting, and it is influenced by lighting parameters. If value g is given for the RGB wavelengths, it can be intuitively interpreted as the color of the medium.

Thus, the absorption and out-scattering terms are characterized by extinction coefficient τ and the emission and in-scattering are covered by source term g. We will call these two together the *optical parameters* of the medium. With these, the change of radiance dL over distance ds can be written as

$$dL = g \cdot ds - \tau L \cdot ds,$$

yielding the differential equation

$$\frac{dL}{ds} = g - \tau L, \tag{5.1}$$

for which the particular solution with $L(0) = L_{background}$ is

$$L(s) = \frac{g \cdot (1 - e^{-s\tau})}{\tau} + L_{background} \cdot e^{-s\tau}. \tag{5.2}$$

This formula gives us the radiance contribution of a homogenous medium segment of thickness s and the attenuation factor for the background radiance. Note that the analytic solution of the differential equation is possible because we assume that the medium is homogeneous. With linear or quadratic functions for $\tau(s)$ and $g(s)$, we would get integral formulas, the evaluation of which would no longer appear beneficial, having ray marching as an alternative.

5.3   Ray Decomposition

In order to find the color of a pixel, we need to evaluate the radiance along the ray shot from the eye through the pixel. The scene objects are either opaque or

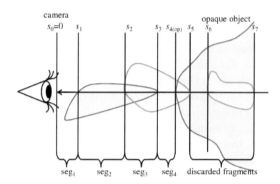

Figure 5.2.   Ray decomposition into homogenous segments.

homogenously transparent solids. Let us consider the ray interval between the
eye and the first intersected opaque surface. As depicted in Figure 5.2, this interval is divided into homogenous segments by the points where the ray intersects
surfaces of transparent objects. Such a segment may be empty, contain medium
from one object, or have multiple objects overlapping. Our goal is to identify
all these segments, compute the optical properties for them, and evaluate their
contributions to the observed radiance.

Where two objects overlap, the optical parameters of the mixed medium must
be found. If the chance that a photon travels the distance ds without collision is
$1 - \tau_A \cdot ds$ in one medium and $1 - \tau_B \cdot ds$ in the other, the probability of no collision
in either is the product $(1 - \tau_A \cdot ds)(1 - \tau_B \cdot ds)$, meaning collision probability $\tau \cdot ds$
for the combined medium is $\tau_A \cdot ds + \tau_B \cdot ds - \tau_A \tau_B \cdot (ds)^2$. Dividing by ds gives
us the extinction coefficient we must use in the differential equation, but there,
as the remaining ds term approaches zero, this simply becomes $\tau = \tau_A + \tau_B$. It
can be said that the chance that a photon would collide with both media must
not be considered over an infinitesimal distance. Following the same reasoning,
the source terms g_A and g_B can also simply be added to get the mixed medium
source term g.

Let us denote the distances where the ray intersects the surfaces of transparent
objects in increasing order by s_i, with $i = 1 \ldots n$, where n is the number of
intersections, and prepend $s_0 = 0$ to this ordered list. The intersections divide
the ray into homogenous segments. Let τ_i and g_i be the extinction coefficient and
source term of the combined medium in segment $[s_i, s_{i+1})$. As explained above,
these are simply the sums of the medium parameters of the objects overlapping in
the segment. Along the ray, $\tau(s)$ and $g(s)$ increase at every *entry point*, at which
the ray enters an object, and decrease at every *exit point*, at which it leaves one.
The change is equal to the optical parameters of the entered or exited object.
Let us denote the changes at s_i with $\Delta \tau_i$ and Δg_i, respectively. The values are

positive for entry points and negative for exit points. The optical parameters at the eye can be found as the negated sum of all changes, as all objects are finite and both parameters are zero at infinity:

$$\tau_0 = -\sum_{i=1}^{n} \Delta\tau_i, \qquad g_0 = -\sum_{i=1}^{n} \Delta g_i.$$

Consequent segment parameters can simply be found by applying the changes due to entered or exited objects:

$$\tau_i = \tau_{i-1} + \Delta\tau_i, \qquad g_i = g_{i-1} + \Delta g_i. \tag{5.3}$$

If $L(s_n)$ is the background radiance that enters at the end of the last segment, and $L(s_i)$ is the radiance that leaves segment $[s_i, s_{i+1})$ toward the eye, then using Equation (5.2) we can write for $i < n$ that

$$L(s_i) = \frac{g_i \cdot \left(1 - e^{(s_{i+1} - s_i)\tau_i}\right)}{\tau_i} + L(s_{i+1})e^{(s_{i+1} - s_i)\tau_i},$$

which yields a recursive formula for $L(s_0)$, the incoming radiance at the eye. We can evaluate this formula in an iterative manner, by accumulating the contribution of segments into variable L while maintaining the total transparency of all processed segments in variable T. We start with $L = 0$ and $T = 1$, and for every segment, in order, we perform

$$L \leftarrow L + T \cdot \frac{g_i \cdot \left(1 - e^{(s_{i+1} - s_i)\tau_i}\right)}{\tau_i},$$

$$T \leftarrow T \cdot e^{(s_{i+1} - s_i)\tau_i}.$$

After the last segment has been processed, L will contain the radiance at the eye. Note that the process can be terminated early when T becomes negligibly small, meaning that the processed segments completely occlude any features further away.

5.4 Finding Intersections with Ray Casting

In order to render an image like the one in Figure 5.3, the radiance has to be evaluated as described above, for every pixel. Thus, for every pixel, we need to assemble an ordered list of all intersections with transparent object surfaces, storing intersection distances s_i. Optical parameter changes $\Delta\tau_i$ and Δg_i can either be stored directly in the list records or just be referenced by the object ID and an enter/exit flag. If the objects are such that ray–object intersection is easy to compute, building this ordered list can be done in a pixel shader when rendering a full-viewport quad.

Figure 5.3. Transparent spheres in the *Crytek Sponza* scene [Dabrovic and Meinl 02].

In this section, we discuss an algorithm for the case when the transparent objects are spheres. This is an important special case, because sets of spheres can be used to render particle systems. Although overlapping is allowed, presorting the spheres can help minimize local shader memory usage and sorting overhead, because it allows us to process partial intersection lists. The algorithm renders a frame as follows:

1. We render opaque scene color and depth into a texture. This texture is accessible for later shaders.

2. Spheres are sorted according to their distance from the camera, in ascending order. Note that this is not the distance to the sphere center, but the distance to the sphere, which is one radius less. The sorted array is uploaded to the GPU.

3. A full-viewport quad is rendered. For every pixel, the shader does the following:

    (a) Running variables extinction coefficient τ, source term g, and radiance contribution L are initialized to zero. Aggregate transparency T is initialized to one.

(b) For every sphere in the array, the following is true:

    i. The sphere is intersected with the ray through the pixel. Intersected intervals are clipped to between zero and the opaque depth. Intersection records (s_i, sphere ID, and an enter/exit flag) are inserted into a list ordered by depth. This list is short and it is stored in a fixed-sized local-memory array.

    ii. *Safe* intersection records are those intersections in the list that are within the eye-to-sphere distance of the next, yet unprocessed, sphere (in the *safe zone*). As spheres are ordered, intersections with further spheres cannot precede the safe ones. For these safe intersections, the radiance contribution L and the transparency T are accumulated. The extinction coefficient and source term are maintained in the running variables, adding the $\Delta\tau_i$ and Δg_i terms as the intersection points are processed. The processed intersections are discarded from the ordered list. If no spheres are left, we can evaluate all remaining intersections.

(c) We return L as the pixel color, adding T times the opaque surface color.

We store the elements of the ordered list in the local-memory array in reverse order. Elements are removed simply by decreasing the element count. For every intersected sphere we need to insert two records in known order, meaning records of a lesser distance have to be moved only once.

The fixed-size local memory array may be insufficient to hold intersections from too many overlapping spheres, forcing us to discard some intersections or, preferably, process nonfinal ones. This creates a trade-off between performance and the amount of overlapping we can handle robustly. However, as intersection records can be kept small, typical particle system scenarios can be handled easily.

The above brute force algorithm can be accelerated dramatically, if we render a set of smaller quadrilateral tiles that cover the viewport instead of a single viewport-sized quad. For every such tile, we can find in advance those spheres that intersect the frustum defined by the tile and the eye position. Only these spheres have to be considered for intersection in the shader. This allows the method to scale to higher particle counts and smaller particle diameters.

Other tweaks are also possible. Note that the shader now implicitly computes the optical properties at the eye in every pixel. These could be precomputed, but then we should handle intersections behind the eye as a special case, producing a more complex shader and more divergent execution. Likewise, intersections with spheres that happen completely in the safe zone could be processed immediately, skipping the list. This could save us a few operations, but at the cost of introducing new conditionals.

Figure 5.4. Particle system rendered with plain spheres (left), with impostors (center), and with colorful particles (right).

5.5 Application for Particle System Rendering

Using the above ray-casting algorithm, we are able to render perfect, intersecting, transparent spheres without billboard artifacts. We no longer require a large number of billboards to approximate a continuous effect. However, constant-density spheres have sharp apparent boundaries, and we cannot hope to compete with the detail of billboard rendering without texturing.

We can get rid of sharp sphere contours by artificially attenuating particle density near the edges. A sophisticated way of adding detail through textures is to use a *distance impostor* cube map [Szirmay-Kalos et al. 05], which can define the geometry of particles. Intersection with the sphere is then replaced by intersection with the distance impostor. Particle data sent to the shader can be augmented with a particle orientation quaternion, used to rotate the impostor providing proper 3D behavior. (See Figure 5.4 for results.) We found that executing a single iteration step of the intersection algorithm is sufficient to provide the required detail. In our implementation, we query the distance map with the intersection point on the sphere, and re-execute ray–sphere intersection with the obtained radius, as depicted in Figure 5.5. The sphere center is de-

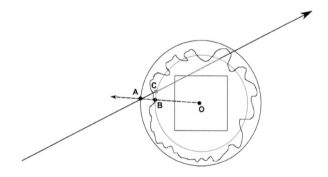

Figure 5.5. Using a distance impostor to add detail to particles.

noted by O, the original intersection point is A, the cube map texture is queried to return the distance OB, and the actual intersection point is approximated as C.

5.6   Finding Intersections with Rasterization

The ray-casting approach is only feasible if the transparent objects can be defined by few primitives, and even then an acceleration structure—like the tile decomposition described above—is necessary. For arbitrary-shaped objects, defined by manifold triangle meshes, we need to exploit the power of hardware rasterization. Gathering a list of fragments for image pixels is possible with Shader Model 5 hardware, as it has been demonstrated in the Order-Independent Transparency (OIT) method [Everitt 01]. In the OIT method the fragments are gathered so that they can be sorted by depth to evaluate alpha-blending-like transparency. We are going to use similar fragment lists to evaluate volumetric transparency, realizing that the front-face fragments correspond to entry points while back-face fragments are exit points.

The algorithm consists of three passes. First, we render the opaque scene into a render target texture, also storing surface distance from the eye. Second, we render transparent objects, collecting fragments into linked lists. Then, in the final pass, the lists are sorted and evaluated using the volumetric transparency method to get the pixel colors.

5.6.1   Data Structures

We store the fragment records in a *read/write structured buffer* called the *fragment&link buffer*. This contains linked list elements complete with an index referencing the buffer element that is the next in the linked list. This index is set to -1 in the final element of a list. The locations of the head elements of linked lists for specific pixels are given by *byte address buffers* called *start offset buffers*. The start offset buffer must have as many elements as there are pixels in the framebuffer.

When rasterizing the transparent objects, we need to be able to insert elements into these linked lists. This means adding new elements to the fragment&link buffer, which is possible using the built-in, synchronized-increment counter for structured buffers (consult the Direct3D documentation for details), in which we will maintain the element count. The buffer has to be large enough to accomodate all fragments. The required size can be estimated as the number of pixels multiplied by the average depth complexity.

Every fragment record in the fragment&link buffer stores the s_i distance, a front/back facing flag, and an index of the rendered object, allowing access to optical properties stored in a constant buffer.

5.6.2   Shader Passes

The first shader pass is called the *deferring* pass, as it is similar to the first pass of *deferred shading* [Policarpo and Fonseca 05]. It simply renders opaque scene elements with regular shaders into a render target texture and stores the eye-to-surface distance in the alpha channel. Regular Z-buffering is used, producing scene depth in the depth buffer.

The second pass (called the *storing* pass, as it stores the fragments into linked lists) renders transparent objects. There is no render target set; the frag-ment&link buffer is accessible as an initially empty, zero-element-count, unordered-access resource. Culling is disabled to get back-facing fragments. Depth writes are disabled, and depth tests might be enabled to discard frag-ments behind opaque objects. In the pixel shader, a new record is allocated in the fragment&link buffer by incrementing the buffer counter. The eye-to-surface distance, the facing flag, and the object ID are combined into this new fragment record, which is inserted as the new head element into the linked list of the pixel. For this, the index of the former head record in the start address buffer must be exchanged with the address of the new record. As multiple fragments for the same pixel might be processed at the same time, we need to use an *inter-locked exchange* operation, which is also a feature of Shader Model 5 structured buffers.

The third, *sorting and rendering* pass renders a full-viewport quad onto the framebuffer. The pixel shader traces linked lists reading fragments into a local array and sorts them according to their distance. Finally, it evaluates volumetric transparency for the segments between the fragments just like in the ray-casting case.

The sorting algorithm needs to work well with relatively few—surely less than 100—fragments. Thus, computational complexity is trumped by less storage and administration overhead, making insertion sort the optimal choice [Estivill-Castro and Wood 92].

If the camera is allowed within transparent objects, the optical properties at the eye—or rather, in this case, at the near clipping plane—are required. Find-ing them in the shader is possible if all fragments between the near clipping plane and infinity have been rendered into the linked lists: changes at the in-tersections have to be summed and negated. This requires that depth testing is disabled in the storing pass (meaning longer linked lists to store and sort) and that transparent objects do not extend over the far clipping plane. If we do not want to make these concessions, we need an extra pass that renders transpar-ent geometry, blend-adding optical properties into a texture and yielding near-plane optical properties for every pixel. The storing pass can also be modified to produce this texture if the depth test is performed in the shader, filtering hidden fragments from the linked list but letting them through to the render target.

Figure 5.6. Transparent objects with added surface reflection.

5.7 Adding Surface Reflection

Surfaces of transparent objects may also reflect light, just like opaque ones. To handle this, the surface reflection must be evaluated in the storing phase, and fragment records must store the additional radiance reflected toward the eye from the intersection point. When processing the intersections in the sorting and rendering pass, these also have to be added to the total radiance, weighted by the accumulated transparency. Figure 5.6 shows some examples.

5.8 Shadow Volumes

We assumed the source term to be constant in objects, meaning that lighting is uniform everywhere. However, we can maintain the concept of a piecewise-constant source term if the lighting is not uniform but piecewise constant itself. This is the case for directional or distant unattenuated point-like light sources. To augment the original algorithm, we need to factorize the source term to a product of the medium *albedo* α and the lighting irradiance I. Both of these can simply be added where multiple objects or lighted volumes overlap. Thus, optical properties τ, α, and I are handled just like τ and g were before. Naturally, a transparent object contributes nothing to lighting, making ΔI_i at intersections zero.

For a light source, the volume that it illuminates is given by its shadow volume [Yen Kwoon 02]. Shadow volumes can be rendered in the storing pass just like regular transparent objects. They contribute nothing to the extinction coefficient or the albedo, thus $\Delta \tau_i$ and $\Delta \alpha_i$ are zero. However, entering a shadow volume decreases irradiance by the value associated with the light source, and exiting increases it by the same. Irradiance at the eye is the sum of the changes along a ray added to the total irradiance due to all light sources.

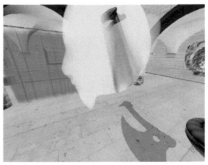

Figure 5.7. Volumetric shadows on transparent objects.

Note that the shadow volumes can be rendered by sending mesh-adjacency-enabled shadow caster geometry to the GPU and extruding silhouette edges in the geometry shader (see Figure 5.7 for screenshots).

5.9 Conclusion

Rendering complex transparent objects in real time became possible with Shader Model 5 and order-independent transparency. In this chapter, we have shown how the approach can be extended to volumetric transparency, and even intersecting objects. The algorithm can also be used—even with ray casting instead of linked-list rasterization—to render particles systems, thus eliminating all intersection and popping artifacts and reducing the required particle count to represent continuous volumetric phenomena. Thus, volumetric transparency can be seen both as a relatively low-cost improvement to order-independent transparency and as a sophisticated approach to replace billboards in particle rendering. Figure 5.8 shows a complex scene where the method performs in real time.

Figure 5.8. A complex scene with transparent objects.

Bibliography

[Bahnassi and Bahnassi 06] H. Bahnassi and W. Bahnassi. *ShaderX^5: Advanced Rendering Techniques*, Chapter Volumetric Clouds and Mega-Particles, pp. 295–302. Hingham, MA: Charles River Media, 2006.

[Bunyk et al. 97] P. Bunyk, A. Kaufman, and C. T. Silva. "Simple, Fast, and Robust Ray Casting of Irregular Grids." In *Scientific Visualization Conference*, pp. 30–30. Los Alamitos, CA: IEEE, 1997.

[Dabrovic and Meinl 02] M. Dabrovic and F. Meinl. "Crytek Sponza Model." http://www.crytek.com/cryengine/cryengine3/downloads, 2002.

[Estivill-Castro and Wood 92] V. Estivill-Castro and D. Wood. "A Survey of Adaptive Sorting Algorithms." *ACM Computing Surveys (CSUR)* 24:4 (1992), 441–476.

[Everitt 01] C. Everitt. "Interactive Order-Independent Transparency." *Nvidia* 2:6 (2001), 7. White paper.

[Ikits et al. 04] M. Ikits, J. Kniss, A. Lefohn, and C. Hansen. *Volume Rendering Techniques*, pp. 667–692. Reading, MA: Addison Wesley, 2004.

[Policarpo and Fonseca 05] F. Policarpo and F. Fonseca. "Deferred shading tutorial." Technical report, 2005.

[Szirmay-Kalos et al. 05] L. Szirmay-Kalos, B. Aszódi, I. Lazányi, and M. Premecz. "Approximate Ray-Tracing on the GPU with Distance Impostors." *Computer Graphics Forum (Eurographics '05)* 24:3 (2005), 695–704.

[Szirmay-Kalos et al. 11] L. Szirmay-Kalos, B. Tóth, and M. Magdics. "Free Path Sampling in High Resolution Inhomogeneous Participating Media." In *Computer Graphics Forum*. Wiley Online Library, 2011. Available online (onlibrary.wiley.com).

[Umenhoffer et al. 06] T. Umenhoffer, L. Szirmay-Kalos, and G. Szijártó. "Spherical Billboards and their Application to Rendering Explosions." In *Graphics Interface*, pp. 57–64. Toronto: Canadian Information Processing Society, 2006.

[Yen Kwoon 02] Hun Yen Kwoon. "The Theory of Stencil Shadow Volumes." http://www.gamedev.net/reference/articles/article1873.asp, 2002.

6

Practical Binary Surface and Solid Voxelization with Direct3D 11
Michael Schwarz

6.1 Introduction

Regular, discrete representations of potentially complex signals are routinely used in many fields. They provide a comfortable domain in which to work, often facilitate processing, and are largely independent from the represented signal's complexity. In computer graphics, we encounter such representations mainly in the form of two-dimensional images, like the final rendering result or a shadow map. Their three-dimensional analog, and the focus of this chapter, is *voxelizations* stored in voxel grids. They offer a volumetric representation of a scene, where each grid cell, referred to as a *voxel*, encodes that part of the scene that is located within the cell. In case of a *binary voxelization*, this encoding is particularly simple: merely two states are distinguished, where a set voxel indicates the presence of some, and an unset voxel the absence of any, scene object.

Largely orthogonal to this encoding, two main flavors of voxelizations can be distinguished (see Figure 6.1). In a *surface voxelization* (also called boundary voxelization), the scene is interpreted as consisting solely of surfaces, that is, all closed objects are assumed hollow. Therefore, only voxels overlapped by a surface (like a scene triangle) will be nonempty. By contrast, a *solid voxelization* treats all objects as solids, and hence, any voxel interior to an object will be set. Note that this basically requires the objects to be closed.

Binary voxelizations are useful for many applications, ranging from collision detection [Zhang et al. 07, Eisemann and Décoret 08] to ambient occlusion [Reinbothe et al. 09], soft shadows [Forest et al. 10], area light visibility [Nichols et al. 10], and volumetric shadows [Wyman 11]. Unless confined to static settings, they all mandate that the voxelization be created on the fly at real-time speed. This chapter describes how this goal can be achieved using Direct3D 11, covering the process of turning an input scene, given as a collection

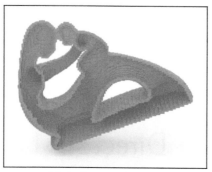

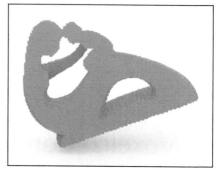

(a) Surface voxelization.   (b) Solid voxelization.

Figure 6.1. In a surface voxelization (a), the voxels overlapping the scene's surfaces are set, whereas in a solid voxelization (b), the voxels that are inside a scene object are set. (For illustration purposes, the fronts of the voxelizations have been cut away, revealing the interiors.)

of triangles, into a binary surface or solid voxelization. We first discuss implementations that build on the standard graphics pipeline and its rasterization stage; these are rather simple and easy to implement but also suffer from several shortcomings. Addressing some of them, we subsequently investigate alternative realizations that employ DirectCompute.

6.2 Rasterization-Based Surface Voxelization

With surface voxelization basically being a three-dimensional extension of rasterization, it is natural to try to pose this process in terms of rasterization and harness the according existing hardware units. Assuming a target voxel grid of size $w \times h \times d$, a simple approach is to render the scene into a deep framebuffer of resolution $w \times h$ with (at least) d bits per pixel (see Figure 6.2). Hence, for each triangle, all pixels covered are determined, and a fragment is generated for each of them. In the invoked pixel shader, those voxels within the voxel column represented by the according deep pixel are identified that are actually covered by the triangle. The resulting voxel-column pixel value is then output by the shader and incorporated into the existing framebuffer.

6.2.1 Challenges

Unfortunately, this appealing approach faces several problems in practice. A major issue is that in ordinary rasterization, a pixel is only considered to be covered by a triangle if the triangle overlaps the pixel's center. This implies that no fragments are generated for all those pixels that a triangle partially overlaps without simultaneously overlapping their centers. Consequently, no voxels are

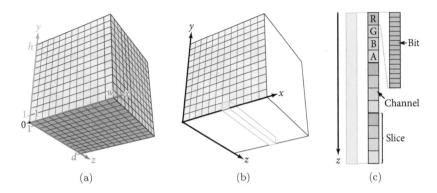

Figure 6.2. (a) We assume a voxel grid of size $w \times h \times d$ and define the *voxel space* such that each voxel has a footprint of size 1^3 and the grid covers the range $[0, w] \times [0, h] \times [0, d]$. (b) The grid can be thought of as a 2D image with deep pixels (each representing a voxel column). (c) These deep pixels may be encoded in multiple multichannel texture slices.

set in these cases, making resulting voxelizations routinely suffer from gaps and miss thin structures (see Figure 6.3). The situation can be somewhat alleviated by rendering the scene not just from one side of the grid (xy) but from three orthogonal sides (xy, xz, and yz) [Forest et al. 10]. This necessitates additional temporary buffers and a merging step, though, and still easily misses many voxels. The only real solution is to always generate a fragment if any part of a pixel's area is overlapped by a triangle. Current hardware, however, does not provide for this so-called *conservative rasterization*. While it can be emulated in software by enlarging each triangle appropriately [Hasselgren et al. 05] (e.g., in the geometry shader), this obviously incurs a significant overhead. Therefore, it is not surprising that an according voxelization algorithm [Zhang et al. 07] turns out to often be rather slow (and it also suffers from some robustness issues). For now, we will simply ignore this problem, but we will tackle it later in Section 6.4 when adopting a compute-based approach.

Another issue arises from updating the voxel grid to incorporate the voxel column output for a fragment. For correct results, obviously a bitwise OR operation is needed. One solution is to realize the deep framebuffer by multiple multichannel render targets, using the single bits of all the channels for encoding the voxel states (see Figure 6.2(c)), and to perform bitwise-OR blending. This was first demonstrated by Dong et al. [Dong et al. 04] (using additive blending, though); the specific framebuffer encoding is sometimes referred to as *slicemap* [Eisemann and Décoret 06]. While this approach works well when using OpenGL, it is not possible with Direct3D, as recent versions no longer expose the hardware's still-existing bitwise blending functionality (also known as logical pixel operations), which once was used for color-index rendering.

(a) Rasterized (1 dir).   (b) Rasterized (3 dirs).   (c) Conservative.

Figure 6.3. (a) If surface voxelization is performed with ordinary rasterization, voxels are frequently missed, leading to perforated surfaces and unconnected voxel clouds. (b) Executing this process from three orthogonal directions and combining the results helps in the case of closed surfaces (like the torus knot), but generally still fails badly if thin structures are involved (like in the leaf-deprived Italian maple). (c) By contrast, conservative voxelization yields correct results.

6.2.2 Approach

Fortunately, Direct3D 11 introduces the ability to write to arbitrary positions of a resource from within the pixel shader and further supports atomic updates to this end. These new features finally allow for pursuing a rasterization-based surface voxelization approach with Direct3D. The basic idea is to replace the bitwise blending of the pixel shader output into the deep framebuffer by performing atomic bitwise update operations on the voxel grid within the pixel shader.

This leads to the following overall approach: First, a resource for storing the voxel grid of size $w \times h \times d$, along with an according unordered access view (UAV), needs to be created. This can be a texture (array) or a buffer, with the latter

```
RWBuffer<uint> g_rwbufVoxels;

struct PSInput_Voxelize {
  float4 pos     : SV_Position;
  float4 gridPos : POSITION_GRID;
};

PSInput_Voxelize VS_Voxelize(VSInput_Model input) {
  PSInput_Voxelize output;
  output.pos = mul(g_matModelToClip, input.pos);
  output.gridPos = mul(g_matModelToVoxel, input.pos);
  return output;
}

float4 PS_VoxelizeSurface(PSInput_Voxelize input) : SV_Target {
  int3 p = int3(input.gridPos.xyz / input.gridPos.w);
  InterlockedOr(g_rwbufVoxels[p.x * g_stride.x + p.y * g_stride.y +
                              (p.z >> 5)], 1 << (p.z & 31));

  discard;
  return 0.0;
}
```

Listing 6.1. Vertex and pixel shaders for rasterization-based surface voxelization.

being the best choice for most applications. As for data format, a 32-bit integer type has to be chosen to allow for atomic updates. Furthermore, either a render target or a depth/stencil target of minimum size $w \times h$ needs to be available.

For creating the voxelization, this target is bound as the only output-merger-stage target, and a viewport of size $w \times h$ is set. Moreover, the voxel grid is reset by clearing its UAV with zeroes, and this UAV is bound. We then render the scene, using the vertex and pixel shaders from Listing 6.1, which adopt the buffer layout shown in Figure 6.4 as a concrete example. The vertex shader transforms

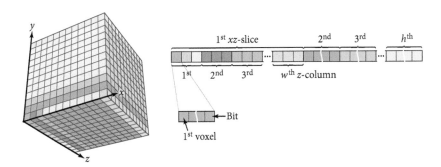

Figure 6.4. To store the voxel grid in a buffer, we linearize it first along the z-direction, packing 32 consecutive voxels into the bits of a 32-bit (unsigned) integer buffer value, then along the x-direction, and finally along the y-direction.

the vertex position into clip space, mapping the grid's xyz-extent to the clip volume (i.e., to $[-1, 1]^2 \times [0, 1]$), and into voxel space, mapping the grid's xyz-extent to $[0, w] \times [0, h] \times [0, d]$. Based on the clip-space coordinates, each triangle is rasterized, and a fragment is generated for each pixel (voxel column) whose center is overlapped. In the pixel shader, the voxel-space coordinate is used to directly set the according voxel in the voxel grid with an atomic OR operation. Subsequently, the fragment is discarded. Note that even though the render or depth/stencil target is thus never updated, it is still required, as otherwise no fragments would be generated.

6.2.3 Discussion

Compared to approaches using bitwise blending, confining them to OpenGL, the presented technique is similarly easy to implement and has both advantages and disadvantages. On the downside, it is often somewhat slower, especially in case of larger voxel grids. This is because random atomic updates to the voxelization are less optimized and efficient than blending executed by the graphics hardware's dedicated raster operation (ROP) units.

A big advantage of the described approach, however, is that the data organization is significantly nicer. Using a buffer resource and storing the voxel grid as a linearized 3D array, each voxel can be easily accessed via simple indexing into this buffer. In particular, this makes working with the generated voxelization rather straightforward. Moreover, it decouples the voxel grid from the side of the grid from which the scene is rendered. Consequently, if the scene is rendered from all three axis directions in order to reduce the artifacts resulting from non-conservative rasterization, a single voxelization buffer can be shared, both saving space and avoiding a final merging step.

By contrast, a deep framebuffer consisting of multiple multichannel render targets, typically stored in a texture array, makes addressing cumbersome because within a render target (texture slice) individual channels cannot be accessed via indexing; instead, conditional expressions are required. Furthermore, as the concrete number of render targets and channels depends on d, supporting variable grid depths d necessitates multiple pixel shaders—one for each render target count. Finally, for large values of d, the needed number of render targets can exceed the maximum number supported by the hardware, requiring multiple passes to fill the voxel grid.

6.3   Rasterization-Based Solid Voxelization

In solid voxelization, we seek to determine all voxels that are interior to some object. Typically, a voxel is considered interior if its center is interior, and we adopt this criterion, too. This leaves us with the task of computing, for each voxel center, whether or not it is located inside some scene object. Assuming that the

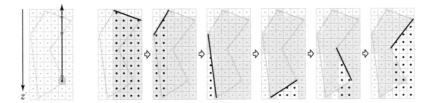

Figure 6.5. A voxel is inside an object if a ray shot upward from its center intersects the scene an odd number of times (far left). These intersection parities can be determined by rendering all triangles, each time flipping all voxels whose centers are below the respective triangle.

scene consists solely of closed, watertight objects and that no object is contained in another one, a point can be classified accordingly by shooting a ray from this point in an arbitrary direction and counting the number of intersections with the scene. If this number is even, the ray entered as many objects as it exited, and hence, the point must be outside. Conversely, an odd count indicates that the point is interior.

Instead of shooting a ray from each voxel center, the parity of the intersection count can be determined equally well using the following approach [Fang and Chen 00, Eisemann and Décoret 08]: First, all voxels are initialized to unset. Subsequently, we loop over all triangles. For each, the state of all voxels whose center is "below" this triangle is flipped. This accounts for the fact that if a ray would be shot from such a center "upward," it would intersect the triangle, increasing the intersection count and hence flipping its parity. Consequently, the final voxel state correctly reflects the parity of the total intersection count and thus the voxel's inside/outside classification (see Figure 6.5).

Using ordinary rasterization from the voxel grid's xy-side, identifying the voxels "below" a triangle is straightforward: for each fragment, corresponding to a whole voxel column, we merely have to select all voxels in this column whose z-index is larger than the fragment's voxel-space z-coordinate minus 0.5.[1]

Consequently, for a practical implementation, the same code as for the surface voxelization can be used. The only modification required affects the pixel shader: instead of setting the voxel corresponding to the fragment's voxel-space coordinates via a bitwise OR, we now have to flip the state of all voxels whose center is below the fragment via atomic XOR operations. Moreover, depth clipping should be turned off (or the clip-space z-coordinate set to a constant $\tilde{z} \in [0, 1]$ in the vertex shader); otherwise, some intersections may be missed if part of the scene is in front of the grid, potentially leading to wrong results.

Note that because a voxel's state is determined solely by the inside/outside classification of its center, accurate results are obtained with ordinary rasteri-

---

[1]This half-voxel adjustment is because we consider the voxel's center.

zation. This is unlike the situation with surface voxelization, where, instead, conservative rasterization is generally required for correctness.

6.4　Conservative Surface Voxelization with DirectCompute

Having seen that using the existing rasterization hardware for voxelization is rather simple, we now turn to an alternative approach based on DirectCompute.[2] It basically boils down to writing our own 3D software rasterizer, which is directly executed on the GPU. This allows us to adapt the rasterizer to the specific problem of voxelization and to exploit arising optimization potential. Being no longer bound to the design decisions and behavior of the graphics hardware's rasterizer, we are, in particular, free to adopt any criterion we want to determine whether a triangle covers a pixel or voxel. Consequently, the fundamental problem of surface voxelization encountered in Section 6.2 can be addressed, namely that the hardware rasterizer does not generate fragments for pixels that are partially covered without their respective centers being covered. Recall that this causes many voxels to incorrectly not be set, severely restricting the usefulness of according techniques.

6.4.1　Approach

Our software surface voxelizer processes all scene triangles in parallel, spending one thread per triangle. In the executed compute shader, at first, the triangle's vertices are fetched and transformed into voxel space. The bounding box of the transformed triangle is then determined and subsequently clipped against the voxel grid. In the case that the clipped bounding box is empty, the triangle is entirely outside the voxel grid, and we are done. Otherwise, the shader loops over all voxels within the bounding box that are potentially overlapped by the triangle. For each of these candidate voxels, an overlap test is performed, and, if the test passes, the voxel is set with an atomic OR operation.

To facilitate a practical implementation of this basic approach, some details should be pointed out. Firstly, the input scene geometry may be made available to the voxelizer in various forms. This could be a list of transformed vertex triplets, each representing a triangle, possibly collected in a stream-output buffer after vertex processing with an ordinary vertex shader. Another possibility is to provide a vertex buffer and an index buffer, and to perform any vertex processing in the compute shader together with the transformation into voxel space.

The chosen set of potentially overlapped voxels may basically be any superset of the actually overlapped voxels. Thus, a simple, conservative approach is just to consider all voxels that are (partially) within the triangle's bounding box. As

---

[2]This approach heavily builds on our previous CUDA-based work [Schwarz and Seidel 10].

each candidate voxel needs to be further investigated, subjecting it to an overlap test, and this test is far from free, performance benefits from better strategies that reduce the number of tested voxels that fail the test and that, hence, would ideally not have been considered in the first place. We will come back to this in Section 6.4.2.

Concerning the overlap test, we are fairly free to choose any criterion we like to define when an overlap occurs. For instance, by testing whether the triangle overlaps the voxel's 3D extent at least partially, a *conservative surface voxelization* is obtained. An according fast triangle/voxel overlap test is detailed in Section 6.4.2.

Finally, when looping over multiple voxels that are represented by different bits of the same 32-bit buffer value, it is advantageous to not immediately update the voxelization buffer for each set voxel among them. Instead, these updates should be buffered in a local 32-bit register and, once the last voxel has been processed, collectively written to the voxelization buffer with a single atomic OR operation.

6.4.2 Triangle/Voxel Overlap Testing

For conservative surface voxelization, we need to determine which voxels are at least partially overlapped by a certain triangle. To this end, we adopt a triangle/box overlap test [Schwarz and Seidel 10] that lends itself to a GPU implementation. It comprises several simpler tests that all have to succeed for an overlap to occur; if any of them fails, the voxel is not covered by the triangle.

Bounding box overlap. Given a triangle T and a voxel V, it is first checked whether the bounding box of T and V overlap. Since, by construction, we only test voxels that are (at least partially) within T's bounding box, this check is redundant and can be omitted.

Plane overlap. Subsequently, we have to test whether the plane of T overlaps V. Suppose that T has the three vertices $\mathbf{v}_0$, $\mathbf{v}_1$, and $\mathbf{v}_2$, all specified in voxel-space coordinates, and that V is located at index (x, y, z) within the voxel grid, thus corresponding to the box defined by the two voxel-space corners $\mathbf{x} = [x, y, z]$ and $\mathbf{x}' = [x+1, y+1, z+1]$. We then compute the normal $\mathbf{n}$ of T and determine that pair of opposing voxel corners $(\mathbf{c}_1, \mathbf{c}_2)$ that best aligns with $\mathbf{n}$ (see Figure 6.6):

$$c_{1,x} = \begin{cases} 1, & n_x > 0, \\ 0, & n_x \leq 0, \end{cases} \qquad c_{1,y} = \begin{cases} 1, & n_y > 0, \\ 0, & n_y \leq 0, \end{cases} \qquad c_{1,z} = \begin{cases} 1, & n_z > 0, \\ 0, & n_z \leq 0; \end{cases}$$

$$c_{2,x} = 1 - c_{1,x}, \qquad c_{2,y} = 1 - c_{1,y}, \qquad c_{2,z} = 1 - c_{1,z}.$$

Note that these corners are expressed relative to $\mathbf{x}$. If and only if they lie on different sides of the triangle's plane (or one lies exactly on the plane), the plane

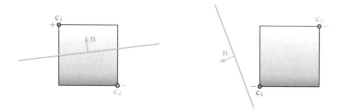

Figure 6.6. For testing whether a plane overlaps a voxel, the two opposing voxel corners c_1 and c_2 for which the vector $c_1 - c_2$ best aligns with the plane normal n are determined. An overlap occurs if they are located in different half spaces of the plane (as on the left).

overlaps V. This can be easily checked by inserting the two voxel extrema $\mathbf{x} + \mathbf{c}_1$ and $\mathbf{x} + \mathbf{c}_2$ into the plane equation and comparing the results' signs:

$$\big(\mathbf{n} \cdot (\mathbf{x} + \mathbf{c}_1 - \mathbf{v}_0)\big)\big(\mathbf{n} \cdot (\mathbf{x} + \mathbf{c}_2 - \mathbf{v}_0)\big) = (\mathbf{n} \cdot \mathbf{x} + d_1)(\mathbf{n} \cdot \mathbf{x} + d_2) \le 0, \qquad (6.1)$$

where $d_k = \mathbf{n} \cdot (\mathbf{c}_k - \mathbf{v}_0)$. If the signs differ, the product of the results is negative; it is zero if one of the corners is located on the plane.

2D triangle/box overlap. Finally, we have to test whether the triangle and the voxel overlap in all three, mutually orthogonal, 2D main projections (xy, xz, and yz). Such a 2D test can be efficiently realized with *edge functions* [Pineda 88]. An edge function is simply (the left-hand side of) a 2D line equation for one triangle edge:

$$e_i(\mathbf{p}) = \mathbf{m}_i \cdot (\mathbf{p} - \mathbf{w}_i), \qquad (6.2)$$

where $i \in \{0, 1, 2\}$ is the index of the edge going from $\mathbf{w}_i$ to $\mathbf{w}_{(i+1) \bmod 3}$, $\{\mathbf{w}_i\}$ are the 2D triangle's vertices, and $\mathbf{m}_i$ denotes the edge's normal. This normal points to the inside of the triangle and is given by

$$\mathbf{m}_i = \big[w_{(i+1) \bmod 3, y} - w_{i,y}, w_{i,x} - w_{(i+1) \bmod 3, x}\big]$$

if the triangle is oriented clockwise and by

$$\mathbf{m}_i = \big[w_{i,y} - w_{(i+1) \bmod 3, y}, w_{(i+1) \bmod 3, x} - w_{i,x}\big]$$

in the case of counterclockwise orientation. Consequently, a point $\mathbf{p}$ is inside a triangle if the edge functions for all three edges yield a nonnegative result.

Taking the xy-projection as a concrete example, the triangle's 2D projection T^{xy} is given by the vertices $\mathbf{w}_i = [v_{i,x}, v_{i,y}]$. Its orientation can easily be determined by checking the triangle's normal $\mathbf{n}$; if $n_z > 0$, it is oriented counterclockwise. The voxel's 2D footprint V^{xy} corresponds to the box with corners $\mathbf{b} = [x, y]$ and $\mathbf{b}' = [x + 1, y + 1]$.

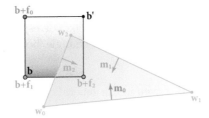

Figure 6.7. To determine whether a box (defined by corners $\mathbf{b}$ and $\mathbf{b}'$) and a triangle (with vertices $\mathbf{w}_0$, $\mathbf{w}_1$, and $\mathbf{w}_2$) overlap, for each triangle edge, we check whether the corresponding critical box corner $\mathbf{b} + \mathbf{f}_i$, implied by the edge's normal $\mathbf{m}_i$, is on the interior side of the edge line.

To test whether T^{xy} and V^{xy} overlap, we determine for each edge i that corner $\mathbf{f}_i$ of V^{xy} to which the edge's normal $\mathbf{m}_i$ points, that is,

$$f_{i,x} = \begin{cases} 1, & m_{i,x} > 0, \\ 0, & m_{i,x} \le 0, \end{cases} \qquad f_{i,y} = \begin{cases} 1, & m_{i,y} > 0, \\ 0, & m_{i,y} \le 0 \end{cases}$$

(see Figure 6.7), and evaluate the edge function for it. It is easy to see that only if $\mathbf{f}_i$ is on the interior side of the edge, that is, $e_i(\mathbf{b} + \mathbf{f}_i) \ge 0$, can there be any overlap of T^{xy} and V^{xy}. Hence, we have to check whether this is fulfilled for all three edges. Actually, it turns out that this is also sufficient for an overlap to occur if the bounding box of T^{xy} and V^{xy} overlap, which is always the case in our setup.

Single-triangle, many-voxel testing. Since, in general, a triangle is tested against multiple voxels for overlap, it is reasonable to compute all quantities that depend only on the triangle in the beginning and then to reuse them for the individual voxel overlap tests. Employing the reformulation

$$e_i(\mathbf{b} + \mathbf{f}_i) = \mathbf{m}_i \cdot (\mathbf{b} + \mathbf{f}_i - \mathbf{w}_i) = \mathbf{m}_i \cdot \mathbf{b} + g_i,$$

with $g_i = \mathbf{m}_i \cdot (\mathbf{f}_i - \mathbf{w}_i)$, this means that in a setup phase, the triangle normal $\mathbf{n}$, the distances d_1 and d_2, as well as the quantities $\mathbf{m}_i$ and g_i (for $i = 0, 1, 2$ and each of the three projections xy, xz, and yz) are determined. The actual per-voxel overlap test then merely requires checking whether the expression in Equation (6.1) holds and if $\mathbf{m}_i \cdot \mathbf{b} + g_i \ge 0$ for all edges and 2D projections.

Simplifications. In several situations, it is possible to simplify the described triangle/voxel overlap test and thus reduce its cost. For instance, if the bounding box of the triangle (before clipping to the voxel grid) covers just a one-voxel-thick

line of voxels, all voxels are overlapped by the triangle and no further per-voxel
test is necessary. Similarly, if the bounding box corresponds to a one-voxel-thick
voxel grid slice, only the corresponding 2D triangle/box overlap subtest needs to
be performed for each voxel.

Candidate voxel selection. But even in the general case, a noticeable simplification
is possible by integrating the overlap test with the selection of potentially overlapped voxels. Key is the observation that a triangle's voxelization is basically
two-dimensional and that, hence, visiting all voxels in its bounding box, a 3D volume, is wasteful. This leads to the following strategy: First, determine the grid
side that best aligns with the triangle's plane. Then look at the corresponding 2D
projection, and loop over the voxel columns covered by the triangle's bounding
box, applying the according 2D triangle/box overlap subtest to each. If a column
passes the test, determine the range of voxels overlapped by the triangle's plane;
their number is at most three per column. If the range comprises just a single
voxel, it is guaranteed to be overlapped. Otherwise, the voxels are subjected to
the two remaining 2D triangle/box overlap subtests to derive their final overlap
status. More details are given in our original publication [Schwarz and Seidel 10].

6.4.3 Discussion

In conservative surface voxelization, generally, significantly more voxels are set
than in rasterization-based surface voxelization. In Figure 6.3, for instance, increases of 132% and 305% for the torus knot and the Italian maple, respectively,
occur (with respect to rasterization from one direction). Moreover, unlike in
ordinary rasterization, all voxels overlapped by an edge shared by multiple triangles are set by each of these triangles, further increasing the number of voxel
updates. Together with the fact that the overlap test is much more expensive,
this causes conservative voxelization to be slower than surface voxelization using
the rasterization-based overlap criterion.

Concerning performance, it is important to understand the implications of
pursuing a triangle-parallel approach. First, the scene has to feature a large
enough number of triangles to provide enough data parallelism. Moreover, the
triangles should produce roughly the same amount of work. For instance, if
the scene has a ground plane consisting of only two triangles, the two threads
dedicated to their voxelization have to process an excessive number of voxels,
easily causing all other threads to finish early, leaving many shader cores idle.
In the case of such unfavorable configurations, a simple remedy is to tessellate
the scene accordingly. Another option is to distribute the voxelization of a single
triangle over multiple threads. This can be achieved by a blocking approach,
where each triangle is assigned to those macro grid cells it overlaps, or a tiling
approach, where each of the three grid front sides is split into coarse tiles, and
each triangle is assigned to those tiles it overlaps from that side to which it aligns

best. Each macrocell and tile, respectively, is then processed by a thread group, looping over all assigned triangles. An according implementation is left as an exercise for the interested reader.

As DirectCompute offers less opportunities for fine-tuning than CUDA, reaching performance comparable to optimized CUDA-based implementations is often hard to achieve and is partially at the mercy of the runtime and the driver. Hence, the accompanying source code does not focus on utmost performance but on legibility and structural cleanness, hopefully facilitating both adaptations and retargeting to other compute languages or platforms.

6.5 Solid Voxelization with DirectCompute

Obviously, realizing a software voxelizer using DirectCompute is not restricted to surface voxelization. In this section, we demonstrate an according approach for solid voxelization, which combines ideas from our previous solid and hierarchical, sparse solid voxelization algorithms [Schwarz and Seidel 10].

Similar to the rasterization-based algorithm from Section 6.3, we perform a 2D rasterization of the scene from one side of the voxel cube (xz this time, assuming the data layout from Figure 6.4). For each pixel whose center is covered, we determine the first voxel in the corresponding voxel column whose center is below the processed triangle and flip the state of this voxel with an atomic XOR operation. The other voxels in the column that are below this voxel are not flipped; instead, their update is deferred to a separate propagation pass that is executed once all triangles have been rendered (see Figure 6.8). This means that, after the rasterization, a set voxel indicates that all voxels below should be flipped. To obtain the final solid voxelization, these flips are carried out by the subsequent propagation pass. For each voxel column, it visits all voxels from top to bottom, flipping a voxel's state if the preceding voxel is set. This

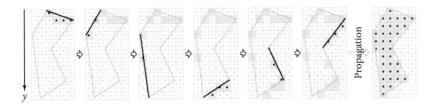

Figure 6.8. During the solid voxelization's initial rasterization pass, in each voxel column covered by a triangle, the state of the first voxel whose center is below the triangle is flipped. The state of the other voxels below is only updated in a subsequent propagation pass, which progresses from top to bottom, flipping a voxel's state if its neighbor directly above is set.

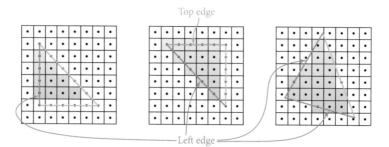

Figure 6.9. In standard rasterization, a pixel is covered by a triangle if its center is located within the triangle. In case the pixel center lies exactly on a triangle edge, it is not considered inside unless the edge is a left or a top edge.

distribution of voxel flips over two passes saves memory bandwidth and reduces the number of atomic update operations and random memory accesses compared to a single-pass approach that directly flips all voxels below, which helps performance.

For the rasterization, we again pursue a triangle-parallel approach, dedicating one thread per triangle. In the compute shader, the triangle's vertices are fetched and transformed, and their bounding box is computed and clipped against the voxel grid. If the bounding box is nonempty, we subsequently loop over all voxel columns (extending in the y-direction) within the xz-extent of the bounding box. For each column, we test in the 2D xz-projection whether the center is overlapped by the triangle. If that is the case, we compute the first voxel in this column whose center is below the triangle and flip the voxel's state.

The 2D overlap test can be efficiently realized by employing the edge functions e_i from Equation (6.2) and evaluating them at the column's 2D center position $\mathbf{q} = [x + \frac{1}{2}, z + \frac{1}{2}]$; if all three results $e_i(\mathbf{q})$ are nonnegative, $\mathbf{q}$ is inside. There is a caveat, though: if $\mathbf{q}$ lies exactly on a triangle's edge, $\mathbf{q}$ is not only inside this triangle but also inside the adjacent triangle with which this edge is shared.[3] Hence, two surface intersections are reported, with the according voxel flips canceling out each other. Except for the case of a silhouette edge, this obviously leads to wrong results because actually only one intersection with the multitriangle surface occurs. A robust remedy is to adopt a consistent fill-rule as employed in hardware rasterization, which assigns an on-edge point to exactly one side of the edge. Using Direct3D's top-left convention, an on-edge point only belongs to a triangle if the edge is a left edge or a horizontal top edge (see Figure 6.9). This can be checked by looking at the edge's normal $\mathbf{m}_i$, leading to the following

---

[3]Since we are assuming closed, watertight geometry, this is always the case.

overlap criterion:

$$\bigwedge_{i=0}^{2}\left(\underbrace{e_i(\mathbf{q}) > 0}_{\text{interior}} \vee \left(\underbrace{e_i(\mathbf{q}) = 0}_{\text{on edge}} \wedge \left(\underbrace{m_{i,x} > 0}_{\text{left edge}} \vee \underbrace{(m_{i,x} = 0 \wedge m_{i,y} < 0)}_{\text{top edge}}\right)\right)\right).$$

Since the edge-classification terms solely depend on the edge's normal, they need only be evaluated once. However, for all this to work, it is necessary that when processing the triangles sharing an edge, consistent numerical results are obtained for the common edge. One way to achieve this is to enforce a consistent ordering of an edge's two vertices.

The subsequent propagation pass proceeds slice-wise in the y-direction, operating on all voxel columns in parallel. A single thread simultaneously processes 32 columns that are consecutive in the z-direction. By design, for each y-slice, the voxels of these columns are represented by different bits of the same 32-bit buffer value; this also provides the motivation for selecting to perform rasterization from the xz-side. The employed compute shader loops over all slices from top to bottom. At each slice, it fetches the buffer value encoding the according voxel states for the 32 columns. This value is then XORed with the value for the previous slice, thus propagating state flips, and written back to the buffer.

6.6 Conclusion

This chapter has shown that (and how) GPU-accelerated binary surface and solid voxelization can be realized with Direct3D 11. On the one hand, we explored how the existing rasterization hardware can be harnessed for this task and how to cope with the absence of bitwise blending. The presented solution is characterized by random atomic buffer writes from within a pixel shader to update the voxelization. While accurate results are obtained for solid voxelization, the quality of surface voxelizations suffers from the inappropriate overlap test performed by ordinary rasterization, which is inherent to all such approaches.

Partially motivated by this shortcoming, we also, on the other hand, looked into how the whole voxelization process can be implemented in software using DirectCompute. Pursuing a simple triangle-parallel approach, for each triangle, all potentially affected voxels or voxel columns, respectively, are considered, applying an overlap test for each to determine their state. For surface voxelization, we detailed a triangle/voxel overlap test that yields a conservative surface voxelization, which obviates the deficiencies of its rasterization-based cousin. By contrast, solid voxelization relies on consistent rasterization, and we described an according approach that defers voxel state flips to a separate pass to improve performance. Overall, the covered techniques demonstrate that resorting to a compute-based software implementation for executing the voxelization offers a large degree of flexibility, and it is up to the reader to explore new overlap criteria, load balancing schemes, and voxel grid representations.

Bibliography

[Dong et al. 04] Zhao Dong, Wei Chen, Hujun Bao, Hongxin Zhang, and Qunsheng Peng. "Real-time Voxelization for Complex Polygonal Models." In *Proceedings of Pacific Graphics 2004*, pp. 43–50. Washington, DC: IEEE Computer Society, 2004.

[Eisemann and Décoret 06] Elmar Eisemann and Xavier Décoret. "Fast Scene Voxelization and Applications." In *Proceedings of ACM SIGGRAPH Symposium on Interactive 3D Graphics and Games 2006*, pp. 71–78. New York: ACM Press, 2006.

[Eisemann and Décoret 08] Elmar Eisemann and Xavier Décoret. "Single-Pass GPU Solid Voxelization for Real-Time Applications." In *Proceedings of Graphics Interface 2008*, pp. 73–80. Toronto: Canadian Information Processing Society, 2008.

[Fang and Chen 00] Shiaofen Fang and Hongsheng Chen. "Hardware Accelerated Voxelization." *Computers & Graphics* 24:3 (2000), 433–442.

[Forest et al. 10] Vincent Forest, Loic Barthe, and Mathias Paulin. "Real-Time Hierarchical Binary-Scene Voxelization." *Journal of Graphics, GPU, and Game Tools* 14:3 (2010), 21–34.

[Hasselgren et al. 05] Jon Hasselgren, Tomas Akenine-Möller, and Lennart Ohlsson. "Conservative Rasterization." In *GPU Gems 2*, edited by Matt Pharr, Chapter 42, pp. 677–690. Reading, MA: Addison-Wesley, 2005.

[Nichols et al. 10] Greg Nichols, Rajeev Penmatsa, and Chris Wyman. "Interactive, Multiresolution Image-Space Rendering for Dynamic Area Lighting." *Computer Graphics Forum* 29:4 (2010), 1279–1288.

[Pineda 88] Juan Pineda. "A Parallel Algorithm for Polygon Rasterization." *Proc. SIGGRAPH '88 (Computer Graphics)* 22:4 (1988), 17–20.

[Reinbothe et al. 09] Christoph K. Reinbothe, Tamy Boubekeur, and Marc Alexa. "Hybrid Ambient Occlusion." In *Eurographics 2009 Annex (Areas Papers)*, pp. 51–57, 2009.

[Schwarz and Seidel 10] Michael Schwarz and Hans-Peter Seidel. "Fast Parallel Surface and Solid Voxelization on GPUs." *ACM Transactions on Graphics* 29:6 (2010), 179:1–179:9.

[Wyman 11] Chris Wyman. "Voxelized Shadow Volumes." In *Proceedings of High Performance Graphics 2011*, 2011.

[Zhang et al. 07] Long Zhang, Wei Chen, David S. Ebert, and Qunsheng Peng. "Conservative Voxelization." *The Visual Computer* 23:9–11 (2007), 783–792.

Interactive Ray Tracing Using the Compute Shader in DirectX 11

Arturo García, Francisco Ávila, Sergio Murguía, and Leo Reyes

7.1 Introduction

Currently, the most widely used technique for real-time 3D rendering is rasterization, mainly because of its low computational cost and the availability of efficient hardware implementations. DirectX and OpenGL are the most common rasterization-based APIs used for high-end video game graphics programming. Rasterization is well suited for handling animated scenes, and no auxiliary data structures are needed to display geometrical changes. On the other hand, ray tracing is traditionally associated with high computational costs, although it could eventually become the video game rendering algorithm of the future as hardware becomes more powerful and ray-tracing techniques grow more sophisticated. Recent advances in ray-tracing engines, acceleration structures, and GPU programmability are making interactive frame rates possible for ray-tracing applications.

This chapter presents an original GPU ray-tracing application running solely on the compute shader and Shader Model 5.0 in DirectX 11. (DirectX 11.1 was released shortly after this writing. The demo uses only DX11.0 features, and a few implementation details may change in DX11.1) The implementation includes gloss mapping, normal mapping, texturing, shadowing, reflections, and a bounding volume hierarchy (BVH) for fast ray-intersection discovery. We analyze the advantages and disadvantages of using multipass ray tracing for handling a number of infinite concurrent textures versus a strategy that handles a limited number of textures in one pass. The ray tracer achieves interactive frame rates on high-end video cards and can be used as a starting point to implement more advanced rendering techniques. (See Figure 7.1.)

Figure 7.1. Sample picture generated by the ray tracer explained in this chapter.

7.2 Ray Tracing

Ray tracing is an advanced illumination technique that simulates the effects of light by tracing rays through the screen on an image plane. The degree of visual realism of the images generated via this technique is considerably higher than that obtained through other rendering methods such as rasterization. However, the computational cost is so high that ray tracing has mostly been used for offline rendering. Nevertheless, real-time ray-tracing applications are available today thanks to constant hardware improvements and algorithmic advances, which ultimately yield more efficient algorithms.

Ray tracing is traditionally known to be a trivially parallel-implementation problem given that the color computation for each pixel is independent of its neighbors. Both CPUs and GPUs are becoming more powerful year after year; however, they have intrinsically different architectures, so it is necessary to have a proper understanding of the interaction between algorithms and hardware in order to achieve optimal performance. In any case, memory handling remains a constant bottleneck, and it is one of the key points that needs to be addressed in order to attain high frame rates.

Efficient data structures are therefore required in order to solve the memory bottleneck. These structures should allow fast memory access and fast ray-geometry intersection discovery. Currently, acceleration structures are frequently used to avoid unnecessary calculations during ray traversal, the most common of which are kd-trees, BVHs, grids, and their variants.

Kd-trees are more efficient for actual rendering but tend to be slower for construction. Grids are their counterpart, having fast construction with an inefficient traversal. The BVH is a trade-off between grid construction velocity and kd-tree performance. It can be built faster than a kd-tree and can still manage to maintain competitive rendering performance.

In the real world, light travels from light sources, bounces between objects, and then reaches our eyes. This is called *forward ray tracing*, since it follows the natural path of the light rays. However, in a ray-tracing implementation, forward ray tracing leads to unnecessary computation. Imagine that you are inside your bedroom and the sun rays enter through your window; such a scene, from your point of view, would be composed of everything your eyes could see inside your room and maybe near your window. What about the rays that are thrown to the roof of your house or to your neighbor's yard? From a computational standpoint, ray-tracing calculations performed for places outside of the rendered scene are obviously a waste of resources. So, to save resources, rays are cast from the eye into the scene and then bounced back to the light sources, following an inverse path. Fittingly, the process can be labeled as *backward ray tracing*; however, current state-of-the-art implementations simply refer to it as *ray tracing*.

The algorithm begins by throwing rays (called *primary rays*) from the point representing the eye into each pixel of the image. The acceleration structure tests each ray on the scene looking for the nearest intersection to the eye—which is the most computationally intensive part of the ray-tracing algorithm. Finally, the algorithm computes the color of the pixel.

Color calculation can be as complex as required by the application. For the computation of shadows, each pixel throws a new ray to each light source to check if an object is blocking the light ray's path. The computation of reflections and refractions requires new calls to the ray-tracing function using the intersected point as the new ray origin. The new direction is the reflected or the refracted direction of the original ray. The pixel color is calculated after all ray bounces (which are called *secondary rays*) have been traversed. If the ray never intersected

```
for each pixel {
   throw ray from the camera position to the pixel;
   if( ray intersects an object ) {
      if( the object is nearer than last one found) {
         nearestObject = object;
      }
   }

   if ( ray hits a primitive ) {
      foreach light {
         throw ray from intersection to light;
         calculate shadow;
      }

      recursively calculate reflections and refractions;
      calculate other desired effects;
      calculate color of the pixel;
   } else {
      pixelColor = backgroundColor;
   }
}
```

Listing 7.1. Whitted-style ray-tracing algorithm.

```
// Primary Rays Stage
generate primary rays;
for each pass {
   for each pixel {
      // Intersection Stage
      if( ray intersects an object ) {
         if( the object is nearer than last one found) {
            nearestObject = object;
         }
      }

      //Color Stage
      if ( ray hits a primitive ) {
         for each light {
            throw ray from intersection to light;
            calculate shade;
         }
         calculate normal mapping;
         calculate gloss mapping;
         calculate reflection;
         accumulate into result;
      }
      else {
         accumulate background color;
         kill pixel;
      }
   }
}
```

Listing 7.2. Our ray-tracing algorithm.

an object, the color of that pixel would be the background color (or whatever the programmer decides).

The ray-tracing algorithm described in this section is shown as pseudocode in Listing 7.1. However, the algorithm was initially proposed for CPU architectures and some adjustments are required in order to make it fit into a GPU-based architecture implementation. Listing 7.2 shows the pseudocode for our ray-tracing algorithm. The main difference between CPU and GPU implementations is that the latter requires various rendering passes to simulate recursion.

7.3 Our Implementation

This chapter describes the implementation of a real-time demo using DirectX 11.0 and Shader Model 5.0 (see also Figure 7.2):

1. The demo builds an acceleration structure (a BVH) on the CPU and sends it through a buffer to the GPU.

2. The ray-tracing algorithm writes the output on an unordered-access-view (UAV) texture as a render target directly from the compute shader.

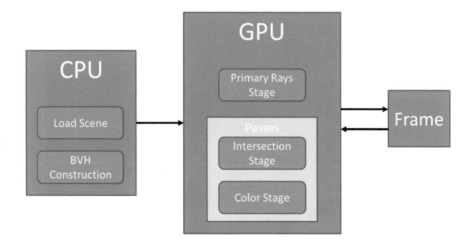

Figure 7.2. The current pipeline of our implementation is divided into three main sections: the CPU preprocess, the GPU rendering, and the final frame. The CPU preprocess consists of loading a scene and building an acceleration structure. The GPU rendering consists of three stages that perform the ray tracing algorithm. Finally, the frame is the output of this pipeline.

7.3.1 The Compute Shader

Current 3D pipelines (Figure 7.3) operate by moving data in a predetermined order through different stages called *shaders*. One of the main characteristics of the compute shader is that it "is not a part" of the pipeline. The compute shader is capable of performing calculations and rendering simultaneously, via the use of general structures similar to C++. Therefore, it is not necessary to render geometry or to ingeniously cast information into textures in order to use the compute shader.

Prior understanding of four of the concepts of the DirectX API is necessary before proceeding: the shader resource view (SRV), the unordered access view (UAV), the render target view (RTV), and the constant buffer.

- An SRV is a read-only resource that can be used as input into any shader. Textures are usually SRVs. The data that will not change during the application execution can be set as SRVs. For example, since our current application is not rebuilding the acceleration structure on each frame, it is sent as SRV to the GPU. In other words, an SRV is the knowledge base of the application.

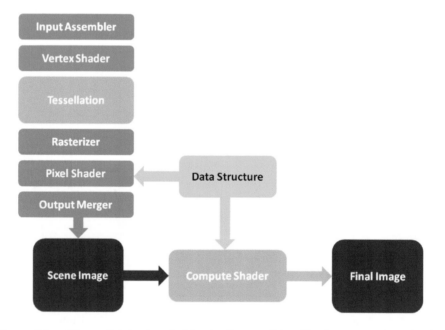

Figure 7.3. Microsoft introduced this pipeline on DirectX 10.1, and it was further improved on DirectX 11.0. Although the compute shader is physically a part of the DirectX pipeline, from the programmer's perspective, the compute shader is, for practical purposes, an independent stage.

- A UAV is a resource that can be read and written on both pixel and compute shaders (textures are usually read-only elements and the only output is set at the end of shader execution). The UAV structures are dynamic; they change throughout the application execution. This feature was introduced with DirectX 11, and it is the key for future GPGPU applications such as the ray-tracer implementation described in this chapter.

- An RTV is a resource that will be presented onscreen as a rendered frame. Optionally, the texture bound as an RTV can also be an SRV or a UAV. In the problem presented in this chapter, the RTV is a UAV since the texture is dynamically filled using the compute shader.

- A constant buffer (or cbuffer) is optimized for storing information that remains constant during the execution of shaders in the GPU, but that can be updated frequently by the CPU between calls to the GPU. It is a read-only resource with a low latency access from the GPU, which is commonly used to store the camera data—which usually changes at every frame—and other small-sized constants.

The current application cannot work on older versions of DirectX because they do not support UAVs, which are extensively used in this application. A workaround for this issue is to use the pixel shader instead. However, this is the technique that has been used to implement (non-CUDA) GPU ray tracers so far. The compute shader is a stage specifically designed for GPGPU programming, and it is ideal for applications like ray tracing. This is because the compute shader is capable of using structures similar to C++, performing reading and writing of different objects defined as UAVs or SRVs and storing the result as either a texture or a structure.

As of this writing, *GPU Pro 3* will be the first publication that includes a compute shader–based ray-tracing application. Independent researchers can use this ray tracer as a starting point to implement more advanced techniques and acceleration structures. Currently, widely available GPU ray tracers force the user to use vendor-specific APIs (like CUDA). Since this ray tracer is not linked to any video card in particular, the user may use whatever platform he or she wishes.

7.3.2 Bounding Volume Hierarchies (BVHs)

BVHs are tree-based acceleration structures that are grounded in a geometric dissection; primitives are stored on leaf nodes, and each internal node stores a bounding box of the primitives contained within it. While traversing the tree, subdivisional tests continue until an intersection with the scene geometry is found, or the test is skipped if the node box is not hit by the ray. BVHs tend to be efficiently built and deliver good performance since they can adapt to irregular primitive distributions across scene geometry.

When used in dynamic scenes, BVHs perform better than kd-trees [Gunther et al. 07], which is why interest in BVHs has grown recently. It is true that grids can be rebuilt from scratch due to their extraordinarily fast construction [Wald et al. 09], but their traversal time is neither comparable with BVH nor with kd-trees [Havran 00, Zlatuska and Havran 10]. Therefore, the BVH offers a fast traversal time in comparison with the performance of kd-trees, but with significantly faster construction time. The BVH is also a compact structure that fits GPU requirements for good performance [Zlatuska and Havran 10].

Construction. After loading the model, the acceleration structure construction is the next task to be performed. Construction is done using one core of the CPU before GPU initialization. When construction is complete, the BVH is sent as SRVs, through two structured buffers, to the GPU. The SRVs contain an ordered array of primitives, as well as an array of nodes. The first structure stores an ordered list of triangle indices used by the BVH during traversal. The second structure is a list of binary tree nodes representing a BVH.

The scope of this chapter does not cover CPU-based construction of a BVH. Our implementation is based on the BVH of the PBRT framework [Pharr and Humphreys 04], which can be consulted for further details. Briefly, the BVH construction consists of the following steps:

1. Select a primitive partition scheme—surface area heuristic (SAH) is highly recommended.

2. Create a bounding box for each primitive.

3. Recursively partition the primitives either left or right depending on the partition scheme selected until all primitives have been allocated.

7.3.3 GPU Initialization

DirectX requires certain initialization of context and resources for an application to be executed. However, it is beyond the scope of this chapter to explain this in detail. The interested reader should consult the latest DirectX documentation from Microsoft for more details. Additionally, the code provided should be self-explanatory.

The SRVs store eight data structures used in the stages of the ray-tracing algorithm. They are divided into three major categories: model information, acceleration structure data, and textures:

- *Vertices SRV*. Stores the vertex data of the model.

- *Indexes SRV*. Every three indices (referencing three vertices) represent a triangle.

- *Materials SRV*. Stores the material ID for each primitive.

- *BVH nodes SRV.* Stores the BVH node data.

- *BVH primitives information SRV.* Store the primitive information of the BVH structure.

- *Textures SRV.* Stores the textures of the scene materials.

- *Normal maps SRV.* Stores the normal maps of the textures loaded.

- *Specular maps SRV.* Stores the specular maps of the textures loaded.

The UAVs store four dynamic data structures. Each frame rendered overwrites the values of each buffer:

- *Rays buffer UAV.* Stores the rays generated in the primary rays stage and their bounces.

- *Intersections buffer UAV.* Stores the nearest intersection found by the intersection stage.

- *Accumulation texture UAV.* DirectX disallows accumulations of colors on textures that are simultaneously bound as RTV and UAV, so instead, this texture is used as a workaround.

- *Result texture UAV.* Stores final frame color and is present onscreen after each iteration.

7.4 Primary Rays Stage

The first step of the ray-tracing algorithm is the primary rays generation. This stage is fairly simple since it creates a ray per pixel with the origin located at the camera position and the direction given by the pixel position. Besides position and direction, the ray structure has one `float` indicating the maximum distance t where the ray has hit, a `float3` representing the light intensity of the current ray, and an `int` storing the `id` of the last triangle hit to prevent errors due to floating point rounding. Also, both the accumulation buffer and the result buffer are initialized during this stage.

The pinhole camera model is used to generate the primary rays. The square with coordinates $(-1, -1, 2)$ and $(1, 1, 2)$ is divided into cells that represent the pixels; the ray that starts at the point $(0, 0, 0)$ and passes through the center of that cell is used as the primary ray. In order to allow rotations and translations, the origin and cell coordinates are first transformed using the world matrix.

On this stage, the `maxT` component of the ray is initialized to a large number. This value is used on the intersection stages to only consider hits that occur at a distance in the range [`origin`,`maxT`]. An example of its use is when there is a light source and one needs to find out if that light source is visible from a hit point.

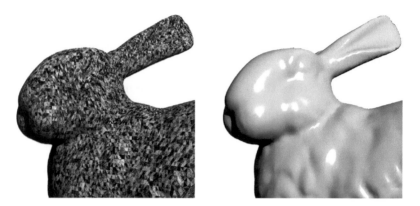

Figure 7.4. Effect of a floating-point precision error when intersecting secondary rays with primitives (left), and the image rendered after fixing this error (right). (See Listing 7.7 for details.)

In such a case, the intersection should only consider triangles that are between the hit point and the light source.

Also during this stage the `TriangleId` component is initialized to −1. This variable is used to store an identifier of the last triangle hit by the ray to prevent a secondary ray hitting the same triangle used to generate it. For instance, when projecting a ray at a mirror, the reflected ray may hit the same mirror sometimes due to numerical errors. In order to prevent such errors (see Figure 7.4), the intersection stage will only check triangles with an `id` different to `TriangleId`. Another component initialized on this stage is the reflective factor; this variable stores a `float3` that is used on the color stage before accumulating the color to the accumulation buffer. It is used to simulate how much light a surface can reflect or refract. (See Listing 7.3.)

```
//generate pixel coordinates
float inverse = 1.0f/(float(N));
float y = -float(2.f * DTiId.y + 1.f - N) * inverse;
float x = float(2.f * DTiId.x + 1.f - N) * inverse;
float z = 2.0f;

// Create new ray from the camera position to the pixel position
Ray ray;
float4 aux = (mul(float4(0,0,0,1.f),g_mfWorld));
ray.vfOrigin = aux.xyz/aux.w;
float3 vfPixelPosition = mul(float4(x,y,z,1.f),
   g_mfWorld).xyz;
ray.vfDirection = normalize(vfPixelPosition-ray.vfOrigin);
ray.fMaxT = 10000000000000000.f;
ray.vfReflectiveFactor = float3(1.f,1.f,1.f);
ray.iTriangleId = -1;
ray.iPadding = 0;
```

```
unsigned int index = DTiId.y * N + DTiId.x;
// Copy ray to global UAV
g_uRays[index] = ray;
g_uAccumulation[index] = 0.0f;
```

Listing 7.3. Primary rays stage.

7.5 Intersection Stage

Whenever a new ray (either primary or secondary) is generated, it must search through the scene to find the closest intersection with the camera space. This stage calls the function that computes the intersection between a single ray and the current geometry using an acceleration structure. A buffer stores the ID of the nearest triangle hit since this information is used by the next stage: the color computation stage.

The intersection stage code is shown in Listing 7.4. It calls the traversal function and assigns the intersection information to the corresponding buffer for each pixel. It is important to remember that the UAV buffers store the information for each pixel. Then, each pixel knows its color, its best intersection, and its primary ray.

Certainly, the acceleration structure function could be called directly instead of using an intermediary function to start traversal; however, this scheme allows for a more flexible approach where different acceleration structures or traversal algorithms can easily be added to the framework.

```
if ( g_uRays[index].iTriangleId > (-2) )
    g_uIntersections[index] = BVH_IntersectP(g_uRays[index]);
else
    g_uIntersections[index].iTriangleId = -2;
```

Listing 7.4. Intersection stage. When **iTriangleId** is equal to -2, the ray on the current pixel is no longer active.

7.5.1 Simple Traversal

The simple traversal is the naïve approach for searching the nearest intersection. Each ray tests each primitive in the scene. In other words, this function does not use an acceleration structure and might be used for debugging purposes. Bear in mind, however, that this debugging approach is only practical for scenes with only a few primitives.

```
Intersection cIntersection;
Intersection bIntersection;
bIntersection.iTriangleId = -1;
bIntersection.fT = 10000.f;
bIntersection.fU = -1;
bIntersection.fV = -1;

const int iNumPrimitives = 10;

for(int i = 0; i < iNumPrimitives; ++i)
{
    unsigned int offset = i*3;
    float3 A = g_sVertices[g_sIndices[offset]].vfPosition;
    float3 B = g_sVertices[g_sIndices[offset+1]].vfPosition;
    float3 C = g_sVertices[g_sIndices[offset+2]].vfPosition;

    cIntersection = getIntersection(ray,A,B,C);
    if(ray.iTriangleId != i &&
       RayTriangleTest(cIntersection) &&
       cIntersection.fT < bIntersection.fT)
    {
        bIntersection = cIntersection;
        bIntersection.iTriangleId = i;
    }
}
```

Listing 7.5. Simple traversal.

The traversal algorithm in Listing 7.5 returns the best intersection (the nearest intersection). The traversal iterates on each primitive of the scene (for each pixel) and tests the primitives looking for an intersection. If the ray intersects the primitive, the current intersection compares itself against the best intersection until that moment to check whether the newest intersection is better than all others previously found. This is repeated until all the primitives have been analyzed. That is the reason why this method is only for debug purposes. It does not make real-time applications possible since the traversal is the most time-consuming part of any ray-tracing algorithm.

7.5.2 BVH Traversal

The BVH traversal is what makes real-time performance possible. In this case, we chose to have one primitive per leaf node (at most) since overall performance revealed better results this way. Just like a classic BVH, the ray traverses down the structure testing against node boxes to check whether or not a ray intersects the box. The function shown in Listing 7.6 returns two distance t values, representing the nearest and farthest intersection points. It is important to note that if/else-based implementations do not perform optimally on the GPU. Instead,

```
float2 BVH_IntersectBox(float3 vfStart,float3 vfInvDir,
    unsigned int uiNodeNum)
{
    float2 T;

    float3 vfDiffMax = g_sNodes[uiNodeNum].vfMax-vfStart;
    vfDiffMax *= vfInvDir;
    float3 vfDiffMin = g_sNodes[uiNodeNum].vfMin-vfStart;
    vfDiffMin *= vfInvDir;

    T[0] = min(vfDiffMin.x,vfDiffMax.x);
    T[1] = max(vfDiffMin.x,vfDiffMax.x);

    T[0] = max(T[0],min(vfDiffMin.y,vfDiffMax.y));
    T[1] = min(T[1],max(vfDiffMin.y,vfDiffMax.y));

    T[0] = max(T[0],min(vfDiffMin.z,vfDiffMax.z));
    T[1] = min(T[1],max(vfDiffMin.z,vfDiffMax.z));

    //empty interval
    if (T[0] > T[1])
    {
        T[0] = T[1] = -1.0f;
    }

    return T;
}
```

Listing 7.6. Bounding box intersection function.

a min/max-based implementation must be used and a manual unroll is recommended since ray tracing is commonly performed on a three-dimensional space.

The traversal algorithm consists of the following steps:

1. Initialize variables.

2. Pop a node from the stack.

3. Perform a ray-box intersection with the current node box.

4. If an intersection is found, check if the node is either a leaf or an internal node. If it is a leaf, test the primitives inside the node. If it is an internal node, push its children into the stack.

5. Repeat Steps 2–4 until the stack is empty (no more nodes left).

The BVH implementation shown in Listing 7.7 is stack based. An array, called stack, stores the nodes-to-visit and simulates the behavior of a stack. If the ray does not intersect the node box, the stack pops a node for the next iteration. On the other hand, if the ray does intersect the node, two actions may be performed depending on whether the node is a leaf or an internal node.

- If the node is a leaf, the ray tests the primitive, looking for an intersection. If the leaf node contains more than one primitive, then an extra ray-box intersection test is recommended before testing the primitives themselves. That operation would also add more execution branches and increase the number of comparisons, which is the main reason why the authors suggest just one primitive per leaf node.

- If the node is an internal node, its children are added to the stack for future tests. The push order of the left and right children depends on the ray direction. If the direction of the ray on the current axis is negative, then the right child is pushed first and vice versa. This process repeats itself until the stack is empty. In other words, the loop ends when the array offset becomes zero.

```
[allow_uav_condition]while(true)
{
    // Perform ray-box intersection test
    float2 T = BVH_IntersectBox(ray.vfOrigin,vfInvDir,iNodeNum);

    // If the ray does not intersect the box
    if ((T[0] > bIntersection.fT) || (T[1] < 0.0f))
    {
        // If the stack is empty, the traversal ends
        if(iStackOffset == 0) break;
        // Pop a new node from the stack
        iNodeNum = stack[--iStackOffset];
    }
    // If the intersected box is a Leaf Node
    else if(g_sNodes[nodeNum].nPrimitives > 0)
    {
        // Get the triangle iId contained by the node
        iTrId = g_sNodes[iNodeNum].primitivesOffset;
        iTrId = g_sPrimitives[iTrId];

        // Get the triangle data
        int offset = iTrId*3;

        float3 A=g_sVertices[g_sIndices[offset]].vfPosition;
        float3 B=g_sVertices[g_sIndices[offset+1]].vfPosition;
        float3 C=g_sVertices[g_sIndices[offset+2]].vfPosition;

        cIntersection = getIntersection(ray,A,B,C);
        // Search for an intersection:
        // 1. Avoid float-precision errors.
        // 2. Perform ray-triangle intersection test.
        // 3. Check if the new intersection is nearer to
        // the camera than the current best intersection.
        if((ray.iTriangleId != iTrId)
            && (RayTriangleTest(cIntersection)  )
            && (cIntersection.fT < bIntersection.fT))
        {
            bIntersection = cIntersection;
```

```
            bIntersection.iTriangleId = iTrId;
            bIntersection.iRoot = iNodeNum;
        }

        // If the stack is empty, the traversal ends
        if(iStackOffset == 0) break;
        // Pop a new node from the stack
        iNodeNum = stack[--iStackOffset];
    }
    // If the intersected box is an Inner Node
    else
    {
        // Depending on the ray direction and the split-axis,
        // the order of the children changes on the stack.
        int dirIsNeg[3] = { vfInvDir < 0 };
        const int iAxis = -g_sNodes[iNodeNum].nPrimitives;
        const int aux = dirIsNeg[iAxis];
        stack[iStackOffset++] = (iNodeNum+1)*aux + (1-aux)*
            g_sNodes[iNodeNum].primitivesOffset;
            aux + (1-aux)*(iNodeNum+1);
    }
}
```

Listing 7.7. BVH traversal.

Due to floating-point precision errors, secondary rays might hit the primitive where the secondary rays were generated. In order to prevent such errors, the secondary ray checks if the primitive intersected in the previous pass is different from the current primitive analyzed. If both primitives are the same, the primitive being tested is skipped. Figure 7.4 shows the effects of this glitch, which produces a noisy image.

Some specific tags must be added to the code to allow the correct compilation of the shader. The [allow_uav_condition] tag indicates that the loop termination depends on a UAV buffer that changes dynamically during execution. This will not change the application's behavior; in fact, it should be thought of as a warning tag of something that must be carefully coded.

7.6   Color Stage

The color stage computes the color for each pixel. It uses different effects to add realism to the final frame. Those effects require secondary rays and more than one pass to accomplish a better visual impact. The ray tracer described in this chapter includes phong or flat shading, texturing, normal mapping, gloss mapping, environment mapping, and reflections.

7.6.1   Common Rasterization Techniques

The ray tracer implements several techniques that are common in rasterization engines, such as flat and phong shading, texturing, normal mapping, gloss mapping, and environment mapping. When implementing these techniques in a common rasterizer, the 3D rasterization pipeline takes care of interpolating values between adjacent vertices (using the GPU), so that the information needed to compute these effects is already present at each pixel to be rendered. The ray tracer, however, runs on the compute shader, so this vertex information is not interpolated by the pipeline. Instead, the triangle-ray intersection function returns the barycentric coordinates of the intersection, and these coordinates are then used to interpolate the information needed at each pixel.

An interesting side effect of the ray-tracing engine is that it already behaves as a rasterizer that uses "deferred shading." In deferred shading, the rasterizer prerenders the scene to know which pixels are ultimately visible, so as not to waste resources computing effects for pixels that will be obscured by other geometry. With the ray-tracing engine, this comes free since the closest intersection to the camera is always computed.

Another point that must be noted is that the implementation of environment mapping is also slightly different. This is detailed next.

7.6.2 Environment Mapping

Environment mapping is a technique that provides a texture-based representation of a scene's surrounding environment. It is often used to simulate reflections on a closed surface or to represent the horizon and the sky of an open scene. Two techniques can be used to do environment mapping: spherical mapping and cube mapping. We used the latter in the ray tracer, since it is more accurate. The

Figure 7.5. Images rendered by the ray tracer using environment mapping with three reflections. The Stanford Bunny (left) is running at 47 frames per second and the Stanford Dragon (right) at 22 frames per second.

```
const float4 tx_Environment = g_sEnvironmentTx.SampleLevel(
    g_ssSampler, g_uRays[index].vfDirection.xyz,0);
//Environment mapping
vfFinalColor.xyz = vfFactor.xyz * tx_Environment.xyz;
// This indicates that the Environment Mapping has
// been applied to the current pixel.
g_uRays[index].iTriangleId = -2;
```

Listing 7.8. Environment mapping.

impact on the performance is negligible and it adds an interesting effect, as shown in Figure 7.5.

In order to implement environment mapping, rays must be cast from the scene into the environment. Then, the direction of the ray is used to sample the environment map and get a color. However, the ray tracer already casts rays, so implementing this technique in the framework is rather straight-forward: whenever a ray misses the geometry (i.e., when the ray-triangle intersection is void), the environment map is sampled once. If the ray is primary, then the color will end up in the "background"; if the ray comes from a reflection or a refraction, then the color sampled from the environment map will be mixed with the color of the surface and will be back-propagated through all the previous bounces. In any case, the environment map must be sampled exactly once, and this is indicated in the code by setting a flag in the iTriangleID field of the current ray. The code in Listing 7.8 is self-explanatory. Basically, environment mapping enables a predetermined background texture and allows the background to be reflected into the scene.

7.6.3 Ray Bounces

A ray bounce might be understood as a reflection or a refraction. However, the current ray tracer only includes reflections due to performance issues when using both effects at the same time. It is an interesting challenge to add material support for both refractive and reflective objects while maintaining a real-time frame rate.

The naïve implementation for both reflections and refractions is based on throwing a new ray for each effect. In other words, an extra rendering pass for each ray bounce is required. This leads to computing n images to create one frame (where n is the number of ray bounces), which translates into a high computational cost. Performance can be traded for realism; however, in the ray tracer provided, the number of ray reflections is controlled by the user via a global parameter.

Implementing reflections in code is quite simple, as shown in Listing 7.9. The CPU function controlling the rendering must add an extra pass to compute a

```
g_uRays[index].vfReflectiveFactor *= tx_SpecularColor;
g_uRays[index].vfOrigin = vfHitPoint;
g_uRays[index].vfDirection = vfNewDirection;
g_uRays[index].iTriangleId = iTriangleId;
```

Listing 7.9. Ray bounces.

frame. If three reflections are simulated, then three extra passes are added. It
is important to notice that the primary-rays shader must not be executed since
a reflection is a secondary ray. Both the intersection stage and the color stage
are executed for each pass. However, at the end of the color stage execution, the
ray's buffer must be modified. The new origin is the intersection found by the
last ray stored in that pixel. The new direction is given by the reflection of the
last ray stored in that pixel. The reflective factor is diminished a little bit after
each bounce according to the specular map. This is done to account for the fact
that, in nature, only a portion of the incident light is reflected.

Computing pixel color. The color at each pixel is computed using the well-known
Phong illumination equation. Then, two more rays are cast from the current
point: one ray is sent to the light source in order to figure out if the current
point is shadowed and another ray is reflected according to the current normal
(an example of this simple illumination scheme is shown in Figure 7.6). This

Figure 7.6. Happy Buddha (1,087,716 triangles) and Welsh Dragon (2,210,673 triangles)
ray-traced with phong shading and shadows.

```
// Apply color to texture
g_uAccumulation[index] += vfFinalColor;
g_uResultTexture[DTid.xy] = g_uAccumulation[index];
```

Listing 7.10. Compute color.

reflected ray is recursively traced and accumulated with the current color as
shown in Listing 7.10.

7.7 Multipass Approach

A multipass approach is not about having multiple ray bounces. Currently, a single
pass is enough to compute all pixel colors no matter what material is attached
to the intersected primitive thanks to texture arrays. A multipass approach renders
one material per pass, which is useful when limited resources are available
such as number of textures or texture memory.

Older versions of DirectX were limited to allocating eight textures simultaneously,
and the last version released in June 2010 is capable of allocating up to
128 textures. However, it is possible to have an infinite number of textures using
a multipass approach by changing the material-to-render on each pass. Obviously,
performance is impacted by this approach and some code reordering will
be needed.

The shader needs to know what the current rendered material is in advance.
The constant buffer is the best choice since it is optimized for constant variables
and for changing its values constantly on the CPU (which the multipass
approach will perform). The shader computes the pixel color just as if the current
intersected primitive had the current-material-to-render attached to itself. Otherwise,
the shader is skipped. On each pass, the SRVs, or any buffer that stores
the texture information, should be updated with the current-material-to-render
information.

Another feasible approach that balances resource availability and performance
would be to load 128 materials after each pass. This way, 256 materials could
be rendering by performing two passes—but the code becomes even more complicated.

7.8 Results and Discussion

The tests were executed on an Nvidia GTX 480. The Stanford Dragon, the
Happy Buddha, and the Welsh Dragon are used to directly measure the frames
per second (FPS) of our framework so that it may be compared against other
ray tracers. The Crytek Sponza was used to measure the performance on a

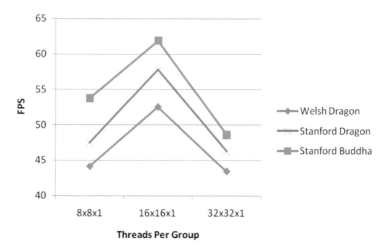

Figure 7.7. Performance of different compute shader threads per group configurations. The tests were executed with shadows, phong shading, and gloss mapping but without environment mapping, reflections, or normal mapping. The x-axis shows the number of threads per group and the y-axis the number of frames per second.

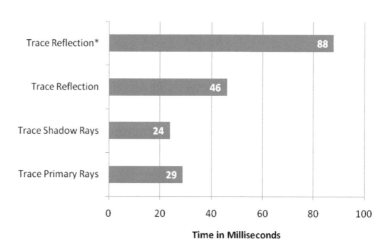

Figure 7.8. Time needed to execute each render step for a single frame. The x-axis shows the time in milliseconds, and the individual rendering steps are plotted in the y-axis. The results are averaged using six different cameras on the Crytek Sponza model. The tracing algorithm includes both ray generation and ray-triangle intersection. Each step is computed independently, and two different measures were computed for tracing one reflection: with and without normal mapping and shadows.

more realistic context with an averaged FPS given different camera positions and directions. The grid size is $64 \times 64 \times 1$, and the group size is $16 \times 16 \times 1$ to launch a total of 1,048,576 threads in the compute shader. The resolution is set to $1,024^2$, where each thread computes the color of one pixel.

The best configuration for evenly distributed threads is a grid size of $64 \times 64 \times 1$ groups and a group size of $16 \times 16 \times 1$ threads. This is shown in Figure 7.7, where this tendency remains regardless of the model used.

The full capabilities of the ray-tracing framework are exploited by scenes such as Crytek Sponza. Figure 7.8 shows the time needed by each render step to produce a single frame. Ray-box and ray-triangle intersections are the most time-consuming operations and rely heavily on the effectiveness of the acceleration structure employed. Based on recent publications (such as [Pantaleoni and Luebke 10, Kalojanov et al. 11, Garanzha et al. 11]), these render times still allow a full BVH/grid reconstruction on the GPU at every frame while still maintaining real-time frame rates.

7.9 Optimization

In order to reduce branches, the color stage skips if the ray does not intersect any primitive. Since each group computes the color of a 16×16 pixel patch, the primary rays on the same warp test against similar objects reducing the number of branches. However, secondary rays are not coherent, which impacts significantly the final execution time when shading, reflections, or both are active. The ray stage could be decomposed in different kernels for reordering, which would improve ray coherence [Garanzha and Loop 10].

Although current hardware supports double-precision floating-point variables, it is preferable to use single-precision floating-point variables in order to speed up the ray tracer. A ray-tracing algorithm does not require high-precision calculations, and the differences in the images produced using either method are not noticeable.

In a GPU application, it is very important to properly set up the grid/group/thread configuration. The GPU computation tasks are commonly addressed as grids. A grid is conformed by one or more thread groups. A thread group is conformed by one or more threads. Since GPUs were created for massive parallel execution, the hardware must have a large workload divided into small tasks. Three rules should be met to take full advantage of the power of the GPU [Fung 10]:

1. The ratio of the number of thread groups per multiprocessor should be greater than 2. The number of thread groups in the ray tracer is 4,096 and the number of multiprocessors is 16. The ratio is 256, which is clearly greater than 2.

2. The number of thread groups should be greater than 100 in order to scale well to future devices and greater than 1,000 to scale across multiple generations. The number of thread groups in the ray tracer is 4,096, which is more than four times the number of thread groups suggested to scale to multiple generations.

3. The number of threads per thread group should be a multiple of the warp size. The number of threads per group in the ray tracer is 256, which is a multiple of 32 (the warp size) since $256/32 = 8$.

7.10   Conclusion

This chapter described a step-by-step ray-tracing implementation in the compute shader using Shader Model 5.0 in DirectX 11.0. The application includes the most-used effects in ray tracing and allows programmers to add their own code or to modify the existing code in order to improve the visual effects and their performance.

The compute shader capabilities will improve video game quality and other real-time DirectX-based applications. The techniques described in this chapter can be easily attached to different stages of current commercial applications. Furthermore, similar research fields such as radiosity, ambient occlusion, or global illumination can take advantage of the framework described here.

7.11   Further Work

We are currently interested in developing dynamic scenes, refractions, and global illumination effects on the ray tracer. The BVH might be rebuilt on each frame [Pantaleoni and Luebke 10] in order to accomplish dynamic scenes and enable interactive applications, such as video games, with a ray tracing–based renderer. It would be desirable to build a CPU–GPU hybrid to take advantage of the CPU power as well, given that the current ray tracer does not use the CPU during the frame calculation.

A Monte Carlo approach has been implemented on the current ray tracer, pursuing global illumination effects like those shown in Figure 7.9 (the implementation of global illumination is not included in the demo). However, rendering a single frame takes several minutes. Currently, decreasing the rendering time of global illumination effects in order to produce photorealistic images is an open challenge in computer graphics. Due to the GPU architecture and the capabilities of the compute shader, this DirectCompute stage seems like a desirable target with which to try out global illumination approaches.

Figure 7.9. Global illumination.

7.12   Acknowledgments

The authors would like to thank the Stanford Computer Graphics Laboratory for the Happy Buddha, the Stanford Dragon, and the Stanford Bunny models; Bangor University for the Welsh Dragon model (released for Eurographics 2011); Crytek for its modified version of the Sponza model; and Matt Pharr and Greg Humphreys for their permission to base the BVH implementation on the PBRT framework [Pharr and Humphreys 04].

Bibliography

[Fung 10] James Fung. "DirectCompute Lecture Series 210: GPU Optimizations and Performance." http://channel9.msdn.com/Blogs/gclassy/DirectCompute-Lecture-Series-210-GPU-Optimizations-and-Performance, 2010.

[Garanzha and Loop 10] Kirill Garanzha and Charles Loop. "Fast Ray Sorting and Breadth-First Packet Traversal for GPU Ray Tracing." *Computer Graphics Forum* 29:2 (2010), 289–298.

[Garanzha et al. 11] Kirill Garanzha, Simon Premož, Alexander Bely, and Vladimir Galaktionov. "Grid-based SAH BVH Construction on a GPU." *The Visual Computer* 27 (2011), 697–706. Available online (http://dx.doi.org/10.1007/s00371-011-0593-8).

[Gunther et al. 07] Johannes Gunther, Stefan Popov, Hans-Peter Seidel, and Philipp Slusallek. "Realtime Ray Tracing on GPU with BVH-based Packet Traversal." In *Proceedings of the 2007 IEEE Symposium on Interactive Ray Tracing*, pp. 113–118. Washington, DC: IEEE Computer Society, 2007.

[Havran 00] Vlastimil Havran. "Heuristic Ray Shooting Algorithms." Ph.d. thesis, Czech Technical University in Prague, 2000.

[Kalojanov et al. 11] Javor Kalojanov, Markus Billeter, and Philipp Slusallek. "Two-Level Grids for Ray Tracing on GPUs." In *EG 2011: Full Papers*, edited by Oliver Deussen Min Chen, pp. 307–314. Llandudno, UK: Eurographics Association, 2011.

[Pantaleoni and Luebke 10] J. Pantaleoni and D. Luebke. "HLBVH: Hierarchical LBVH Construction for Real-Time Ray Tracing of Dynamic Geometry." In *Proceedings of the Conference on High Performance Graphics, HPG '10*, pp. 87–95. Aire-la-Ville, Switzerland: Eurographics Association, 2010.

[Pharr and Humphreys 04] Matt Pharr and Greg Humphreys. *Physically Based Rendering: From Theory to Implementation*. San Francisco: Morgan Kaufmann Publishers, 2004.

[Wald et al. 09] Ingo Wald, William R Mark, Johannes Günther, Solomon Boulos, Thiago Ize, Warren Hunt, Steven G Parker, and Peter Shirley. "State of the Art in Ray Tracing Animated Scenes." *Computer Graphics Forum* 28:6 (2009), 1691–1722.

[Zlatuska and Havran 10] M. Zlatuska and V. Havran. "Ray Tracing on a GPU with CUDA: Comparative Study of Three Algorithms." http://dcgi.felk.cvut.cz/home/havran/ARTICLES/ZlatuskaHavran2010wscg.pdf, 2010. Proceedings of WSCG '10, Communication Papers.

8

Bit-Trail Traversal for Stackless LBVH on DirectCompute

Sergio Murguía, Francisco Ávila, Leo Reyes, and Arturo García

8.1 Introduction

Rendering dynamic scenes with ray tracing is a major challenge on current hardware and software implementations. Fast construction algorithms are usually needed to rebuild acceleration structures from scratch on each frame in current state-of-the-art implementations. However, these algorithms tend to have poor traversal performance.

This chapter describes an improvement to the stackless linear bounding volume hierarchy (SLBVH) presented in [Murguia et al. 11], which is a new way for traversing and constructing a linear bounding volume hierarchy (LBVH). The SLBVH enables dynamic scenes relying on a fast construction algorithm while maintaining traversal performance for real-time ray tracing. Furthermore, a naive Monte Carlo algorithm allows the framework to produce high-quality global illumination effects.

The current implementation is the continuation of the chapter "Interactive Ray Tracing Using the Compute Shader on DirectX 11" published in *GPU Pro 3* [Garcia et al. 12]. The core of this new chapter is the heap-based structure. The main contributions of the chapter are

1. a tutorial on how to implement a SLBVH running solely on the GPU using DirectCompute and DirectX 11;

2. a stackless binary heap as an LBVH, reducing memory accesses while maintaining traversal performance;

3. four arithmetic operations that compute the left, right, parent, and next-to-visit nodes (which depend on the direction of the ray);

4. a traversal that can restart from the last node hit instead of the root using a bit trail (intersections for secondary rays are computed faster).

8.2   Ray Tracing Rendering

The SLBVH implementation adds a new stage to the original work of [Garcia et al. 12]. Instead of preloading a stack-based BVH from the CPU, an SLBVH is built from scratch on each frame using the available mesh data on the GPU. The process is the following:

1. Initialize the application on the CPU.

2. Send data to the GPU.

3. Build a SLBVH from scratch.

4. Render:

    (a) Throw primary rays.

    (b) Compute intersections.

    (c) Throw secondary rays.

    (d) Compute color.

5. Repeat Steps 3–4.

The coloring process includes phong shading, flat shading, texturing, normal mapping, gloss mapping, reflections, environment mapping, and shadows. These algorithms are common on rasterization implementations and introductory computer graphics topics.

During the primary ray stage, one ray is thrown through each pixel. The origin is located at the current camera position, and the direction is given by the destination pixel. Each ray, either primary or secondary, travels the structure's tree searching for the closest intersection on the camera space. The ID of the *best intersection* is stored on a buffer in order to calculate the color of the current pixel using the properties of the intersected triangle. The coloring of the pixel takes place on the last stage.

8.3   Global Illumination

In order to generate global illumination effects, the framework uses a Monte Carlo approach. It generates multiple images and renders the average of all of them. The way it presents the images is incremental. First, only one image is generated and displayed. Then, a second image is generated, combined with the previous one, and displayed on the screen. This is repeated until the camera position

```
if (Pdiff>=randomDir.w){
    // Take diffuse reflection.
    g_uRays[index].vfReflectiveFactor *= tx_TextureColor.xyz;
    g_uRays[index].vfDirection = normalize(randomDir.xyz);
}
  else
  {
    // Take specular reflection.
    g_uRays[index].vfReflectiveFactor *= tx_SpecularColor.xyz;
    g_uRays[index].vfDirection =
        normalize(reflect(g_uRays[index].vfDirection,vfNormal));
}
```

Listing 8.1. Reflection in global illumination.

changes or the shaders are reloaded. When the nth image is generated, every pixel p_a in the accumulated image is updated following the formula

$$p_a = \frac{n-1}{n}p_a + \frac{1}{n}p_n.$$

The main difference from conventional ray tracing is that each time a ray hits a primitive, the reflected direction is generated from a random distribution based on the properties of the material. Under global illumination, the reflected ray can be either a diffuse or a specular reflection. When it is reflected in a diffuse way, the new direction is sampled from a unitary sphere; while in the specular reflection, it is computed by taking the reflection around the normal at the hit point. The decision on whether to follow a diffuse reflection over the specular reflection is based on a material parameter called *Pdiff*, which is a number between 0 and 1 that represents the probability of doing a diffuse reflection. The code in Listing 8.1 shows the details on how it is implemented.

Since there are no explicit functions for computing random values in the compute shaders, all the random values are computed in the CPU and sent to the compute shader using a texture. Updating that texture on every frame would be very expensive and could cause the application to slow down. To prevent this, only a two-dimensional offset is updated in every frame and the texture is sampled using that offset combined with the *thread ID*, causing different threads to use a different pixel of the random texture on the same dispatch. Also, since the offset is updated every time a random value is going to be used, the pixel used by an specific thread will be different every time.

Once Monte Carlo is used, it can also be extended to handle other effects; for example, to reduce aliasing, the ray direction can be computed using a point around the center of the pixel causing a subsampling on the pixel. Another effect is depth of field; instead of taking the ray origin as the same point for all the rays as in a pinhole model, the ray origin is taken as a random point around a circle centered at the camera position. Figure 8.1 demonstrates the use of those effects.

(a)   (b)

Figure 8.1. Comparison of the same scene using (a) Whitted-style ray tracing and (b) Monte Carlo for global illumination. Notice how other effects such as caustics, soft shadows, depth of field, and antialiasing are present when using Monte Carlo.

The current implementation is not fully optimized for global illumination. It produces a high-quality render in 15–30 minutes on large scenes such as the Welsh Dragon and Thai Statue. However, this approach can be used as a starting point for optimized algorithms, as demonstrated in [Ernest and Woop 11], to yield better performance.

8.4   Stackless LBVH

The SLBVH is a stackless and pointerless binary heap that uses a middle split approach based on the Morton code of primitives [Lauterbach et al. 09]. While traversing, the next node to be visited is computed using arithmetic operations. One 32-bit integer is used to store the trail of each ray, which allows restarting the traversal from the last node hit instead of the root [Laine 10]. Also, using the split axis and the direction of the ray, the trail can be used to decide whether the left or right child must be visited first.

The resulting tree is a *heap*. In a heap, the left child of node n is located at $2n$ and the right child is at $2n + 1$. The tree representation assumes that the depth of the tree D will be constant, thus the number of nodes will also remain fixed (regardless of the scene complexity). In this approach, a heap with depth D requires an array of $2^D - 1$ elements. The scene could have either 1 or 1,000,000 primitives, yet the number of nodes remains the same. This introduces some disadvantages since empty nodes must be stored (yet are never visited) in order to satisfy the arithmetic operations that relate the nodes in the heap. On the other hand, the memory footprint of the SLBVH is lower than other stackless approaches [Popov et al. 07] since no extra information is stored in the tree; at the same time, SLBVH has more advantages than similar BVH algorithms [Laine 10] using a bit trail.

Besides the common properties of a heap, the SLBVH possesses the following characteristics:

- The root node is at position $i = 1$. The node at position $i = 0$ is invalid. In this way, the arithmetic operations to traverse the tree are simpler.

- The first right ancestor of node n is found by removing all the least significant bits that are 0 in the binary notation of n.

- The binary notation of an auxiliary 32-bit integer (the "trail") can be used to substitute the stack (commonly used to store the visited nodes during ray traversal). Each bit represents one level in the tree. A 0 means that the level still has unvisited nodes, while a 1 means that all nodes in that level have already been visited.

The tree uses a breadth-first scheme. A depth-first construction scheme was also considered, but the traversal formula becomes more complex and an extra variable is needed to keep track of which side of the subtree is being traversed.

8.4.1 Construction

The size of each node is 32 bytes. Six 32-bit floats are stored per node representing an axis-aligned bounding box (AABB), two 32-bit integers storing the number of primitives (`PrimCount`), and a primitive offset (`PrimPos`). Additionally, `PrimCount` stores the split axis and whether the node is leaf or internal, as shown in Figure 8.2. The axis is stored on the two least-significant bits of `PrimCount`, and the node flag (leaf $= 1$, internal $= 0$) is stored on its third least-significant bit. Two bits are enough to store the axis and the flag, but this would increase the number of comparisons when traversing the structure.

Figure 8.2. Binary breakdown of the `PrimCount` variable. The two least-significant bits are used to store the axis: $x = 00$, $y = 01$, and $z = 10$. The third least-significant bit is used to mark a node as leaf. The rest of the bits store the number of primitives in that node.

The construction stage is divided in four steps:

1. Generate AABBs and 32-bit Morton codes for each primitive.

2. Sort primitives using their Morton codes as their keys.

3. Build the tree.

4. Generate AABBs for each node.

Generate AABBs and Morton codes for each primitive. The first step is straight-forward. Each thread computes the Morton code of one primitive. This process assumes that the bounding box for the whole model is known. Since we know the boundaries of the bounding box of the root, it is possible to initialize node 0 (which is invalid) and node 1, which "contains" the whole model. The output of this stage is the input of the sorting algorithm. Each primitive is represented by a Morton code in order to take advantage of its space coherence. The code used is shown in Listing 8.2.

```
// The centroid is not divided by 3
// so we have to adjust the points of the box.
float3 bbMin = (3*g_vfMin);
float3 bbMax = (3*g_vfMax);

// inverse of the boundaries (size of the grid)
float3 invBox = 1024.0f / (bbMin - bbMax);

// Set initial bits according to the position of the primitive.
int3 primComp = int3((vfCentroid - bbMin) * invBox);
uint zComp = (primComp.z & 1);
uint yComp = ((primComp.y & 1) << 1);
uint xComp = ((primComp.x & 1) << 2);

// Initialize Morton code's components.
uint mCode = zComp | yComp | xComp;

int shift3 = 2;
int shift = 2;

// 30 bits for the Morton code (xyz=3 shifts*10)
for (int j = 1; j < 10; j++)
{
  mCode |= (tmp.z & shift) << (shift3++);
  mCode |= (tmp.y & shift) << (shift3++);
  mCode |= (tmp.x & shift) << (shift3);
  shift <<= 1;
}

// Copy to global memory.
g_uMortonCode[index].primitiveId = index;
g_uMortonCode[index].code = mCode;
```

Listing 8.2. Computation of the Morton code for each primitive.

Sort primitives. Our current implementation uses a modified version of the bitonic sort included in the DirectX 11 software development kit (SDK) [Microsoft 10]. According to [Satish et al. 09], radix sort currently seems to be the fastest sorting algorithm on GPU platforms. However, it is not within the scope of the current chapter to discuss the advantages of radix sort against bitonic sort. Bitonic sort allows the current application to build models as big as 2^{18} (262,144) primitives.

A proper sorting implementation would allow the building of bigger models from scratch every frame. The algorithm sorts the primitives in ascending order based on the Morton code computed on the previous stage. For bigger models, the framework uses a CPU-based BVH.

Build the tree. On the third step, the tree is built in a top-down fashion. Each thread computes the data of two nodes, left and right. Since two children share the same parent, race conditions are avoided. The number of passes is equal to the depth of the tree because each pass computes the nodes of one level. It is easy to see that the first levels are poorly parallelized, which represents a serious issue on hierarchical structures. The algorithm stores three types of nodes: invalid, leaf, and internal nodes. For invalid nodes, the algorithm checks the parent of the current nodes. If `PrimCount` is negative, it means that the parent is invalid. Since an invalid node cannot contain valid nodes underneath it, both children are marked as invalid. When the ith node is less than 2^{D-1}, the node is internal. If it is greater than that, then it is a leaf node (as shown in Listing 8.3). There are exceptions to this rule. Internal nodes may be marked as leaf nodes and their children would be marked as invalid (which will never be visited) when

1. a branch finishes all possible geometry partitions before reaching the maximum depth of the tree, D (in this case, the primitives are stored in an internal node, and the node is marked as a leaf node);

2. two or more primitives have the same Morton code (in this case, all primitives with the same Morton code are stored in the same node; if the node is an internal node, then the same process described previously is followed).

The first exception improves traversal performance by 20% because it avoids unnecessary comparisons on deeper branches. In this way, the SLBVH emulates an adaptive BVH by storing primitives in internal nodes. These internal nodes have all the properties of a leaf node. The second exception has the same advantage. If two primitives have the same Morton code, then in the end, they will be stored on the same node. Instead of waiting until the last level of the tree, the primitives are stored on a node as soon as possible.

Leaf nodes are also created when computing the nodes on the last level of the tree, as shown in Listing 8.3. All remaining primitives are stored on either the left or the right child. This is a disadvantage due to memory constraints. On large models, in order to decrease the number of comparisons per ray, the depth

```
int isLeaf = 0;

// If the index corresponds to the lastLevel -1, it is leaf.
if( index >= ( 1 << (g_Depth -1)) )
{
  // Set flag for leaf as true.
  isLeaf = 4;
}

// Check if the node should be leaf.
int primCount = (g_uNodes[parent].iPrimCount >> 3) - 1;
int a = g_uNodes[parent].iPrimPos;
int b = g_uNodes[parent].iPrimPos + primCount;
int mask = g_uMortonCode[a].iCode ^ g_uMortonCode[b].iCode;

// It is leaf.
if( mask == 0 )
{
  // Make both children invalid.
  // left child
  g_uNodes[index].iPrimPos = -MAX_INT;
  g_uNodes[index].iPrimCount = -MAX_INT;
  // right child
  g_uNodes[index+1].iPrimPos = -MAX_INT;
  g_uNodes[index+1].iPrimCount = -MAX_INT;

  // Set the node as leaf.
  g_uNodes[parent].iPrimCount |= 4;
  return;
}
[...]
```

Listing 8.3. Check for if a node is a leaf node.

of the tree is increased. However, the depth is constrained by GPU memory. Most practical implementations will store more data besides the structure (like the model itself and the textures), which limits the size of the SLBVH built on the GPU. Although increasing the depth of the tree improves the traversal performance, it increases construction time as well. On dynamic scenes, a tradeoff between construction and traversal times is needed. After a certain depth, the traversal performance barely increases.

The cut is done on the longest axis, which improves traversal performance on heterogeneous models such as the Sponza model. On models with uniform primitive size, the gain is minimal. A round-robin approach is also an option, and it works almost as fast as using the longest axis. The axis is stored in the two least-significant bits of `PrimCount` where $x = 00$, $y = 01$, and $z = 10$ in binary notation. If nodes are neither invalid nor leaf, then both nodes are considered internal. The boxes will be computed on the next step of construction. Therefore, this step must store the primitives' offset `PrimPos` and the number of primitives `PrimCount`.

Generate AABBs for each node. Finally, after the tree is completely built, the AABBs for each node are computed. Contrary to the previous step, the tree is now traversed in a bottom-up fashion. This step considers two type of nodes: internal nodes and leaf nodes. If the node is leaf, then the box is built using the box of each primitive. If the node is internal, then the thread takes the boxes of both left and right nodes to create a new box. Using this approach, race conditions are avoided and no synchronization barriers are needed.

8.4.2 Traversal

The traversal algorithm has two important characteristics: it uses a bit trail instead of a stack, and ray traversal restarts on the last node hit (instead of the root). As far as the authors know, the SLBVH is the first algorithm that uses a heap representation and arithmetic operations in order to avoid the use of stacks and pointers. The traversal is similar to a classical BVH. A ray is casted through the scene. The ray performs ray-box intersection tests until it reaches a node marked as leaf. At that point, the ray performs ray-primitive intersection tests and stores the closest intersection to the camera. The difference relies on how the ray visits the next node and on how the ray comes back to a previous nonvisited node. The algorithm stops if the ray comes back to the root. This means that the ray cannot find more intersections.

The trail, which is a "hidden" stack, is a 32-bit integer. Each bit in the trail represents a level on the tree. Each bit in the trail has the following meanings:

- bit $= 0$. The level on the current subtree contains unvisited nodes. They might be on either the left or the right branches.

- bit $= 1$. All nodes in the current level of the subtree have been visited.

The initial value of `trail` is `1 << firstbithigh(nodeNum)`.

- The `firstbithigh` function is an intrinsic DirectX function available in Shader Model 5. It returns the location of the first bit set starting from the highest-order bit and working downwards.

- The output of the `firstbithigh` function returns the depth of the current node.

- If a function similar to `firstbithigh` is not available, the following formula can be used instead:
$$\frac{n+1}{((n+1) \oplus n)\&(n+1)},$$
where n is `nodeNum` and $\&$ is the bitwise AND operator.

- `nodeNum` is the last hit node. It is initially set to 1 (the root).

After the first intersection is found, the traversal stores the intersected `nodeNum` and it is passed to the next traversal iteration. The trail *pushes* nodes when an internal node is intersected (just as a classical BVH) and *pops* nodes when either an intersection was not found or when a leaf node is intersected. A `push` is computed using a bitwise shift-left operation and a `pop` using a bitwise shift-right operation.

The algorithm starts with both `nodeNum` and `trail` set to 1. When going down the tree, the algorithm checks the ray's sign along the current split axis. If the ray is positive, it appends a 0 to `nodeNum` and 1 otherwise. In this case, it also appends a 0 to `trail` (because if the ray goes down the tree, that means that there was an intersection, which is a push). It is also possible to check which of the boxes is hit first by the ray (in case an intersection exists). If the left node is hit first, a 0 should be "pushed" into `nodeNum` and a 1 otherwise.

When going up the tree, `trail = trail + 1`; and then the number n of consecutive 0's starting from the least significant bit (LSB) in `trail` is counted. Next, the algorithm sets `trail = trail >> n` (which corresponds to a pop) and `nodeNum = nodeNum >> n`. Finally, `nodeNum`'s LSB is inverted (to mark the other branch as visited). The regular BVH traversal checks are also performed. At each internal node, the ray is intersected with the current box. If there is an intersection, we go "down" the tree. If there is no intersection, we go "up" the tree. Traversal ends when `nodeNum = 1`, which means that the ray returns to the root and no intersections were found.

To illustrate the algorithm, let us walk through an example. Figure 8.3 shows an SLBVH built with 3-bit codes. Each node in the tree is labeled with its index (in binary notation) and, for internal nodes, the split axis is also specified. Note, for instance, that the root is labeled 001 so the left child is $1 \times 2 = 2 \, (010_2)$ and the right child is $1 \times 2 + 1 = 3 \, (011_2)$. Figure 8.3 also shows the signs of an example ray across each axis. In this case, we have a ray that is positive on the x-axis and negative on the y- and z-axes. Positive signs for the ray map to 0 and negative signs to 1. In order to illustrate a full traversal, we will assume that no primitive intersections are found along the ray but all internal nodes intersect the ray. In this way, we are forced to visit all the nodes.

Let n and t stand for the current node and the trail, respectively. Initially, $n = 001_2$ and $t = 001_2$ (Figure 8.3(a)). The current node is the root and its split axis is the x-axis (positive sign $= 0$), so the traversal appends a 0 to n (n is now 010_2). The trail is always appended with a 0 when going down. Thus, we end up with $n = 010_2$ and $t = 010_2$ (which means we went down the left child, see Figure 8.3(b)). For the current node ($n = 010_2$), the split was done along the z-axis (negative sign $= 1$), so we append a 1 to the current node (n is now 101_2) and a 0 to the trail (t is now 100_2). We now have $n = 101_2$ and $t = 100_2$ (Figure 8.3(c)). Node $n = 101_2$ is leaf, so we test the primitives contained in it for an intersection. Assuming no intersection was found, we need to "backtrack" to the next sibling.

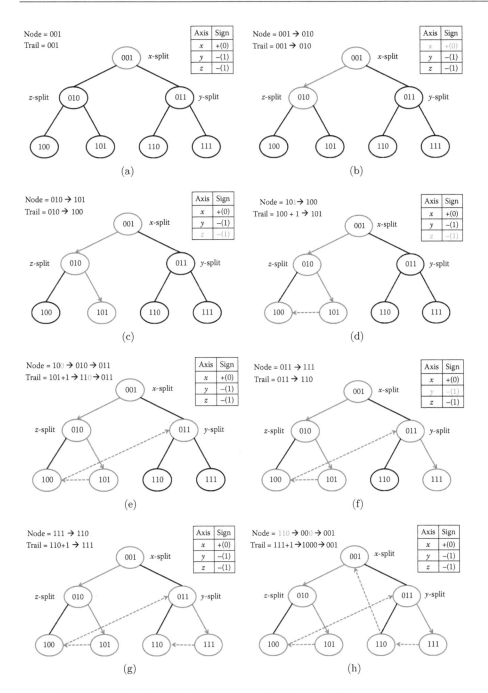

Figure 8.3. Walkthrough, following steps (a)–(h), for a stackless traversal using a bit trail.

```
bool isLeaf = (g_uNodes[nodeNum].iPrimCount & 4);
// Traverse the tree until we find a leaf node.
[allow_uav_condition]
while( !isLeaf )
{
  hit = intersectBox(ray.vfOrigin, invDir, nodeNum);
  p = firstbitlow(trail + 1);

  // Intersection is better than the current one
  // and it's not behind the camera.
  if ((hit[0] > bestIntersection.t) ||
  (hit[1] < 0.0f))
    {
      // does not intersect
      // "Pop" node from trail.
      trail = (trail >> p) + 1;
      // Change to next node.
      nodeNum = (nodeNum >> p) ^ 1;
    }
  else
    {
      // "Push" node to trail.
      trail = trail << 1;
      int axis = g_uNodes[nodeNum].iPrimCount&3;
      int direction = dirIsNeg[axis];
      // Set next node to visit.
      nodeNum = (nodeNum << 1) | direction );
    }
  // If we finish on the root, stop traversal.
  if(trail <= 1) break;
}
```

Listing 8.4. Setting the next node.

To find the next sibling, we add 1 to the trail, yielding $t = 101_2$, and we count the number of 0's starting from the LSB until we find a 1. In this case, there are no trailing zeros, so we simply invert the node's LSB, yielding $n = 100_2$ and $t = 101_2$ (Figure 8.3(d)). Node $n = 100_2$ is another leaf node. Assuming no intersections, we again must find the next sibling. We add 1 to the trail yielding $t = 110_2$. In this case, we get 1 trailing 0, so we remove one bit from the node and the trail and then invert the node's LSB, yielding $n = 011_2$ and $t = 011_2$ (Figure 8.3(e)). Node $n = 011_2$ is internal with a split along the y-axis (negative sign $= 1$). We append 1 to the node and 0 to the trail, yielding $n = 111_2$ and $t = 110_2$ (Figure 8.3(f)). Node $n = 111_2$ is leaf. Assuming no intersections, we add 1 to the trail to yield $t = 111_2$. Since there are no trailing 0's, we invert the node's LSB to yield $n = 110_2$ and $t = 111_2$ (Figure 8.3(g)). Node $n = 110_2$ is leaf. Assuming no intersections, we again need to find the next sibling. Adding 1 to the trail yields $t = 000_2$ with three trailing 0's. Removing three bits from the node and the trail, and inverting the node's LSB, yields $n = 001_2$ and $t = 000_2$ (Figure 8.3(h)). We have returned to the root, so this is the end of the algorithm. Listing 8.4 is the code for the walkthrough of Figure 8.3.

Figure 8.4. The Stanford Bunny (left, 94 fps), Welsh Dragon (center, 31 fps), and Happy Buddha (right, 49 fps) models rendered in real time using the SLBVH. The application uses gloss mapping, phong shading, and one ray for shadows with one light source.

8.5 The SLBVH in Action

The tests were executed on an NVIDIA GTX 590 but using just one of its GPUs. The models compared are the Stanford Bunny (69,451 primitives), Crytek Sponza (279,163 primitives), Conference Room (282,759 primitives), and Welsh Dragon (2,097,152 primitives). The data is normalized and scaled to fit within a sphere of radius 0.8. An average of six different camera positions are used to measure performance.

The grid size is $64 \times 64 \times 1$, and the group size is $16 \times 16 \times 1$ to launch a total of 1,048,576 threads in the compute shader. The resolution is set to $1,024 \times 1,024$ pixels where each thread computes the color of one pixel. The tests shown in Figure 8.5 were executed using shadows, phong shading, and gloss mapping. Reflections were not activated on benchmarks. Shadow rays are not coherent, which heavily impacts on performance. When deactivating shadows, the frame is computed up to two times faster. However, a ray reordering [Garanzha and Loop 10] scheme could improve rendering times.

A BVH using a surface area heuristic (SAH-BVH) is used to compare traversal performance with our SLBVH. The BVH is based on the one provided on the PBRT framework [Pharr and Humphreys 04] and it is built on the CPU.

8.5.1 Traversal Frame Rate

The rendering times are shown in Figure 8.5. Three models are traversed using an SLBVH and a stack-based SAH-BVH. On small models with constant primitive sizes, the SLBVH is as fast as a stack-based SAH-BVH. Since the algorithm is not using a stack, cache memory usage is significantly lower than a BVH with higher tree quality. However, on larger models such as the Welsh Dragon, a high number of primitives occupy the same leaf node, which decreases rendering time.

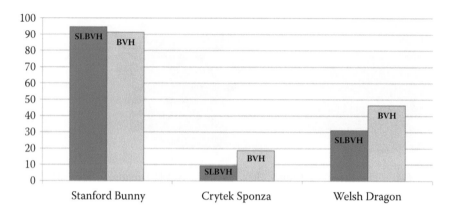

Figure 8.5. Three different-sized models are compared (frames per second) using SLBVH and regular stack-based BVH traversal: Stanford Bunny (depth = 18), Crytek Sponza (depth = 21), and Welsh Dragon (depth = 23).

Two options might yield better results: building a two-level SLBVH or using the surface area heuristic (SAH) as a partition scheme. The first one would produce a "deeper" tree and primitives would disperse on more nodes. The second one would increase tree quality and should be less complex to introduce in the current construction algorithm.

The SLBVH suffers with heterogeneous models such as the Conference Room and Crytek Sponza. Hundreds of small triangles are stored in leaf nodes, which impacts enormously on traversal times. One interesting option would be using the DirectX tessellator in order to partition large triangles into small ones. The number of primitives would increase, but as shown with large models, the traversal performance allows real-time frame rates.

8.5.2 Memory Footprint

The SLBVH is a stackless structure with less memory overhead than the ropes scheme for the stackless kd-trees [Popov et al. 07]. For example, the Stanford Bunny occupies 23 MB in Popov's SKD-Tree. As shown in Figure 8.6, an SLBVH of depth 18 uses only 8 MB of memory, which is enough to store this model due to its small size. This is just one third of the SKD-Tree size. The Conference Room and the Crytek Sponza models have similar characteristics. In the SKD-Tree, the Conference Room occupies 85 MB, while the SLBVH just needs 64 MB. Just as on the Bunny Model, SLBVH shows a better utilization of memory on a stackless approach. However, the SLBVH has a bigger memory footprint than a regular BVH. We are currently working on ways to lower this footprint for the SLBVH.

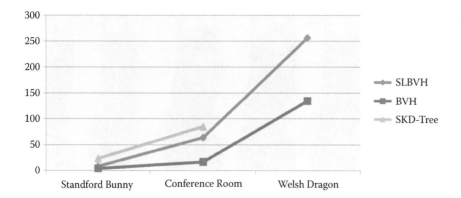

Figure 8.6. Memory footprint (MB) for different structures: SLBVH with varying depth, SAH-based BVH, and SKD-Tree.

8.5.3 Empty Nodes

Contrary to common structures, the SLBVH stores empty nodes in order to satisfy the arithmetic operations (which allow us to traverse the heap without a stack). The percentage of occupied nodes versus empty nodes is considerably low, as shown in Figure 8.7. However, the geometry is not well partitioned given that the middle-split scheme based on Morton codes is not optimal for balanced distributions. On the other hand, using SAH for all levels (or perhaps just the first few levels) of the structure might improve the tree quality. Yet, a tradeoff between construction time and traversal performance must be accomplished. A faster traversal does not mean a more effcient structure on dynamic scenes.

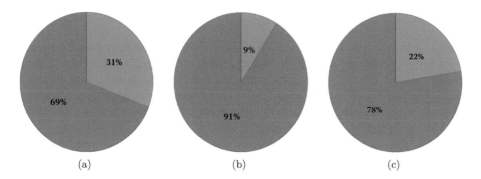

Figure 8.7. SLBVH nodes distribution. The red and blue colors represent empty nodes and occupied nodes, respectively on the (a) Stanford Bunny (depth = 18), (b) Crytek Sponza (depth = 21), and (c) Welsh Dragon (depth = 23) models. The primitive-per-leaf ratio is 1.72, 2.98, and 2.35, respectively.

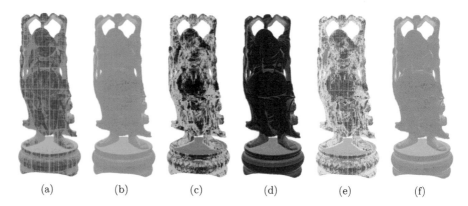

(a)   (b)   (c)   (d)   (e)   (f)

Figure 8.8. Number of intersections per box (a–b, red) and per primitive (c–d, green). The images show the differences between the SLBVH (a,c,e) and the BVH (b,d,f). The last two images (e–f) combine the intersections of both boxes and primitives.

Intersections per box and per primitive. Besides the memory waste occasioned by the heap's scheme, the nonuniform primitives' distribution is not handled optimally by the partition algorithm. Many primitives end up sharing the same leaf node, leading to an unbalanced tree. As a result, rays intersect few boxes but a lot of primitives. As shown in Figure 8.8, the BVH does a better job traversing the structure than the SLBVH, though the comparison is a little unfair since they are using different partitioning schemes. By decreasing the number of intersected primitives, the overall performance of the structure should improve. One of the options to decrease the number of intersected primitives per pixel is using the SAH algorithm instead of a middle split.

8.6   Conclusion

As far as the authors know, the SLBVH traversal is the first heap-based structure used for real-time ray tracing. In this approach, traversing the tree can be done easily with bit-wise operations, removing the need for additional information like a stack or the "ropes" in the SKD-Tree. This scheme has the additional advantage that the traversal can be restarted at any point in the tree, which is useful when computing reflections or refractions.

Even though the memory usage for the SLBVH is higher than the regular LBVH, its memory footprint is lower when compared with other stackless approaches—even when storing empty nodes. The weakest part of the algorithm it its poor partition on complex scenes. This is due to the fixed partition scheme we used (the Morton codes) that ends up with big boxes for a wide range of primitive sizes. However, using a better partition scheme (like SAH) could conceivably solve this problem.

Besides the partition issue, the memory consumption could be optimized by decreasing or removing the empty space on the structure. However, doing this might lead to having an extra look-up table or to a lack of simple arithmetic operations to traverse the tree. We are currently looking for ways to remove the empty nodes in the SLBVH while retaining the simple stackless traversal scheme.

We have also shown a very simple way to extend the framework to do global illumination. Although naive, this implementation could also serve as a starting point to create more optimized global illumination algorithms.

Even though the SLBVH was used on a ray-tracing environment, the data structure may be used in other, more generic geometric search problems where performance relies on effciently traversing a uniform set of data tokens represented in a heap. For instance, fast geometric search algorithms are widely used in video games for collision detection and scene culling.

8.7 Acknowledgments

The authors would like to thank the Stanford Computer Graphics Laboratory for the Happy Buddha and the Stanford Bunny models, the Bangor University for the Welsh Dragon model (released for Eurographics 2011), and Crytek for its modified version of the Sponza model.

Bibliography

[Ernest and Woop 11] Manfred Ernest and Sven Woop. "Embree—Photo-Realistic Ray Tracing Kernels." *Intel Software*, http://software.intel.com/en-us/articles/embree-photo-realistic-ray-tracing-kernels/, 2011.

[Garanzha and Loop 10] Kirill Garanzha and Charles Loop. "Fast Ray Sorting and Breadth-First Packet Traversal for GPU Ray Tracing." *Computer Graphics Forum* 29:2 (2010), 289–298.

[Garcia et al. 12] Arturo Garcia, Francisco Avila, Sergio Murguia, and Leo Reyes. "Interactive Ray Tracing Using DirectX11 on the Compute Shader." In *GPU Pro 3*, edited by Wolfgang Engel, pp. 353–376. Boca Raton, FL: CRC Press, 2012.

[Laine 10] Samuli Laine. "Restart Trail for Stackless BVH Traversal." In *Proceedings of the Conference on High Performance Graphics*, pp. 107–111. Aire-la-Ville, Switzerland: Eurographics Association, 2010.

[Lauterbach et al. 09] Christian Lauterbach, Michael Garland, Shubhabrata Sengupta, David Luebke, and Dinesh Manocha. "Fast BVH Construction on GPUs." *Computer Graphics Forum* 28:2 (2009), 375–384.

[Microsoft 10] Microsoft. "DirectX Software Development Kit." *Microsft Download Center*, http://www.microsoft.com/en-us/download/details.aspx?id= 6812, June 2010.

[Murguia et al. 11] Sergio Murguia, Arturo Garcia, Francisco Avila, and Leo Reyes. "Stackless LBVH Traversal for Real-Time Ray Tracing." Short paper, Computer Graphics International 2011, Ottawa, Canada, June 15, 2011. (Available at https://docs.google.com/file/d/ 0BxcYFN7UTqwWeWQ4MWh1WXhKdTQ/edit?usp=sharing.)

[Pharr and Humphreys 04] Matt Pharr and Greg Humphreys. *Physically Based Rendering: From Theory to Implementation*. San Francisco: Morgan Kaufmann Publishers Inc., 2004.

[Popov et al. 07] Stefan Popov, Johannes Günther, Hans-Peter Seidel, and Philipp Slusallek. "Stackless KD-Tree Traversal for High Performance GPU Ray Tracing." *Computer Graphics Forum* 26:3 (2007), 415–424.

[Satish et al. 09] Nadathur Satish, Mark Harris, and Michael Garland. "Designing Effcient Sorting Algorithms for Manycore GPUs." In *Proceedings of the 2009 IEEE International Symposium on Parallel and Distributed Processing*, pp. 1–10. Washington, DC: IEEE Computer Society, 2009.

Real-Time JPEG Compression Using DirectCompute

Stefan Petersson

Transporting frames within a DirectX application to a target destination is a nontrivial task. For example, both low latency and available bandwidth are important factors when streaming image frames via a network connection. By using the technique presented in this chapter, JPEG image data can be encoded in real time. The resulting data may thereafter be streamed to a network destination, saved as an image file, or appended to a movie sequence.

9.1 Introduction

Since the advent of DirectCompute, it is possible to execute more general algorithms using Direct3D with full cross-vendor support. In this chapter a technique is presented that uses DirectCompute to encode baseline JPEG images. The technique is implemented using C++ and Direct3D 11.0, which ease integration into existing rendering systems. By using standard quantization and Huffman tables, a majority of encoding steps can be computed in the GPU and encoded images may be stored as still image JPEG files or appended to a motion-JPEG (MJPEG) movie sequence file. This technique has advantages when source images are generated by the GPU, for example, taking a screenshot or recording gameplay video. GPU encoding can outperform CPU encoding when modern hardware is used.

9.1.1 Baseline JPEG Encoding

JPEG is a digital image compression standard created by the Joint Photographic Experts Group. The standard was accepted in 1992 and supports both lossless and lossy compression modes. Lossy versions are frequently used in, for example, digital cameras and web pages. The image compression method is used in multiple data formats such as the JPEG file interchange format (JFIF) [Hamilton 92]. Files with JFIF information are often referred to as "jpg-files." This section describes

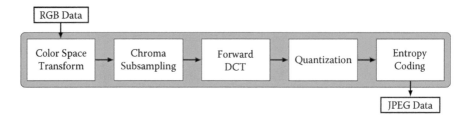

Figure 9.1. Baseline JPEG compression scheme.

the process of encoding uncompressed RGB data into compressed JPEG data. The sequential baseline is the codec implemented in the presented GPU technique. The JPEG codec is widely used and suffcient for most applications. Several encoding steps are required and a brief introduction to each step is presented. Figure 9.1 outlines the main steps that are applied to 8×8 blocks of pixels independently in each color-space component plane. Images with dimensions that are not multiples of 8 have border pixels padded by repeating the edge color. Processed blocks are appended to a final JPEG bit stream.

9.1.2 Color-Space Transform

This first step in the encoding process is optional as the JPEG algorithm is not bound to any specific color space, such as RGB or YC_bC_r. Encoders often sample and convert source-image RGB data into YC_bC_r color-space data, where luminance and chrominance information are separated. Luminance data is stored in the Y component and chrominance data in the C_b and C_r components. RGB to YC_bC_r conversion—see Equation (9.1)—is defined in the *ITU-R BT.601* standard:

$$
\begin{aligned}
Y &= & & 0.299R &+& 0.587G &+& 0.114B, \\
Cb &= 128 &-& 0.168736R &-& 0.331264G &+& 0.5B, \\
Cr &= 128 &+& 0.5R &-& 0.418688G &-& 0.081312B.
\end{aligned}
\tag{9.1}
$$

9.1.3 Chroma Subsampling

Chroma subsampling describes different sampling patterns used to lower resolution of the C_bC_r planes. Chroma resolution can be reduced because human vision is more sensitive to luminance variations than to chrominance variations [Pennebaker and Mitchell 93]. Luminance information is rarely modified, normally maintaining source-image resolution. One common approach to lower chrominance resolution is by averaging adjacent chroma components together [Kerr 12]. Sampling patterns are described as $W : H : V$, where W represents sampling width, H represents the number of horizontal samples, and V represents the

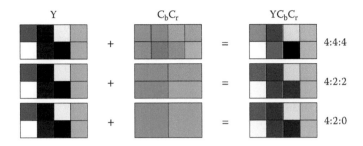

Figure 9.2. Chroma subsampling patterns.

number of vertical samples. Example results of chroma subsampling are illustrated in Figure 9.2, where decoded samples are shown by combining luminance and chrominance information.

9.1.4   Forward Discrete Cosine Transform

After chroma subsampling, a forward discrete cosine transform (FDCT) is applied to each 8×8 block. Before applying FDCT, color components are level shifted to the range $[-128,127]$. The level shift is applied by subtracting 128 from each component. Subsampled and level-shifted components are grouped into an 8×8 matrix referred to as M. The FDCT is calculated by matrix multiplications, seen in Equation (9.3), where matrices F and F^{T} are defined using Equation (9.2):

$$F_{i,j} = \begin{cases} \dfrac{1}{\sqrt{8}} & \text{if } i = 0, \\[2ex] \sqrt{\dfrac{2}{8}} \cos\left[\dfrac{(2j+1)i\pi}{16}\right] & \text{if } i > 0, \end{cases} \tag{9.2}$$

$$D = FMF^{\mathrm{T}}. \tag{9.3}$$

FDCT converts color information to a frequency domain where more efficient encoding schemes can be used. When applying FDCT, components are divided into differing intensity frequencies. The frequency values are referred to as *DCT coefficients*. Coefficients are usually grouped in a 8×8 matrix, which is referred to as D. The coefficient D_{00} is called the *DC coefficient*, which has zero frequency in both dimensions. The remaining 63 coefficients are called *AC coefficients*, which have nonzero frequency information. FDCT concentrates most signal information in the lower spatial frequencies, which often results in multiple coefficients with zero or near-zero amplitude. Frequency amplitudes that are zero or near-zero are ignored in the following steps.

$$\begin{bmatrix}
16 & 11 & 10 & 16 & 24 & 40 & 51 & 61 \\
12 & 12 & 14 & 19 & 26 & 58 & 60 & 55 \\
14 & 13 & 16 & 24 & 40 & 57 & 69 & 56 \\
14 & 17 & 22 & 29 & 51 & 87 & 80 & 62 \\
18 & 22 & 37 & 56 & 68 & 109 & 103 & 77 \\
24 & 35 & 55 & 64 & 81 & 104 & 113 & 92 \\
49 & 64 & 78 & 87 & 103 & 121 & 120 & 101 \\
72 & 92 & 95 & 98 & 112 & 100 & 103 & 99
\end{bmatrix}
\qquad
\begin{bmatrix}
17 & 18 & 24 & 47 & 99 & 99 & 99 & 99 \\
18 & 21 & 26 & 66 & 99 & 99 & 99 & 99 \\
24 & 26 & 56 & 99 & 99 & 99 & 99 & 99 \\
47 & 66 & 99 & 99 & 99 & 99 & 99 & 99 \\
99 & 99 & 99 & 99 & 99 & 99 & 99 & 99 \\
99 & 99 & 99 & 99 & 99 & 99 & 99 & 99 \\
99 & 99 & 99 & 99 & 99 & 99 & 99 & 99 \\
99 & 99 & 99 & 99 & 99 & 99 & 99 & 99
\end{bmatrix}$$

(a) Luminance Q_{50} (b) Chrominance Q_{50}

Figure 9.3. Standard quantization tables for (a) luminance and (b) chrominance.

9.1.5 Quantization

Small changes in high-frequency intensity are not perceived by human vision [Pennebaker and Mitchell 93]. Some DCT coefficient precision may therefore be discarded without major impact in the perception of a decoded image for a viewer. Each DCT coefficient is divided by a corresponding factor in a precalculated quantization table, where each table entry is an integer ranging from 1 to 255. The resulting value is thereafter rounded to the nearest integer. This quantization process loses information and will affect the JPEG data size output. Luminance and chrominance components are quantized using different tables because of the differences explained in Section 9.1.3. The JPEG standard provides optional standard quantization tables—see Figure 9.3—for both luminance and chrominance components. In Equation (9.4), standard table Q_{50} is used to derive tables of different quality levels:

$$Q_{\text{quality}} = \begin{cases} Q_{50} \dfrac{(100 - \text{quality})}{50} & \text{if quality} > 50, \\[2em] Q_{50} \dfrac{50}{\text{quality}} & \text{if quality} < 50. \end{cases} \tag{9.4}$$

After quantization all coefficients are ordered in a zigzag sequence; see Figure 9.4. The zigzag ordering is used to place low-frequency coefficients, which have higher probability to be nonzero, before high-frequency coefficients.

9.1.6 Entropy Coding

After quantization the coefficients are entropy-coded to compact coefficient information into a bit stream. Each nonzero coefficient is encoded as the concatenation of two symbols, wherein the first symbol is Huffman coded. Huffman tables may be computed per image before compression or predefined and used for all images. In this chapter two predefined, JPEG standard, Huffman coding tables are used. There is one DC coefficient code table and one AC coefficient code table. DC coefficients are coded as deltas from the previous block in that color plane. The

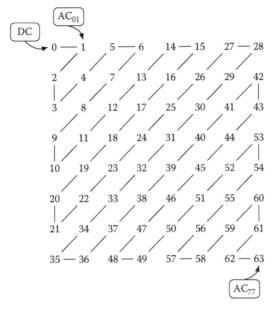

Figure 9.4. Zigzag sequence order.

first DC symbol includes the bit count and the second symbol includes the amplitude information. The first AC symbol contains preceding zeros and the number of bits needed to represent the second AC symbol, in which amplitude information is stored. Figure 9.5 illustrates how symbols are represented in memory,

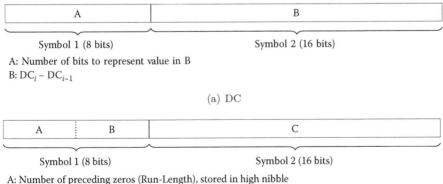

Figure 9.5. Code symbol structure for (a) DC and (b) AC coefficients.

before Huffman coding is applied. Coefficient symbols are sequentially variable length encoded (VLE) and concatenated into a JPEG bit stream. Special marker symbols are used in the following conditions:

1. for every preceding 16 zeros of an AC coefficient,

2. when an additional 0x00 byte is appended directly after bytes that equals 0xFF,

3. to indicate end of block (EOB) or end of image (EOI).

Further entropy coding details are beyond the scope of this chapter.

9.2   Implementation

Based on the description in Section 9.1.1, this section describes the implementation of a baseline JPEG encoder using DirectX 11.0 and Shader Model 5.0. The encoder is designed and implemented using C++ and the Direct3D 11.0 API, making it trivial to use in an existing DirectX 11.0-based renderer. Shader preprocessor directives are used in the example implementation to control the output index and texture sampling behavior: this makes it possible to use the same shader program for all YC_bC_r components. Each thread group consists of 8×8 threads—see Listing 9.3—and the number of dispatched thread groups is based on the source-image dimensions and chroma subsampling mode. The following features of Direct3D are beneficial to encoding JPEG data:

- full interoperability with all Direct3D resources,

- execution of group threads synchronization,

- computations' access to group shared memory,

- read and write capabilities on resources via *unordered access views*,

- automatic bounds check when reading from or writing to *shader resource views* and unordered access views,

- atomic intrinsic functions,

- source texture rescaling by hardware.

9.2.1   Performance Considerations

This encoder technique is designed and implemented to minimize global memory accesses. Global accesses may considerably lower performance if overused, for example, when the same data is processed in multiple dispatch calls. Therefore only one dispatch call per color plane is invoked. Loops accessing memory are manually unrolled to help the compiler. To maintain computation performance, shared memory registers are reused. The total size of shared members is 32 KB for data. Group shared memory is smaller in size than 16 KB and may therefore make it possible for a multiprocessor to execute two thread groups simultaneously [Fung 10]. Global memory accesses are, whenever possible, coalesced to avoid multiple transactions.

9.2.2   Challenges

Source-image data is stored in `Texture2D` resource objects. To encode `Texture2D` resource data, three technical problems may arise. Also challenges may occur, for example, if the output-image dimensions differ from the source-image dimensions.

No shader resource. When creating a texture resource in Direct3D, different *bind flags* are set. Bind flags tell how a resource is bound to the pipeline. After resource creation, it is no longer possible to modify any bind flag settings. This means that a nonshader resource texture has to be copied to a resource with the flag set. Compatible resources can copy data to and from each other using the device method `CopyResource`. Swap-chain buffers (back buffer) can be created with the `DXGI_USAGE_SHADER_INPUT` flag that maps to `D3D11_BIND_SHADER_RESOURCE`. Back-buffer data can then be sampled directly without copying to another resource. It is not possible to sample textures that are currently bound to the output merger stage, and therefore the back buffer has to be unbound before encoding starts.

Multisampling enabled. Texture resources with multisampling enabled have to be processed before encoding starts. A multisampled resource, of same dimensions and compatible format, is copied into a nonmultisampled resource by using the device context method `ResolveSubresource`. The target resource may thereafter be encoded.

Image dimensions not multiples of 8 or 16. Depending on the chroma subsampling mode, image dimensions have to be multiples of either 8 or 16. One solution to the problem is to repeat edge pixels until evenly divisible values are met. In this technique edge pixels are repeated by dispatching threads outside texture boundaries. Threads sample source-texture color data using the `D3D11_TEXTURE_ADDRESS_CLAMP` address mode. The sampling mode automatically repeats border-color values, avoiding the need for conditional behavior in the shader. Texture coordinates are calculated from `SV_DispatchThreadID` values; see Listing 9.1. Border-pixel data is also entropy coded and actual image dimensions are specified in the JFIF header. Padded image dimensions are now referred to as *computation dimensions*.

```
float2 GetTexCoord(uint3 DispatchThreadID)
{
    return float2(DispatchThreadID.x / ImageWidth,
                  DispatchThreadID.y / ImageHeight);
}
```

Listing 9.1. Texture coordinate calculation used with chroma subsampling 4:4:4.

Element	Resource Type
Image dimensions	Constant buffer
Computation dimensions	Constant buffer
Output block size	Constant buffer
Source texture	Shader resource view
Quantization table	Shader resource view
AC Huffman table	Shader resource view
GPU output result	Unordered access view

Table 9.1. Shader resources used in different instances.

9.2.3 GPU Initialization

Some Direct3D resources can be created at encoding system initialization, while others have to be created based on encoding parameters. The necessary resource types used are either textures, *constant buffers*, or *structured buffers* that utilize cache functionality. Constant buffers are used when multiple threads read the same data. Structured buffers are used when multiple threads read different data. The output buffer size is calculated based on the JPEG quality and the chroma subsampling mode, since lower chroma resolution results in fewer computation blocks and less memory to be copied from the GPU to the CPU. Textures and structured buffers are accessed as shader resource views, and the output buffer is accessed as an unordered access view. One compute shader instance is created per color plane, and the shader resources in Table 9.1 are used in each instance.

9.2.4 Execution

Figure 9.1 illustrates a generic encoding process where only some of the steps are suited for GPU processing. The execution path used in this technique involves both GPU and CPU processing. The GPU is used to compute a majority of encoding steps, and the CPU is used to stitch together final JPEG data. Encoding can take place when all required resources are created. The input data to each encode invocation includes image width, image height, source-image resource, data block size, and JPEG quality. Quantization tables are calculated based on JPEG quality, while computation dimensions are calculated from image dimensions and subsampling mode. Figure 9.6 illustrates an execution of a single thread group, where the final output is one DC coefficient, a bit-stream of entropy coded AC coefficients, and the number of bits occupied by the AC data.

Dispatch thread groups. For each color plane, thread groups are spawned by calling the device context method `Dispatch`; see the C++ code in Listing 9.2. The method takes three input parameters that specify how many thread groups to spawn in each dimension. Each thread group consists of 64 threads, 8 threads per x- and y-dimension, as the main HLSL function in Listing 9.3 shows. The

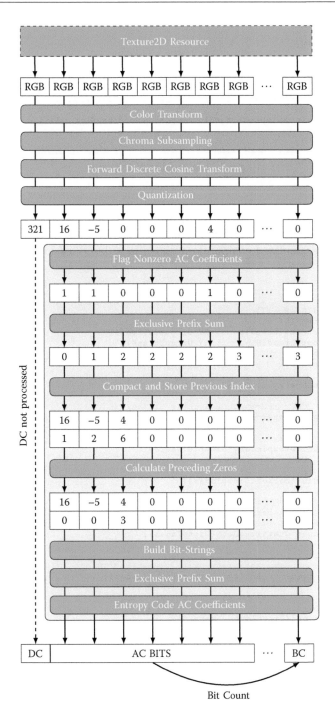

Figure 9.6. Thread group execution flow example.

```
void Dispatch()
{
    ...
    d3dContext->Dispatch(numBlocksY_x, numBlocksY_y, 1);
    ...
    d3dContext->Dispatch(numBlocksCb_x, numBlocksCb_y, 1);
    ...
    d3dContext->Dispatch(numBlocksCr_x, numBlocksCr_y, 1);
}
```

Listing 9.2. Dispatching of thread groups.

group thread count is a multiple of 32, which is recommended to maximize hardware occupancy [Bilodeau 11, Fung 10]. The number of spawned thread groups equals the precalculated computation dimensions described in Section 9.2.2. Af-

```
[numthreads(8, 8, 1)]
void ComputeJPEG(
  uint3 DispatchThreadID     : SV_DispatchThreadID,
  uint3 GroupThreadID        : SV_GroupThreadID,
  uint3 GroupID              : SV_GroupID,
  uint GroupIndex            : SV_GroupIndex)
{
  InitSharedMemory(GroupIndex);

  //RGB -> YCbCr component and level shift
  ComputeColorTransform(GroupIndex, DispatchThreadID);

  //Apply forward discrete cosine transform.
  ComputeFDCT(GroupIndex, GroupThreadID);

  //Quantize DCT coefficients.
  ComputeQuantization(GroupIndex);

  //Move nonzero quantized values to
  //beginning of shared memory array
  //to be able to calculate preceding zeros.
  StreamCompactQuantizedData(GroupIndex);

  //Initiate bitstrings, calculate number of
  //bits to occupy, and identify if thread represents EOB.
  BSResult result = BuildBitStrings(GroupIndex);

  //Do entropy coding to shared memory
  //using atomic operation.
  EntropyCodeAC(GroupIndex, result);

  //Move result from shared memory to device memory.
  CopyToDeviceMemory(GroupIndex, GroupID, result);
}
```

Listing 9.3. Main compute shader function.

```
float Get_YCbCr_Component_From_RGB(float3 RGB)
{
#ifdef COMPONENT_Y
  return dot(RGB,float3(0.299,0.587,0.114)) * 255.0f;
#elif COMPONENT_CB
  return dot(RGB,float3(-0.168736,-0.331264,0.5)) * 255.0f + 128.0f;
#elif COMPONENT_CR
  return dot(RGB,float3(0.5,-0.418688,-0.081312)) * 255.0f + 128.0f;
#endif
}
```

Listing 9.4. RGB to $YC_b C_r$ conversion.

ter finished execution, each group has computed one 8×8 block of partial JPEG data that is later processed by the CPU. One `Dispatch` method call per color plane is invoked. All relevant shader resources are set before each invocation.

Compute color transform and chroma subsampling. Source texture data is sampled using the clamp addressing mode; see details in Section 9.2.2. Depending on the chroma subsampling mode, each thread group may simulate a different group size by sampling multiple texture elements per thread. When encoding using, for example, 4:2:0 subsampling, each thread block acts over a 16×16 pixel block by having each thread sample four pixels each. Sampled RGB color values are converted to $YC_b C_r$ color space using Equation (9.1). Listing 9.4 shows how this conversion is done using HLSL, where defines are used to differentiate between the shaders for the different color planes. Converted values are averaged and finally rescaled to the range $[0, 255]$.

Compute forward discrete cosine transform. Before DCT is applied, color values are level shifted and grouped in an 8×8 color matrix M. The DCT matrix multiplications, as in Equation (9.3), are computed in parallel [Kirk and Hwu 10]. Each thread calculates a matrix element result by adding corresponding row and column element multiplications together. To avoid data dependency errors, threads are synchronized before the second multiplication takes place. The HLSL implementation is listed in Listing 9.5.

Compute quantization. After DCT computation, the resulting matrix is quantized. Quantization is computed by dividing each DCT coefficient by a corresponding quantization table element. The resulting floating-point value is rounded to the nearest integer and copied in the zigzag order, shown in Figure 9.4, to an integer array. See the quantization HLSL code in Listing 9.6.

Calculation of preceding zeros. AC coefficients are, for any chroma subsampling and quality level, entropy coded as described in Section 9.1.6. To comply with the JPEG standard, run-length zeros are counted. Scan primitives provide a method

```
void ComputeFDCT(uint GroupIndex, uint3 GroupThreadID)
{
  DCT_MatrixTmp[GroupIndex] = 0;
  [unroll] for(int k = 0; k < 8; k++)
    DCT_MatrixTmp[GroupIndex] += DCT_matrix[GroupThreadID.y*8+k] *
            TransformedPixelData[k*8+GroupThreadID.x];

  GroupMemoryBarrierWithGroupSync();

  DCT_Coefficients[GroupIndex] = 0;
  [unroll] for(int k = 0; k < 8; k++)
    DCT_Coefficients[GroupIndex] += DCT_MatrixTmp[GroupThreadID.y*8+k] *
            DCT_matrix_transpose[k*8+GroupThreadID.x];

  GroupMemoryBarrierWithGroupSync();
}
```

Listing 9.5. Forward cosine transform computed in parallel.

```
void ComputeQuantization(uint GroupIndex)
{
  //Divide and round to nearest integer.
  QuantizedComponents[GroupIndex] =
          round( DCT_Coefficients[ZigZagIndices[GroupIndex]] /
                  Quantization_Table[GroupIndex]);
}
```

Listing 9.6. Quantization code.

```
void StreamCompactQuantizedData(uint GroupIndex)
{
  //Set to 0 when a DC component or AC == 0.
  if(GroupIndex > 0 && QuantizedComponents[GroupIndex] != 0)
    ScanArray[GroupIndex] = 1;
  else
    ScanArray[GroupIndex] = 0;

  GroupMemoryBarrierWithGroupSync();

  Scan(GroupIndex);

  if(GroupIndex > 0 && QuantizedComponents[GroupIndex] != 0)
  {
    RemappedValues[ScanArray[GroupIndex]] = QuantizedComponents[GroupIndex];
    PrevIndex[ScanArray[GroupIndex]] = GroupIndex;
  }

  GroupMemoryBarrierWithGroupSync();
}
```

Listing 9.7. Calculate run-length zeros and stream compact AC coefficients.

for performing stream compaction in parallel, which is used in the counting process [Harris et al. 07]. First the DC coefficient and all nonzero AC coefficients are flagged and copied to a separate array in shared memory. The collected values are accumulated by computing an exclusive scan. Each nonzero AC coefficient is, together with its current index position, copied to a new array where the destination index position is equal to the corresponding scan result value; see the HLSL implementation in Listing 9.7.

Build bit strings. After stream compaction, entropy bit strings are constructed. Here each thread group is responsible for generating a bit stream of encoded AC coefficients that complies to the JPEG standard. Each thread identifies which, if any, bit strings to construct and append to the thread-group bit stream. Threads also keep track of the total bit count of all constructed bit strings. Bit count is retrieved by using the Shader Model 5.0 intrinsic function firstbithigh. Total bit count is used when calculating output positions, to calculate where bit strings should be concatenated. The bit-string construction HLSL code is in Listing 9.8.

```
typedef int BitString; // <-- numbits stored in high 16 bits

struct BSResult
{
  int NumEntropyBits;
  BitString BS[6];
};

BSResult BuildBitStrings(uint GroupIndex)
{
  BSResult result = (BSResult)0;

  static const uint mask[] = {1,2,4,8,16,32,64,128,256,
              512,1024,2048,4096,8192,16384,32768};

  // special marker symbols
  BitString M_16Z = AC_Huffman[0xF0];
  BitString M_EOB = AC_Huffman[0x00];

  if(GroupIndex == 0 && RemappedValues[0] == 0)
  {
    result.BS[5] = M_EOB;
  }
  else if(RemappedValues[GroupIndex] != 0)
  {
    uint PrecedingZeros = (PrevIndex[GroupIndex] -
              PrevIndex[GroupIndex-1] - 1);

    //Append 16 zeros markers.
    for(int i = 0; i < PrecedingZeros / 16; i++)
    {
      result.BS[i] = M_16Z;
    }

    int tmp = RemappedValues[GroupIndex];

    //Get number of bits to represent number.
    uint nbits = firstbithigh(abs(tmp)) + 1;
```

```
//AC symbol 1
result.BS[3] = AC_Huffman[((PrecedingZeros % 16) << 4) + nbits];

//AC symbol 2
if(tmp < 0) tmp --;
result.BS[4] = (nbits << 16) | (tmp & (mask[nbits] - 1));

//Insert end of block (EOB) symbol?
if(PrevIndex[GroupIndex] != 63 && RemappedValues[GroupIndex+1] == 0)
{
  result.BS[5] = M_EOB;
}
}

//Calculate total bit count.
[unroll] for(int i = 0; i < 6; i++)
{
  if(result.BS[i] != 0)
  {
    result.NumEntropyBits += (result .BS[i] >> 16);
  }
}

return result;
}
```

Listing 9.8. Construction of bit strings.

Entropy code AC coefficients. When using precomputed Huffman tables, VLE on GPU hardware has previously been shown to be efficient [Balevic 09]. Each constructed bit string is appended to a bit stream in shared memory. Bits are appended using the atomic intrinsic function `InterlockedOr`. When all threads have finished entropy coding, as seen in Listing 9.9, the final block output is copied to device memory. The last group thread is also responsible for outputting the bit count of the AC entropy data.

```
void EntropyCodeAC(uint GroupIndex, BSResult result)
{
  ScanArray[GroupIndex] = result.NumEntropyBits;

  Scan(GroupIndex);

  uint bitpos = ScanArray[GroupIndex];
  [unroll] for(int i = 0; i < 6; i++)
  {
    if(result.BS[i] != 0)
    {
      Write(result.BS[i], bitpos);
      bitpos += result.BS[i] >> 16;
    }
  }

  GroupMemoryBarrierWithGroupSync();
}
```

Listing 9.9. Entropy coding of group AC coefficients.

```
void CopyToDeviceMemory(uint GroupIndex, uint3 GroupID, BSResult result)
{
  uint outIndex = GetOutputIndex(GroupIndex, GroupID);

  if(GroupIndex > 0 && GroupIndex < EntropyBlockSize-1)
    EntropyOut[outIndex] = ConvertEndian(EntropyResult[GroupIndex-1]);

  else if(GroupIndex == 0)
    EntropyOut[outIndex] = QuantizedComponents[0];
  else if(GroupIndex == 63)
    EntropyOut[outIndex - 64 + EntropyBlockSize] = ScanArray[63];
}
```

Listing 9.10. Copying group result to device memory.

Copy to device memory. Each thread that has valid output data is responsible for copying that data to device memory, as shown in Listing 9.10. Endianness conversion is applied to optimize the final CPU coding step where each byte is treated separately. Block data copied to the output buffer is ordered in a pattern based on the chroma subsampling mode used. Figure 9.7 illustrates how YC_bC_r blocks are copied to device memory at different chroma subsampling modes.

Final CPU coding. After GPU computation, the data is copied to a staging buffer resource for final CPU processing. Each GPU generated block is processed by coding delta DC values and appending to the final JPEG bit stream, as described in Section 9.1.6. No modifications are done to already entropy-coded AC data. The CPU process is briefly illustrated in Figure 9.7. The GPU is not suited to do this concatenation because of challenges with delta DC calculations and special cases when an appended byte equals 0xFF. Every 0xFF byte has to be directly followed by a 0x00 byte, otherwise it would be confused with a JPEG marker symbol. After all blocks have been appended to the stream, an end of image (EOI) marker is appended and the JPEG data is complete.

The CPU is also creating the corresponding JFIF header, which is used when decoding generated baseline JPEG data [Hamilton 92]. The following, relevant encoding data is stored in the JFIF header structure:

- quantization tables,

- Huffman tables,

- chroma subsampling factors,

- image dimensions,

- number of color components,

- sample precision (8 bits).

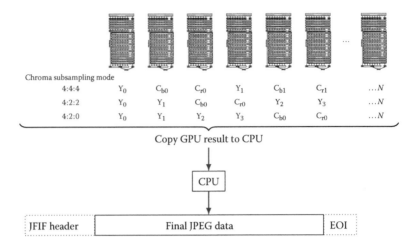

Chroma subsampling mode							
4:4:4	Y_0	C_{b0}	C_{r0}	Y_1	C_{b1}	C_{r1}	$...N$
4:2:2	Y_0	Y_1	C_{b0}	C_{r0}	Y_2	Y_3	$...N$
4:2:0	Y_0	Y_1	Y_2	Y_3	C_{b0}	C_{r0}	$...N$

Copy GPU result to CPU

CPU

JFIF header	Final JPEG data	EOI

Figure 9.7. GPU to CPU process showing thread group output order based on chroma subsampling mode.

9.3   Performance

Performance tests were performed by compressing back-buffer data into JPEG data. Two source images, of dimensions 2,268 × 1,512 pixels, were encoded with different settings using the presented technique and libjpeg-turbo version 1.2.0.[1] The back buffer has the relevant flags to be treated as a shader resource. The source `Texture2D` resource is created by loading RGB data from a file. This texture is mapped to a full screen quad, which is rendered to the back buffer in each test run. For libjpeg-turbo tests, back-buffer data is copied to a CPU-accessible staging resource and thereafter encoded. The DirectCompute tests are done by sampling back-buffer data directly. Resulting JPEG data size was always smaller when encoding using the DirectCompute encoder. Encoded images, with chroma subsampling disabled and JPEG quality 100, were decoded and thereafter compared to source-image data. The comparison showed that the decoded version was almost identical to the source image; details are presented in the following sections for each benchmark scenario.

The 32-bit test application was executed using a computer equipped with Microsoft Windows 7 Professional x64, Intel i7 860 CPU at 2.8 GHz, 8 GB RAM, and AMD Radeon 7970 GPU. Each run was executed 50 times, in which each run was performance timed. The test results show that the presented technique outperforms libjpeg-turbo in all test cases.

---

[1]libjpeg-turbo 1.2.0 uses SIMD instructions to encode baseline JPEG image data and is one of the fastest CPU encoders available today.

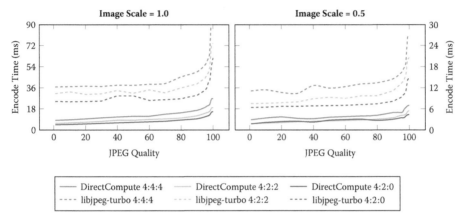

Figure 9.8. Benchmark Scenario 1 results.

9.3.1 Benchmark Scenario 1

The source image[2] used was selected to benchmark how the technique performs when encoding nonartificial image data, such as a photograph. Benchmark results are presented in Figure 9.8. Resulting data sizes at JPEG quality 100 and chroma subsampling 4:4:4 were 1,973 KiB when encoding using DirectCompute and 2,602 KiB when encoding using libjpeg-turbo. A comparison between encoded results and source-image data is presented in Table 9.2.

	Color Channel Difference Tolerance				
	0	1	2	3	4
DirectCompute	56.99%	97.52%	99.98%	100.00%	100.00%
libjpeg-turbo	59.30%	95.72%	99.54%	99.98%	100.00%

Table 9.2. Decoded Scenario 1 data compared to source-image data. JPEG data was encoded with chroma subsampling 4:4:4 and quality 100. The cell values represent the match percentages at different tolerance levels in the range $[0, 255]$.

---

[2]The source image was taken from www.imagecompression.info, where images have been "carefully selected to aid in image compression research and algorithm evaluation."

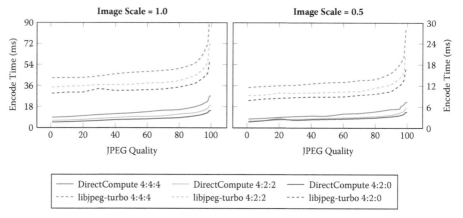

Figure 9.9. Benchmark Scenario 2 results.

9.3.2 Benchmark Scenario 2

The source image[3] used was selected to benchmark how the technique performs
when encoding artificial image data, such as a game screenshot. Benchmark
results are presented in Figure 9.9. Resulting data sizes at JPEG quality 100
and chroma subsampling 4:4:4 were 1,926 KiB when encoding using DirectCompute and 2,519 KiB when encoding using libjpeg-turbo. A comparison between
encoded results and source-image data is presented in Table 9.3.

	Color Channel Difference Tolerance				
	0	1	2	3	4
DirectCompute	63.58%	98.62%	99.99%	100.00%	100.00%
libjpeg-turbo	66.84%	97.27%	99.77%	99.99%	100.00%

Table 9.3. Decoded Scenario 2 data compared to source-image data. JPEG data was
encoded with chroma subsampling 4:4:4 and quality 100. The cell values represent the
match percentages at different tolerance levels in the range $[0, 255]$.

---

[3]The source image was taken from a game called *Screen Space Combat*, which has been
developed by the author.

9.4 Conclusion

This chapter demonstrates how to encode JPEG standard compliant images using DirectCompute. The technique supports both chroma subsampling and varying quality settings, which broadens usage scenarios. Benchmark scenarios show that this GPU-based encoder is well suited, compared to using a CPU encoder, when transforming uncompressed back-buffer data into JPEG image data. A demo application is supplied that can be trivially adapted and integrated into existing Direct3D 11.0-based renderers.

9.5 Acknowledgments

I would like to thank Andrew Moss, Francisco Lopez Luro, Håkan Grahn, and Jonas Petersson for their valuable input and support.

Bibliography

[Balevic 09] Ana Balevic. "Parallel Variable-Length Encoding on GPGPUs." In *Euro-Par'09: Proceedings of the International Conference on Parallel Processing*, pp. 26–35. Berlin: Springer-Verlag, 2009.

[Bilodeau 11] Bill Bilodeau. "Effcient Compute Shader Programming." Presentation, Game Developers Conference, San Francisco, CA, 2011.

[Fung 10] James Fung. "DirectCompute Lecture Series 210: GPU Optimizations and Performance." http://channel9.msdn.com/Blogs/gclassy/DirectCompute-Lecture-Series-210-GPU-Optimizations-and-Performance, 2010.

[Hamilton 92] Eric Hamilton. "JPEG File Interchange Format: Version 1.02." *JPEG*, http://www.jpeg.org/public/jfif.pdf, September 1, 1992.

[Harris et al. 07] Mark Harris, Shubhabrata Sengupta, and John D. Owens. "Parallel Prefix Sum (Scan) with CUDA." In *GPU Gems 3*, edited by Hubert Nguyen, Chapter 39. Reading, MA: Addison-Wesley Professional, 2007.

[Kerr 12] Douglas A. Kerr. "Chrominance Subsampling in Digital Images." http://dougkerr.net/pumpkin/articles/Subsampling.pdf, January 19, 2012.

[Kirk and Hwu 10] David Kirk and Wen-mei Hwu. *Programming Massively Parallel Processors: A Hands-on Approach*. San Francisco: Morgan Kaufmann, 2010.

[Pennebaker and Mitchell 93] William B. Pennebaker and Joan L. Mitchell. *JPEG Still Image Data Compression Standard*. Norwell, MA: Kluwer Academic Publishers, 1993.

10

Hair Simulation in TressFX
Dongsoo Han

10.1 Introduction

A human has around 120,000 strands of hair, and due to its high cost of rendering and lack of real-time simulation technique, it has been a challenge to present human hair inside real-time video games. Therefore, many artists and game developers have to choose alternative approaches such as simple polygons and textures.

In this chapter, I will explain the hair simulation method in TressFX, which has been used in the recent *Tomb Raider* and AMD *Ruby* demos. (See Figure 10.1.) It can simulate around 19,000 strands consisting of 0.22 million vertices in less than a millisecond in high-end GPUs. TressFX was developed specifically for video games. Therefore, performance was the highest concern, over physical accuracy.

Figure 10.1. Example of hair simulation in *Tomb Raider*.

10.2 Simulation Overview

When TressFX simulation was developed, the main focus was to simulate styled hair, which is much harder than straight hair because it requires strong bending and twisting effects. Regardless of hair style, it should be safe to consider human hair as inextensible. To simulate those three effects, there are generally two ways to represent them, as either stiff spring or constraint.

In VFX, stiff spring is commonly used for various simulations such as hair or cloth. However, for real-time physics simulation, stiff spring is not practical because the integration of strong spring force can easily make the mass-spring-damper system unstable unless a complicated integration scheme such as implicit backward integrator is used [Baraff and Witkin 98, Selle et al. 08]. Also, it becomes hard to deal with stretching, bending, and twisting springs in the same solver, especially in GPUs. In TressFX, all springs are replaced with hard and soft constraints. For inextensibility, we use a simple iterative position-based distance constraint. Bending and twisting are considered as a single effect for simplicity, and local and global shape constraints were developed. We also sometimes resort to ad-hoc constraints to deal with fast-moving characters.

Besides bending and twisting effects, the rest of hair simulation is similar to cloth simulation. However, in terms of GPU computing, hair has more benefits because there are a lot of hair strands and they are independent as long as inter-hair collisions are ignored. Also the topology of vertex connection is straightforward. By exploiting them, TressFX can achieve strand- and vertex-level parallelism without complex data structure.

> **Input:** hair data
> precompute rest-state values;
> **while** *simulation running* **do**
>   integrate;
>   apply Global Shape Constraints;
>   **while** *iteration* **do**
>   apply Local Shape Constraints;
>   **end**
>   **while** *iteration* **do**
>   apply Edge Length Constraints;
>   **end**
>   apply wind;
>   collision handling;
>   update position;
>   pass updated vertex buffer to rendering pipeline;
> **end**

Algorithm 10.1. Hair simulation outline.

10.3 Definitions

Basically, each hair strand is a poly line. We will use the terms *local* and *global* often when we explain local shape constraints. Global is in world frame and local is in local frame, which is attached to the starting point of a line segment.

The index of vertices starts from the root of a hair strand that is attached to a scalp. P_i is the position of vertex i in the current time step. The zeroth time step is the rest state, and we use a right superscript to express it explicitly (i.e., P_i^0). Here, we focus only on vertices in one strand when we explain algorithms. Therefore, vertex index i is always unique.

In case we need to explicitly clarify which coordinate system we are using, we specify it using a left superscript (i.e., $^{i-1}P_i$ means the position of vertex i in the current time step defined in the local frame $i-1$). When the position is defined in the world coordinate system, we can drop the frame index (i.e., $^w P_i = P_i$).

In terms of transforms, we define $^{i-1}T_i$ as a full transformation containing rotation $^{i-1}R_i$ and translation $^{i-1}L_i$. It transforms $^i P_{i+1}$ to $^{i-1}P_{i+1}$ such that $^{i-1}P_{i+1} = {}^{i-1}T_i \cdot {}^i P_{i+1}$. Because of careful indexing of vertices in the strand, the following equation holds:

$$^w T_i = {}^w T_0 \cdot {}^0 T_1 \cdot {}^1 T_2 ... \cdot {}^{i-2}T_{i-1} \cdot {}^{i-1}T_i.$$

In this chapter, we call $^{i-1}T_i$ a local transform and $^w T_i$ a global transform. In the case of vertex 0, local transform and global transform are the same such that $^{-1}T_0 = {}^w T_0$.

In Figure 10.2, local frames are defined at each vertex. Vectors x_i, y_i, and z_i are basis vectors of the local frame of vertex i in the current time step. x_i is simply defined as a normalized vector of $P_i - P_{i-1}$. As an exception, $x_0 = (P_1 - P_0) / \|P_1 - P_0\|$. In Figure 10.3, basis vectors are shown in red, yellow, and blue.

To describe the head transform, we use $^w T_H$, which transforms the head from the rest state to the current state and is an input from user or predefined animations.

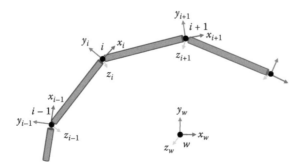

Figure 10.2. Local frames in a hair strand.

Figure 10.3. Black is a hair stand. Red, yellow, and blue are x, y, and z axes, respectively.

10.4   Integration

To integrate the motion of hair dynamics, we use the Verlet integration scheme because it is simple and shows good numerical stability compared to the explicit Euler method. External forces such as gravity are applied during this step. The damping coefficient is multiplied by velocity to simulate a damping effect.

We integrate only particles whose inverse mass is nonzero. If the inverse mass is zero, we consider it non-movable, update its positions following its attached objects (such as a head), and skip the rest of the steps for those particles. We assign zero inverse mass for vertex 0 and 1 so they can be animated following the head movement.

10.5   Constraints

There are three types of constraints. ELC (edge length constraint) is a hard constraint to simulate inextensible hair. LSC (local shape constraint) is a soft constraint for bending and twisting. GSC (global shape constraint) is complementary to LSC and helps keep the initial hair shape preserved with very minimum computation cost.

10.5.1   Edge Length Constraint

ELC enforces edges to keep their rest lengths. Figure 10.4 shows how position corrections are computed for each edge. To be simple, we set an equal mass to all vertices except the first two vertices. To apply this constraint in parallel, we create two batches. Each batch is independent of the other so that it is

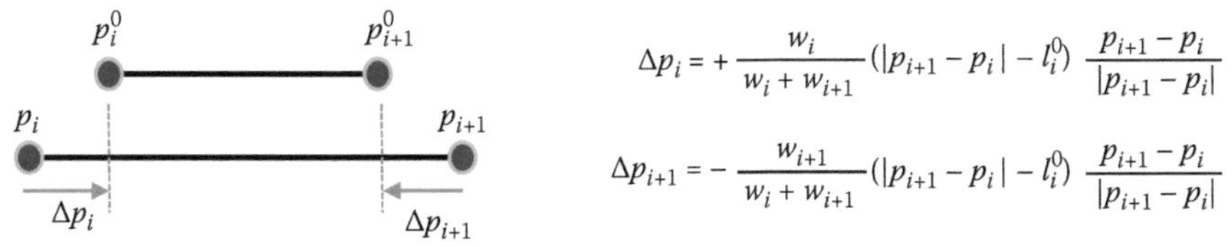

$$\Delta p_i = + \frac{w_i}{w_i + w_{i+1}} (|p_{i+1} - p_i| - l_i^0) \frac{p_{i+1} - p_i}{|p_{i+1} - p_i|}$$

$$\Delta p_{i+1} = - \frac{w_{i+1}}{w_i + w_{i+1}} (|p_{i+1} - p_i| - l_i^0) \frac{p_{i+1} - p_i}{|p_{i+1} - p_i|}$$

Figure 10.4. Edge length constraint: w_i and w_{i+1} are inverse masses of p_i and p_{i+1}, respectively.

safe to update vertex positions without conflict. In hair, it is easy to create the two batches as an even edge index group and an odd edge index group. We run the first batch followed by the second one. This approach gives us a good parallelism. Unfortunately, the trade-off is that it has poor convergence, so we iterate it multiple times to make all edges reach their rest lengths.

In *Tomb Raider*, the main character can move and turn very fast. Basically, users can create a strong acceleration, which causes very long elongation to hair. In this case, ELC does not converge well even with more than 20 iterations. It is easy to check the convergence by measuring the first movable edge length and comparing it with its rest length. To fix this problem, we switch to the ad-hoc constraints, which update only one vertex position, p_{i+} in Figure 10.4. By updating one vertex position per edge starting from the root of the hair strand, we can simply satisfy ELC by one iteration. However, this approach can add extra energy to the system and cause unnatural simulation results. To remove this extra energy, we add high damping. Due to this, we only use this approach when it is really necessary. The interested reader is referred to [Müller et al. 12] for deeper understanding of this problem and different solutions.

10.5.2   Global Shape Constraint

The main idea of GSC is quite simple. We take the initial hair shape as a target and try to move vertices to it. It is similar to shape matching. Probably the easy way to understand it is to think of the initial hair shape as a cage and GSC enforcing hair to trap inside it. Before simulation begins, we save the rest positions of vertices P_i^0. We use these rest positions as goal positions to apply global shape constraints. In equation (10.1), S_G is a stiffness coefficient for the global shape constraint. It ranges between 0 and 1. If S_G is 0, there is no effect; if it is 1, the hair becomes completely rigid, frozen to the initial shape:

$$P_i \mathrel{+}= S_G({}^w T_H \cdot P_i^0 - P_i). \tag{10.1}$$

In many cases, we apply global shape constraints on a part of the hair strand such as close to the root. We can also gradually reduce S_G from the root of the hair to the end. This is because hair seems to behave more stiffly close to the root; also, it maintains the hair style more efficiently without bringing unnecessary extra stiffness to overall hair simulation.

The benefit of global shape constraints is that it keeps the global shape with minimum cost. Combined with local shape constraints, it takes almost no time to settle the simulation and there is no visual perturbation when simulation starts. Designers can expect that their authored hair shape will be the initial shape. Global shape constraints also ensure that hair does not get tangled in weird shapes during fast-moving gameplay.

10.5.3   Local Shape Constraint

Even though GSC can effectively manage the hair shape, we need a way to simulate bending and twisting forces for individual hair strands. In real-time cloth simulation, the bending effect is often represented as a soft distance constraint connecting two vertices across the bent edge. It is also possible to use the same approach for a bending effect in hair, but twisting is not really easy.

For simplicity and high performance, we combine bending and twisting effects as one soft distance constraint. To define this constraint, the target goal positions are computed using the local frames as in Figures 10.2 and 10.3.

Equation (10.2) may look complex due to its subscripts and superscripts but the concept is the same as ELC. The first equation computes $^{i-1}d_i$, which is a distance between the current position and its target goal position. The left superscript $i-1$ indicates that those positions are defined within the local frames. In the end, when we calculate the position correction, we actually use world frame but equation (10.2) is written in local frame to simplify it:

$$^{i-1}d_i = {}^{i-1}P_i^0 - {}^{i-1}P_i$$

$$^{i-1}P_{i-1} -= \frac{1}{2}S_L{}^{i-1}d_i \qquad (10.2)$$

$$^{i-1}P_i += \frac{1}{2}S_L{}^{i-1}d_i.$$

As explained in ELC, we divide the position correction by the mass ratio and apply it to two connected vertices ($^{i-1}P_{i-1}$ and $^{i-1}P_i$). Here, we already assume that all mass is equal so the ratio is $1/2$.

10.6   Wind and Collision

Wind is an important part of simulation since it makes the hair interact with the environment and gives the game character dynamics even during idle states. To generate more randomized effects and prevent hair from getting clumped, a single wind input gets converted to four cone-shape directions as in Figure 10.5. Also,

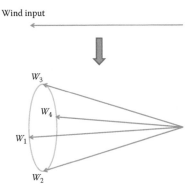

Figure 10.5. A single wind input is converted to four wind directions to generate randomized effects and prevent hair clumping.

wind magnitude gets modulated by using the sine function and frame number as below:

$$\text{wind magnitue} \times = (\sin^2(\text{frame} \times 0.05) + 0.5).$$

Equation (10.6) shows how wind force is calculated and applied to position update. W_1, W_2, W_3, and W_4 are the four wind vectors, and the strand index is used to add more randomization:

$$\begin{aligned}
a &= ((\text{strand index})\%20)/20, \\
W &= a \times W_1 + (1-a) \times W_2 + a \times W_3 + (1-a) \times W_4, \\
V &= P_i - P_{i+1}, \\
f &= -(V \times W) \times V, \\
P_i &+= f \times \Delta t^2.
\end{aligned} \tag{10.3}$$

The number 20 in the first equation is an arbitrary choice, W is an interpolated wind vector by a from four wind vectors, and Δt is timestep.

The wind is applied after the shape constraints and is not a part of integration because shape constraints are too strong and could cancel its effect if it is applied as an external force during integration. The key point of calculating wind is to create randomized direction and periodic magnitude. So it is more empirical than physically correct.

10.7 Authoring Hair Asset

The TressFX demo and Lara Croft's hair assets were created using Autodesk Maya. (See Figure 10.6.) However, it can be authored using any DCC (digital content creation) tools. Once the hair strands are authored as splines, a custom

Figure 10.6. Authoring Lara Croft's hair in Autodesk Maya.

python script exports them as poly lines. In the TressFX demo, hair is divided into four groups as front, top, side, and ponytail and each group is saved as a separate file.

10.8   GPU Implementation

TressFX uses compute shader in DirectX 11 to run hair simulation in the GPU. There are a total of five compute shader kernels. Listing 10.1 shows the `Simulate Hair_A` kernel, which handles integration and GSC. This kernel computes one vertex per thread. Since `GROUP_SIZE` is defined as 64, one thread group can compute four hair strands if one strand has 16 vertices. With `maxPossibleVertsInStrand`, it is possible to control how many strands can be computed in one thread group. Since `GROUP_SIZE` is 64, the maximum number of vertices in a strand is 64. By changing `GROUP_SIZE` to 128 or 256, we can have more vertices. However, more vertices could take a longer time to enforce ELC and LSC. Therefore, it is recommended to use 16 or 32 vertices per strand for real-time purposes.

Listing 10.2 shows the `SimulateHair_A` kernel, which does LSC. This kernel computes one strand per thread and thus there is a `for` loop. `strandType` is a variable showing to which group the strand belongs. With this, we can assign different simulation parameters such as stiffness or damping to hair groups.

The `SimulateHair_C` kernel computes one vertex per thread, enforces ELC, and applies wind. Finally, `SimulateHair_D` takes care of collision and computes tangents of line segments for the rendering pipeline.

```
// Integrate and global shape constraints
// One thread computes one vertex
[numthreads(GROUP_SIZE, 1, 1)]
void SimulateHair_A(uint GIndex : SV_GroupIndex,
                    uint3 GId : SV_GroupID,
                    uint3 DTid : SV_DispatchThreadID)
{
    int offset = 0;
    int strandType = 0;

    uint globalStrandIndex = 0;
    uint localVertexIndex = 0;
    uint indexForSharedMem = GIndex;
    uint numOfStrandsPerThreadGroup = 2;
    uint maxPossibleVertsInStrand = (GROUP_SIZE /
      numOfStrandsPerThreadGroup);

    // If maxPossibleVertsInStrand is 64, one thread group
    // computes one hair strand.
    // If it is 32, one thread group computes two hair
    // strands. Below code takes care of strand and vertex
    // indices based on how many strands are computed
    // in one thread group.
    if ( GIndex < maxPossibleVertsInStrand )
    {
        globalStrandIndex = 2 * GId.x;
        localVertexIndex = GIndex;
    }
    else
    {
        globalStrandIndex = 2 * GId.x + 1;
        localVertexIndex = GIndex - maxPossibleVertsInStrand;
    }

    if( globalStrandIndex > 0 )
    {
        offset =  g_GuideHairVerticesOffsetsSRV
                           .Load(globalStrandIndex - 1);
        strandType = g_GuideHairStrandType
                           .Load(globalStrandIndex - 1);
    }

    uint globalVertexIndex = offset + localVertexIndex;
    uint numVerticesInTheStrand = g_GuideHairVerticesOffsetsSRV
                           .Load(globalStrandIndex) - offset;

    // Copy data into shared memory
    // Integrate
    // Global shaping matching style enforcement
    // update global position buffers
}
```

Listing 10.1. SimulateHair_A compute shader kernel.

In case hair simulation should be skipped, SkipSimulateHair kernel does this job. It may be possible to assign 1.0 GSC stiffness but it would waste lots of computation. The SkipSimulateHair kernel applies only the head transform to vertices and makes the hair do rigid motion.

```
// Local shape constraints
// One thread computes one strand
[numthreads(GROUP_SIZE, 1, 1)]
void SimulateHair_B(uint GIndex : SV_GroupIndex,
                    uint3 GId : SV_GroupID,
                    uint3 DTid : SV_DispatchThreadID)
{
    uint globalStrandIndex = GROUP_SIZE*GId.x;
    globalStrandIndex += GIndex;

    int offset = 0;
    int strandType = 0;

    if ( globalStrandIndex > 0 )
    {
        offset =   g_GuideHairVerticesOffsetsSRV
                                  .Load(globalStrandIndex - 1);
        strandType = g_GuideHairStrandType
                                  .Load(globalStrandIndex - 1);
    }

    uint numVerticesInTheStrand = g_GuideHairVerticesOffsetsSRV
                          .Load(globalStrandIndex) - offset;

    // Local shape constraint for bending/twisting
    {
        float4 pos_minus_one = g_GuideHairVertexPositions
                                                  [offset];
        float4 pos = g_GuideHairVertexPositions[offset+1];
        float4 pos_plus_one;
        uint globalVertexIndex = 0;
        float4 rotGlobal = g_GlobalRotations[offset];

        for ( uint localVertexIndex = 1; localVertexIndex <
                numVerticesInTheStrand-1; localVertexIndex++ )
        {
            globalVertexIndex = offset + localVertexIndex;
            pos_plus_one = g_GuideHairVertexPositions
                                          [globalVertexIndex+1];

            // Update position i and i_plus_1

            // Update local/global frames
        }
    }

    return;
}
```

Listing 10.2. SimulateHair_B compute shader kernel.

10.9 Conclusion

The hair simulation of TressFX is optimized for real-time games in many aspects, such as using shape constraints and limits on the number of vertices per strand. Therefore, it is required to understand its basic approaches to maximize its performance and quality.

Lastly, for readers who want to know more details, we refer them to [Han and Harada 12].

Bibliography

[Baraff and Witkin 98] David Baraff and Andrew Witkin. "Large Steps in Cloth Simulation." In *Proceedings of the 25th Annual Conference on Computer Graphics and Interactive Techniques*, pp. 43–54. New York: ACM, 1998.

[Han and Harada 12] Dongsoo Han and Takahiro Harada. "Real-Time Hair Simulation with Efficient Hair Style Preservation." In *VRIPHYS*, edited by Jan Bender, Arjan Kuijper, Dieter W. Fellner, and Eric Guérin, pp. 45–51. Aire-la-Ville, Switzerland: Eurographics Association, 2012.

[Müller et al. 12] Matthias Müller, Tae-Yong Kim, and Nuttapong Chentanez. "Fast Simulation of Inextensible Hair and Fur." In *VRIPHYS*, edited by Jan Bender, Arjan Kuijper, Dieter W. Fellner, and Eric Guérin, pp. 39–44. Aire-la-Ville, Switzerland: Eurographics Association, 2012.

[Selle et al. 08] Andrew Selle, Michael Lentine, and Ronald Fedkiw. "A Mass Spring Model for Hair Simulation." In *ACM SIGGRAPH 2008 Papers*, pp. 64:1–64:11. New York: ACM, 2008.

11

Object-Order Ray Tracing for Fully Dynamic Scenes

Tobias Zirr, Hauke Rehfeld,
and Carsten Dachsbacher

11.1 Introduction

This chapter presents a method for tracing incoherent secondary rays that integrates well with existing rasterization-based real-time rendering engines. (See Figure 11.1.) In particular, it requires only linear scene access and supports fully dynamic scene geometry. All parts of the method that work with scene geometry are implemented in the standard graphics pipeline. Thus, the ability to generate, transform, and animate geometry via shaders is fully retained. Our method does not distinguish between static and dynamic geometry.

Figure 11.1. Arbitrary reflection rays traced using our method.

Moreover, shading can share the same material system that is used in a deferred shading rasterizer. Consequently, our method allows for a unified rendering architecture that supports both rasterization and ray tracing. The more expensive ray tracing can easily be restricted to complex phenomena that require it, such as reflections and refractions on arbitrarily shaped scene geometry. Steps in rendering that do not require the tracing of incoherent rays with arbitrary origins can be dealt with using rasterization as usual.

11.1.1   The Classic Divide between Rasterization and Ray Tracing

Ray tracing is a robust and flexible approach to image synthesis that elegantly solves many problems that are hard to solve using rasterization. Since light typically travels in straight lines, most light transport problems can be decomposed into finding the next point along a straight line, starting at a point that emits or receives light. The ability to determine intersections with the scene geometry for arbitrary rays therefore allows for a trivial implementation of many light transport phenomena.

Recent advances in the performance and flexibility of graphics processing hardware have made ray tracing a viable option even for real-time rendering applications. Yet, integrating ray tracing into existing rasterization-based real-time rendering solutions poses significant challenges. Modern rasterization-based rendering engines (Figure 11.2) typically use the capabilities of modern GPUs to generate, transform, and amplify geometry on the fly. In contrast, efficient ray tracing techniques typically depend on pre-built spatial acceleration data structures that allow for fast random access to the scene geometry (Figure 11.3).

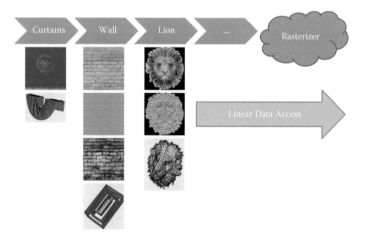

Figure 11.2. Linear batch-based rendering. A rasterizer sequentially iterates over all primitives and their resources to project them onto the image plane.

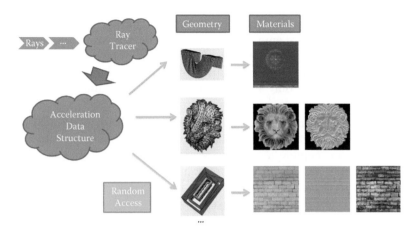

Figure 11.3. Ray-order ray tracing using a global acceleration data structure accesses the primitives and their resources in quasi-random order.

Our method bridges this divide: It allows for the precise tracing of arbitrary rays while only using linear render passes of triangle soups, just like rasterizing renderers do. Thus, it remains trivial to render dynamic geometry. Both geometry and shading can even be manipulated on the fly by shaders as usual. Hence, enhancing existing graphics engines with ray tracing becomes much easier.

11.2   Object-Order Ray Tracing Using the Ray Grid

To determine which pixels are overlapped by geometric primitives (typically triangles), rasterization projects them onto an image raster. Similarly, our algorithm determines which rays potentially intersect geometric primitives using a *ray grid*. Grid- and tree-based ray scheduling has been explored before in work on out-of-core ray tracing [Pharr et al. 97, Hanika et al. 10] and coherent image-order ray tracing [Guntury and Narayanan 12, Bikker 12].

The ray grid is a coarse voxel grid that encloses the scene. Each cell in the grid stores links to all rays that intersect it. Before any actual intersection testing is performed, the grid is filled by ray marching through the grid and storing a link to the traversing ray in each of the traversed grid cells.

In a subsequent intersection testing stage, all primitives in the scene are rendered into this ray grid. For every grid cell intersected by a primitive, we simply look up all the rays that traversed this particular grid cell during the prior ray grid construction stage and then test the primitive for intersection with only those rays. If an intersection is detected, the corresponding ray is updated with the nearest hit information.

Sparseness. The amount of memory consumed by a naively constructed ray grid would be high. Hence, we employ a conservative binary voxel approximation of the scene to restrict the generation of ray links to only those cells that are actually overlapped by geometry. Empty cells are simply skipped during ray marching, so that the resulting grid is only sparsely populated with ray links.

Occlusion. Rasterization typically uses a depth buffer with early depth testing to economically discard fragments that are hidden by geometry closer to the eye. Similarly, we employ a multi-pass approach that expands rays front to back: In each pass, rays are inserted only into a small number of ray grid cells each, and then tested for intersection. Rays for which a hit point is detected are terminated and no longer considered in subsequent passes. Thus, we can eliminate intersection tests with primitives behind the first (few) points of intersection. Moreover, this further reduces the size of the ray grid. In each pass, only very few links per ray (typically four) need to be stored, which makes our technique viable even in memory-constrained environments (about 14 MiB of ray links at 720p with full-resolution reflections).

11.3 Algorithm

Our algorithm consists of the following steps, illustrated in Figure 11.4:

1. *Scene voxelization:* We first build a coarse binary *voxel representation* of the scene by conservatively voxelizing all primitives. Affected voxels are flagged occupied.

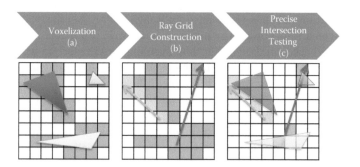

Figure 11.4. Algorithm steps: (a) Conservative binary voxel approximation of the scene (occupied voxels are marked in grey). (b) Links to traversing rays are inserted into the cells of a ray grid using ray marching (marked in the color of the rays). Unoccupied grid cells are skipped. (c) The scene is rendered into the ray grid. Each primitive is tested against the rays stored in all cells it overlaps.

2. *Ray grid construction:* Given a list of rays, we march along every ray to construct the *ray grid*. For every traversed grid cell, we first check if this cell is occupied by geometry by looking up the corresponding voxel in our voxel representation. A ray link is enqueued if the grid cell is occupied; empty cells are ignored.

3. *Intersection testing:* Using the ray grid, we perform precise intersection testing with the actual scene geometry. Again, we voxelize all scene geometry conservatively. For every voxel affected by a primitive, we look up all the rays that were enqueued in the corresponding ray grid cell during ray grid construction. We test the primitive for intersection only with these rays.

Note that in none of the steps are there any global dependencies on the primitives in the scene. Each batch of triangles can be rendered independently just as with rasterization.

11.3.1 Intersect Early: Multi-pass Scheme

Ray marching and intersection testing are repeated alternately to allow for front-to-back expansion of rays. Figure 11.5 illustrates this multi-pass scheme. Clearly, the right-hand ray (marked red) is obstructed by the second triangle it encounters. As we are only interested in the closest hit, intersection tests and ray links behind that triangle would be wasted.

Therefore, in the first pass, we start by expanding all rays into only the first few occupied cells of the ray grid each. Then, we immediately perform intersection testing using the resulting (incomplete) ray grid. A lot of rays will already intersect primitives in these first few occupied cells and are terminated. These rays can be ignored in subsequent passes, as we are progressing front to back. The remaining rays are expanded further in the next pass. Since the red ray in Figure 11.5 is terminated in the first pass, we only consider the yellow ray in the subsequent passes.

Bounded memory. We repeat intersection testing and ray grid construction alternately until all rays have either hit some geometry or have traversed the entire grid. The number of layers expanded in each pass can be increased as the number of active rays decreases. The fewer active rays that remain, the more ray links can be stored per ray without increasing the overall memory consumption of the ray grid. In the last pass, all remaining rays are fully expanded. Thus, we achieve both bounded time (typically three passes) and bounded memory (typically four links per ray).

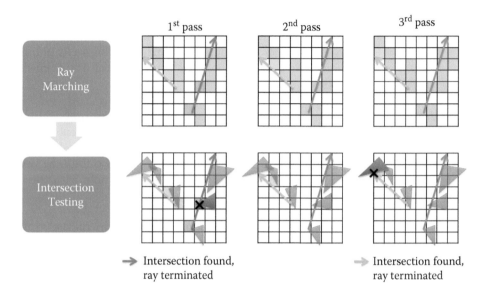

Figure 11.5. Three-pass intersection testing. Each pass builds a different partial ray grid (ray links are marked in the color of the rays). The red ray intersects a triangle in the first pass and is no longer considered afterward (grayed-out). The voxel representation of the scene is underlaid in grey to improve readability.

11.4 Implementation

In the following, we provide details on the implementation of our method. While some remarks may be specific to DirectX 11, everything that is required has its counterparts in other GPU programming APIs and thus can easily be implemented in different environments just as well.

11.4.1 Voxelization

We make use of voxelization both to build the coarse voxel representation of the scene and to identify overlapped ray grid cells during intersection testing. In both cases, voxelization has to be conservative, i.e., every voxel fully or partially overlapped by a triangle needs to be identified. Thus, we ensure that a *voxel fragment* (pixel shader thread) is generated for every voxel touched by a primitive. Otherwise, we could miss intersections with the rays of cells that are only partially overlapped.

Projection to 2D rasterization. We have implemented conservative voxelization in the standard graphics pipeline, similar to [Crassin et al. 11]. We use the hardware rasterizer to rasterize primitives into a two-dimensional othographic projection of the voxel grid. Every pixel corresponds to one column of voxels that expands into the third dimension. As we only get one linearly interpolated depth value per pixel, the third dimension needs to be discretized manually.

To make effective use of parallel rasterization, we want to maximize the number of fragments per triangle. Since the rasterizer parallelizes over two dimensions only, this number depends on the orientation of the triangle and the chosen direction of projection. Fortunately, we can easily change the projection direction per triangle in the geometry shader. The triangle's normal tells us which of the three cardinal axes best fits the triangle's plane and thus will allocate the most fragments.

Conservative triangle modification. Rasterization has to be altered in a way that ensures that a pixel shader thread is executed for each intersected voxel column, even those where the fragment center itself is not covered by the projected triangle. Such modification of standard rasterization is appropriately called *conservative rasterization* and has been described in some detail in [Hasselgren et al. 05].

We use the vertex shader to transform positions into grid space. The geometry shader ensures conservative rasterization, essentially shifting all triangle edges outward by half a pixel diagonal. The resulting triangle will cover the *centers* of all pixels that were only partially covered by the original triangle (see Figure 11.6).

We do not construct a precise and minimal conservative hull for each voxelized triangle, as this would result in multiple triangles per input triangle. Instead, we only construct one over-conservative triangle and manually clip fragments outside the minimal conservative hull in the pixel shader. For this, an axis-aligned bounding box (AABB) of the minimal conservative triangle hull is computed alongside

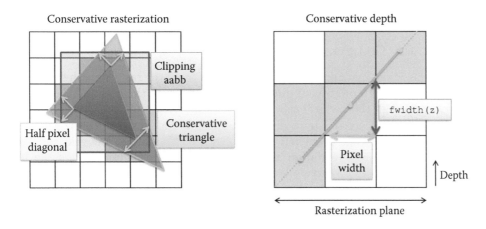

Figure 11.6. Over-conservative triangle modification with screen-space bounding box to clip unneeded fragments in the pixel shader (left). Depth bounds estimation using the derivatives of the linear triangle depth values (right).

the overestimating conservative bounding triangle in the geometry shader and is passed to the pixel shader as well. Note that modifying the triangle may change its depth derivatives, unless the resulting triangle is realigned with the plane of the original triangle.

To be able to reconstruct the proper grid space coordinates of a rasterized triangle, we also need to pass the chosen direction of projection to the pixel shader. This only requires two bits, so we reuse the storage of the four `float`s required to pass the clipping AABB to the pixel shader. As all fragment coordinates in screen space are nonnegative, we encode the three possible directions in the unused sign bits of two of the AABB components.

Conservative depth bounds estimation. During rasterization, a pixel shader is executed for each voxel column covered by the projected triangle. To conservatively find which voxels are intersected, we need to compute a depth range spanning from the closest to the farthest point on the projected triangle inside each voxel column. We can then iterate over all (fully or partially) overlapping voxels in the pixel shader.

To compute this depth range we use the pixel shader gradient instructions provided by HLSL. The intrinsic function `fwidth` returns the sum of the absolute partial derivatives for a given variable. The derivatives are evaluated at the location for which the pixel shader was executed, scaled to pixel steps. Since our projection is orthographic and thus our depth values are linear, this sum coincides with the maximum depth delta of the triangle inside a fully covered voxel column. As rasterization yields depth values interpolated at pixel centers (green in Figure 11.6), we add and subtract one half of the depth derivative to obtain a conservative estimate for the depth range that contains all potentially touched voxels.

11.4.2 Ray Grid Construction

We do classic ray marching in a compute shader to fill the ray grid with ray links. We transform both origin and direction of each ray into the grid and then work our way through the ray grid cell by cell.

For every cell crossed by a given ray, we first check if that cell is actually occupied by any scene geometry. In our implementation, the ray grid and the grid of the voxel representation always align, therefore this information can be retrieved using a single texture lookup in the voxel representation. For occupied cells, the ray is queued into the respective ray grid cell, to be tested against the actual triangle geometry overlapping that cell in the subsequent precise intersection testing stage. For empty cells, no further action is taken and marching simply continues to the next cell.

Note that filling the ray grid requires a conservative ray marching that does not skip cells in passing. Hence, it would not be sufficient to use a fixed step size,

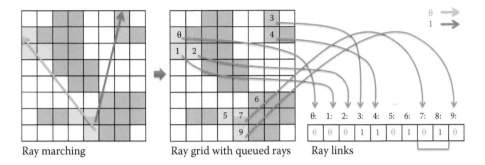

Figure 11.7. Ray grid construction by ray marching, adding ray links to traversed cells.

but rather the distance to the next cell has to be recalculated in every marching step. This is easily achieved by maintaining a vector of the three offsets to the next cell on every axis, always choosing the smallest of these as the next step offset. Thus, we ensure that no ray-cell intersection is missed.

Storage options. We can queue the rays into ray grid cells in several ways; the most straightforward solution is to construct linked lists. Every time a new ray is enqueued, a volumetric list head texture is atomically updated with the link to a new head element. HLSL's `InterlockedExchange()` also yields the previous head link, which can be stored in the new element to establish a singly linked list.

However, we have found that in our case a more compact and coherent layout is desirable: Once we enter the intersection testing stage, primitives will be intersected with all rays in each overlapped ray grid cell. For optimal memory access patterns, the links to rays enqueued in the same cell should lie next to each other in memory. As primitives typically come in connected batches of triangles, we can furthermore expect that a lot of them occupy similar sets of neighboring cells. To make good use of caches, the rays of neighboring cells should also lie next to each other in memory.

Storing the rays enqueued in the ray grid consecutively along a space-filling Z curve fulfills these requirements (see Figure 11.7). Such a Z layout can be directly obtained by applying a 3D parallel prefix sum scan to a grid of cell ray counts. However, for decently sized grids, this approach would have to work through too many empty cells to be efficient.

Construction using sorting. Recent research has shown that it is feasible to use sorting for grid construction [Kalojanov and Slusallek 09].[1] Using the optimized GPU sorting implementation provided by the B40C library [Merrill and Grimshaw 11], this turns out to be both simple and efficient.

---

[1] Also see [Kalojanov et al. 11] for multi-level grids.

During ray marching, enqueued rays are output in an arbitrary order, making use of structured unordered access views enhanced with a global atomic counter (`D3D11_BUFFER_UAV_FLAG_COUNTER` creation flag). A slot in the buffer is reserved by calling `RWStructuredBuffer.IncrementCounter()`. The function yields an index where the enqueued ray may be stored. Note that this is much more efficient than using `InterlockedAdd()` on a counter value stored in a global memory buffer, as `IncrementCounter()` is optimized for highly concurrent access.

For each occupied grid cell crossed during ray marching, we output the ray index annotated with the morton code of the crossed cell. The morton code is constructed by interleaving the bits of the three integers forming the grid cell index. Sorting data by morton code yields the desired coherent Z-order memory layout described in Section 11.4.2.

After sorting, each grid cell's range of ray links (ray indices with cell codes) is extracted in another compute shader pass. This pass simply compares the morton codes of successive ray links. Whenever these differ, the end of the previous cell's range and the beginning of the next cell's range have been found. Decoding the morton codes yields the grid indices of each cell, which allows for the begin and the end ray link indices to be stored in the respective cells of a volume texture.

Compacted ray inlining. During intersection testing all rays stored in a ray grid cell need to be fetched and tested against each overlapping primitive. Following the ray indices stored as ray links, this would repeatedly cause random indirect memory accesses. To further increase memory access coherency, we therefore *compact and inline* enqueued rays after sorting. Instead of following ray links again and again for each primitive, we follow the ray links in every cell once up front and store compacted clones of the referenced rays in an array parallel to the ray link array.

For compacted storage, we pack the ray origins into cell-relative 21-bit triples. The ray directions are packed into 16-bit tuples using the octahedron normal vector encoding described in [Meyer et al. 10]. Together, these require a total of three 32-bit integers per ray.

Persistent threads. During ray marching, we make use of the observations by Aila et al. regarding GPU work distribution [Aila and Laine 09]: just like in their BVH ray traversal algorithm, ray lengths in our ray marching stage may vary. On current GPUs, the work distribution unit always waits for an entire unit of work to be finished before distributing new units. For that reason, a single thread working on a particularly long ray may block all other processing units in the same processing group.

We therefore launch a fixed number of persistent GPU worker threads that continually fetch new rays whenever ray-marching along a previous ray has been finished. This alleviates work distribution delays. Due to the SIMD nature of GPUs, the problem cannot be completely avoided, but we can at least take advantage of more fine-grained scheduling mechanisms.

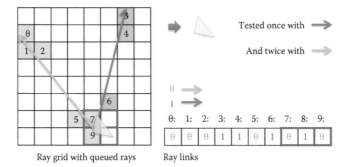

Figure 11.8. Intersection testing with one triangle using the ray grid. Ray grid cells are marked in the colors of the rays enqueued. Voxelization of the light-blue triangle generates the blue-framed voxel fragments. A lookup in the array of ray links returns both rays in one cell and only the yellow ray in another cell.

11.4.3 Precise Intersection Testing

After the ray grid has been constructed, we have direct access to all rays intersecting a particular cell just by indexing into a volume texture using the cell coordinates. In order to compute precise ray-triangle intersections with all triangles in the scene, we simply re-voxelize the scene into the ray grid as described in Section 11.4.1: For every fragment generated by conservative rasterization, we iterate over all cells in the corresponding voxel column that are touched by the respective triangle. For each cell, we check for intersection with all rays that have been enqueued there. Figure 11.8 shows an example.

Whenever a ray-triangle intersection is detected, the intersection information of the corresponding ray has to be updated. If the new intersection is closer than a previous intersection, the ray intersection information is locked, triangle attributes are interpolated, hit data is stored, and finally the closest distance is updated. If a thread finds the intersection information locked by another thread, it temporarily skips ray update and re-checks the ray state in a subsequent iteration (see Listing 11.1).

Ray hit information. Our ray hit information records consist of the distance, normal, and color(s) of each ray's current closest hit point. The records are stored in an array parallel to that storing the ray descriptions and may thus be indexed by ray links.

Apart from the distance attribute, these attributes may be replaced or extended freely to suit any rendering engine's need. We store typical G-buffer information to allow for simple deferred shading as described in Section 11.4.6.

To allow for atomic updating and synchronization with minimal memory overhead, we reuse the distance attribute to mark records locked. A negative sign indicates that the record is locked, while the absolute value of the attribute

```
1  // Distance of the new hit point,
2  // asuint() retains the order of positive floats
3  int newDist = asuint(floatingPointHitDistance);
4
5  int lastDistOrLocked = 0;
6  do
7  {
8    // The absolute value always corresponds to the current
9    // closest hit. Immediately discard farther hits
10   if (newDist >= abs(RayDistBuffer[rayIdx]))
11     break;
12
13   // Atomically compare new hit to the current closest hit
14   // and check if the ray is locked at the same time
15   InterlockedMin(
16       RayDistBuffer[rayIdx], newDist, lastDistOrLocked);
17
18   // Only entered if ray is unlocked (lastDistOrLocked >= 0)
19   // and new distance is less than old distance
20   if (newDist < lastDistOrLocked)
21   {
22     // Atomically lock ray via the distance buffer
23     // (= set distance to a negative value)
24     int lastDist = 0;
25     InterlockedCompareExchange(
26         RayDistBuffer[rayIdx], newDist, -newDist, lastDist);
27
28     // Check if exchg successful and new distance still closest
29     if (lastDist == newDist)
30     {
31       <Update hit data>
32       // Unlock the ray by updating the distance buffer
33       InterlockedExchange(RayDistBuffer[rayIdx], newDist);
34     }
35   }
36 // Re-iterate until the ray has been unlocked
37 } while(lastDistOrLocked < 0);
```

Listing 11.1. HLSL code for the ray update synchronization.

always corresponds to the current distance to the closest hit point. This enables us to both atomically compare the distance of a new hit point against the current closest distance and check the respective record's lock state at the same time.

Ray update synchronization. We make use of the atomic operations on unordered access views that have become available in shader model 5.0 to implement a spin lock mechanism that allows for the atomic updating of more than just one unsigned integer quantity. Listing 11.1 shows the HLSL code skeleton.

We first check whether the distance of the new hit point is actually smaller than the current absolute value of the record's distance attribute (line 8). Hits with greater distances are skipped right away. We then use InterlockedMin() in its *signed* integer version to atomically update the distance attribute with the *positive* distance of the new hit point (line 13). If the record is currently locked, the update fails, as negative values are always smaller than the given positive distance. In this case, updating is temporarily skipped (line 18) and will be retried in a subsequent loop iteration (`while` checks the lock state in line 37).

Note that just waiting for the record to become unlocked by looping until all other concurrent updates have been finished would not work. The SIMT execution model of current GPUs implies that threads skipping certain instructions have to wait on other threads that execute these instructions until all threads are back in sync and can continue to operate in *lockstep*. Therefore, it is important to implement the spin lock by skipping instructions in the waiting threads. Otherwise, waiting threads would actively hold back the unlocked threads from performing the work they are waiting on.

In case of a successful atomic distance update, the entire record is locked using `InterlockedCompareExchange()` (line 22). The distance of the hit point is passed for comparison. If no closer point of intersection has been found in the meantime, the negated distance will be written to the record, acquiring the lock on the hit data. If the exchange fails, the hit point is discarded. In this case, a closer point has already been found by some other thread. If the exchange succeeds, all the other hit information is updated. Afterwards, the record is unlocked using `InterlockedExchange()` to reset the distance attribute to the positive distance value (line 32).

Input register pressure and incoherence. Our first implementation simply passed entire triangles from geometry to pixel shader using many `nointerpolation` registers. This proved to be problematic in two ways. Firstly, as we exceeded a certain number of pixel shader input registers, performance greatly deteriorated. High register pressure limits the number of concurrent pixel shader threads that can be started. Secondly, the number of rays enqueued per voxel varies. It turned out to be too incoherent for SIMD parallelism to work on a per-voxel level: some threads were looping through large numbers of rays while others were mostly idling.

Load balancing using geometry shaders. To keep threads from idling, we implemented a two-pass load balancing scheme that makes use of geometry shaders to achieve full parallelism on a per-ray and per-triangle level. The scheme is illustrated in Figure 11.9.

In the first pass, the current batch of triangles is voxelized. During this pass, both the transformed triangles and pairs of ray grid cell and triangle indices for all touched voxels are streamed out into auxiliary buffers. In the second pass, all cell-triangle pairs are read in parallel using null-input vertex and geometry shaders. The primitive ID (retrieved using the `SV_PrimitiveID` shader system value input semantic) indicates which pair to process.

DirectX 11 provides `DrawInstancedIndirect()` to issue draw calls where the number of vertices and instances resides in a GPU buffer. This allows us to trigger

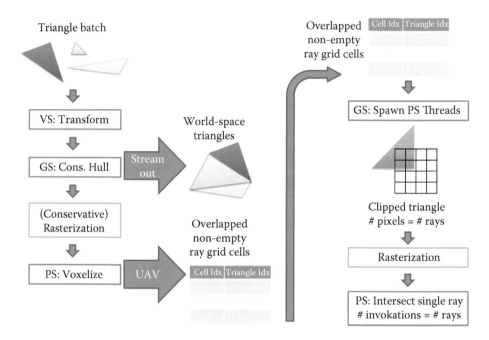

Figure 11.9. Intersection testing load balancing using the geometry shader.

the right number of vertex shader executions and thus process the right number of cell-triangle pairs without having to do a CPU read back. In the geometry shader of the second pass, a rectangle is generated for each pair. This *dispatch rectangle* is scaled to make the number of covered viewport pixels equal to the number of rays queued in the pair's ray grid cell. Consequently, for each *ray*, a fragment is generated and a pixel shader thread is spawned. We have to make sure that the viewport we rasterize the *dispatch rectancles* into is large enough to contain pixels for every ray in the fullest ray grid cell.

In each of the pixel shader threads, we now only have to perform intersection testing with one single ray against one single triangle. This way, we achieve fully concurrent intersection testing, independent of the number of rays queued per ray grid cell.

Unfortunately, we have to provide auxiliary buffers, one (created with D3D11_BIND_STREAM_OUTPUT) to store the streamed out pre-transformed geometry and another one (bound via counter-enhanced UAV) to store the intermediate cell-triangle pairs for one batch of triangles. However, these buffers only need to provide storage for the largest batch of triangles in the scene. The amount of storage can be strictly limited by enforcing a maximum triangle batch size, e.g., by partitioning larger batches using multiple draw calls.

11.4.4 Multi-pass Tracing

To properly implement the multi-pass intersection testing scheme described in
Section 11.3, we need to store some additional information and take some additional precautions. First of all, we need to remember the ray grid cell in which
the expansion of each ray stopped in the previous pass of ray grid construction.
As we only ever continue ray expansion for rays that have not yet hit any geometry in the previous passes, we can simply reuse some of the ray hit information
storage for that purpose. In each ray-marching pass we store the ray offset of the
last grid cell each ray was expanded to and continue expansion with that offset
in the next pass.

Active ray filtering. To keep track of which rays are still active and which rays may
be terminated, we check the distance attribute of their hit information record.
We use two special values to distinguish between rays that have already left the
scene bounds without any intersections and rays for which no intersection has
been found yet, but which are still in bounds. Recall that for atomic ray update to work, our distance attribute is a signed integer. Therefore, we may use
`MissedRayDepth = 0x7ffffffe` and `MaxRayDepth = 0x7fffffff`, respectively. Before we continue expanding rays in subsequent ray grid construction passes, we
filter out all terminated rays and compact the indices of remaining active rays
into one consecutive array. This array is then processed by the ray marching
shader.

Hit point ordering. Finally, it is important to enforce strict front-to-back intersection testing. Just like in classic ray tracing where an acceleration data structure
is traversed in an ordered fashion, we may find intersection points that lie beyond
the cells that the ray has been expanded to in the current pass. In other words,
the intersection is found on a section of the ray that would only be tested in a
later pass.

   This is especially likely for large triangles that span many ray grid cells, when
rays slowly converge toward the triangle plane and are inserted into several cells
that hold the triangle but not the actual point of intersection. If we accepted these
premature hit points, we would be prone to missing other in-between geometry
that lies only in cells beyond those the ray has thus far been expanded to. We
can remedy this problem by strictly accepting only those hit points that lie inside
the cell that caused their detection. Rejected points will then be re-detected in
the proper cells, possibly during a later pass. Thus, rays will not be terminated
prematurely.

11.4.5 Ray Generation

In our implementation, we demonstrate the tracing of incoherent secondary rays
with reflection rays. We simply generate these rays from the G-buffer created by

our traditional deferred shading pipeline. We reconstruct reflecting surface points using the depth and the normal stored in the G-buffer and reflect the camera rays to spawn reflection rays.

11.4.6   Shading

We use standard deferred shading to process the closest hit point information collected for each ray. The result is composited with the shading of the point that spawned the ray, blended using Schlick's fresnel approximation.

We implemented sunlight for demonstration purposes. For other, spatially bounded light sources, it would make sense to limit the influence of these lights to a certain subset of grid cells. Shading can then be restricted to few lights per cell just like in screen-space deferred shading approaches.

11.5   Results

We have implemented the described algorithm with DirectX 11 Graphics and Compute, and we use the radix sorting implementation provided by the B40C library implemented in CUDA 5 [Merrill and Grimshaw 11]. The algorithm is implemented in a typical rasterization-based deferred shading engine, using rasterization for primary and shadow rays and using the described method for tracing reflection rays. All tests were run on a NVIDIA GeForce GTX 560 GPU and an Intel Core i7-2600K CPU. Images were rendered at a resolution of 1280×720. The ray and voxel grids had a resolution of $128 \times 128 \times 128$ each.

We tested our method in the Crytek Sponza scene (270k tris), the Sibenik Cathedral scene (75k tris), and a simple test scene composed of a bumpy reflective cube and some low-poly objects (2k tris). The Sponza scene generates highly incoherent reflection rays due to the heavy use of normal maps on the scene's brickwork. Reflection rays were spawned everywhere except on the curtains and the sky.

To increase the data locality of spacially adjacent geometry, we have used the mesh optimization post-processing step provided by the Open Asset Import Library [Gessler et al. 09]. All quantities were measured for a selection of view points that vary in complexity by both ray coherence and surrounding geometry.

Table 11.1 shows the average time spent per frame in each of the major stages. With less than 2 ms, conservative voxelization is rather cheap. Naive ray marching and ray sorting are pretty much independent of the scene complexity, constantly taking about 10 ms each. Intersection testing, on the other hand, is highly sensitive to the number of triangles, as all triangles are processed linearly.

Table 11.2 details the time spent in the intersection testing stage. Together, stream out (GS) and emission of cell-triangle pairs (PS) in pass 1 make for a cross-shader communication overhead of about 10 ms. This can likely be reduced in future graphics pipelines (see Section 11.6). Intersection testing itself (pass 2) is compute-bound. Due to our carefully chosen memory layout, this is to be

	Frame	Voxelize	Ray March	Ray Sort	Testing
Sponza	92.6 ms	2.0 ms	9.9 ms	12.7 ms	54.2 ms
Sibenik	65.9 ms	0.6 ms	12.7 ms	15.4 ms	24.5 ms
Simple	31.3 ms	0.1 ms	9.2 ms	7.7 ms	5.4 ms

Table 11.1. Time spent in each of the stages per frame. Total frame time includes G-buffer generation, rendering of shadow maps, and deferred shading.

	VS	GS	PS	Total
Pass 1 (trafo + cell-tri pairs)	0.9 ms	2.3 ms	7.8 ms	11.0 ms
Pass 2 (ray-tri intersections)	1.3 ms	3.0 ms	38.2 ms	42.4 ms

Table 11.2. Time spent in each of the shaders in the two-pass load-balancing scheme illustrated in Figure 11.9 (measured in the Sponza scene and summed for all batches of triangles).

expected. Both geometry and rays are processed linearly and are therefore always accessed in a perfectly coherent fashion.

Table 11.3 shows some additional figures for the number of ray links and intersection tests. As can be seen, storage requirements for the ray grid typically stay below four links per ray. Across all passes, rays are enqueued to four to eight occupied cells on average, depending on the scene complexity. As expected, the number of hit tests per ray greatly depends on the number of triangles in the scene.

Table 11.4 shows how rays and triangles are distributed across all ray grid cells that are occupied by geometry and traversed by at least one ray. These numbers vary greatly for different scenes. They depend on the way the geometry is laid out, what parts are occluded, and how evenly the scene is tessellated.

	Tests	Hits	Hit Ratio	Max Links	Total Links
Sponza	121.1	1.5	1.72%	3.8	7.5
Sibenik	27.9	1.1	4.1%	3.7	6.4
Simple	8.0	0.4	4.65%	2.5	3.9

Table 11.3. Per ray, the hit tests, hits, maximum number of ray links per pass, and total number of ray links (not stored) across all passes.

		# rays/cell				
	# cells	μ	σ	$> 10\mu$	max	# tris/cell
Sponza	150K	32.9	261.6	1.66%	11670	15.4
Sibenik	138K	45.5	282.1	1.37%	9180	4.4
Simple	43K	58.8	461.3	1.95%	4131	2.1

Table 11.4. Number of ray grid cells active during intersection testing, with distribution of rays and triangles per cell; μ is the expected value and σ the standard deviation.

The high average number of hit tests per ray as well as the high average number of triangles per grid cell in the Sponza scene suggests that a more adaptive ray grid could be beneficial for more complex scenes with uneven tessellation. The great number of small triangles on the Sponza curtains fill the rather coarse fixed-size grid cells with loads of unstructured geometry, resulting in many hit tests for the rays passing nearby.

11.6   Conclusion

In this chapter, we have proposed a GPU-based object-order ray-tracing algorithm that allows for the tracing of incoherent secondary rays at interactive speeds. We have shown that this is possible in the context of a typical rasterization-based deferred shading rendering engine, without changing the architecture from linear batch processing to global pooling of randomly accessible scene data.

The presented algorithm is another step toward mingling rasterization and ray-tracing approaches. In future work, this mingling could be taken even further by re-introducing fixed-size shallow geometric hierarchies inside triangle batches. This way, the coherency that is present in most chunks of triangles could be exploited further and the linear cost of crowded ray grid cells with many triangles could be improved upon.

Future work could also apply multi-level grids as described by [Kalojanov et al. 11] to adapt grid resolution to uneven tessellation. This would additionally help in skipping potentially larger empty spaces in vast scenes. Furthermore, transferring occlusion culling as it is commonly used in rasterization-based rendering to secondary ray tracing could be an interesting topic.

The presented algorithm makes extensive use of the flexibility that is offered by the DirectX 11 graphics pipeline. With the tessellation and geometry shader stages, the graphics pipeline currently offers two junction points for load balancing, redistributing work across parallel GPU threads on the fly. However, passing data between these stages is still difficult. Currently, there does not appear to be an efficient way of passing entire triangles down to the pixel shader stage without resorting to a separate geometry stream out pass. DirectX 11.1 introduced unordered resource writes in all shader stages, which slightly improves the situation. While the feature is not widely available on PCs yet, it is likely to spread with the introduction of the next console generation. Still, having to resort to global memory writes seems like a suboptimal solution considering the availability of fast on-chip shared memory on today's graphics hardware.

Bibliography

[Aila and Laine 09] Timo Aila and Samuli Laine. "Understanding the Efficiency of Ray Traversal on GPUs." In *Proceedings of the Conference on High Performance Graphics 2009*, pp. 145–149. New York: ACM, 2009.

[Bikker 12] J. Bikker. "Improving Data Locality for Efficient In-Core Path Tracing." *Computer Graphics Forum* 31:6 (2012), 1936–1947.

[Crassin et al. 11] Cyril Crassin, Fabrice Neyret, Miguel Sainz, Simon Green, and Elmar Eisemann. "Interactive Indirect Illumination Using Voxel-Based Cone Tracing: An Insight." In *ACM SIGGRAPH 2011 Talks*, p. Article no. 20, 2011.

[Gessler et al. 09] Alexander Gessler, Thomas Schulze, Kim Kulling, and David Nadlinger. "Open Asset Import Library." http://assimp.sourceforge.net, 2009.

[Guntury and Narayanan 12] Sashidhar Guntury and P.J. Narayanan. "Raytracing Dynamic Scenes on the GPU Using Grids." *IEEE Transactions on Visualization and Computer Graphics* 18 (2012), 5–16.

[Hanika et al. 10] Johannes Hanika, Alexander Keller, and Hendrik P. A. Lensch. "Two-Level Ray Tracing with Reordering for Highly Complex Scenes." In *Proceedings of Graphics Interface 2010*, pp. 145–152. Toronto: Canadian Information Processing Society, 2010.

[Hasselgren et al. 05] Jon Hasselgren, Tomas Akenine-Möller, and Lennart Ohlsson. "Conservative Rasterization." In *GPU Gems 2: Programming Techniques for High-Performance Graphics and General-Purpose Computation*, edited by Matt Pharr and Randima Fernando, Chapter 42. Upper Saddle River, NJ: Addison-Wesley Professional, 2005.

[Kalojanov and Slusallek 09] Javor Kalojanov and Philipp Slusallek. "A Parallel Algorithm for Construction of Uniform Grids." In *Proceedings of the Conference on High Performance Graphics 2009*, pp. 23–28. New York: ACM, 2009.

[Kalojanov et al. 11] Javor Kalojanov, Markus Billeter, and Philipp Slusallek. "Two-Level Grids for Ray Tracing on GPUs." In *EG 2011 Full Papers*, pp. 307–314. Aire-le-Ville, Switzerland: Eurographics Association, 2011.

[Merrill and Grimshaw 11] Duane Merrill and Andrew Grimshaw. "High Performance and Scalable Radix Sorting: A Case Study of Implementing Dynamic Parallelism for GPU Computing." *Parallel Processing Letters* 21:2 (2011), 245–272.

[Meyer et al. 10] Quirin Meyer, Jochen Sußmuth, Gerd Sußner, Marc Stamminger, and Günther Greiner. "On Floating-Point Normal Vectors." *Computer Graphics Forum* 29:4 (2010), 1405–1409.

[Pharr et al. 97] Matt Pharr, Craig Kolb, Reid Gershbein, and Pat Hanrahan. "Rendering Complex Scenes with Memory-Coherent Ray Tracing."

In *Proceedings of the 24th Annual Conference on Computer Graphics and Interactive Techniques, SIGGRAPH '97*, pp. 101–108. New York: ACM Press/Addison-Wesley Publishing Co., 1997.

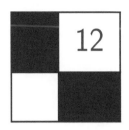

12

Quadtrees on the GPU
Jonathan Dupuy, Jean-Claude Iehl,
and Pierre Poulin

12.1 Introduction

Finding an appropriate mathematical representation for objects is a fundamental problem in computer graphics. Because they benefit from hardware acceleration, polygon meshes provide an appealing solution and are widely adopted by both interactive and high-quality renderers. But in order to maintain optimal rendering performance, special care must be taken to guarantee that each polygon projects into more than a few pixels. Below this limit, the Z-buffer starts aliasing, and the rasterizer's efficiency decreases drastically [AMD 10]. In the movie industry, this limitation is alleviated by using very high sampling rates, at the expense of dissuasive computation times. For applications that target interactivity, however, such as video games or simulators, such overhead is unaffordable.

Another solution is to adapt the mesh to produce optimal on-screen polygons. If it can be simplified and/or enriched on the fly, it is said to be a scalable representation. Quadtrees provide such a scheme for grids and have been used extensively since the early days of rendering, especially for terrain synthesis. Despite their wide adoption, though, the first full GPU implementation was only introduced last year [Mistal 13]. This is due to two main reasons. First, quadtrees are usually implemented recursively, which makes them hard to handle in parallel by their very nature (see the implementation of Strugar [Strugar 09], for instance). Second, they require a T-junction removal system, which may result in an increase of draw calls [Andersson 07], adding non-negligible overhead to the CPU. As an alternative to quadtrees, instanced subdivision patches have been investigated [Cantlay 11, Fernandes and Oliveira 12]. Although such solutions can run entirely on the GPU, their scalability is currently too limited by the hardware.

In this chapter, we present a new implementation suitable for the GPU, which completely relieves the CPU without sacrificing scalability. In order to update the quadtree in parallel, we use the linear quadtree representation, which is presented

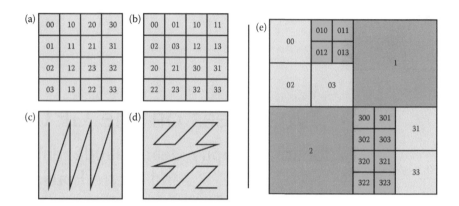

Figure 12.1. (a) Column major ordering versus (b) Morton ordering and (c,d) the curves they form. The curve formed by Morton ordering in (d) is often denoted as a Z-order curve. (e) Bit codes of a linear quadtree, built from the ordering of (b). The subdivision levels for the blue, green, and red nodes are respectively 1, 2, and 3.

in the next section. At render time, a square subdivision patch is instanced with a unique location and scale for each node. By employing a distance-based LOD criterion, we will show that T-junctions can be removed completely using a simple tessellation shader.

12.2   Linear Quadtrees

Linear quadtrees were introduced by Gargantini as a nonrecursive alternative to regular quadtrees [Gargantini 82]. In this data structure, each node is represented by its subdivision level and a unique bit code, and only the leaves are stored in memory. The code is a concatenation of 2-bit words, each identifying the quadrant in which the node is located relative to its parent. If these words are chosen so as to form a Z-order curve, then their concatenation forms a Morton code. In Figure 12.1, for instance, the codes 0, 1, 2, and 3 are mapped to the upper left (UL), upper right (UR), lower left (LL), and lower right (LR) quadrants, respectively. This last property allows direct translation to row/column major numbering (Figure 12.1(e)) by bit de-interleaving the code.

12.2.1   Representation

Similarly to Shaffer [Shaffer 90], we use a single integer to represent each node. The rightmost bits are reserved for the subdivision level, and the adjacent bits are left for the bit code. Below is the bit representation of the 32-bit word encoding the red node whose code is 321 in Figure 12.1. Bits irrelevant to the code are denoted by the "_" character.

```
// de-interleave a 32-bit word using the Shift-Or algorithm
uint lt_undilate_2(in uint x) {
  x = (x | (x >> 1u)) & 0x33333333;
  x = (x | (x >> 2u)) & 0x0F0F0F0F;
  x = (x | (x >> 4u)) & 0x00FF00FF;
  x = (x | (x >> 8u)) & 0x0000FFFF;
  return (x & 0x0000FFFF);
}

// retrieve column major position and level from a 32-bit word
void lt_decode_2_15(in uint key, out uint level, out uvec2 p) {
  level = key & 0xF;
  p.x = lt_undilate_2((key >> 4u) & 0x05555555);
  p.y = lt_undilate_2((key >> 5u) & 0x05555555);
}
```

Listing 12.1. GLSL node decoding routines. There are many ways to de-interleave a word. For a thorough overview of existing methods, we refer to [Raman and Wise 08].

```
msb                                          lsb
---- ---- ---- ---- ---- --11 1001 0011
```

The first four bits store the level ($0011_b = 3$ in this example), leaving the remaining 28 bits for the code. Using this configuration, a 32-bit word can store up to a $28/2 + 1 = 15$-level quadtree, including the root node. In Listing 12.1, we provide the procedures to retrieve the column major numbering from this representation. Naturally, more levels require longer words. Because longer integers are currently unavailable on many GPUs, we emulate them using integer vectors, where each component represents a 32-bit wide portion of the entire code. For more details, please see our implementation, where we provide a 30-level quadtree using the GLSL uvec2 datatype.

12.2.2 Updating the Structure

When relying on quadtrees to generate progressive meshes, efficient updates are critical. Fortunately, node splitting and merging can be accomplished in a very straightforward manner with linear trees. The following bit representations match the parent of the node given in the previous example with its four children:

```
         msb                                      lsb
parent:  ---- ---- ---- ---- ---- ---- 1110 0010
node:    ---- ---- ---- ---- ---- --11 1001 0011
UL:      ---- ---- ---- ---- ---- 1110 0100 0100
UR:      ---- ---- ---- ---- ---- 1110 0101 0100
LL:      ---- ---- ---- ---- ---- 1110 0110 0100
LR:      ---- ---- ---- ---- ---- 1110 0111 0100
```

```
// generate children nodes from a quadtree encoded
// in a 32-bit word
void lt_children_2_15(in uint key, out uint children[4]) {
  key = (++key & 0xF) | ((key & ~0xF) << 2u);
  children[0] = key;
  children[1] = key | 0x10;
  children[2] = key | 0x20;
  children[3] = key | 0x30;
}

// generate parent node from a quadtree encoded
// in a 32-bit word
uint lt_parent_2_15(in uint key) {
  return ((--key & 0xF) | ((key >> 2u) & 0x3FFFFFF0));
}
```

Listing 12.2. Splitting and merging procedures in GLSL.

Note that compared to the node representation, the levels differ by 1 and the bit codes are either 2-bit expansions or contractions. The GLSL code to generate these representations is shown in Listing 12.2. It simply consists of an arithmetic addition, a bitshift, and logical operations and is thus very cheap.

12.2.3 GPU Implementation

Managing a linear quadtree on the GPU requires two buffers and a geometry shader. During initialization, we store the base hierarchy (we start with the root node only) in one of the buffers. Whenever the nodes must be updated, the buffer is iterated over by the geometry shader, set to write into the second buffer. If a node needs to be split, it emits four new words, and the original code is deleted. Conversely, when four nodes must merge, they are replaced by their parent's code. In order to avoid generating four copies of the same node in memory, we only emit the code once from the UL child, identified using the test provided in Listing 12.3. For the nodes that do not require any intervention, their code is simply emitted, unchanged.

```
// check if node is the upper left child
// in a 32-bit word
bool lt_is_upper_left_2_15(in uint key) {
  return ((key & 0x30) == 0x00);
}
```

Listing 12.3. Determining if the node represents the UL child of its parent representation. Only the first 2-bit word of the Morton code has to be tested.

It is clear that this approach maps very well to the GPU. Note, however, that an iteration only permits a single split or merge operation per node. Thus when more are needed, multiple buffer iterations should be performed. At each new iteration, we swap the first and second buffer so that the newest hierarchy is processed by the geometry shader. This strategy is also known as double, or ping-pong, buffering. In our implementation, a single buffer iteration is performed at the beginning of each frame.

12.3 Scalable Grids on the GPU

So far, we have only discussed a parallel implementation of a quadtree. In this section, we present a complete OpenGL pipeline to extract a scalable grid from this representation, which in turn can be used to render terrains, as well as parametric surfaces.

12.3.1 LOD Function

Similarly to [Strugar 09], we essentially exploit the quadtree to build the final grid by drawing multiple copies of a static grid mesh. Each copy is associated with a node, so that it can be translated and scaled to the correct location. Listing 12.4 shows how the transformations are extracted from the codes and applied to each vertex of the instanced grid in a vertex shader.

```glsl
layout(location = 0) in vec2 i_mesh; // instanced vertices
layout(location = 1) in uint i_node; // per instance data

// retrieve normalized coordinates and size of the cell
void lt_cell_2_15(in uint key, out vec2 p, out float size) {
    uvec2 pos;
    uint level;

    lt_decode_2_15(key, level, pos);
    size = 1.0 / float(1u << level); // in [0,1]
    p = pos * size; // in [0,1)
}

void main() {
    vec2 translation;
    float scale;

    // pass on vertex position and scale
    lt_cell_2_15(i_node, translation, scale);
    vec2 p = i_mesh * scale + translation;
    gl_Position = vec4(p, scale, 1.0);
}
```

Listing 12.4. GLSL vertex shader for rendering a scalable grid.

In order to guarantee that the transformed vertices produce rasterizer-friendly polygons, a distance-based criterion can be used. Indeed, under perspective projection, the image plane size s at distance z from the camera can be determined analytically with the relation

$$s(z) = 2z \tan \left(\frac{\alpha}{2} \right),$$

where $\alpha \in (0, \pi]$ is the horizontal field of view. Thus if polygons scale proportionally to s, they are guaranteed to be of approximately constant size in screen space. Based on this observation, we derived the following routines to determine whether a node should be split or merged:

```
float z1 = distance(eye, node_center);
float z2 = distance(eye, parent_center);

if( k * node_size > s(z1) ) split();
else if( k * parent_size < s(z2) ) merge();
else keep();
```

Here, k is an arbitrary positive constant that controls the average number of on-screen cells. We found that using $k = 8$ produces good results, resulting in roughly 36 (6×6) cells in the image plane. Therefore, when the instanced grid has $n \times n$ polygons, the average on-screen polygon density is $36n^2$.

12.3.2   T-Junction Removal

The core of our meshing scheme closely resembles that of [Strugar 09]; both methods rely on mesh instancing and a distance-based LOD function to build a scalable grid. As such, Strugar's vertex morphing scheme can be used to avoid T-junctions. We suggest next an alternative solution, which relies on tessellation shaders.

Before transforming the vertices of the instanced grid, we invoke a tessellation control shader and evaluate the LOD function at each edge of its polygons. We then divide their length by the computed value and multiply the result by $\sqrt{2}$. This operation safely refines the grid polygons nearing neighbor cells of smaller resolution; its output is illustrated in Figure 12.2. Our GLSL tessellation control shader code is shown in Listing 12.5.

12.3.3   OpenGL Pipeline

Our OpenGL implementation consists of three passes. The first pass updates the quadtree, using the algorithm described in Section 12.2. After the tree has been updated, a culling kernel iterates over the nodes, testing their intersection with the view frustum. Note that we can reuse the buffer holding the nodes before

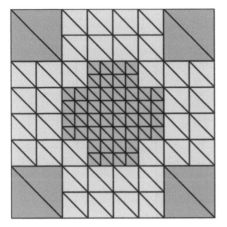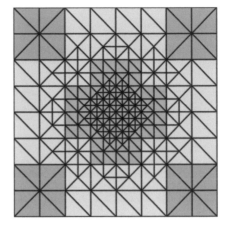

Figure 12.2. Multiresolution mesh before (left) and after (right) tessellation. T-junctions have been completely removed.

the first pass to store the results. Since we only have access to the leaf nodes, no hierarchical optimizations can be performed, so each node is tested independently. This scheme still performs very well nonetheless, as it is very adequate for the parallel architecture of the GPU. Finally, the third pass renders the scalable grid to the back buffer, using the algorithms described earlier in this section. The full pipeline is diagrammed in Figure 12.3.

```glsl
layout(vertices = 4) out; // quad patches
uniform vec3 u_eye_pos; // eye position
void main() {
  // get data from vertex stage
  vec4 e1 = gl_in[gl_InvocationID].gl_Position;
  vec4 e2 = gl_in[(gl_InvocationID+1)%4].gl_Position;

  // compute edge center and LOD function
  vec3 ec = vec3(0.5 * e1.xy + 0.5 * e2.xy, 0);
  float s = 2.0 * distance(u_eye_pos, ec) * u_tan_fov;

  // compute tessellation factors (1 or 2)
  const float k = 8.0;
  float factor = e1.z * k * sqrt(2.0) / s;
  gl_TessLevelOuter[gl_InvocationID] = factor;
  gl_TessLevelInner[gl_InvocationID%2] = factor;

  // send data to subsequent stages
  gl_out[gl_InvocationID].gl_Position =
    gl_in[gl_InvocationID].gl_Position;
}
```

Listing 12.5. GLSL tessellation control shader for rendering a scalable grid.

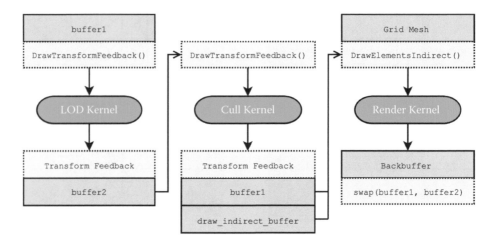

Figure 12.3. OpenGL pipeline of our method.

12.3.4 Results

To demonstrate the effectiveness of our method, we wrote a renderer for terrains and another one for parametric surfaces. Some results can be seen in Figures 12.4 and 12.5. In Table 12.1, we give the CPU and GPU timings of a zoom-in/zoom-out sequence using the terrain renderer at 720p. The camera's orientation was fixed, looking downward, so that the terrain would occupy the whole frame buffer, thus maintaining constant rasterization activity. The testing platform is an Intel Core i7-2600K, running at 3.40 GHz, and a Radeon 7950 GPU. Note that the CPU activity only consists of OpenGL uniform variables and driver management. On current implementations, such tasks run asynchronously to the GPU.

As demonstrated by the reported numbers, the performance of our implementation is both fast and stable. Naturally, the average GPU rendering time depends on how the terrain is shaded. In our experiment, we use solid wireframe shading [Gateau 07] which, despite requiring a geometry shader, is fairly cheap.

Kernel	CPU (ms)	GPU (ms)	CPU stdev	GPU stdev
LOD	0.096	0.067	0.039	0.026
Cull	0.068	0.077	0.035	0.032
Render	0.064	1.271	0.063	0.080

Table 12.1. CPU and GPU timings and their respective standard deviation over a zoom-in sequence of 1000 frames.

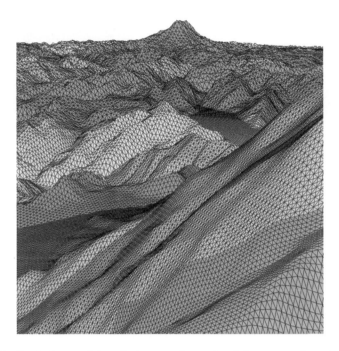

Figure 12.4. Crack-free, multiresolution terrain rendered from a quadtree implemented entirely on the GPU. The alternating colors show the different levels of the quadtree.

12.4 Discussion

This section provides a series of answered questions, which should give better insights on the properties and possible extensions of our implementation.

How much memory should be allocated for the buffers containing the nodes? This depends on the α and `k` values, which control how fast distant nodes should be merged. The buffers should be able to store at least $3 \times$`max_level`$+1$ nodes and do not need to exceed a capacity of $4^{\texttt{max\_level}}$ nodes. The lower bound corresponds to a perfectly restricted quadtree, where each neighboring cell differs by one level of subdivision at most. The higher bound gives the number of cells at the finest subdivision level.

Is the quadtree prone to floating-point precision issues? There are no issues regarding the tree structure itself, as each node is represented with bit sequences only. However, problems may occur when extracting the location and scale factors applied to the instanced grid during the rendering pass, in Listing 12.4. The 15-level quadtree does not have this issue, but higher levels will, eventually. A simple solution to delay the problem on OpenGL4+ hardware is to use double precision, which should provide sufficient comfort for most applications.

Figure 12.5. Crack-free, multiresolution parametric surfaces produced on the GPU with our renderer.

Could fractional tessellation be used to produce continuous subdivisions? If the T-junctions are removed with the CDLOD morphing function [Strugar 09], any mode can be used. Our proposed alternative approach does not have restrictions regarding the inner tessellation levels, but the outer levels must be set to exact powers of two. Therefore, fractional odd tessellation will not work. The even mode can be used, though.

Are there any significant reasons to use tessellation rather than the CDLOD morphing function for T-junctions? The only advantage of tessellation is flexibility, since arbitrary factors can be used. For some parametric surfaces, tessellation turned out to be essential because the quadtree we computed was not necessarily restricted. The phenomenon is visible in Figure 12.5, on the blue portions of the trefoil knot. If we had used the CDLOD method, a crack would have occurred. For terrains, the distance-based criterion ensures that the nodes are restricted, so both solutions are valid.

There are two ways to increase polygon density: either use the GPU tessellator, or refine the instanced grid. Which approach is best? This will naturally depend on the platform. Our renderers provide tools to modify both the grid and the GPU tessellation values, so that their impact can be thoroughly measured. On the Radeon 7950, we observed that tessellation levels could be increased up to a factor of 8 without performance penalties, as long as the average on-screen polygon size remained reasonable.

12.5 Conclusion

We have presented a novel implementation for quadtrees running completely on the GPU. It takes advantage of linear trees to alleviate the recursive nature of common tree implementations, offering a simple and efficient data structure for parallel processors. While this work focuses on quadtrees, this representation can also be used for higher dimensional trees, such as octrees. Using the same distance-based criterion, the *Transvoxel* algorithm [Lengyel 10] could be employed to produce a crack-free volume extractor, running entirely on the GPU. We expect such an implementation to be extremely fast as well.

Acknowledgments

This work was partly funded in Canada by GRAND and in France by ANR. Jonathan Dupuy acknowledges additional financial support from an Explo'ra Doc grant from "région Rhône-Alpes," France.

Bibliography

[AMD 10] AMD. "Tessellation for All." http://community.amd.com/ community/amd-blogs/game/blog/2010/11/29/tessellation-for-all, 2010.

[Andersson 07] Johan Andersson. "Terrain Rendering in Frostbite Using Procedural Shader Splatting." In *ACM SIGGRAPH 2007 Courses*, pp. 38–58. New York: ACM, 2007.

[Cantlay 11] Iain Cantlay. "DirectX 11 Terrain Tessellation." White paper, http://developer.nvidia.com/sites/default/files/akamai/gamedev/files/ sdk/11/TerrainTessellation_WhitePaper.pdf, 2011.

[Fernandes and Oliveira 12] António Ramires Fernandes and Bruno Oliveira. "GPU Tessellation: We Still Have a LOD of Terrain to Cover." In *OpenGL Insights*, edited by Patrick Cozzi and Christophe Riccio, pp. 145–162. Boca Raton, FL: CRC Press, 2012.

[Gargantini 82] Irene Gargantini. "An Effective Way to Represent Quadtrees." *Communications of the ACM* 25:12 (1982), 905–910.

[Gateau 07] Samuel Gateau. "Solid Wireframe." http://developer. download.nvidia.com/SDK/10.5/direct3d/Source/SolidWireframe/Doc/ SolidWireframe.pdf, 2007.

[Lengyel 10] Eric Lengyel. "Voxel-Based Terrain for Real-Time Virtual Simulations." Ph.D. thesis, University of California, Davis, CA, 2010.

[Mistal 13] Benjamin Mistal. "GPU Terrain Subdivision and Tessellation." In *GPU Pro 4: Advanced Rendering Techniques*, edited by Wolfgang Engel, Chapter 1. Boca Raton, FL: A K Peters/CRC Press, 2013.

[Raman and Wise 08] Rajeev Raman and David Stephen Wise. "Converting to and from Dilated Integers." *IEEE Transactions on Computers* 57:4 (2008), 567–573.

[Shaffer 90] Clifford A. Shaffer. "Bit Interleaving for Quad or Octrees." In *Graphics Gems*, edited by Andrew S. Glassner, pp. 443–447. San Diego, CA: Academic Press, 1990.

[Strugar 09] Filip Strugar. "Continuous Distance-Dependent Level of Detail for Rendering Heightmaps." *Journal of Graphics, GPU, and Game Tools* 14:4 (2009), 57–74.

13

Two-Level Constraint Solver and Pipelined Local Batching for Rigid Body Simulation on GPUs
Takahiro Harada

13.1 Introduction

GPUs are attractive processors to execute large-scale dynamic physics simulations because of their high bandwidth and computational power. Studies on accelerating relatively simple simulations include particle-based [Harada et al. 07], cloth [Zeller 05], and grid-based fluid [Harris 04] simulations. However, there are few works on accelerating rigid body simulation using GPUs. Rigid body simulation in general consists of broad-phase collision detection, narrow-phase collision detection, and constraint solving [van den Bergen 03]. Each stage has challenges.

This chapter presents a two-level constraint solver designed for the GPU. We first give a general description of the solver and then present a GPU implementation. The two-level constraint solver performs two preparations: global split and local batching. Local batching is especially challenging for GPUs because the naïve implementation of batching is a serial algorithm. We present pipelined local batching, which parallelizes local batching by pipelining the operation and using a SIMD lane as a stage of the pipeline.[1] With pipelined local batching executed on the GPU, the entire constraint solver is completed on the GPU. Constraints in benchmark scenes are solved using the two-level constraint solver on the GPU to analyze the performance. This chapter is an extension of the work presented in [Harada 11]; this chapter also presents pipelined batching, which overcomes issues of local batching presented in [Harada 11], and a detailed performance analysis.

---

[1] We use terminology for AMD GPUs. A SIMD is a compute unit that can operate independently and is called a core on CPUs. An ALU unit in a SIMD is called a SIMD lane.

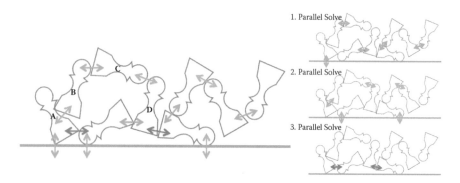

Figure 13.1. Batched constraints (left) and how they are solved in three steps (right).

13.2   Rigid Body Simulation

13.2.1   Simulation Pipeline

Rigid body simulation has been studied for decades. To realize interaction between bodies, colliding pairs must be detected dynamically, and a collision must be resolved for each of the detected pairs. Studies of implementing collision detection on GPUs include [Harada 07, Grand 07, Liu et al. 10].

After colliding pairs are detected, the normal directional component of relative velocity at each contact point must be greater than zero to prevent further penetration [Ericson 04]. This is a condition called velocity constraint and must be satisfied at all the contact points. Because the velocity constraint is not an equality, this is a linear complementarity problem (LCP) [Eberly 03]. LCPs can be solved using the projected Gauss-Seidel method, which is gaining popularity in a real-time application [Catto 05]. The Gauss-Seidel method can solve only a linear system, but the projected Gauss-Seidel method can solve LCP; it adds clamping a solution after solving a row of the system to the Gauss-Seidel method. However, the serial nature of the algorithm makes it difficult to implement in parallel.

13.2.2   Constraint Solver

Batched constraint solver. To solve constraints in parallel, dependency must be checked among the constraints. If we look at the constraints connecting A,B and C,D of the example shown in Figure 13.1, we see that they are independent constraints (i.e., they do not share any body), thus they can be solved in parallel.

We can collect those independent constraints and define a group of constraints, which is called a batch. These constraints in a batch can be solved in parallel because they are independent. After a batch is created, independent constraints are collected from the remaining constraints to create another batch. This operation is repeated until all the constraints are assigned to a batch. Once constraints are divided into batches, we can solve constraints within a batch in parallel, although synchronization is necessary among solving different batches because they have dependency. Figure 13.1 illustrates batched constraints in which constraints in the same batch are drawn using the same color.

Global batching. Batching classifies all the constraints into independent batches. An algorithm for batching is shown in Algorithm 13.1. It iterates through all the constraints in the simulation and checks the dependency of a constraint against the constraints stored in a batch. If a constraint does not have dependency to the constraints in the batch (line 7), the constraint is added to the batch (line 8); otherwise, the constraint is stored in another buffer as a remaining constraint (line 13).

Once all the constraints are checked, the batch is closed (line 16). Then the next batch is opened, the remaining constraints from the previous iteration are processed one by one, and dependency is checked against the current batch as for the first batch. This operation is repeated until all the constraints are assigned to a batch. We call this batching algorithm *global batching*, and a constraint solver that solves constraints using it a *global batch global constraint solver*.

```
 1: pairsSrc ← pairs
 2: pairsDst
 3: while pairsSrc.getSize() do
 4:     nConsumed = 0 // pair count scheduled in the batch
 5:     for pairsSrc.getSize() do
 6:         iPair = pairsSrc[i]
 7:         if !locked(iPair.x) and !locked(iPair.y) then
 8:             batch.add( iPair )
 9:             lock( iPair.x )
10:             lock( iPair.y )
11:             nConsumed++
12:         else
13:             pairsDst.add( iPair )
14:         end if
15:     end for
16:     if nConsumed = 0 then
17:         batch.close()
18:         clear( lockStatus )
19:     end if
20:     swap( pairSrc, pairsDst )
21: end while
22: batch.close()
```

Algorithm 13.1. Batch creation.

13.3   Two-Level Constraint Solver

This section presents the two-level constraint solver, which solves constraints in two stages. The reason for the split is to make the algorithm easy to parallelize and to localize expensive operations to improve the efficiency. This two-level approach is applicable for GPUs as well as for multi-core CPUs. Because the two-level constraint solver solves constraints in two steps, the batching, which is a serial computation, is also split into two steps (global split and local batching), each of which can be implemented in parallel.

13.3.1   Global Split

Constraints are split into several independent groups during the global split (a group is similar in concept to a simulation island). The objective of this split is to process groups in parallel. However, if all the constraints in the simulation are connected—as often happens—it just creates a single big group and we cannot split it into groups. Therefore, we first split constraints into groups, allowing some dependencies. Then independent groups are collected from all the groups to form a set of constraint groups. This operation is repeated until all the groups are assigned to one of the sets. After sets are created, constraint groups in a set can be processed in parallel; however, processing different sets must be serialized because they may depend on each other.

There are several spatial splits we can use, but we employ a two-dimensional regular split as shown in Figure 13.2 because the simplicity of the connectivity of cells of a regular split makes it easy to create sets of constraint groups. Constraints in a cell form a constraint group. Although adjacent cells can have a constraint sharing a body, one-ring neighbor cells do not have a connected constraint. Therefore, cells (or groups) are split into four independent sets (Figure 13.2).

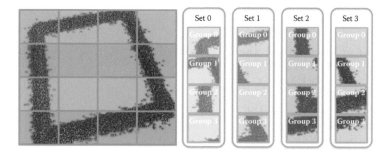

Figure 13.2. Global split creates sets of constraint groups.

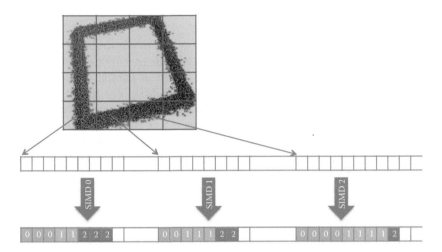

Figure 13.3. Constraints in a group are stored in a contiguous memory. Each group has the offset to the memory and number of constraints. Local batching sorts constraints for a group by batch index using a SIMD.

13.3.2 Local Batching

After the global split, constraint groups are independent in a set. In other words, groups in a set can be processed in parallel. A group is processed by a SIMD of the GPU. There are, however, still dependencies among constraints in a group. Therefore, batching is necessary to process them in parallel in each group. We call this *local batching*, in contrast to the global batching described in Section 13.2.2, because batching for this step must consider only the connectivity of constraints in a group that consists of localized constraints.

One big difference between global and local batching is the width of the batch we must create. For global batching, the optimal batch width is the hardware computation width. For a GPU, which executes thousands of work items concurrently, we have to extract thousands of independent constraints to fill the hardware. However, because we assign a SIMD to solve constraints in a group, local batching requires creating a batch only with the SIMD width (e.g., on a GPU with a 64-wide SIMD, only 64 independent constraints have to be extracted). Creating a narrower batch is easier and computationally cheaper because the wider the batch, the more expensive the dependency check of constraints becomes.

The input of local batching is a set of constraints. Batches are created at this stage and batch index is calculated for each constraint. For the convenience of the constraint solver, constraints are sorted by batch indices. Figure 13.3 illustrates how constraints are stored.

13.3.3   Constraint Solver

Because the global split creates four dependent sets of constraint groups, as discussed in Section 13.3.1, four sequential solves are executed. Within a set of constraint groups, constraint groups can be solved in parallel because they are independent. A constraint group is solved by a SIMD. The SIMD sequentially reads constraints of the group from the beginning of the section of the constraint buffer using a SIMD lane to read a constraint. Once constraints are read by all lanes, it compares batch indices of the constraints. If constraints belong to different batches, they have a dependency and are not able to be solved in parallel. Thus, it selects a batch index to solve and if the batch index of a constraint is different from the batch index, the SIMD lane is masked and the constraint is not solved. After solving constraints in SIMD, it counts the number of constraints solved at this step. Then it adds the count to the offset of the constraint buffer and repeats the operations until all constraints in the group are processed.

13.4   GPU Implementation

The two-level constraint solver has challenges when it comes to implementation on a GPU. In particular, batching described in Section 13.2.2 cannot be parallelized easily. Thus, we propose pipelined local batching that extracts parallelism on the batching by pipelining the algorithm to utilize wide SIMD architecture while keeping the quality of batches high.

13.4.1   Global Split

Because we use a two-dimensional grid for the split, the belonging cell of a constraint can be found from the world position of the constraint. As a unique cell index is assigned for each cell, cell indices are calculated for all constraints. Once that is done, constraints are sorted by cell index [Merrill and Grimshaw 11]. After the sort, bounds of constraints for cells are searched by comparing cell indices of adjacent constraints. We must ensure that the size of the cell is larger than the largest extent of rigid bodies; otherwise, non-adjacent cells can have a dependency because they share the same rigid body.

Host code can be written as follows. It uses parallel primitives such as radix sort and prefix scan. An OpenCL implementation can be found (for example, [Harada and Howes 12] and [Coumans 13]).

```
//    Compute sortData for each contact
execute(SetSortDataKernel, contacts, bodies, sortData);
//    Sort sortData. Keys are cell index
RadixSort(sortData);
//    Count number of entries per cell
BoundSearch(sortData, counts);
//    Convert counts to offsets
```

```
PrefixScan(counts, offsets);
//    Reorder contacts using sortData
execute(ReorderContactKernel, contacts, contactsSorted, sortData);
```

SetSortDataKernel computes the cell index and write a key value pair for each contact as follows.

```
__kernel
void SetSortDataKernel(__global Contact* gContact,
    __global Body* gBodies,
    __global int2* gSortDataOut)
{
    int gIdx = get_global_id(0);
    int aIdx = gContact[gIdx].m_bodyA;
    int bIdx = gContact[gIdx].m_bodyB;

    float4 p = gBodies[aIdx].m_pos;
    int xIdx = convertToCellIdx(p.x);
    int zIdx = convertToCellIdx(p.z);

    gSortDataOut[gIdx].x = computeUniqueId( xIdx, zIdx );
    gSortDataOut[gIdx].y = gIdx;
}
```

Once the key value pairs are sorted, contacts are reordered in `ReorderContactKernel`.

```
__kernel
void ReorderContactKernel(__global Contact* in,
    __global Contact4* out,
    __global int2* sortData)
{
    int gIdx = get_global_id(0);
    int srcIdx = sortData[gIdx].y;
    out[gIdx] = in[srcIdx];
}
```

13.4.2 Pipelined Local Batching

Each constraint group can be processed in parallel; thus, it is assigned to a SIMD of a GPU in a single kernel dispatch. However, the batching algorithm described in Section 13.2.2 is a completely serial process, which is inefficient if it is executed on a GPU. The proposed pipelined local batching transforms the serial batching algorithm into a pipelined parallel algorithm. Pipelined local batching decomposes the `while` loop of Algorithm 13.1 and processes them in parallel. However, each iteration of the `while` loop is dependent on the previous iteration and it is not straightforward to parallelize.

The proposed pipelined local batching uses a SIMD lane as a stage of the pipeline to create a batch. Pipelined local batching starts by reading a constraint of the group from the input buffer at the first stage by SIMD lane 0. The lane checks whether it can be inserted in batch 0. If the constraint is independent from constraints in batch 0, batch index 0 is assigned to the constraint and the constraint is deleted from the pipeline; otherwise, the constraint is forwarded to the next stage of the pipeline, which is processed by SIMD lane 1. This is one cycle of the pipeline. During the first cycle, only SIMD lane 0 is active. On the next cycle, SIMD lane 0 reads the next constraint from the input buffer and other lanes receive constraints from the previous stage of the pipeline. If the first constraint is forwarded from SIMD lane 0 after the first cycle, SIMD lane 1 receives the constraint. Then each lane checks the dependency of the constraint to the batch. If it is independent, it sets the batch index to the constraint and the data is deleted from the pipeline; otherwise, it is delivered to the next stage of the pipeline. As the number of cycles increases, more constraints flow on the pipeline and SIMD lanes at a deeper pipeline stage are filled with data.

While serial batching starts creation of the second batch once the first batch is created, pipelined local batching finishes batching soon after the first batch is created. When the last constraint of the group is processed by lane 0, most of the batches are completed and the pipeline finishes working once all the data in the pipeline is processed.

Figure 13.4 illustrates pipelined local batching, and Algorithm 13.2 shows pseudo code. Local data store (LDS) is used to forward data between stages processed by each lane of a SIMD. The SIMD width of the GPU used for this chapter is 64; therefore, it can create up to 64 batches. If a constraint could not be inserted in the last lane, it overflows the pipeline. Overflowed constraints can be stored in a buffer and processed after all the constraints are processed once. However, we did not implement this because we have not encountered an overflow for our test cases.

```
 1: nRemainings ← pairs.getSize() // number of pairs not batched yet
 2: while nRemainings > 0 do
 3:     iPair ← fetchFromBuffer()
 4:     if !locked(iPair.x) and !locked(iPair.y) then
 5:         batch.add( iPair )
 6:         lock( iPair.x )
 7:         lock( iPair.y )
 8:     else
 9:         forwardPairToNextLane( iPair )
10:     end if
11:     nRemainings = countRemainingPairs()
12: end while
```

Algorithm 13.2. Pipelined batching.

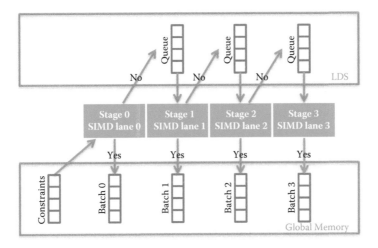

Figure 13.4. Pipelined local batching.

Pipelined local batching always creates the same batches as serial batching, whereas other parallel batching using atomics usually creates different batches and the number of batches is greater than the number created by the serial algorithm. Keeping the number of batches small is important to keep the computation time of the expensive constraint solver low, as discussed in Section 13.2.

OpenCL kernel code for pipelined batching can be found in Listing 13.1.

13.4.3 Constraint Solver

The constraints are solved by four subsequent kernel executions: one kernel execution for each set of constraint groups. Each dispatch assigns a SIMD for a constraint group within a set, and batched constraints are solved in parallel by checking batch indices. While the global constraint solver dispatches a kernel for each batch, the two-level constraint solver always executes four kernels in which a SIMD of the GPU repeats in-SIMD dispatches by itself until all the constraints belonging to the group are solved.

13.5 Comparison of Batching Methods

A batching method can be evaluated by two aspects: batching computation time and the performance of the constraint solver. Batching computation time is shorter when local batching is used because it can be executed in parallel and it needs to create batches only with the hardware SIMD width, while global batching must create batches with the processor width (the SIMD width times the number of SIMDs on the hardware).

```
__kernel
void PipelinedBatchingKernel()
{
  int start = gOffsets[get_group_id(0)];
  int i = start;
  int lIdx = get_local_id(0);

  //  0.  initialize
  nPairsInQueue(lIdx) = 0;
  clearLocks();

  if( lIdx == 0 )
  {
    ldsNRemainings = countRemainingPairs();
  }

  while( ldsNRemainings != 0 )
  {
    //  1. fetch one pair from buffer
    int4 iPair = make_int4(-1,0,0,0);
    if( lIdx == 0 )
    { //  SIMD lane 0 fetches from global memory
      iPair = make_int4( gPairs[i].x, gPairs[i].y, i, 0 );
    }
    else
    { //  other lanes fetch from queues
      if( nPairsInQueue(lIdx-1) != 0 )
      {
        iPair = ldsBuf[lIdx-1];
        nPairsInQueue(lIdx-1)--;
      }
    }

    //  2. check dependency of iPair to the batch
    bool notLocked = !locked( iPair.x ) && !locked( iPair.y );

    //  3. process iPair
    if( iPair.x != -1 )
    {
      if( notLocked )
      { //  iPair was independent. add to the batch
        lock( iPair.x ); lock( iPair.y );
        gBatchOut[iPair.z] = lIdx;
      }
      else
      { //  forward iPair to next lane
        ldsBuf[lIdx] = iPair;
        nPairsInQueue(lIdx)++;
      }
    }

    i++;
    if( lIdx == 0 )
      ldsNRemainings = countRemainingPairs();
  }
}
```

Listing 13.1. Simplified kernel code of pipelined local batching.

A measure of performance of a constraint solver is the total number of batches created by a batching method. As the number of batches increases, the number of serial computations and synchronization increases, which results in longer constraint solving time. When a rigid body in the simulation is connected by n constraints, at least n batches are necessary to batch these constraints because all of them must be executed in different batches. Thus, the number of batches created by global batching is more than $n_{\text{max}}^{\text{global}} = \max(n_0, n_1, \cdots, n_m)$ for a simulation with m rigid bodies where n_i is the number of constraints connected to body i. When constraints are solved by the two-level constraint solver with local batching, it splits constraints into four constraint sets. The number of batches required for the set i is $n_{\text{max}}^{\text{local}_i} = \max(n_0^i, n_1^i, \cdots, n_{m_i}^i)$. Constraint sets must be processed sequentially; thus, the number of batches for the two-level constraint solver is $\sum_0^4 n_{\text{max}}^{\text{local}_i}$.

If all the constraints of the rigid body having $n_{\text{max}}^{\text{global}}$ constraints belong to constraint set 0, $n_{\text{max}}^{\text{local}_0} = n_{\text{max}}^{\text{global}}$. Therefore, the total number of batches of the two-level constraint solver cannot be less than the number of batches created by global batching ($\sum_0^4 n_{\text{max}}^{\text{local}_i} \geq n_{\text{max}}^{\text{local}_0} = n_{\text{max}}^{\text{global}}$).

If a simulation is executed on a highly parallel processor like a GPU, a large number of constraints can be solved at the same time. If the number of constraints in a batch is less than the hardware parallel width, the solving time for each batch should be roughly the same. Therefore, the number of batches can be an estimation of the computation time of a constraint solver. From the comparison of the number of batches, the two-level constraint solver cannot, in theory, outperform a parallel constraint solver using the optimal global batching.

13.6 Results and Discussion

The presented method is implemented on the GPU and constraints in six benchmark scenes (shown in Figure 13.5) are solved using an AMD Radeon HD7970 GPU. Table 13.1 shows the data from those simulations. We also implemented the global constraint solver, which uses the CPU for global batching and the GPU for solving constraints, to evaluate the performance of the two-level constraint solver. In our implementation, constraints are not stored one by one; instead, up to four constraints for a colliding pair are stored as a constraint pair.

13.6.1 Evaluation of Global Split

The space is split into 64×64 for a global split for all benchmarks. The number of splits is the only parameter we need to specify to implement our constraint solver, other than the physical parameters for a constraint solver. It is not likely that rigid bodies are distributed evenly in the simulation space (i.e., it is unlikely that all cells are populated in a simulation). Therefore, we want to set the number of

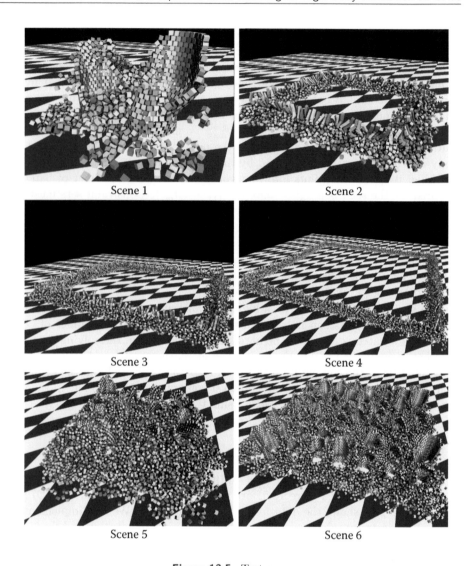

Figure 13.5. Test scenes.

nonempty cells to be about equal to the number of SIMDs on the GPU to assign a computation for each SIMD.

We assumed that the ratio of non-empty cells to all cells is about 0.5. Thus, when a 64×64 split is used, there are 2,048 non-empty cells in total, or 512 non-empty cells for each constraint set on average. The GPU we used for the experiments has 128 SIMDs. Therefore, the number of non-empty cells for each set is more than the number of SIMDs if the population ratio is 0.5. Figure 13.6

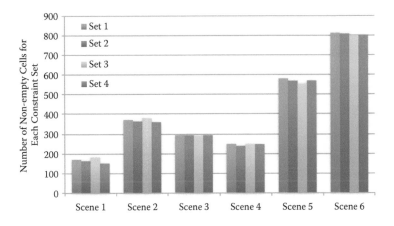

Figure 13.6. The number of non-empty cells for each scene.

shows the number of non-empty cells for each benchmark scene. Although scene 6 has about 800 non-empty cells for each set, scene 1 has less than 200 cells. Thus, all the SIMDs on the GPU are active. When the number of non-empty cells is small, we could increase the resolution of the spatial split. However, this results in a reduction of the number of constraints in a cell. At the same time, we do not want to reduce the number of constraints in a cell to fill SIMD lanes of each SIMD.

13.6.2 Computation Time

Computation times for pipelined local batching and constraint solvers are shown in Table 13.1. Pipelined local batching takes longer for a simulation with more constraints. Because constraints are processed by the pipeline one by one, the

	Scene 1	Scene 2	Scene 3	Scene 4	Scene 5	Scene 6
Number of bodies	1,200	6,240	12,640	19,040	9,600	38,400
Number of constraint pairs	1,763	13,203	21,904	33,209	16,684	67,263
Number of global batches	11	16	14	16	13	25
Pipelined local batching time	0.105	0.357	0.524	0.735	0.376	1.16
Global solver time (1 iter.)	0.264	0.415	0.45	0.552	0.367	0.999
Two-level solver time (1 iter.)	0.162	0.387	0.433	0.540	0.359	0.839
Max batch count in set1	6	12	11	16	13	17
Max batch count in set2	5	14	16	16	11	12
Max batch count in set3	5	12	14	14	11	13
Max batch count in set4	5	12	12	14	12	14

Table 13.1. Benchmark data (time in milliseconds).

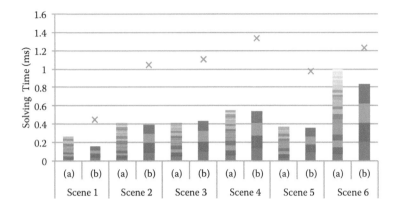

Figure 13.7. Time to solve constraints once in benchmarks using (a) the global and (b) the two-level constraint solvers. The plots show estimated time for the two-level constraint solver. Each color corresponds to a single-kernel execution. The global constraint solver requires several kernel executions, but the two-level constraint solver requires only four kernel executions. This graph plots the estimated computation time for the two-level constraint solver.

time taken for pipelined local batching is linear to the number of constraints in a group. Thus, batching for scene 6 takes longer than for other scenes.

A comparison of the computation time for the two-level and the global constraint solvers shown in Table 13.1 completely contradicts the expectation discussed in Section 13.5. For most scenes, the two-level constraint solver outperforms the global constraint solver, which needs the CPU for batching. The first potential explanation for the superior performance is that the number of batches for the two-level solver is smaller in the test scenes. We counted the number of batches for solvers for all scenes and confirmed that the total number of batches for the two-level constraint solver is more than that of the global constraint solver (Table 13.1).

To get a better understanding of this result, we performed more detailed analyses on the global constraint solver. The solving time for each batch is measured in Figure 13.8, and the number of constraints in each batch is counted in Figure 13.9. Figure 13.9 shows that no batch has more than 8,000 constraint pairs. The maximum number of concurrent works the GPU can execute is more than the number of SIMDs times the SIMD lane width: $128 \times 64 = 8,192$ for the GPU. Therefore, all constraints in a batch are processed concurrently. Batches with larger batch indices have constant computation times for all benchmarks; batches with smaller batch indices do not.

Figures 13.8 and 13.9 also show that batches that take longer to solve have more constraints. Batches with longer execution times, however, should have the same number of ALU operations per SIMD lane. The difference must come from

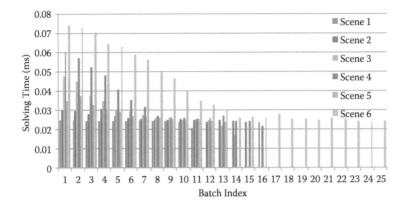

Figure 13.8. Solving time for a batch created by global batching.

memory access latency. As the number of constraint pairs increases, so does the demand for more memory operations. We can guess that the increase saturates the memory system at the point at which solver time exceeds the constant time.

We can also see solving time starts increasing when more than 2,000 constraint pairs are scheduled in a batch. As the number of constraints increases further, performance gradually decreases.

From Figure 13.8, we can get a lower bound of a batch's solving time as 0.021 ms. Multiplying the minimum time required to solve a batch by the number of batches for each benchmark scene, we can estimate the lower bound of the time required for the two-level constraint solver plotted in Figure 13.7. However, we can see that the measured solving time using the two-level constraint solver is

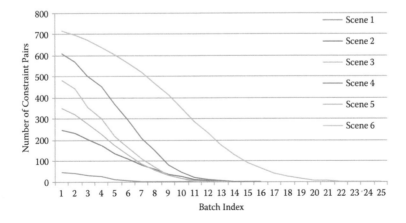

Figure 13.9. The number of constraint pairs in each batch when global batching is used.

more than twice as fast as the estimate. Because ALU operation time cannot be shortened, the only reason for superior performance is that the two-level constraint solver has faster memory access. This is possible only because of better utilization of the cache hierarchy.

Cache utilization is low for the global constraint solver because a rigid body is processed only once in a kernel and the assignment of a constraint to a SIMD is random for each kernel. Therefore, it cannot reuse any cached data from previous kernel executions. In contrast, localized constraint solving and in-SIMD batch dispatch of the two-level solver enable it to use cache efficiently. When a rigid body has multiple constraints in the region, it accesses the same body multiple times. Also, in-SIMD batch dispatch keeps a SIMD running until all the batches are processed; therefore, it is guaranteed that all batches of a constraint group are always solved by the same SIMD. This means that cached data remains in a SIMD, whereas the global constraint solver can assign any constraint from the entire simulation domain to a SIMD, which likely trashes the data in the cache for every batch solve.

Another advantage of in-SIMD dispatch is that it reduces GPU processing overhead by reducing the number of kernel dispatches. For scene 1, the global constraint solver executes 11 kernels (Table 13.1) while the two-level constraint solver executes four kernels to solve the system once. The two-level constraint solver has an advantage on the overhead as well.

From these analyses, we found that higher ALU occupancy is not the most important factor for achieving high performance of a constraint solver for a rigid body simulation on the GPU. To improve performance further, we need to reduce the memory traffic using optimizations such as memory compression and cache-aware ordering of constraint data.

The constraint solver using local batching is a persistent thread style implementation because a SIMD keeps processing until all constraints in a constraint group are solved [Aila and Laine 09]. They chose this implementation to improve the occupancy of the GPU, but we found that it has another positive impact: performance improvement because of better cache utilization.

Dispatching small kernels like the global constraint solver is simple to implement and worked well on old GPU architectures that do not have a memory hierarchy. However, today's GPUs have evolved and are equipped with a cache hierarchy. Our study has shown that the old GPU programming style, in which small kernels are dispatched frequently, cannot exploit current GPU architectures. Thus, a persistent thread style implementation is preferable for today's GPUs. An alternative solution would be to provide an API to choose a SIMD to run a computation so the GPU can benefit from the cache from different kernel executions.

This solver has been integrated to the Bullet 3 physics simulation library and it is used as a basis for the GPU rigid body simulation solver. Full source code is available at [Coumans 13].

Bibliography

[Aila and Laine 09] Timo Aila and Samuli Laine. "Understanding the Efficiency of Ray Traversal on GPUs." In *Proceedings of the Conference on High Performance Graphics 2009, HPG '09*, pp. 145–149. New York: ACM, 2009.

[Catto 05] E Catto. "Iterative Dynamics with Temporal Coherence." Presentation, Game Developers Conference, San Francisco, CA, March, 2005.

[Coumans 13] Erwin Coumans. "Bullet 3." http://bulletphysics.org/, 2013.

[Eberly 03] Dave H. Eberly. *Game Physics*. New York: Elsevier Science Inc., 2003.

[Ericson 04] Christer Ericson. *Real-Time Collision Detection*. San Francisco, CA: Morgan Kaufmann Publishers Inc., 2004.

[Grand 07] Scotte Le Grand. "Broad-Phase Collision Detection with CUDA." In *GPU Gems 3*, edited by Hubert Nguyen, pp. 697–722. Upper Saddle River, NJ: Addison-Wesley, 2007.

[Harada and Howes 12] Takahiro Harada and Lee Howes. "Heterogeneous Computing with OpenCL: Introduction to GPU Radix Sort." http://www.heterogeneouscompute.org/?page_id=7, 2012.

[Harada et al. 07] T. Harada, S. Koshizuka, and Y. Kawaguchi. "Smoothed Particle Hydrodynamics on GPUs." Presentation, Computer Graphics International Conference, Rio de Janeiro, Brazil, May, 2007.

[Harada 07] Takahiro Harada. "Real-Time Rigid Body Simulation on GPUs." In *GPU Gems 3*, edited by Hubert Nguyen, pp. 611–632. Upper Saddle River, NJ: Addison-Wesley, 2007.

[Harada 11] Takahiro Harada. "A Parallel Constraint Solver for a Rigid Body Simulation." In *SIGGRAPH Asia 2011 Sketches*, pp. 22:1–22:2. New York: ACM, 2011.

[Harris 04] Mark Harris. "Fast Fluid Dynamics Simulation on the GPU." In *GPU Gems*, edited by Randima Fernando, pp. 637–665. Upper Saddle River, NJ: Addison-Wesley, 2004.

[Liu et al. 10] Fuchang Liu, Takahiro Harada, Youngeun Lee, and Young J. Kim. "Real-Time Collision Culling of a Million Bodies on Graphics Processing Units." *ACM Transactions on Graphics* 29 (2010), 154:1–154:8.

[Merrill and Grimshaw 11] Duane Merrill and Andrew Grimshaw. "High Performance and Scalable Radix Sorting: A Case Study of Implementing Dynamic Parallelism for GPU Computing." *Parallel Processing Letters* 21:2 (2011), 245–272.

[van den Bergen 03] Gino van den Bergen. *Collision Detection in Interactive 3D Environments.* San Francisco, CA: Morgan Kaufmann, 2003.

[Zeller 05] Cyril Zeller. "Cloth Simulation on the GPU." In *ACM SIGGRAPH 2005 Sketches, SIGGRAPH '05*, p. Article no. 39. New York: ACM, 2005.

Non-separable 2D, 3D, and 4D Filtering with CUDA
Anders Eklund and Paul Dufort

14.1 Introduction

Filtering is an important step in many image processing applications such as image denoising (where the goal is to suppress noise, see Figure 14.1), image registration (where the goal is to align two images or volumes, see Figure 14.2), and image segmentation (where the goal is to extract certain parts of an image or volume, see Figure 14.3). In medical imaging, the datasets generated are often 3D or 4D and contain a large number of samples, making filtering a computationally demanding operation. A high-resolution magnetic resonance (MR) scan of a human head normally contains on the order of $256 \times 256 \times 200$ voxels (a voxel is the 3D equivalent of a pixel). Functional magnetic resonance imaging (fMRI) is used for studying brain function, and the generated 4D datasets can easily contain 300 volumes over time with $64 \times 64 \times 30$ voxels each. Ultrasound machines are increasingly affordable and can output volume data at 20–30 Hz. Computed tomography (CT) scanners can yield even higher spatial resolution than MR scanners, at the cost of ionizing radiation. A 4D CT dataset of a beating heart can be of the size $512 \times 512 \times 445 \times 20$ samples [Eklund et al. 11]. Reducing the amount of radiation in CT leads to higher noise levels, but this can be remedied by applying image denoising algorithms. However, to apply 11 non-separable denoising filters with $11 \times 11 \times 11 \times 11$ coefficients to a dataset of size $512 \times 512 \times 445 \times 20$, for example, requires approximately 375,000 billion multiply-add operations using a convolution approach. Fortunately, graphics processing units (GPUs) can now easily be used to speed up a large variety of parallel operations [Owens et al. 07].

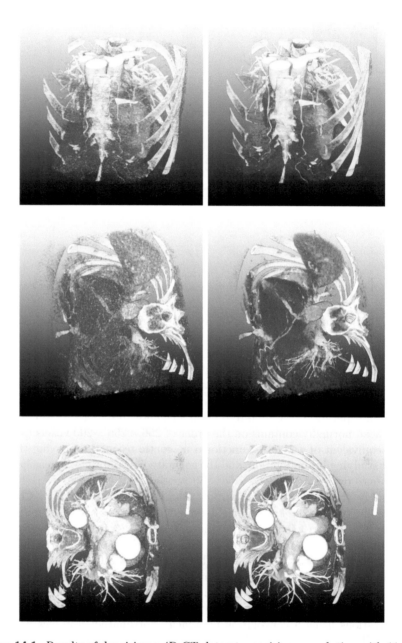

Figure 14.1. Results of denoising a 4D CT dataset, requiring convolution with 11 non-separable 4D filters of size $11 \times 11 \times 11 \times 11$. See [Eklund et al. 11] for further information about the denoising algorithm. The left images show the original data, and the right images show the denoised data.

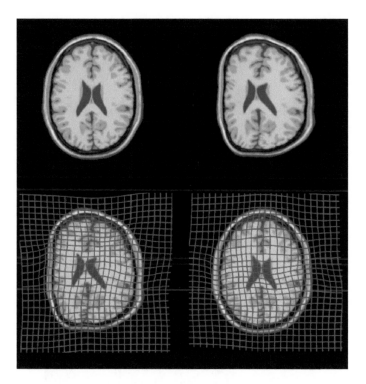

Figure 14.2. An example of image registration where the goal is to align two images or volumes. The registration algorithm used here is called the Morphon; it takes advantage of quadrature filters to detect edges and lines to estimate the displacement between two images or volumes. Quadrature filters are non-separable and can for example be of size $9\times9\times9$ voxels for volume registration. An axial brain MRI image is shown at the top left, with an artificially warped version of the same image at the top right. The task for the registration algorithm is to align the two images by finding an optimal field deforming one into the other. At the bottom left, the warped image is shown again, overlaid with the artificial deformation field used to create it. The output of the registration procedure appears at the bottom right, overlaid by its computed deformation field. The algorithm has recovered the original image and also generated a deformation field that inverts or cancels the artificial field. [This example was kindly provided by Daniel Forsberg.]

14.2 Non-separable Filters

Filtering can be divided into separable and non-separable variants. Popular separable filters are Gaussian filters (used for smoothing/blurring to reduce noise and details) and Sobel filters (used for detection of edges). Filter kernels for Gaussian (G) smoothing and edge detection along x and y using Sobel (S) filters can be

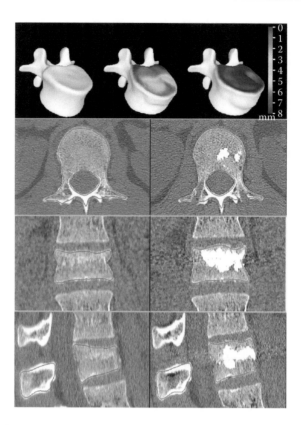

Figure 14.3. Three-dimensional segmentation of a fractured vertebra before and after a surgical procedure to restore its height, using the SpineJack device from Vexim SA of Toulouse, France. The bottom three rows show before (left) and after (right) images overlaid with the contours of the 3D segmentations. The top row shows 3D renderings of the segmentations, color-coded to indicate the change in height pre- and post-surgery. The reference (leftmost) 3D vertebra is a pre-trauma reconstruction—a prediction of the vertebra's shape before it was fractured. Filtering is used here to detect the edges of the vertebra. [Image used with permission courtesy of Dr. David Noriega, Valladolid, Spain, and Vexim SA.]

written as

$$G = \begin{bmatrix} 1 & 2 & 1 \\ 2 & 4 & 2 \\ 1 & 2 & 1 \end{bmatrix} /16\,, \quad S_x = \begin{bmatrix} 1 & 0 & -1 \\ 2 & 0 & -2 \\ 1 & 0 & -1 \end{bmatrix}, \quad S_y = \begin{bmatrix} 1 & 2 & 1 \\ 0 & 0 & 0 \\ -1 & -2 & -1 \end{bmatrix}.$$

Separability means that these filters can be decomposed as one 1D filter along x and one 1D filter along y. The Sobel filter used for edge detection along x can for example be decomposed as

$$S_x = \begin{bmatrix} 1 & 0 & -1 \\ 2 & 0 & -2 \\ 1 & 0 & -1 \end{bmatrix} = \begin{bmatrix} 1 \\ 2 \\ 1 \end{bmatrix} \begin{bmatrix} 1 & 0 & -1 \end{bmatrix}.$$

A separable filter of size 9×9 requires 18 multiplications per pixel and can be applied in two passes. One pass performs convolution along the rows, and the other pass performs convolution along the columns. A non-separable filter of size 9×9, on the other hand, requires 81 multiplications per pixel and is applied in a single pass.

While separable filters are less computationally demanding, there are a number of image processing operations that can only be performed using non-separable filters. The best-known non-separable filter is perhaps the Laplace (L) filter, which can be used for edge detection. In contrast to Gaussian and Sobel filters, it cannot be decomposed into two 1D filters. Laplace filters of size 3×3 and 5×5 can, for example, be written as

$$L_{3 \times 3} = \begin{bmatrix} 0 & 1 & 0 \\ 1 & -4 & 1 \\ 0 & 1 & 0 \end{bmatrix}, \quad L_{5 \times 5} = \begin{bmatrix} 1 & 1 & 1 & 1 & 1 \\ 1 & 1 & 1 & 1 & 1 \\ 1 & 1 & -24 & 1 & 1 \\ 1 & 1 & 1 & 1 & 1 \\ 1 & 1 & 1 & 1 & 1 \end{bmatrix}.$$

The quadrature filter is another popular non-separable filter, which is complex valued in the spatial domain. The real part of the filter is a line detector and the imaginary part is an edge detector. A 1D quadrature filter is given in Figure 14.4, but quadrature filters of any dimension can be created. The name *quadrature* comes from electronics and describes the relation between two signals having the same frequency and a phase difference of 90 degrees. An edge detector is an odd function similar to a sine wave, while a line detector is an even function similar to a cosine wave. A sine and a cosine of the same frequency always differ in phase by 90 degrees and a filter that can be described as one sine wave and one cosine wave is therefore called a *quadrature filter*. The interested reader is referred to [Granlund and Knutsson 95, Knutsson et al. 99] for further information about quadrature filters and filter design. Quadrature filters can be applied for a wide range of applications, such as image registration [Knutsson and Andersson 05, Eklund et al. 10, Forsberg et al. 11], image segmentation [Läthen et al. 10], and image denoising [Knutsson et al. 83, Knutsson 89, Granlund and Knutsson 95, Westin et al. 01]. Quadrature filters are very similar to Gabor filters [Granlund 78, Jain and Farrokhnia 91], which are also complex valued in the spatial domain.

For most algorithms using Gabor or quadrature filters, several filters are applied along different directions. For example, estimation of a structure tensor [Knutsson 89, Knutsson et al. 11] in 3D requires filtering with at least six

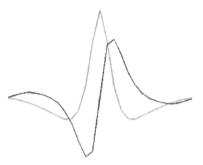

Figure 14.4. A 1D quadrature filter; the real part (green) is a line detector (a cosine modulated with a Gaussian window) and the imaginary part (blue) is an edge detector (a sine modulated with a Gaussian window).

complex valued quadrature filters, i.e., a total of 12 filters (six line detectors and six edge detectors). The Morphon [Knutsson and Andersson 05] is an image registration algorithm that uses quadrature filters to estimate the displacement between two images or volumes. To improve the registration, estimation of a structure tensor is performed in each iteration, thus requiring an efficient implementation of filtering. Monomial filters [Knutsson et al. 11, Eklund et al. 11] are a good example of filters appropriate for non-separable filtering in 4D.

14.3   Convolution vs. FFT

Images and filters can be viewed directly in the image domain (also called the spatial domain) or in the frequency domain (also denoted Fourier space) after the application of a Fourier transform. Filtering can be performed as a convolution in the spatial domain or as a multiplication in the frequency domain, according to the convolution theorem

$$F[s * f] = F[s] \cdot F[f],$$

where $F[\,]$ denotes the Fourier transform, s denotes the signal (image), f denotes the filter, $*$ denotes convolution, and $\cdot$ denotes pointwise multiplication. For large non-separable filters, filtering performed as a multiplication in the frequency domain can often be faster than convolution in the spatial domain. The transformation to the frequency domain is normally performed using the fast Fourier transform (FFT), for which very optimized implementations exist. However, FFT-based approaches for 4D data require huge amounts of memory and current GPUs have only 1–6 GB of global memory. Spatial approaches can therefore be advantageous for large datasets. Bilateral filtering [Tomasi and Manduchi 98], which is a method for image denoising, requires that a range function is evaluated for each filter coefficient during the convolution. Such an operation is hard to do with a FFT approach, since bilateral filtering in its original form is a nonlinear operation and the Fourier transform is linear. For optimal performance, FFTs often also require that the dimensions of the data are a power of 2. Additionally, there is no direct support for 4D FFTs in the Nvidia CUFFT library. Instead, one has to apply two batches of 2D FFTs and change the order of the data between these (since the 2D FFTs are applied along the two first dimensions).

14.4 Previous Work

A substantial body of work has addressed the acceleration of filtering using GPUs. Two of the first examples are the work by Rost, who used OpenGL for 2D convolution [Rost 96], and Hopf and Ertl, who used a GPU for separable 3D convolution [Hopf and Ertl 99]. For game programming, filtering can be used for texture animation [James 01]. A more recent example is a white paper from Nvidia discussing separable 2D convolution [Podlozhnyuk 07]. See our recent review about GPUs in medical imaging for a more extensive overview of GPU-based filtering [Eklund et al. 13]. GPU implementations of *non-separable* filtering in 3D, and especially 4D, are less common. For example, the NPP (Nvidia performance primitives) library contains functions for image processing, but for convolution it only supports 2D data and filters stored as integers. The CUDA SDK contains two examples of separable 2D convolution, one example of FFT-based filtering in 2D, and a single example of separable 3D convolution.

The main purpose of this chapter is therefore to present optimized solutions for non-separable 2D, 3D, and 4D convolution with the CUDA programming language, using floats and the fast shared memory. Our code has already been successfully applied to a number of applications [Eklund et al. 10, Forsberg et al. 11, Eklund et al. 11, Eklund et al. 12]. The implementations presented here have been made with CUDA 5.0 and are optimized for the Nvidia GTX 680 graphics card. Readers are assumed to be familiar with CUDA programming, and may avail themselves of the many books available on this topic if not (e.g. [Sanders and Kandrot 11]). All the code for this chapter is available under GNU GPL 3 at https://github.com/wanderine/NonSeparableFilteringCUDA.

14.5 Non-separable 2D Convolution

Two-dimensional convolution between a signal s and a filter f can be written for position $[x, y]$ as

$$(s * f) [x, y] = \sum_{f_x = -N/2}^{f_x = N/2} \sum_{f_y = -N/2}^{f_y = N/2} s [x - f_x, y - f_y] \cdot f [f_x, f_y], \qquad (14.1)$$

where $N + 1$ is the filter size. The most important aspect for a GPU implementation is that the convolution can be done independently for each pixel. To

```
__global__  void Convolution_2D_Texture(float* Filter_Response,
int DATA_W, int DATA_H)
{
    int x = blockIdx.x * blockDim.x + threadIdx.x;
    int y = blockIdx.y * blockDim.y + threadIdx.y;

    if (x >= DATA_W || y >= DATA_H)
        return;

    float sum = 0.0f;
    float y_off = -(FILTER_H - 1)/2 + 0.5f;
    for (int f_y = FILTER_H - 1; f_y >= 0; f_y--)
    {
        float x_off = -(FILTER_W - 1)/2 + 0.5f;
        for (int f_x = FILTER_W - 1; f_x >= 0; f_x--)
        {
            sum += tex2D(texture,x + x_off,y + y_off) *
            c_Filter[f_y][f_x];
            x_off += 1.0f;
        }
        y_off += 1.0f;
    }

    Filter_Response[Get2DIndex(x,y,DATA_W)] = sum;
}
```

Listing 14.1. Non-separable 2D convolution using texture memory: each thread calculates the filter response for one pixel. The filter kernel is stored in cached constant memory and the image is stored in cached texture memory. If the filter size is known at compile time, the inner loop can be unrolled by the compiler. The addition of 0.5 to each coordinate is because the original pixel values for textures are actually stored between the integer coordinates.

obtain high performance, it is also important to take advantage of the fact that filter responses for neighboring pixels are calculated from a largely overlapping set of pixels. We will begin with a CUDA implementation for non-separable 2D convolution that uses texture memory, as the texture memory cache can speed up local reads. Threads needing pixel values already accessed by other threads can thus read the values from the fast cache located at each multiprocessor (MP), rather than from the slow global memory. The filter kernel is put in the constant memory (64 KB) as it is used by all the threads. For Nvidia GPUs the constant memory cache is 8 KB per MP, and 2D filters can thus easily reside in the fast on-chip cache during the whole execution. The device code for texture-based 2D convolution is given in Listing 14.1.

The main problem with using texture memory is that such an implementation is limited by the memory bandwidth, rather than by the computational performance. A better idea is to instead take advantage of the shared memory available at each MP, which makes it possible for the threads in a thread block to cooperate very efficiently. Nvidia GPUs from the Fermi and Kepler architectures have 48 KB of shared memory per MP. If one only considers the number of valid filter responses generated per thread block, the optimal solution is to use all the shared memory for a single thread block, since this would waste a minimum of memory on the "halo" of invalid filter responses at the outer edges. According to the CUDA programming guide, GPUs with compute capability 3.0 (e.g., the Nvidia GTX 680) can maximally handle 1024 threads per thread block and 2048 concurrent threads per MP. Using all the shared memory for one thread block would therefore lead to 50% of the possible computational performance, as only 1024 threads can be used in one thread block. Full occupancy can be achieved by instead dividing the 48 KB of shared memory into two thread blocks. For floating point convolution, 96×64 pixel values can be fitted into 24 KB of shared memory. The 1024 threads per thread block are arranged as 32 threads along x and 32 threads along y, to achieve coalesced reads from global memory and to fit the number of banks in shared memory (32). Each thread starts by reading six values from global memory into shared memory ($96 \times 64/1024 = 6$). For a maximum filter size of 17×17 pixels, 80×48 valid filter responses can then be calculated from the 96×64 values in shared memory, since a halo of size 8 on all sides is required. All threads start by first calculating two filter responses, yielding 64×32 values. Half of the threads then calculate an additional three filter responses, giving a total of 48×32 filter responses. Finally, a quarter of the threads are used to calculate the filter responses for the last 16×16 pixels. The division of the 80×48 values into six blocks is illustrated in Figure 14.5. The first part of the code for non-separable 2D convolution using shared memory is given in Listing 14.2 and the second part is given in Listing 14.3. The device function that performs the 2D convolution is very similar to the kernel for texture-based convolution; interested readers are therefore referred to the repository.

If more than one filter is to be applied, e.g., four complex valued quadrature filters oriented along 0, 45, 90, and 135 degrees, all the filter responses can be calculated very efficiently by simply performing several multiplications and additions each time a pixel value has been loaded from shared memory to a register. This results in a better ratio between the number of memory accesses and floating point operations. By reducing the maximum filter size to 9×9, the number of valid filter responses increases to 88×56 since the halo size shrinks to 4. This will also result in a higher occupancy during the convolution. For the first case yielding 80×48 valid filter responses, the mean occupancy for the six blocks is $(32 \cdot 32 \cdot 2 + 32 \cdot 32 \cdot 2 + 32 \cdot 16 \cdot 2 + 32 \cdot 16 \cdot 2 + 16 \cdot 32 \cdot 2 + 16 \cdot 16 \cdot 2)/(6 \cdot 2048) = 62.5\%$, and for the second case yielding 88×56 valid filter responses, the mean occupancy increases to $(32 \cdot 32 \cdot 2 + 32 \cdot 32 \cdot 2 + 32 \cdot 24 \cdot 2 + 32 \cdot 24 \cdot 2 + 24 \cdot 32 \cdot 2 + 24 \cdot 24 \cdot 2)/(6 \cdot 2048)$ $= 80.2\%$.

The required number of thread blocks in the x- and y-directions are for the shared memory implementation *not* calculated by dividing the image width and height with the number of threads in each direction (32). The width and height should instead be divided by the number of valid filter responses generated in each

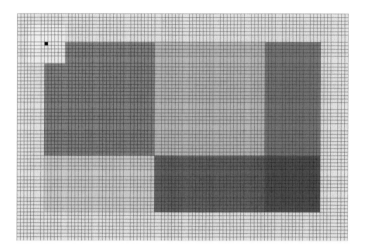

Figure 14.5. The grid represents 96×64 pixels in shared memory. As 32×32 threads are used per thread block, each thread needs to read six values from global memory into shared memory. The gray pixels represent the filter kernel and the black pixel represents where the current filter response is saved. A yellow halo needs to be loaded into shared memory to be able to calculate all the filter responses. In this case 80×48 valid filter responses are calculated, making it possible to apply at most a filter of size 17×17. The 80×48 filter responses are calculated as six runs, the first 2 consisting of 32×32 pixels (marked light red and light blue). Half of the threads calculate three additional filter responses in blocks of 32×16 or 16×32 pixels (marked green, dark blue, and dark red). A quarter of the threads calculates the filter response for a last block of 16×16 pixels (marked purple). If the halo is reduced from eight to four pixels, 88×56 valid filter responses can instead be calculated as two 32×32 blocks, one 24×32 block, two 32×24 blocks, and one 24×24 block. In addition to increasing the number of valid filter responses, such an implementation will also increase the mean occupancy during convolution from 62.5% to 80.2%. The only drawback is that the largest filter that can be applied drops from 17×17 to 9×9.

direction, since each thread block generates more than one valid filter response per thread. The calculation of the x- and y-indices inside the kernel also needs to be changed from the conventional

```
int x = blockIdx.x * blockDim.x + threadIdx.x;
int y = blockIdx.y * blockDim.y + threadIdx.y;
```

to

```
int x = blockIdx.x * VALID_RESPONSES_X + threadIdx.x;
int y = blockIdx.y * VALID_RESPONSES_Y + threadIdx.y;
```

```
#define HALO 8

__global__ void Convolution_2D_Shared(float* Filter_Response,
float* Image, int DATA_W, int DATA_H)
{
    int x = blockIdx.x * VALID_RESPONSES_X + threadIdx.x;
    int y = blockIdx.y * VALID_RESPONSES_Y + threadIdx.y;

    __shared__ float s_Image[64][96]; // y, x

    // Reset shared memory
    s_Image[threadIdx.y][threadIdx.x]           = 0.0f;
    s_Image[threadIdx.y][threadIdx.x + 32]      = 0.0f;
    s_Image[threadIdx.y][threadIdx.x + 64]      = 0.0f;
    s_Image[threadIdx.y + 32][threadIdx.x]      = 0.0f;
    s_Image[threadIdx.y + 32][threadIdx.x + 32] = 0.0f;
    s_Image[threadIdx.y + 32][threadIdx.x + 64] = 0.0f;

    // Read data into shared memory
    if ( ((x-HALO) >= 0) && ((x-HALO) < DATA_W)
       && ((y-HALO) >= 0) && ((y-HALO) < DATA_H) )
        s_Image[threadIdx.y][threadIdx.x] =
        Image[Get2DIndex(x-HALO,y-HALO,DATA_W)];

    if ( ((x+32-HALO) < DATA_W)
       && ((y-HALO) >= 0) && ((y-HALO) < DATA_H) )
        s_Image[threadIdx.y][threadIdx.x + 32] =
        Image[Get2DIndex(x+32-HALO,y-HALO,DATA_W)];

    if ( ((x+64-HALO) < DATA_W)
       && ((y-HALO) >= 0) && ((y-HALO) < DATA_H) )
        s_Image[threadIdx.y][threadIdx.x + 64] =
        Image[Get2DIndex(x+64-HALO,y-HALO,DATA_W)];

    if ( ((x-HALO) >= 0)
       && ((x-HALO) < DATA_W) && ((y+32-HALO) < DATA_H) )
        s_Image[threadIdx.y + 32][threadIdx.x] =
        Image[Get2DIndex(x-HALO,y+32-HALO,DATA_W)];

    if ( ((x+32-HALO) < DATA_W) && ((y+32-HALO) < DATA_H) )
        s_Image[threadIdx.y + 32][threadIdx.x + 32] =
        Image[Get2DIndex(x+32-HALO,y+32-HALO, DATA_W)];

    if ( ((x+64-HALO) < DATA_W) && ((y+32-HALO) < DATA_H) )
        s_Image[threadIdx.y + 32][threadIdx.x + 64] =
        Image[Get2DIndex(x+64-HALO,y+32-HALO,DATA_W)];

    __syncthreads();
```

Listing 14.2. Non-separable 2D convolution using shared memory. This listing represents the first part of the kernel, where data is loaded into shared memory. Each thread block consists of 32×32 threads, such that each thread has to read six values into shared memory (storing 96×64 values). The parameter HALO can be changed to control the size of the largest filter that can be applied (HALO*2 + 1). Before the actual convolution is started, synchronization of the threads is required to guarantee that all values have been loaded into shared memory.

```
if ( (x < DATA_W) && (y < DATA_H) )
  Filter_Response[Get2DIndex(x,y,DATA_W)] =
  Conv2D(s_Image,threadIdx.y+HALO,threadIdx.x+HALO);

if ( ((x + 32) < DATA_W) && (y < DATA_H) )
  Filter_Response[Get2DIndex(x+32,y,DATA_W)] =
  Conv2D(s_Image,threadIdx.y+HALO,threadIdx.x+32+HALO);

if (threadIdx.x < (32 - HALO*2))
{
  if ( ((x + 64) < DATA_W) && (y < DATA_H) )
    Filter_Response[Get2DIndex(x+64,y,DATA_W)] =
    Conv2D(s_Image,threadIdx.y+HALO,threadIdx.x+64+HALO);
}

if (threadIdx.y < (32 - HALO*2))
{
  if ( (x < DATA_W) && ((y + 32) < DATA_H) )
    Filter_Response[Get2DIndex(x,y+32,DATA_W)] =
    Conv2D(s_Image,threadIdx.y+32+HALO,threadIdx.x+HALO);
}

if (threadIdx.y < (32 - HALO*2))
{
  if ( ((x + 32) < DATA_W) && ((y + 32) < DATA_H) )
    Filter_Response[Get2DIndex(x+32,y+32,DATA_W)] =
    Conv2D(s_Image,threadIdx.y+32+HALO,threadIdx.x+32+HALO);
}

if ( (threadIdx.x < (32 - HALO*2)) &&
     (threadIdx.y < (32 - HALO*2)) )
{
  if ( ((x + 64) < DATA_W) && ((y + 32) < DATA_H) )
    Filter_Response[Get2DIndex(x+64,y+32,DATA_W)] =
    Conv2D(s_Image,threadIdx.y+32+HALO,threadIdx.x+64+HALO);
}
}
```

Listing 14.3. Non-separable 2D convolution using shared memory. This listing represents the second part of the kernel where the convolutions are performed, by calling a device function for each block of filter responses. For a filter size of 17×17, HALO is 8 and the first two blocks yield filter responses for 32×32 pixels, the third block yields 16×32 filter responses, the fourth and fifth blocks yield 32×16 filter responses and the sixth block yields the last 16×16 filter responses. The parameter HALO can easily be changed to optimize the code for different filter sizes. The code for the device function Conv2D is given in the repository.

14.6   Non-separable 3D Convolution

Three-dimensional convolution between a signal s and a filter f for position $[x, y, z]$ is defined as

$$(s * f)[x, y, z] = \sum_{f_x = -N/2}^{f_x = N/2} \sum_{f_y = -N/2}^{f_y = N/2} \sum_{f_z = -N/2}^{f_z = N/2} s[x - f_x, y - f_y, z - f_z] \cdot f[f_x, f_y, f_z].$$

This weighted summation can be easily implemented by using texture memory just as for 2D convolution. The differences between 3D and 2D are that an additional `for` loop is added and that a 3D texture is used instead of a 2D texture. The code will therefore not be given here (but is available in the github repository). Using shared memory for non-separable 3D convolution is more difficult, however. A natural extension of the 2D implementation would be, for example, to load $24 \times 16 \times 16$ voxels into shared memory. This would make it possible to calculate $16 \times 8 \times 8$ valid filter responses per thread block for a filter of size $9 \times 9 \times 9$. But the optimal division of the 1024 threads per thread block along x, y, and z is not obvious. One solution is to use $24 \times 16 \times 2$ threads per thread block, giving a total of 1536 threads per MP and 75% occupancy. However, only $16 \times 8 \times 2$ threads per thread block will be active during the actual convolution, giving a low occupancy of 25%. To use 24 threads along x will also result in shared memory bank conflicts, as there are 32 banks. To avoid these conflicts, one can instead load $32 \times 16 \times 12$ values into shared memory and, for example, use thread blocks of size $32 \times 16 \times 2$. The number of valid filter responses drops to $24 \times 8 \times 4 = 768$ per thread block (compared to 1024 for the first case) while the occupancy during convolution will increase to 37.5%. It is not obvious how the different compromises will affect the total runtime, making it necessary to actually make all the different implementations and test them. We will leave 3D convolution for now and instead move on to 4D convolution.

14.7 Non-separable 4D Convolution

There are no 4D textures in the CUDA programming language, so a simple texture implementation is impossible for non-separable 4D convolution. Possible solutions are to use one huge 1D texture or several 2D or 3D textures. One-dimensional textures can speed up reads that are local in the first dimension (e.g., x), but not reads that are local in the other dimensions (y, z, t). A solution involving many 2D or 3D textures would be rather hard to implement, as one cannot use pointers for texture objects. The use of shared memory is even more complicated than for 3D convolution, and here it becomes obvious that it is impossible to continue on the same path. The shared memory cannot even store $11 \times 11 \times 11 \times 11$ values required for a filter of size $11 \times 11 \times 11 \times 11$.

Let us take a step back and think about what a 4D convolution involves. To perform non-separable 4D convolution requires eight `for` loops, four to loop through all the filter coefficients and four to loop through all voxels and time points. To do all the `for` loops on the GPU is not necessarily optimal. A better way to divide the `for` loops is to do four on the CPU and four on the GPU, such that the four loops on the GPU correspond to a non-separable 2D convolution. Thus, four loops on the CPU are used to call the 2D convolution for two image dimensions and two filter dimensions (e.g., z and t). During each call to the 2D

```
// Loop over time points in data
for (int t = 0; t < DATA_T; t++)
{
  // Reset filter response for current volume
  cudaMemset(d_FR, 0, DATA_W * DATA_H * DATA_D * sizeof(float));

  // Loop over time points in filter
  for (int tt = FILTER_T - 1; tt >= 0; tt--)
  {
    // Loop over slices in filter
    for (int zz = FILTER_D - 1; zz >= 0; zz--)
    {
      // Copy current filter coefficients to constant memory
      CopyFilterCoefficients(zz,tt);

      // Perform 2D convolution and
      // accumulate the filter responses inside the kernel,
      // launch kernel for several slices simultaneously
      Convolution_2D_Shared<<<dG, dB>>>(d_FR);
    }
  }
}
```

Listing 14.4. Host code for non-separable 4D convolution, by performing non-separable 2D convolution on the GPU and accumulating the filter responses inside the kernel (dG stands for dimGrid, dB stands for dimBlock, and FR stands for filter responses). The CPU takes care of three for loops and the GPU five for loops.

convolution kernel, the filter responses are accumulated inside the kernel. Before each 2D convolution is started, the corresponding 2D values of the 4D filter are copied to constant memory.

A small problem remains; for a 4D dataset of size $128 \times 128 \times 128 \times 128$, the 2D convolution will be applied to images of size 128×128 pixels. If 80×48 valid filter responses are calculated per thread block, only five thread blocks will be launched. The Nvidia GTX 680 has eight MPs and each MP can concurrently handle two thread blocks with 1024 threads each. At least 16 thread blocks are thus required to achieve full occupancy. To solve this problem one can launch the 2D convolution for all slices simultaneously, by using 3D thread blocks, to increase the number of thread blocks and thereby the occupancy. This removes one loop on the CPU, such that three loops are taken care of by the CPU and five by the GPU. As some of the slices in the filter response will be invalid due to border effects, some additional time can be saved by only performing the convolution for the valid slices. The host code for non-separable 4D convolution is given in Listing 14.4 and the complete code is available in the github repository.

14.8   Non-separable 3D Convolution, Revisited

Now that an implementation for non-separable 4D convolution has been provided, 3D convolution is very easy. The host code is given in Listing 14.5 and the

```
// Loop over slices in filter
for (int zz = FILTER_D - 1; zz >= 0; zz--)
{
    // Copy current filter coefficients to constant memory
    CopyFilterCoefficients(zz);

    // Perform 2D convolution and
    // accumulate the filter responses inside the kernel,
    // launch kernel for several slices simultaneously
    Convolution_2D_Shared<<<dG, dB>>>(d_FR);
}
```

Listing 14.5. Host code for non-separable 3D convolution, by performing non-separable 2D convolution on the GPU and accumulating the filter responses inside the kernel (dG stands for dimGrid, dB stands for dimBlock, and FR stands for filter responses). Just as for the non-separable 4D convolution, the 2D convolution is launched for all slices at the same time to increase the occupancy.

complete code is available in the repository. The only difference compared to 4D convolution is that the CPU for 4D also loops over time points (for data and filters). Just as for 4D convolution, the 2D convolution is launched for all slices at the same time to increase the occupancy.

14.9 Performance

We will now list some performance measures for our implementations. All the testing has been done with an Nvidia GTX 680 graphics card with 4 GB of memory.

14.9.1 Performance, 2D Filtering

Performance estimates for non-separable 2D filtering are given in Figures 14.6–14.7. Time for transferring the data to and from the GPU is not included. The first plot is for a fixed image size of 2048×2048 pixels and filter sizes ranging from 3×3 to 17×17. The second and third plots are for fixed filter sizes of 9×9 and 17×17, respectively. The image sizes for these plots range from 128×128 to 4096×4096 in steps of 128 pixels. All plots contain the processing time for spatial convolution using texture memory (with and without loop unrolling), spatial convolution using shared memory (with and without loop unrolling), and FFT-based filtering using the CUFFT library (involving two forward FFT's, complex valued multiplication and one inverse FFT).

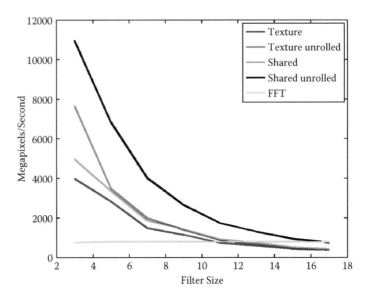

Figure 14.6. Performance, measured in megapixels per second, for the different implementations of 2D filtering, for an image of size 2048×2048 and filter sizes ranging from 3×3 to 17×17. The processing time for FFT-based filtering is independent of the filter size and is the fastest approach for non-separable filters larger than 17×17.

14.9.2   Performance, 3D Filtering

Performance estimates for non-separable 3D filtering are given in Figures 14.8–14.9. Again, time for transferring the data to and from the GPU is not included. The first plot is for a fixed volume size of $256 \times 256 \times 256$ voxels and filter sizes ranging from $3 \times 3 \times 3$ to $17 \times 17 \times 17$. The second and third plots are for fixed filter sizes of $7 \times 7 \times 7$ and $13 \times 13 \times 13$, respectively. The volume sizes for these plots range from $64 \times 64 \times 64$ to $512 \times 512 \times 512$ in steps of 32 voxels. All plots contain the processing time for spatial convolution using texture memory (with and without loop unrolling), spatial convolution using shared memory (with and without loop unrolling), and FFT-based filtering using the CUFFT library (involving two forward FFT's, complex-valued multiplication, and one inverse FFT).

14.9.3   Performance, 4D Filtering

Performance estimates for non-separable 4D filtering are given in Figures 14.10–14.11. Again, time for transferring the data to and from the GPU is not included. The first plot is for a fixed data size of $128 \times 128 \times 128 \times 32$ elements and filter sizes ranging from $3 \times 3 \times 3 \times 3$ to $17 \times 17 \times 17 \times 17$. The second and third plots

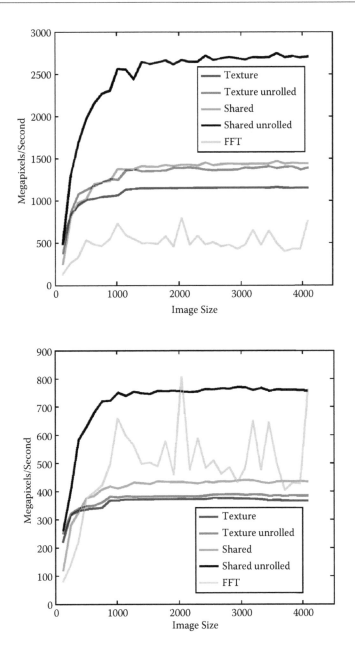

Figure 14.7. Performance, measured in megapixels per second, for the different implementations of 2D filtering and image sizes ranging from 128×128 to 4096×4096. Note the performance spikes for the FFT-based filtering for image sizes that are a power of 2. The results for a 9×9 filter are shown in the upper plot and the results for a 17×17 filter in the lower plot.

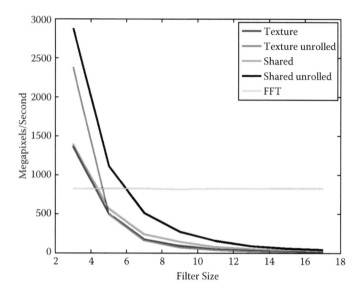

Figure 14.8. Performance, measured in megavoxels per second, for the different implementations of 3D filtering, for a volume of size $256 \times 256 \times 256$ and filter sizes ranging from $3 \times 3 \times 3$ to $17 \times 17 \times 17$. FFT-based filtering is clearly faster than the other approaches for large filters.

are for fixed filter sizes of $7 \times 7 \times 7 \times 7$ and $11 \times 11 \times 11 \times 11$, respectively. The data sizes range from $128 \times 128 \times 64 \times 16$ to $128 \times 128 \times 64 \times 128$ in steps of eight time points. All plots contain the processing time for spatial convolution using shared memory (with and without loop unrolling) and FFT-based filtering using CUFFT. The CUFFT library does not directly support 4D FFTs; it was performed by running two batches of 2D FFTs and changing the order of the data between them from $(x,\ y,\ z,\ t)$ to $(z,\ t,\ x,\ y)$. A 4D FFT developed by Nvidia would, however, probably be more efficient.

14.10   Conclusions

We have presented solutions for fast non-separable floating point convolution in 2D, 3D, and 4D, using the CUDA programming language. We believe that these implementations will serve as a complement to the NPP library, which currently only supports 2D filters and images stored as integers. The shared memory implementation with loop unrolling is approximately twice as fast as the simple texture memory implementation, which is similar to results obtained by Nvidia for separable 2D convolution [Podlozhnyuk 07]. For 3D and 4D data it might seem strange to use convolution instead of an FFT, but the convolution approach

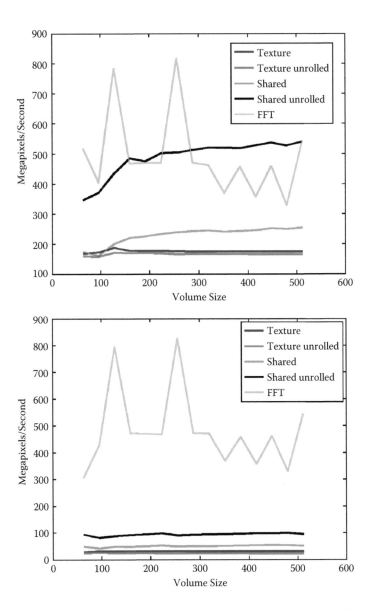

Figure 14.9. Performance, measured in megavoxels per second, for the different implementations of 3D filtering and volume sizes ranging from $64 \times 64 \times 64$ to $512 \times 512 \times 512$. FFT-based filtering is the fastest approach for large filters. The texture-based approach is actually slower for 3D with loop unrolling, which is explained by an increase in the number of registers used. The results for a $7 \times 7 \times 7$ filter are shown in the upper plot the results for a $13 \times 13 \times 13$ filter in the lower plot.

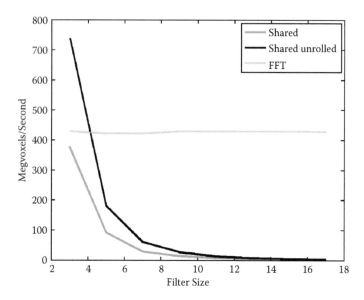

Figure 14.10. Performance, measured in megavoxels per second, for the different implementations of 4D filtering, for a dataset of size $128 \times 128 \times 128 \times 32$ and filter sizes ranging from $3 \times 3 \times 3 \times 3$ to $17 \times 17 \times 17 \times 17$.

can for example handle larger datasets. In our work on 4D image denoising [Eklund et al. 11], the FFT-based approach was on average only three times faster (compared to about 30 times faster in the benchmarks given here). The main reason for this was the high-resolution nature of the data ($512 \times 512 \times 445 \times 20$ elements), making it impossible to load all the data into global memory. Due to its higher memory consumption, the FFT-based approach was forced to load a smaller number of slices into global memory compared to the spatial approach. As only a subset of the slices (and time points) is valid after the filtering, the FFT-based approach required a larger number of runs to process all the slices.

Finally, we close by noting two additional topics that readers may wish to consider for more advanced study. First, applications in which several filters are applied simultaneously to the same data (e.g, six complex valued quadrature filters to estimate a local structure tensor in 3D) can lead to different conclusions regarding performance using spatial convolution versus FFT-based filtering. Second, filter networks can be used to speed up spatial convolution by combining the result of many small filter kernels, resulting in a proportionally higher gain for 3D and 4D than for 2D convolution [Andersson et al. 99, Svensson et al. 05]. All the code for this chapter is available under GNU GPL 3 at https://github.com/wanderine/NonSeparableFilteringCUDA.

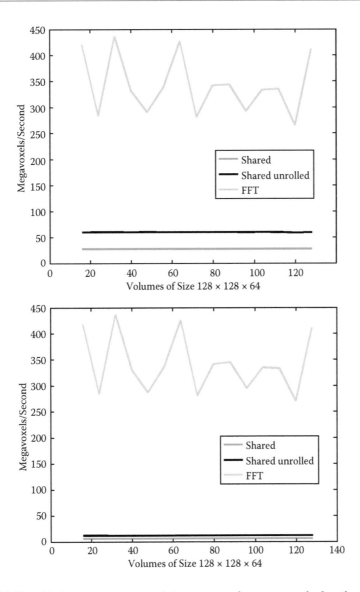

Figure 14.11. Performance, measured in megavoxels per second, for the different implementations of 4D filtering and data sizes ranging from $128 \times 128 \times 64 \times 16$ to $128 \times 128 \times 64 \times 128$. The FFT-based approach clearly outperforms the convolution approaches. The results for a $7 \times 7 \times 7 \times 7$ filter are shown in the upper plot and the results for a $11 \times 11 \times 11 \times 11$ filter in the lower plot.

Bibliography

[Andersson et al. 99] Mats Andersson, Johan Wiklund, and Hans Knutsson. "Filter Networks." In *Proceedings of the IASTED International Conference on Signal and Image Processing (SIP)*, pp. 213–217. Calgary: ACTA Press, 1999.

[Eklund et al. 10] Anders Eklund, Mats Andersson, and Hans Knutsson. "Phase Based Volume Registration Using CUDA." In *IEEE International Conference on Acoustics, Speech and Signal Processing (ICASSP)*, pp. 658–661. Washington, DC: IEEE Press, 2010.

[Eklund et al. 11] Anders Eklund, Mats Andersson, and Hans Knutsson. "True 4D Image Denoising on the GPU." *International Journal of Biomedical Imaging* 2011 (2011), Article ID 952819.

[Eklund et al. 12] Anders Eklund, Mats Andersson, and Hans Knutsson. "fMRI Analysis on the GPU—Possibilities and Challenges." *Computer Methods and Programs in Biomedicine* 105 (2012), 145–161.

[Eklund et al. 13] Anders Eklund, Paul Dufort, Daniel Forsberg, and Stephen LaConte. "Medical Image Processing on the GPU—Past, Present and Future." *Medical Image Analysis* 17 (2013), 1073–1094.

[Forsberg et al. 11] Daniel Forsberg, Anders Eklund, Mats Andersson, and Hans Knutsson. "Phase-Based Non-rigid 3D Image Registration—From Minutes to Seconds Using CUDA." Presentation, Joint MICCAI Workshop on High Performance and Distributed Computing for Medical Imaging, Toronto, Canada, September 22, 2011.

[Granlund and Knutsson 95] Gösta Granlund and Hans Knutsson. *Signal Processing for Computer Vision*. Dordrecht, The Netherlands: Kluwer Academic Publishers, 1995.

[Granlund 78] Gösta Granlund. "In Search of a General Picture Processing Operator." *Computer Graphics and Image Processing* 8 (1978), 155–173.

[Hopf and Ertl 99] Matthias Hopf and Thomas Ertl. "Accelerating 3D Convolution Using Graphics Hardware." In *Proceedings of the IEEE Conference on Visualization*, pp. 471–475. Los Alamitos, CA: IEEE Computer Society, 1999.

[Jain and Farrokhnia 91] Anil Jain and Farshid Farrokhnia. "Unsupervised Texture Segmentation Using Gabor Filters." *Pattern Recognition* 24 (1991), 1167–1186.

[James 01] Greg James. "Operations for Hardware-Accelerated Procedural Texture Animation." In *Game Programming Gems 2*, edited by Mark DeLoura, pp. 497–509. Cambridge, MA: Charles River Media, 2001.

[Knutsson and Andersson 05] Hans Knutsson and Mats Andersson. "Morphons: Segmentation Using Elastic Canvas and Paint on Priors." In *IEEE International Conference on Image Processing (ICIP)*, pp. 1226–1229. Los Alamitos, CA: IEEE Press, 2005.

[Knutsson et al. 83] Hans Knutsson, Roland Wilson, and Gösta Granlund. "Anisotropic Non-stationary Image Estimation and Its Applications—Part I: Restoration of Noisy Images." *IEEE Transactions on Communications* 31 (1983), 388–397.

[Knutsson et al. 99] Hans Knutsson, Mats Andersson, and Johan Wiklund. "Advanced Filter Design." In *SCIA '99: Proceedings of the 11th Scandinavian Conference on Image Analysis*, 1, 1, pp. 185–193. Kangerlussuaq, Greenland: IAPR, 1999.

[Knutsson et al. 11] Hans Knutsson, Carl-Fredrik Westin, and Mats Andersson. "Representing Local Structure Using Tensors II." In *Proceedings of the Scandinavian Conference on Image Analysis (SCIA)*, Lecture Notes in Computer Science, 6688, pp. 545–556. Berlin: Springer, 2011.

[Knutsson 89] Hans Knutsson. "Representing Local Structure Using Tensors." In *SCIA '89: Proceedings of the 6th Scandinavian Conference on Image Analysis*, pp. 244–251. Oulu, Finland: IAPR, 1989.

[Läthen et al. 10] Gunnar Läthen, Jimmy Jonasson, and Magnus Borga. "Blood Vessel Segmentation Using Multi-scale Quadrature Filtering." *Pattern Recognition Letters* 31 (2010), 762–767.

[Owens et al. 07] John Owens, David Luebke, Naga Govindaraju, Mark Harris, Jens Kruger, Aaron Lefohn, and Timothy Purcell. "A Survey of General-Purpose Computation on Graphics Hardware." *Computer Graphics Forum* 26 (2007), 80–113.

[Podlozhnyuk 07] Victor Podlozhnyuk. "Image Convolution with CUDA." White paper, Nvidia, 2007.

[Rost 96] Randi Rost. "Using OpenGL for Imaging." *SPIE Medical Imaging, Image Display Conference* 2707 (1996), 473–484.

[Sanders and Kandrot 11] Jason Sanders and Edward Kandrot. *CUDA by Example: An Introduction to General-Purpose GPU Programming*. Upper Saddle River, NJ: Addison-Wesley, 2011.

[Svensson et al. 05] Björn Svensson, Mats Andersson, and Hans Knutsson. "Filter Networks for Efficient Estimation of Local 3D Structure." In *IEEE International Conference on Image Processing (ICIP)*, pp. 573–576. Los Alamitos, CA: IEEE Computer Society, 2005.

[Tomasi and Manduchi 98] Carlo Tomasi and Roberto Manduchi. "Bilateral Filtering for Gray and Color Images." In *Proceedings International Conference on Computer Vision*, pp. 839–846. Los Alamitos, CA: IEEE Computer Society, 1998.

[Westin et al. 01] Carl-Fredrik Westin, Lars Wigström, Tomas Loock, Lars Sjöqvist, Ron Kikinis, and Hans Knutsson. "Three-Dimensional Adaptive Filtering in Magnetic Resonance Angiography." *Journal of Magnetic Resonance Imaging* 14 (2001), 63–71.

15

Compute-Based Tiled Culling
Jason Stewart

15.1 Introduction

Modern real-time rendering engines need to support many dynamic light sources in a scene. Meeting this requirement with traditional forward rendering is problematic. Typically, a forward-rendered engine culls lights on the CPU for each batch of scene geometry to be drawn, and changing the set of lights in use requires a separate draw call. Thus, there is an undesirable tradeoff between using smaller pieces of the scene for more efficient light culling versus using larger batches and more instancing for fewer total draw calls. The intersection tests required for light culling can also be a performance burden for the CPU.

Deferred rendering better supports large light counts because it decouples scene geometry rendering and material evaluation from lighting. First, the scene is rendered and geometric and material properties are stored into a geometry buffer or G-buffer [Saito and Takahashi 90]. Lighting is accumulated separately, using the G-buffer as input, by drawing light bounding volumes or screen-space quads. Removing lighting from the scene rendering pass eliminates the state switching for different light sets, allowing for better batching. In addition, CPU light culling is performed once against the view frustum instead of for each batch, reducing the performance cost. However, because each light is now accumulated separately, overlapping lights increase bandwidth consumption, which can decrease GPU performance [Lauritzen 10].

This chapter presents a better method for supporting large light counts: compute-based tiled culling. Modern GPUs, including those in Xbox One and Playstation 4, can execute general-purpose computation kernels. This capability allows light culling to be performed on the GPU. The technique can be used with both forward and deferred rendering. It eliminates light state switching and CPU culling, which helps forward rendering, and it calculates lighting in a single pass, which helps deferred rendering. This chapter presents the technique in detail, including code examples in HLSL and various optimizations. The companion code implements the technique for both forward and deferred rendering and includes a benchmark.

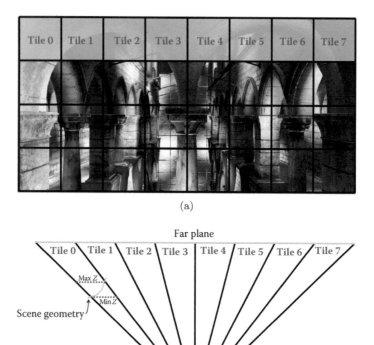

(a)

Far plane

Tile 0   Tile 1   Tile 2   Tile 3   Tile 4   Tile 5   Tile 6   Tile 7

Max Z

Min Z

Scene geometry

Near plane

(b)

Figure 15.1. Partitioning the scene into tiles. (a) Example screen tiles. (b) Fitting view frustum partitions to the screen tiles. For clarity, the tiles shown in this figure are very large. They would typically be 16×16 pixels.

In addition to using the companion code to measure performance, results are presented using Unreal Engine 4, including a comparison of standard deferred rendering versus tiled deferred.

15.2   Overview

Compute-based tiled culling works by partitioning the screen into fixed-size tiles, as shown in Figure 15.1(a). For each tile, a compute shader[1] loops over all lights in the scene and determines which ones intersect that particular tile. Figure 15.1(b) gives a 2D, top-down example of how the tile bounding volume is constructed. Four planes are calculated to represent the left, right, top, and bottom of an

---

[1]This chapter uses Direct3D 11 terminology. In Direct3D 11, the general-purpose computation technology required for tiled culling is called DirectCompute 5.0, and the general-purpose kernel is called a compute shader.

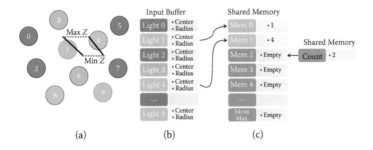

Figure 15.2. Tiled culling overview.

asymmetric partition of the view frustum that fits exactly around the tile. To allow for tighter culling, the minimum and maximum scene depths are calculated for the tile, as shown in Figure 15.1(b) for Tile 0. These depth values form the front and back of the frustum partition. This gives the six planes necessary for testing the intersection between light bounding volumes and the tile.

Figure 15.2 provides an overview of the algorithm. Figure 15.2(a) shows a 2D representation of a tile bounding volume, similar to that shown for Tile 0 in Figure 15.1(b). Several scene lights are also shown. Figure 15.2(b) shows the input buffer containing the scene light list. Each entry in the list contains the center and radius for that light's bounding sphere.

The compute shader is configured so that each thread group works on one tile. It loops over the lights in the input buffer and stores the indices of those that intersect the tile into shared memory.[2] Space is reserved for a per-tile maximum number of lights, and a counter tracks how many entries were actually written, as shown in Figure 15.2(c).

Algorithm 15.1 summarizes the technique.

Referring back to Figure 15.2 as a visual example of the loop in Algorithm 15.1, note from Figure 15.2(a) that two lights intersect the frustum partition: Light 1 and Light 4. The input buffer index (Figure 15.2(b)) of each intersecting light is written to shared memory (Figure 15.2(c)). To make this thread safe, so that lights can be culled in parallel, a counter is stored in shared memory and incremented using the atomic operations available in compute shaders.

15.3 Implementation

This section gives an implementation in HLSL of the compute-based tiled-culling algorithm discussed in the previous section. The three parts of Algorithm 15.1 will be presented in order: depth bounds calculation, frustum planes calculation, and intersection testing.

---

[2]Compute shader execution is organized into thread groups. Threads in the same thread group have access to shared memory.

Input: light list, scene depth
Output: per-tile list of intersecting lights

calculate depth bounds for the tile;
calculate frustum planes for the tile;

for $i \leftarrow$ `thread_index` **to** `num_lights` **do**
    `current_light` $\leftarrow$ `light_list[i]`;
    test intersection against tile bounding volume;
    if *intersection* **then**
        thread-safe increment of list counter;
        write light index to per-tile list;
    end
    $i \leftarrow i +$ `num_threads_per_tile`;
end

Algorithm 15.1. Basic tiled culling.

15.3.1 Depth Bounds Calculation

As mentioned previously (in Footnote 2), compute shader execution is organized into thread groups. You specify the exact organization as part of the compute shader. In HLSL, this is done with the `numthreads` attribute, as shown on line 15 of Listing 15.1. For tiled culling, the thread groups are organized to match the tile size. For example, `TILE_RES` is defined as 16 in Listing 15.1, and the 16×16-pixel tile size results in a 16×16-thread layout in the compute shader.

Compute shaders are executed with the `Dispatch` method, which specifies the number of thread groups to launch. For example, a 1920×1080 screen resolution with 16×16-pixel tiles requires 120×68 tiles to cover the screen. Thus, by calling `Dispatch(120,68,1)` for a compute shader with [`numthreads(16,16,1)`], each thread maps to a particular screen pixel.

To calculate the depth bounds, each thread simply reads its pixel's depth value from the scene depth buffer and performs a thread-safe atomic minimum and maximum in shared memory. The depth buffer read happens on lines 20–21 of Listing 15.1. The `globalIdx` variable used to address the depth buffer is the `SV_DispatchThreadID` value (see line 16), one of the special system-value semantics available to compute shaders. Because the thread group layout from the `Dispatch` call matches the screen tiles and the thread layout from the `numthreads` attribute matches the tile size, the `SV_DispatchThreadID` value corresponds to a screen pixel address and can be used directly with the `Load` function.

One minor complication with the depth bounds calculation is that the scene depth value is floating point, but the atomic minimum and maximum functions (`InterlockedMin` and `InterlockedMax` on lines 43–44) only operate on integer types. Therefore, `asuint` is used to store the raw bits of the floating point depth value,

```
 1  Texture2D<float> g_SceneDepthBuffer;
 2
 3  // Thread Group Shared Memory (aka local data share, or LDS)
 4  groupshared uint ldsZMin;
 5  groupshared uint ldsZMax;
 6
 7  // Convert a depth value from postprojection space
 8  // into view space
 9  float ConvertProjDepthToView(float z)
10  {
11    return (1.f/(z*g_mProjectionInv._34 + g_mProjectionInv._44));
12  }
13
14  #define TILE_RES 16
15  [numthreads(TILE_RES,TILE_RES,1)]
16  void CullLightsCS(uint3 globalIdx : SV_DispatchThreadID,
17                    uint3 localIdx  : SV_GroupThreadID,
18                    uint3 groupIdx  : SV_GroupID)
19  {
20    float depth = g_SceneDepthBuffer.Load(uint3(globalIdx.x,
21                                          globalIdx.y,0)).x;
22    float viewPosZ = ConvertProjDepthToView(depth);
23    uint z = asuint(viewPosZ);
24
25    uint threadNum = localIdx.x + localIdx.y*TILE_RES;
26
27    // There is no way to initialize shared memory at
28    // compile time, so thread zero does it at runtime
29    if(threadNum == 0)
30    {
31      ldsZMin = 0x7f7fffff;  // FLT_MAX as a uint
32      ldsZMax = 0;
33    }
34    GroupMemoryBarrierWithGroupSync();
35
36    // Parts of the depth buffer that were never written
37    // (e.g., the sky) will be zero (the companion code uses
38    // inverted 32-bit float depth for better precision).
39    if(depth != 0.f)
40    {
41      // Calculate the minimum and maximum depth for this tile
42      // to form the front and back of the frustum
43      InterlockedMin(ldsZMin,z);
44      InterlockedMax(ldsZMax,z);
45    }
46    GroupMemoryBarrierWithGroupSync();
47
48    float minZ = asfloat(ldsZMin);
49    float maxZ = asfloat(ldsZMax);
50
51    // Frustum planes and intersection code goes here
52    ...
53  }
```

Listing 15.1. Depth bounds calculation.

and the minimum and maximum are performed against these unsigned bits. This works because the floating point depth is always positive, and the raw bits of a 32-bit floating point value increase monotonically in this case.

```
1  // Plane equation from three points, simplified
2  // for the case where the first point is the origin.
3  // N is normalized so that the plane equation can
4  // be used to compute signed distance.
5  float4 CreatePlaneEquation(float3 Q, float3 R)
6  {
7    // N = normalize(cross(Q-P,R-P)),
8    // except we know P is the origin
9    float3 N = normalize(cross(Q,R));
10   // D = -(N dot P), except we know P is the origin
11   return float4(N,0);
12 }
13
14 // Convert a point from postprojection space into view space
15 float3 ConvertProjToView(float4 p)
16 {
17   p = mul(p,g_mProjectionInv);
18   return (p/p.w).xyz;
19 }
20
21 void CullLightsCS(uint3 globalIdx : SV_DispatchThreadID,
22                   uint3 localIdx  : SV_GroupThreadID,
23                   uint3 groupIdx  : SV_GroupID)
24 {
25   // Depth bounds code goes here
26   ...
27   float4 frustumEqn[4];
28   { // Construct frustum planes for this tile
29     uint pxm = TILE_RES*groupIdx.x;
30     uint pym = TILE_RES*groupIdx.y;
31     uint pxp = TILE_RES*(groupIdx.x+1);
32     uint pyp = TILE_RES*(groupIdx.y+1);
33     uint width =  TILE_RES*GetNumTilesX();
34     uint height = TILE_RES*GetNumTilesY();
35
36     // Four corners of the tile, clockwise from top-left
37     float3 p[4];
38     p[0] = ConvertProjToView(float4(pxm/(float)width*2.f-1.f,
39          (height-pym)/(float)height*2.f-1.f,1.f,1.f));
40     p[1] = ConvertProjToView(float4(pxp/(float)width*2.f-1.f,
41          (height-pym)/(float)height*2.f-1.f,1.f,1.f));
42     p[2] = ConvertProjToView(float4(pxp/(float)width*2.f-1.f,
43          (height-pyp)/(float)height*2.f-1.f,1.f,1.f));
44     p[3] = ConvertProjToView(float4(pxm/(float)width*2.f-1.f,
45          (height-pyp)/(float)height*2.f-1.f,1.f,1.f));
46
47     // Create plane equations for the four sides, with
48     // the positive half-space outside the frustum
49     for(uint i=0; i<4; i++)
50       frustumEqn[i] = CreatePlaneEquation(p[i], p[(i+1)&3]);
51   }
52   // Intersection code goes here
53   ...
54 }
```

Listing 15.2. Frustum planes calculation.

15.3.2 Frustum Planes Calculation

The frustum planes code appears in Listing 15.2 and is straightforward. The four corners of the tile are constructed in postprojection space and converted to view space. These four corners are then used to calculate the planes for the four sides of the frustum partition. Two corners and the origin give the three points needed for each plane equation.

To calculate the pixel locations of the four corners, the `groupIdx` variable is used, which holds the `SV_GroupID` value (see line 23), another of the special system-value semantics available to compute shaders. Because the thread group layout from the `Dispatch` call matches the screen tiles, the `SV_GroupID` value corresponds to the tile number.

One subtlety happens on lines 33–34. Note that the screen size might not be evenly divisible by the tile size, so the screen width and height cannot be used directly in the four corners calculation. Instead, the code calculates the "whole tile" resolution, which is the closest greater-than (or equal-to) value that is evenly divisible by the tile size.

15.3.3 Intersection Testing

The depth bounds and the four plane equations form the six sides of the tile bounding volume. Light culling is accomplished by testing light bounding volumes for intersection against the tile bounding volume. This is shown in Listing 15.3.

In this example, the light bounding volumes are spheres (a natural fit for point lights), and a standard frustum versus sphere intersection test is performed. That is, the sphere is tested against the six planes of the frustum. If it passes, the index of the light in the input buffer is written to shared memory.

Note on line 28 that each thread starts the loop at a different index and increments the loop counter by `NUM_THREADS`, which is 256 for 16×16-pixel tiles. This allows 256 lights to be culled in parallel for each loop iteration. To make the parallel culling thread safe, `InterlockedAdd` is used on line 44 to increment the output list counter.

As mentioned in the introduction, compute-based tiled culling can be applied to forward rendering [Harada et al. 12] and deferred rendering [Andersson 09]. When used with forward rendering, it is commonly called Forward+ [Harada et al. 12]. When used with deferred rendering, it is called tile-based deferred [Lauritzen 10] or simply tiled deferred [Lauritzen 12]. For Forward+, the compute shader writes the per-tile list to an output buffer (i.e., `RWBuffer`). The forward pixel shader then calculates the tile to which it belongs and uses the list for that tile as input to calculate the lighting. For tiled deferred, the same compute shader that does the light culling can then do the lighting, using the list in shared

```
 1  Buffer<float4> g_LightBufferCenterAndRadius;
 2
 3  #define MAX_NUM_LIGHTS_PER_TILE 256
 4  groupshared uint ldsLightIdxCounter;
 5  groupshared uint ldsLightIdx[MAX_NUM_LIGHTS_PER_TILE];
 6
 7  // Point-plane distance, simplified for the case where
 8  // the plane passes through the origin
 9  float GetSignedDistanceFromPlane(float3 p, float4 eqn)
10  {
11    // dot(eqn.xyz, p) + eqn.w, except we know eqn.w is zero
12    return dot(eqn.xyz, p);
13  }
14
15  #define NUM_THREADS (TILE_RES*TILE_RES)
16  void CullLightsCS(...)
17  {
18    // Depth bounds and frustum planes code goes here
19    ...
20    if(threadNum == 0)
21    {
22      ldsLightIdxCounter = 0;
23    }
24    GroupMemoryBarrierWithGroupSync();
25
26    // Loop over the lights and do a
27    // sphere versus frustum intersection test
28    for(uint i=threadNum; i<g_uNumLights; i+=NUM_THREADS)
29    {
30      float4 p = g_LightBufferCenterAndRadius[i];
31      float  r = p.w;
32      float3 c = mul(float4(p.xyz,1), g_mView).xyz;
33
34      // Test if sphere is intersecting or inside frustum
35      if((GetSignedDistanceFromPlane(c,frustumEqn[0]) < r) &&
36        (GetSignedDistanceFromPlane(c,frustumEqn[1]) < r) &&
37        (GetSignedDistanceFromPlane(c,frustumEqn[2]) < r) &&
38        (GetSignedDistanceFromPlane(c,frustumEqn[3]) < r) &&
39        (-c.z + minZ < r) && (c.z - maxZ < r))
40      {
41        // Do a thread-safe increment of the list counter
42        // and put the index of this light into the list
43        uint dstIdx = 0;
44        InterlockedAdd(ldsLightIdxCounter,1,dstIdx);
45        ldsLightIdx[dstIdx] = i;
46      }
47    }
48    GroupMemoryBarrierWithGroupSync();
49  }
```

Listing 15.3. Intersection testing.

memory directly. Even if lights overlap, the G-buffer is only read once for each pixel, and the lighting results are accumulated into shader registers instead of blended into a render target, reducing bandwidth consumption.

15.4 Optimization

This section covers various optimizations to the compute-based tiled-culling technique. Common pitfalls to avoid are presented first, followed by several optimizations to the basic implementation from the previous section.

15.4.1 Common Pitfalls

Part of optimization is avoiding common pitfalls. Two such pitfalls for compute-based tiled culling are described in this section: forgetting to be cache friendly and choosing a suboptimal tile size. The pitfalls are illustrated by making two seemingly small changes to the code in Section 15.3 and showing that those changes hurt performance dramatically.

For the first change, note that line 1 in Listing 15.3 shows that the light bounding spheres (centers and radii) were stored in a buffer with no other data. However, for convenience and code clarity, developers might decide to include other light data in the same buffer, as shown below.

```
struct LightArrayData
{
    float4 v4CenterAndRadius;
    float4 v4Color;
};
StructuredBuffer<LightArrayData> g_LightBuffer;
```

For the second change, recall that line 14 in Listing 15.1 defines TILE_RES as 16, resulting in 16 × 16 threads per thread group, or 256 threads. For AMD GPUs, work is executed in 64-thread batches called *wavefronts*, while on NVIDIA GPUs, work is executed in 32-thread *warps*. Thus, efficient compute shader execution requires the number of threads in a thread group to be a multiple of 64 for AMD or 32 for NVIDIA. Since every multiple of 64 is a multiple of 32, standard performance advice is to configure the thread count to be a multiple of 64. Because 256 is a multiple of 64, setting TILE_RES to 16 follows this advice. Alternatively, setting TILE_RES to 8 (resulting in 8 × 8-pixel tiles) yields 64 threads per thread group, which is certainly also a multiple of 64, and the smaller tile size might result in tighter culling.

Although these two changes seem minor, both decrease performance, as shown in Figure 15.3. The "unoptimized" curve contains both changes (combined light data in a StructuredBuffer and 8 × 8 tiles). For the cache friendly curve, the

---

[3]All performance data in this chapter was gathered on an AMD Radeon R7 260X GPU. The R7 260X was chosen because its performance characteristics are roughly comparable to the Xbox One and Playstation 4.

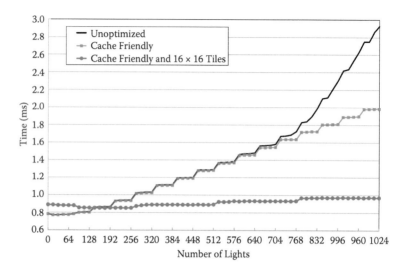

Figure 15.3. Basic optimizations.[3]Tiled-culling compute shader execution time versus number of lights for Forward+ rendering at 1920×1080 using the companion code for this chapter.

`StructuredBuffer` is replaced with the declaration shown in line 1 of Listing 15.3 containing only the data needed for culling. Note that, while performance is similar for much of the chart, performance improves by nearly 1 ms for 1024 lights. Specifically, compute shader execution time decreases from 2.93 ms to 1.99 ms, a 32% reduction.

The "cache friendly" label hints at why this configuration improves performance. Data not needed for culling pollutes the cache during compute shader execution, eventually becoming a bottleneck as light count increases. In general, a structure of arrays (in this case, separate arrays for culling data and light color) is often better for GPU execution than an array of structures, because it allows more cache-friendly memory access.

The "cache friendly and 16×16 tiles" curve keeps the cache-friendly light buffer and changes `TILE_RES` back to 16, resulting in the implementation given in Section 15.3. Because there are now 256 threads, many threads do not have any lights to cull at the lower end of the chart, resulting in a slight performance decrease initially. However, this version scales much better with increasing light counts. At 1024 lights, compute shader execution time is 0.97 ms, a 51% reduction from the previous version and a 67% reduction from the unoptimized version.

The 16×16 configuration is better because more threads per thread group results in more wavefronts/warps in flight per thread group. This allows GPU schedulers to better hide memory latency by switching execution to a new wavefront/warp when the current one hits a high-latency operation.

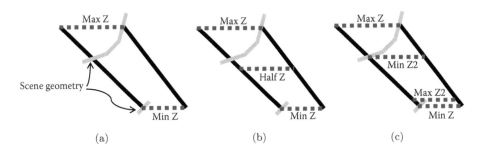

Figure 15.4. Depth discontinuity optimization strategies. (a) Scene depth discontinuities can cause a large depth range in the tile bounding volume. (b) The Half Z method splits the depth range in half and culls against the two ranges. (c) The Modified Half Z method calculates a second minimum and maximum, bounded by the Half Z value.

15.4.2 Depth Discontinuities

Having covered the basic optimizations already present in the code from Section 15.3, additional optimizations will now be presented, starting with those for discontinuities in scene depth.

Figure 15.4 shows 2D representations of a tile bounding volume, similar to that shown for Tile 0 in Figure 15.1(b). As demonstrated in Figure 15.4(a), a foreground object in front of a background object can lead to a large depth range in the tile bounding volume. Lights can intersect the empty space between foreground and background but not actually affect any pixels in the tile. That is, depth discontinuities can lead to an increase in false-positive intersections.

Half Z. Figure 15.4(b) shows a strategy to better handle depth discontinuities called the Half Z method. It simply divides the depth range in two at the midpoint and culls against two depth ranges: one from Min Z to Half Z, and one from Half Z to Max Z. A separate per-tile list is maintained for each depth range. This method requires only two additional plane tests and is a minor change to the code. Listing 15.4 shows the intersection test for this method.

Modified Half Z. Figure 15.4(c) shows a second strategy called the Modified Half Z method. It performs additional atomic operations to find a second maximum (Max Z2) between Min Z and Half Z and a second minimum (Min Z2) between Half Z and Max Z. This can result in tighter bounding volumes compared to the Half Z method, but calculating the additional minimum and maximum is more expensive than simply calculating Half Z, due to the additional atomic operations required.

Light count reduction results. Figure 15.5 shows the reduction in per-tile light count at depth discontinuities from the methods discussed in this section. Note

```
// Test if sphere is intersecting or inside frustum
if ((GetSignedDistanceFromPlane(c,frustumEqn[0]) < r) &&
    (GetSignedDistanceFromPlane(c,frustumEqn[1]) < r) &&
    (GetSignedDistanceFromPlane(c,frustumEqn[2]) < r) &&
    (GetSignedDistanceFromPlane(c,frustumEqn[3]) < r))
{
  if(-c.z + minZ < r && c.z - halfZ < r)
  {
    // Do a thread-safe increment of the list counter
    // and put the index of this light into the list
    uint dstIdx = 0;
    InterlockedAdd(ldsLightIdxCounterA,1,dstIdx);
    ldsLightIdxA[dstIdx] = i;
  }
  if(-c.z + halfZ < r && c.z - maxZ < r)
  {
    // Do a thread-safe increment of the list counter
    // and put the index of this light into the list
    uint dstIdx = 0;
    InterlockedAdd(ldsLightIdxCounterB,1,dstIdx);
    ldsLightIdxB[dstIdx] = i;
  }
}
```

Listing 15.4. Half Z method.

the column in the foreground of the left side of the scene in Figure 15.5(a). This causes depth discontinuities for tiles along the column, resulting in the high light counts shown in red in Figure 15.5(c) for the baseline implementation in Section 15.3.

The results for the Half Z method are shown in Figure 15.5(d). Note that the light counts for tiles along the column have been reduced. Then, for the Modified Half Z method, note that light counts have been further reduced in Figure 15.5(e).

Performance results. Figure 15.6 shows the performance of these methods. Note that, while Figure 15.3 measured only the tiled-culling compute shader, Figure 15.6 measures both the compute shader and the forward pixel shader for Forward+ rendering. More time spent during culling can still be an overall performance win if enough time is saved during lighting, so it is important to measure both here.

The "Baseline" curve is from the implementation in Section 15.3. The "Half Z" curve shows this method at a slight performance disadvantage for lower light counts, because the savings during lighting do not yet outweigh the extra cost of testing two depth ranges and maintaining two lists. However, this method becomes faster at higher light counts. The "Modified Half Z" curve starts out with a bigger deficit, due to the higher cost of calculating the additional minimum and maximum with atomics. It eventually pulls ahead of the baseline method, but never catches Half Z. However, this method's smaller depth ranges can still be useful if additional optimizations are implemented, as shown next.

Figure 15.5. Tiled-culling optimization results using the companion code for this chapter. (a) Scene render. (b) Log scale lights-per-tile legend. (c) Baseline. (d) Half Z. (e) Modified Half Z. (f) Modified Half Z with AABBs.

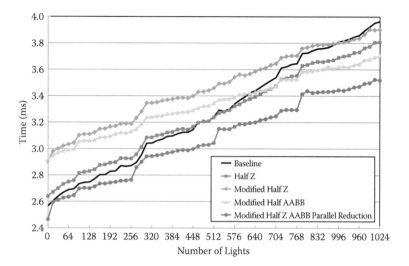

Figure 15.6. Tiled-culling optimizations. GPU execution time versus number of lights using the companion code for this chapter. The vertical axis represents the combined time for the tiled-culling compute shader and the forward pixel shader in Forward+ rendering at 1920×1080.

15.4.3   Frustum Planes versus AABBs

In our previous discussion of the results in Figure 15.5, one result was not mentioned. If view-space axis-aligned bounding boxes (AABBs) are used to bound the tile instead of frustum planes, per-tile light counts can be further reduced, as shown in Figure 15.5(f).

Testing intersection against a frustum using six planes is an approximation. As shown in Figure 15.7(a), the actual intersection volume has curved corners. Regions exist outside the curved corners that will still pass testing against the planes, resulting in false-positive intersections.

Fitting an AABB around the tile's frustum partition will also produce regions where false-positive intersections can occur, as illustrated in Figure 15.7(b). The key difference is that, as the depth range decreases (i.e., as Max Z gets closer to Min Z), these regions get smaller for AABBs, as shown in Figure 15.7(c).

Referring back to Figure 15.5(f), using AABBs with the smaller depth ranges of the Modified Half Z method results in a significant reduction in per-tile light counts. Whereas the previous results showed improvement primarily at depth discontinuities, this method shows an overall improvement. For small depth ranges, the AABB intersection volume nearly matches the true volume, resulting in tighter culling.

Referring back to Figure 15.6, the "Modified Half Z, AABB" curve still starts out at a deficit, due to the increased cost of finding the second minimum and max-

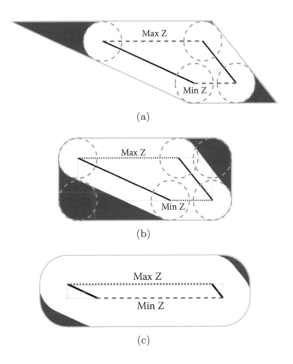

(a)

(b)

(c)

Figure 15.7. Frustum planes versus AABBs. False positive intersections will occur in the shaded regions. (a) Frustum intersection testing. (b) AABB intersection testing. (c) AABB intersection with a small depth range.

imum. However, it scales better as light count increases, eventually overtaking the Half Z method.

15.4.4 Parallel Reduction

Using AABBs with the smaller depth ranges of the Modified Half Z method produces good culling results, but the cost of the second minimum and maximum is significant. There is, however, another way to calculate the depth bounds: parallel reduction. Using the methods first outlined in [Harris 07], as well as the results from [Engel 14], an optimized parallel reduction implementation can be used to produce the smaller depth ranges of the Modified Half Z method, as shown in Listing 15.5.

```
1  Texture2D<float>    g_SceneDepthBuffer;
2  RWTexture2D<float4> g_DepthBounds;
3
4  #define TILE_RES 16
5  #define NUM_THREADS_1D (TILE_RES/2)
```

```
6  #define NUM_THREADS (NUM_THREADS_1D*NUM_THREADS_1D)
7
8  // Thread Group Shared Memory (aka local data share, or LDS)
9  groupshared float ldsZMin[NUM_THREADS];
10 groupshared float ldsZMax[NUM_THREADS];
11
12 // Convert a depth value from postprojection space
13 // into view space
14 float ConvertProjDepthToView( float z )
15 {
16   return (1.f/(z*g_mProjectionInv._34 + g_mProjectionInv._44));
17 }
18
19 [numthreads(NUM_THREADS_1D,NUM_THREADS_1D,1)]
20 void DepthBoundsCS( uint3 globalIdx : SV_DispatchThreadID,
21                     uint3 localIdx  : SV_GroupThreadID,
22                     uint3 groupIdx  : SV_GroupID )
23 {
24   uint2 sampleIdx = globalIdx.xy*2;
25
26   // Load four depth samples
27   float depth00 = g_SceneDepthBuffer.Load(uint3(sampleIdx.x,
28                                           sampleIdx.y,0)).x;
29   float depth01 = g_SceneDepthBuffer.Load(uint3(sampleIdx.x,
30                                           sampleIdx.y+1,0)).x;
31   float depth10 = g_SceneDepthBuffer.Load(uint3(sampleIdx.x+1,
32                                           sampleIdx.y,0)).x;
33   float depth11 = g_SceneDepthBuffer.Load(uint3(sampleIdx.x+1,
34                                           sampleIdx.y+1,0)).x;
35
36   float viewPosZ00 = ConvertProjDepthToView(depth00);
37   float viewPosZ01 = ConvertProjDepthToView(depth01);
38   float viewPosZ10 = ConvertProjDepthToView(depth10);
39   float viewPosZ11 = ConvertProjDepthToView(depth11);
40
41   uint threadNum = localIdx.x + localIdx.y*NUM_THREADS_1D;
42
43   // Use parallel reduction to calculate the depth bounds
44   {
45     // Parts of the depth buffer that were never written
46     // (e.g., the sky) will be zero (the companion code uses
47     // inverted 32-bit float depth for better precision).
48     float minZ00 = (depth00 != 0.f) ? viewPosZ00 : FLT_MAX;
49     float minZ01 = (depth01 != 0.f) ? viewPosZ01 : FLT_MAX;
50     float minZ10 = (depth10 != 0.f) ? viewPosZ10 : FLT_MAX;
51     float minZ11 = (depth11 != 0.f) ? viewPosZ11 : FLT_MAX;
52
53     float maxZ00 = (depth00 != 0.f) ? viewPosZ00 : 0.0f;
54     float maxZ01 = (depth01 != 0.f) ? viewPosZ01 : 0.0f;
55     float maxZ10 = (depth10 != 0.f) ? viewPosZ10 : 0.0f;
56     float maxZ11 = (depth11 != 0.f) ? viewPosZ11 : 0.0f;
57
58     // Initialize shared memory
59     ldsZMin[threadNum] = min(minZ00,min(minZ01,
60                                     min(minZ10,minZ11)));
61     ldsZMax[threadNum] = max(maxZ00,max(maxZ01,
62                                     max(maxZ10,maxZ11)));
63     GroupMemoryBarrierWithGroupSync();
64
65     // Minimum and maximum using parallel reduction, with the
66     // loop manually unrolled for 8x8 thread groups (64 threads
67     // per thread group)
68     if (threadNum < 32)
69     {
```

```
 70        ldsZMin[threadNum] = min(ldsZMin[threadNum],
 71                                 ldsZMin[threadNum+32]);
 72        ldsZMax[threadNum] = max(ldsZMax[threadNum],
 73                                 ldsZMax[threadNum+32]);
 74        ldsZMin[threadNum] = min(ldsZMin[threadNum],
 75                                 ldsZMin[threadNum+16]);
 76        ldsZMax[threadNum] = max(ldsZMax[threadNum],
 77                                 ldsZMax[threadNum+16]);
 78        ldsZMin[threadNum] = min(ldsZMin[threadNum],
 79                                 ldsZMin[threadNum+8]);
 80        ldsZMax[threadNum] = max(ldsZMax[threadNum],
 81                                 ldsZMax[threadNum+8]);
 82        ldsZMin[threadNum] = min(ldsZMin[threadNum],
 83                                 ldsZMin[threadNum+4]);
 84        ldsZMax[threadNum] = max(ldsZMax[threadNum],
 85                                 ldsZMax[threadNum+4]);
 86        ldsZMin[threadNum] = min(ldsZMin[threadNum],
 87                                 ldsZMin[threadNum+2]);
 88        ldsZMax[threadNum] = max(ldsZMax[threadNum],
 89                                 ldsZMax[threadNum+2]);
 90        ldsZMin[threadNum] = min(ldsZMin[threadNum],
 91                                 ldsZMin[threadNum+1]);
 92        ldsZMax[threadNum] = max(ldsZMax[threadNum],
 93                                 ldsZMax[threadNum+1]);
 94      }
 95    }
 96    GroupMemoryBarrierWithGroupSync();
 97
 98    float minZ = ldsZMin[0];
 99    float maxZ = ldsZMax[0];
100    float halfZ = 0.5f*(minZ + maxZ);
101
102    // Calculate a second set of depth values: the maximum
103    // on the near side of Half Z and the minimum on the far
104    // side of Half Z
105    {
106      // See the companion code for details
107      ...
108    }
109
110    // The first thread writes to the depth bounds texture
111    if(threadNum == 0)
112    {
113      float maxZ2 = ldsZMax[0];
114      float minZ2 = ldsZMin[0];
115      g_DepthBounds[groupIdx.xy] = float4(minZ,maxZ2,minZ2,maxZ);
116    }
117  }
```

Listing 15.5. Depth bounds using parallel reduction.

As noted in [Harris 07] and [Engel 14], an optimized parallel reduction implementation requires each thread to work on more than one source value. For the code in Listing 15.5, each thread loads four depth samples in a 2×2 grid instead of just a single sample. However, this requires the thread layout to be 8×8 for 16×16-pixel tiles. That is, the parallel reduction must be executed in a separate compute shader. However, even with the extra overhead of an additional pass, the four-samples-per-thread method is faster than keeping the parallel reduction in the culling compute shader but only loading a single sample per thread.

Referring back to Figure 15.6, the "Modified Half Z, AABB, Parallel Reduction" curve is the fastest method throughout. For 1024 lights, the baseline code executes in 3.97 ms, whereas this final optimized version takes 3.52 ms, a reduction of roughly half a millisecond. This represents an 11% decrease in execution time compared to the baseline.

15.5   Unreal Engine 4 Results

Results to this point have been gathered using the companion code for this chapter. This section presents results using the Unreal Engine 4 *Infiltrator* real-time demo. Unreal Engine 4 is a leading real-time rendering engine that implements the tiled-deferred technique. The *Infiltrator* demo allows results to be gathered using state-of-the-art visuals.

Figures 15.8 and 15.9 show two examples of the per-tile light count reduction achieved by using the Modified Half Z method with AABBs. Note the results for baseline tiled culling, which uses an implementation similar to Section 15.3. In each example, high-light-count areas appear along the silhouette of the infiltrator character, where the transition from foreground to background causes depth discontinuities. These areas are eliminated in the optimized version. In addition, the tighter tile bounding volumes from AABBs with small depth ranges reduce light counts overall.

Figure 15.10 shows the GPU execution time improvement of the optimized method (Modified Half Z with AABBs using parallel reduction for the depth ranges) compared to the baseline implementation similar to Section 15.3. For tiled deferred, the execution time includes the three parts of Algorithm 15.1 (depth bounds calculation, tile bounding volume construction, and intersection testing), as well as the lighting calculations. As shown in Figure 15.10, the optimized version is substantially faster over the entire *Infiltrator* demo. Average cost of the baseline implementation is 5.17 ms, whereas the optimized average cost is 3.74 ms, a reduction of 1.43 ms, or roughly 28% faster.

15.5.1   Standard Deferred versus Tiled Deferred

Unreal Engine 4 can apply lighting using either standard deferred or tiled deferred, offering the opportunity to compare the performance of the two methods. Figure 15.11 shows the GPU execution time improvement of the optimized tiled-deferred method compared to the standard-deferred method. Note that, while tiled deferred is usually faster in the demo, there are areas where standard deferred is faster (i.e., the negative values in the chart). Recall that the primary lighting performance concern with standard deferred is the extra bandwidth consumed when blending overlapping lights. In areas without much light overlap, the savings from tiled deferred's single-pass lighting might not outweigh the cost

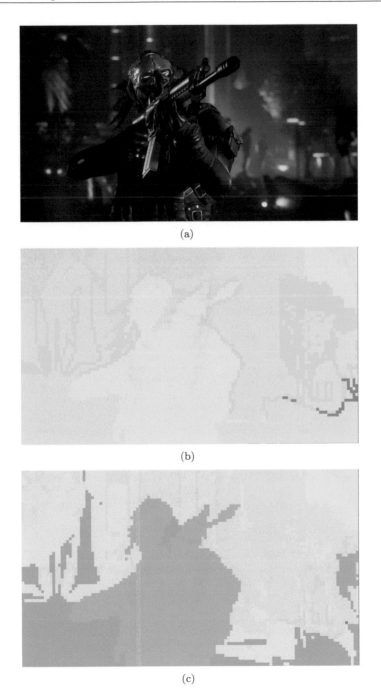

(a)

(b)

(c)

Figure 15.8. Unreal Engine 4 *Infiltrator* demo: Example 1. (a) Scene render. (b) Baseline tiled culling. (c) Modified Half Z with AABBs.

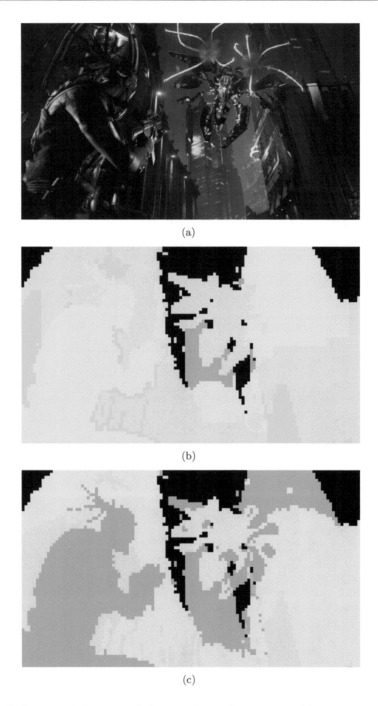

Figure 15.9. Unreal Engine 4 *Infiltrator* demo: Example 2. (a) Scene render. (b) Baseline tiled culling. (c) Modified Half Z with AABBs.

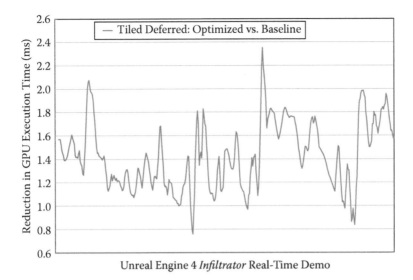

Figure 15.10. Unreal Engine 4 tiled-culling execution time improvement for the optimized version compared to the baseline implementation. Performance was measured over the entire *Infiltrator* demo at 1920×1080.

of calculating the depth bounds and performing the per-tile culling. However, averaged over the entire demo, tiled deferred is still faster overall. Specifically, the average cost of standard deferred is 4.28 ms, whereas the optimized tiled-deferred average cost is 3.74 ms, a reduction of 0.54 ms, or roughly 13% faster.

It is natural to wonder exactly how many lights are needed in a scene with "many lights" before tiled deferred is consistently faster than standard deferred. The answer will depend on several factors including the depth complexity of the scene and the amount of light overlap. For the *Infiltrator* demo, Figure 15.12 is a scatterplot of the data used to generate Figure 15.11 plotted against the number of lights processed during that particular frame. The demo uses a wide range of light counts, from a low of 7 to a high of 980. The average light count is 299 and the median is 218.

For high light counts (above 576), tiled deferred has either comparable or better performance, and is often significantly faster. For example, for counts above 640, tiled deferred is 1.65 ms faster on average. Conversely, for low light counts (below 64), standard deferred is faster. For light counts above 64 but below 576, the situation is less clear from just looking at the chart. Standard deferred values appear both above and below tiled deferred in this range. However, it is worth noting that tiled deferred comes out ahead on average over each interval on the "Number of Lights" axis (i.e., $[0, 64]$, $[64, 128]$, $[128, 192]$, etc.) except $[0, 64]$.

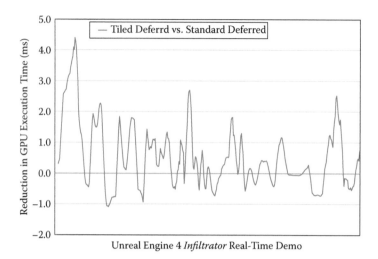

Figure 15.11. Unreal Engine 4 optimized tiled-deferred execution time improvement compared to standard deferred. Performance was measured over the entire *Infiltrator* demo using 1920×1080 screen resolution.

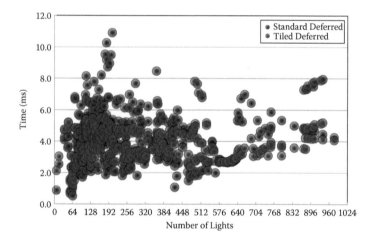

Figure 15.12. Unreal Engine 4 optimized tiled deferred versus standard deferred. GPU execution time versus number of lights. Performance was measured over the entire *Infiltrator* demo at 1920×1080.

To get a clearer picture of average performance, Figure 15.13 applies a moving average to the data in Figure 15.12. The data shows that, while standard deferred is 0.76 ms faster on average for light counts of 70 and below, tiled deferred is on

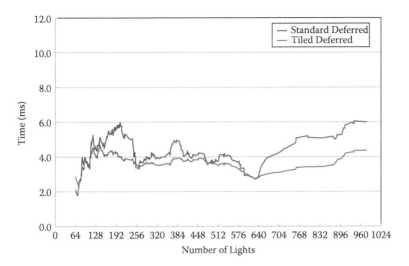

Figure 15.13. Unreal Engine 4 optimized tiled deferred versus standard deferred. GPU execution time versus number of lights. A moving average was applied to the data in Figure 15.12 to show overall trends.

par with or faster than standard deferred for above 70 lights. Thus, for the particular case of the *Infiltrator* demo, 70 is the threshold for when tiled deferred is consistently faster than (or at least comparable to) standard deferred.

Referring back to Figure 15.12, another thing to note about the data is that the standard deviation is lower for tiled deferred. Specifically, the standard deviation is 1.79 ms for standard deferred and 0.90 ms for tiled deferred, a 50% reduction. Note that worst-case performance is also much better for tiled deferred, with no tiled deferred data point appearing above the 6.0 ms line. That is, in addition to getting faster performance on average, tiled deferred also offers more consistent performance, making it easier to achieve a smooth framerate.

15.6   Conclusion

This chapter presented an optimized compute-based tiled-culling implementation for scenes with many dynamic lights. The technique allows forward rendering to support such scenes with high performance. It also improves the performance of deferred rendering for these scenes by reducing the average cost to calculate lighting, as well as the worst-case cost and standard deviation. That is, it provides both faster performance (on average) and more consistent performance, avoiding the bandwidth bottleneck from blending overlapping lights. For more details, see the companion code.

15.7 Acknowledgments

Many thanks to the rendering engineers at Epic Games, specifically Brian Karis for the idea to use AABBs to bound the tiles and Martin Mittring for the initial implementation of AABBs and for the Modified Half Z method. Thanks also go out to Martin for providing feedback for this chapter. And thanks to the Epic rendering team and Epic Games in general for supporting this work.

The following are either registered trademarks or trademarks of the listed companies in the United States and/or other countries: AMD, Radeon, and combinations thereof are trademarks of Advanced Micro Devices, Inc.; Unreal is a registered trademark of Epic Games, Inc.; Xbox One is a trademark of Microsoft Corporation.; NVIDIA is a registered trademark of NVIDIA Corporation.; Playstation 4 is a trademark of Sony Computer Entertainment, Inc.

Bibliography

[Andersson 09] Johan Andersson. "Parallel Graphics in Frostbite—Current and Future." Beyond Programmable Shading, SIGGRAPH Course, New Orleans, LA, August 3–7, 2009.

[Engel 14] Wolfgang Engel. "Compute Shader Optimizations for AMD GPUs: Parallel Reduction." *Diary of a Graphics Programmer*, http://diaryofagraphicsprogrammer.blogspot.com/2014/03/compute-shader-optimizations-for-amd.html, March 26, 2014.

[Harada et al. 12] Takahiro Harada, Jay McKee, and Jason C.Yang. "Forward+: Bringing Deferred Lighting to the Next Level." Paper presented at Eurographics, Cagliari, Italy, May 13–18, 2012.

[Harris 07] Mark Harris. "Optimizing Parallel Reduction in CUDA." NVIDIA, http://developer.download.nvidia.com/compute/cuda/1.1-Beta/x86_website/projects/reduction/doc/reduction.pdf, 2007.

[Lauritzen 10] Andrew Lauritzen. "Deferred Rendering for Current and Future Rendering Pipelines." Beyond Programmable Shading, SIGGRAPH Course, Los Angeles, CA, July 25–29, 2010.

[Lauritzen 12] Andrew Lauritzen. "Intersecting Lights with Pixels: Reasoning about Forward and Deferred Rendering." Beyond Programmable Shading, SIGGRAPH Course, Los Angeles, CA, August 5–9, 2012.

[Saito and Takahashi 90] Takafumi Saito and Tokiichiro Takahashi. "Comprehensible Rendering of 3-D Shapes." *Computer Graphics: Proc. SIGGRAPH* 24:4 (1990), 197–206.

16

Rendering Vector Displacement-Mapped Surfaces in a GPU Ray Tracer
Takahiro Harada

16.1 Introduction

Ray tracing is an elegant solution to render high-quality images. By combining Monte Carlo integration with ray tracing, we can solve the rendering equation. However, a disadvantage of using ray tracing is its high computational cost, which makes render time long. To improve the performance, GPUs have been used. However, GPU ray tracers typically do not have as many features as CPU ray tracers. Vector displacement mapping is one of the features that we do not see much in GPU ray tracers. When vector displacement mapping is evaluated on the fly (i.e., without creating a large number of polygons in the preprocess and storing them in the memory), it allows us to render a highly geometric detailed scene from a simple mesh. Since geometric detail is an important factor for realism, vector displacement mapping is an important technique in ray tracing. In this chapter, we describe a method to render vector displacement-mapped surfaces in a GPU ray tracer.

16.2 Displacement Mapping

Displacement mapping is a technique to add geometric detail to a simple geometry. Although the goal is similar to normal mapping, it actually creates high-resolution geometries, as shown in Figure 16.1, from a low-resolution mesh (Figure 16.2), while normal mapping only changes the normal vector to add an illusion of having a geometric detail. There are two types of displacement mapping. The one we usually call displacement mapping uses textures storing scalar values, which are used as offsets for the displacement using the surface normal as the

Figure 16.1. The "Party" scene with vector displacement-mapped surfaces rendered using the proposed method. The rendering time is 77 ms/frame on an AMD FirePro W9100 GPU. Instancing is not used to stress the rendering algorithm. If pretessellated, the geometry requires 52 GB of memory.

Figure 16.2. The base mesh used for the "Party" scene.

displacement direction. We call this approach *scalar displacement mapping*. The other is *vector displacement mapping*, which uses a texture storing vector values that are used as the displacement vector of the surface. Because the displacement can be an arbitrary direction, it gives a lot of freedom for what we create from a simple geometry. For example, scalar displacement mapping cannot create an overhang as shown in Figure 16.3, but vector displacement mapping can.

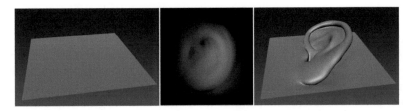

Figure 16.3. Illustration of vector displacement mapping. (a) Simple geometry (a quad). (b) A vector displacement map. (c) Surface after applying vector displacement.

This freedom in vector displacement mapping poses technical challenges when it is ray traced. Although we could use algorithms, such as the method proposed by [Smits et al. 00], for ray tracing a scalar displacement-mapped surface by utilizing the constraint in the displacement direction, we cannot apply it for a vector displacement-mapped surface because the assumption does not apply. In vector displacement mapping, there is no constraint in displacement direction. So when we check the intersection of a ray with a vector displacement patch (VD patch), we cannot avoid creating the detailed geometry by tessellating and displacing vertices and building a spatial acceleration structure for those.

16.3 Ray Tracing a Scene with Vector Displacement Maps

Ray tracing requires identifying a closest hit point for a ray with the scene, which is accelerated by using a spatial acceleration structure. Bounding volume hierarchies (BVHs) as acceleration structures are often employed. When we implement a ray tracer only for simple primitives such as triangles and quads, we compute the intersection to a primitive once we encounter it during BVH traversal. However, an intersection to a VD patch is much more expensive to compute than an intersection test with these simple primitives, especially when direct ray tracing is used (i.e., a VD patch is tessellated and displaced on the fly). To amortize the cost of tessellation and displacement, we want to gather all the rays intersecting the AABB of a VD patch and process them at once rather than subdividing and displacing a VD patch every time a ray hits its AABB, as studied by [Hanika et al. 10].

16.4 Ray Tracing a Vector Displacement Patch

This section focuses on the ray–VD patch intersection, although using it in a ray tracer requires additional changes, which are going to be discussed in Section 16.5. In this section, we first describe a single-threaded implementation of the intersection of a ray with a VD patch to simplify the explanation. We then extend it for a parallel implementation using OpenCL.

16.4.1   Single Ray

To intersect a ray with a VD patch, we first need to build the detailed geometry of the patch by tessellating it to generate vertices, which are then displaced by the value fetched from the vector displacement map. Although there are several ways to generate vertices, we simply generate them uniformly on the patch (i.e., all the generated vertices are on the plane of the patch) without geometry smoothing.

Data structure.   We could find the closest intersection by testing primitives in the scene one by one, but it is better to create a spatial acceleration structure to do this efficiently. As we build it on the fly, the build performance is as important as the intersection performance. Therefore, we employed a simple acceleration structure. A patch is split into four patches recursively to build a complete quad BVH. At the lowest level of the BVH, four vertex positions and texture coordinates are linearly interpolated from the values of the root patch. The displaced vertex position is then calculated by adding the displacement vector value, which is fetched from a texture using the interpolated texture coordinate. Next, the AABBs enclosing these four vertices are computed and used as the geometry at the leaves rather than a quad because we subdivide the patch smaller than a pixel size. This allows us not to store geometries (e.g., vertices), but only store the BVH. Thus, we can reduce the data size for a VD patch. A texture coordinate and normal vector are also computed and stored within a node. Once leaf nodes are computed, it ascends the tree level by level and builds the nodes of the inner level. It does this by computing the union of AABBs and averaging normal vectors and texture coordinates of the four child nodes. This process is repeated until it reaches the root node.

For better performance, the memory footprint for the BVH has to be reduced as much as possible. Thus, an AABB is compressed by quantizing the maximum and minimum values into 2 byte integers $(\max_q, \min_q)$ these as follows:

$$\max_q = 0xfff7 \times (\max_f - \min_{\mathrm{root}})/\mathrm{extent}_{\mathrm{root}} + 1,$$
$$\min_q = 0xfff7 \times (\min_f - \min_{\mathrm{root}})/\mathrm{extent}_{\mathrm{root}},$$
$$\mathrm{extent}_{\mathrm{root}} = \max_{\mathrm{root}} - \min_{\mathrm{root}}.$$

where $\max_f$ and $\min_f$ are uncompressed maximum and minimum values, respectively, of the AABB and $\max_{\mathrm{root}}$ and $\min_{\mathrm{root}}$ are values of the root AABB. We considered compressing them into 1-byte integers, but the accuracy was not high enough since the subdivision level can easily go higher than the resolution limit of 1-byte integers (i.e., eight levels). We also quantized texture coordinates and the normal vectors into 4 bytes each. Therefore, the total memory footprint for a node is 20 bytes (Figure 16.4).

We separate the hierarchy of the BVH from the node data (i.e., a node does not store links to other nodes such as children). This is to keep the memory footprint for nodes small. We only store one hierarchy data structure for all VD

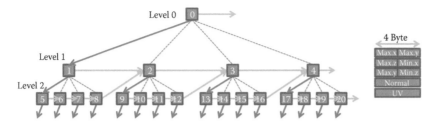

Figure 16.4. Quad BVH. Each node stores two links: one pointing to the first children (red), and one pointing to the skip node (green). To check if a node is a leaf of level i, the node index is compared to $(4^i - 1)/3$, e.g., leaf nodes of level 2 BVH are nodes whose index is greater than 5. Data layout in a node is shown on the left.

patches because we always create a complete quad BVH so that the hierarchy structure is the same for all the BVHs we construct. Although we build a BVH at different depths (i.e., levels), we only compute and store the hierarchy structure for the maximum level we might build. As nodes are stored in breadth-first order, leaf nodes can be identified easily by checking their index. Leaf nodes at the ith level are nodes with indices larger than $(4^i - 1)/3$, as shown in Figure 16.4.

We use stackless traversal for BVH traversal. Thus, a node in the hierarchy structure stores two indices of the first child and the skip node (Figure 16.4). These two indices are packed and stored in 4 bytes of data.

To summarize the data structure we have

- precomputed data for the hierarchy structure,

- BVH (array of nodes) built on the fly.

In Listing 16.1, they are denoted as `gNodes` and `gLinks`, respectively.

Traversal and intersection. The primary reason we employed a stackless traversal is to reduce the memory traffic and register pressure, which affects the performance. Moreover, since the data for the state of the ray is the index of the current node, we could easily shuffle rays to improve the performance, although we have not investigated this optimization yet.

As we have already built the BVH for the patch, the traversal is straightforward. Pseudocode is shown in Listing 16.1. An overview of the process is depicted in Figure 16.5.

16.4.2 OpenCL Implementation

To fully utilize the GPU, we have to parallelize the algorithm described in Section 16.4.1. We implemented our algorithm using OpenCL, and we used AMD GPUs; thus, we follow these respective terminologies in the next explanation.

```
__global Node* gNodes;
__global u32* gLinks;
float f;
u32 n, uv;
int o = getOffset( lodRes );
while( nodeIdx != breakIdx )
{
  Aabb node = NodeGetAabb( gNodes[nodeIdx] ); // reconstruct AABB
  float frac = AabbIntersect( node, &from, &to, &invRay );
  bool isLeaf = nodeIdx >= o;
  if( frac < f )
  {
    if( isLeaf )
    {
      f = frac;
      n = gNodes[nodeIdx].m_n;
      uv = gNodes[nodeIdx].m_uv;
      nodeIdx = LinkGetSkip( gLinks[nodeIdx] );
    }
    else
      nodeIdx = LinkGetChild( gLinks[nodeIdx] );
  }
  else
    nodeIdx = LinkGetSkip( gLinks[nodeIdx] );
}
```

Listing 16.1. Bottom-level hierarchy traversal.

Before we start intersecting rays with VD patches, we gather all the rays hitting the AABB of any VD patches. When a ray hits multiple VD patches, we store multiple hits. These hits are sorted by a VD patch index. This results in a list of VD patches, each of which has a list of rays.

We implemented a kernel doing both BVH build and its traversal. Work groups are launched with the number of work items optimal for the respective GPU architecture. We use AMD GPUs, which are 64-wide SIMD, so 64 work items are executed for a work group. A work group first fetches a VD patch from the list of unprocessed VD patches. This work group is responsible for the intersection of all rays hitting the AABBs of the root patch. First, we use work items executing in parallel for building the BVH. However, as we build a BVH for the patch that has to be stored somewhere, we need to allocate memory for it and therefore the question is where to allocate. The first candidate is in the local data share (LDS), but it is too small if we build a BVH with six levels (64×64 leaf nodes), which requires 108 KB ($= 5400$ nodes $\times$ 20 B). If we limit the number of levels to five (32×32 leaf nodes), we only require 26 KB. Although this is smaller than the maximum allocation size for the LDS (32 KB) for an AMD FirePro W9100 GPU, we can only schedule two work groups per compute unit. (A compute unit has 4 SIMD engines.) Thus, it cannot schedule enough work groups for a SIMD to hide latencies, which results in poor performance. Instead of storing it in the LDS, we store it in the global memory, whose access

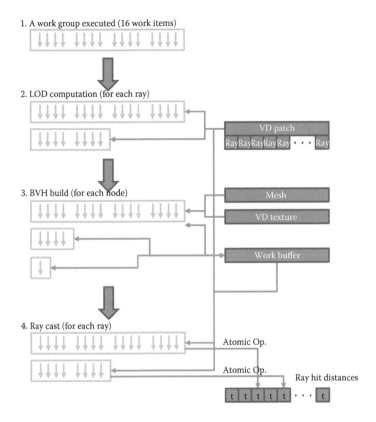

1. A work group executed (16 work items)

2. LOD computation (for each ray)

VD patch

RayRayRayRayRay • • • Ray

3. BVH build (for each node)

Mesh

VD texture

Work buffer

4. Ray cast (for each ray)

Atomic Op.

Atomic Op.

Ray hit distances

t t t t t • • • t

Figure 16.5. Overview of the algorithm. In this illustration, the VD patch has 24 rays intersecting the root AABB; it builds a BVH with depth 3.

latency is higher than the LDS, but we do not have such a restriction in the size for the global memory. Since we do not use the LDS for the storage of the BVH data in this approach, the LDS usage is not the limiting factor for concurrent work group execution in a SIMD. The limiting factor is now the usage of vector general purpose registers (VGPRs). Our current implementation allows us to schedule 12 work groups in a compute unit (CU), which is 3 per SIMD, as the kernel uses 72 VGPRs per SIMD lane.

Because we know the maximum number of work groups executed concurrently in a CU for this kernel, we can calculate the number of work groups executed in parallel on the GPU. We used an AMD FirePro W9100 GPU, which has 44 CUs. Thus, 528 work groups (44 CUs × 12 work groups) are launched for the kernel. A work group processes VD patches one after another and executes until no VD patch is left unprocessed. As we know the number of work groups executed, we allocate memory for the BVH storage in global memory before execution and assign each chunk of memory for a work group as a work buffer. In all the test cases, we limit the maximum subdivision level to 5, and thus a 13-MB (= 26 KB × 528) work buffer is allocated.

After work groups are launched and a VD patch is fetched, we first compute the required subdivision level for the patch by comparing the extent of the AABB of the root node to the area of a pixel at the distance from the camera. As we allow instancing for shapes with vector displacement maps (e.g., the same patch can be at multiple locations in the world), we need to compute the subdivision level for all the rays. Work items are used to process rays in parallel at this step. Once a subdivision level is computed for a ray, the maximum value is selected using an atomic operation to an LDS value.

Then, work items compute the node data, which is the AABB, texture coordinate, and normal vector of a leaf in parallel. If the number of leaf nodes is higher than the number of work items executed, a work item processes multiple nodes sequentially. Once the leaf level of the BVH is built, it ascends the hierarchy one step and computes nodes at the next level of the hierarchy. Work items are used to compute a node in parallel. Since we write node data to global memory at one level and then read it at the next level, we need to guarantee that the write and read order is kept. This is enforced by placing a global memory barrier, which guarantees the order in a work group only; thus, it can be used for this purpose. This process is repeated until it reaches the root of the hierarchy. Pseudocode for the parallel BVH build is shown in Listing 16.2.

```
int localIdx = GET_LOCAL_IDX;
int lIdx = localIdx%8;// Assuming 64 work items in a work group
int lIdy = localIdx/8;
// Compute leaf nodes
for(int jj=lIdy*nn; jj<(lIdy+1)*nn; jj++)
for(int ii=lIdx*nn; ii<(lIdx+1)*nn; ii++)
{
  Aabb aabb;
  for(int j=0; j<2; j++) for(int i=0; i<2; i++)
  {
    float2 w = make_float2( (ii+i)/(float)nSplit, (jj+j)/(float)nSplit );
    float2 uv = interpolateUv( uv0, uv1, uv2, uv3, w );
    float4 v = interpolateVertex( v0, v1, v2, v3, w );
    v += texture_fetch( gVDispMap[faceIdx], uv );// Apply displacement
    AabbIncludePoint( &aabb, v );
  }
  int o = getOffset( tessLevel );
  __global GridCell* dst = &myCells[o + ii + jj*nSplit];
  dst->m_aabb = quantizeAabb( aabb );
  dst->m_n = compressF4( computeNormal(ii,jj) );
  dst->m_uv = compress( computeUv(ii,jj) );
}
GLOBAL_BARRIER;
// Computes internal nodes level by level
for(int level = tessLevel-1; level>=0; level--)
{
  int nc = (1<<level);
  int nf = (1<<(level+1));
```

```
int oc = getOffset( level );
int of = getOffset( level+1 );
while( localIdx < nc*nc )
{
  int ii = localIdx%nc;
  int jj = localIdx/nc;

  GridCell g  = myCells[ of + (2*ii)+(2*jj)*nf ];
  GridCell g1 = myCells[ of + (2*ii+1)+(2*jj+1)*nf ];
  GridCell g2 = myCells[ of + (2*ii+1)+(2*jj)*nf ];
  GridCell g3 = myCells[ of + (2*ii)+(2*jj+1)*nf ];
  myCells[ oc + ii + jj*nc ] = merge( g, g1, g2, g3 );
  localIdx += WG_SIZE*WG_SIZE;
}
GLOBAL_BARRIER;
}
```

Listing 16.2. BVH build, starting with the leaf-level build and then the upper-level build.

Once the hierarchy is built, we switch the work item usage from a work item for a node to a work item for a ray. A work item reads a ray from the list of rays hitting the AABB of the VD patch. A ray is then transformed to the object space of the model and traversed using the hierarchy information. If the current hit is closer than the last found hit, the hit distance, element index, normal vector, and texture coordinate at the hit point are updated. However, we cannot simply write this hit information because a ray can be processed by more than one work item in different work groups. The current OpenCL programming model does not have a mechanism to have a critical section, which would be necessary for our case.[1] Instead, we used 64-bit atomic operations, which are not optimal in terms of performance, but at least we avoided the write hazard. When the element index, quantized normal vector, and quantized texture coordinate are all 32 bit data, the hit distance is converted into a 32-bit integer and appended at the top of those 32 bits to create 64-bit integers. By using an atomic min operation, we can store the closest hit information (Figure 16.5).

Pseudocode for the entire kernel is shown in Algorithm 16.1.

16.5 Integration into an OpenCL Ray Tracer

Although ray tracing one mesh with a vector displacement map is simple, we want to use several meshes with vector displacement maps, together with other triangle meshes, as shown in Figure 16.1. This section describes how the ray tracing of a VD patch is integrated into our OpenCL ray tracer.

---

[1] Note that barrier (`CLK_GLOBAL_MEM_FENCE`) only guarantee synchronization of global memory access from a work group but not for different work groups.

```
while Unprocessed VD patch do
   {Max LOD level computation}
   for rays in parallel do
      level ← computeLODLevel(ray_i)
      maxLevel ← max(level)
   end for
   {Build BVH}
   for leaves in parallel do
      computeLeafNode(leaf_i)
   end for
   for lv = maxLevel − 1, lv > 0 do
      for nodes at level lv in parallel do
         computeNode(node_i)
      end for
   end for
   {BVH traversal and Ray VD patch intersection}
   for rays in parallel do
      level ← computeLODLevel(ray_i)
      hit ← rayCast(level)
      storeHit(ray_i, hit)
   end for
end while
```

Algorithm 16.1. Bottom-level hierarchy build and traversal kernel.

16.5.1 Scene Description

We could store all the primitives in the scene in a single spatial acceleration structure. However, this does not allow us to use techniques such as instancing, which is a powerful method to increase the scene complexity with small overhead. Therefore, we put meshes in the scene and build an acceleration structure storing meshes at leaves. A mesh is a triangle mesh, a quad mesh (some of which might be VD patches), or an instance of one of those with a world transformation. We then build another hierarchy for each mesh in which primitives (e.g., triangles, quads) are stored at leaf nodes. If a primitive is a VD patch, we build another hierarchy in a patch, as we discussed in Section 16.4. Therefore, we have a three-level hierarchy. (See Figure 16.6.) The top and middle stores meshes and primitives, and the bottom exists only for a VD patch, which is generated on the fly.

16.5.2 Preparation

Before rendering starts, we compute AABBs for primitives and build top- and middle-level BVHs. For VD patches, the computation of an accurate AABB is expensive as it requires tessellation and displacement. Instead, we compute the maximum displacement amount from a displacement texture and expand the

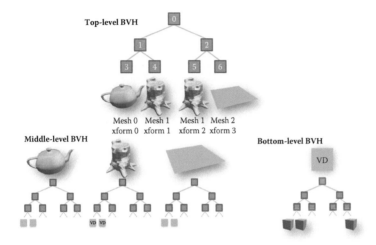

Mesh 0   Mesh 1   Mesh 1   Mesh 2
xform 0   xform 1   xform 2   xform 3

Figure 16.6. Three-level hierarchy. A leaf of the top-level BVH stores an object, which is a middle-level BVH and transform. A leaf of the middle-level BVH stores primitives such as a triangle, a quad, or a VD patch. There is a bottom-level BVH that is built on the fly during the rendering for a leaf storing a VD patch.

AABB of a quad using the value. Although this results in a loose-fitted AABB, which makes ray tracing less efficient than when tight AABBs are computed, it makes the preparation time short.

16.5.3 Hierarchy Traversal

We fused the traversal of top- and middle-level hierarchies into a traversal kernel. When a ray reaches a leaf of the top-level hierarchy, the ray is transformed into object space and starts traversing the middle-level hierarchy. Upon exiting the middle-level hierarchy, the ray is transformed back to world space. Once a ray hits a leaf node of the middle-level hierarchy, it computes a hit the primitive stored at the leaf node immediately if the primitive is a triangle or a quad. As discussed in Section 16.4, we do not compute the intersection of a ray with the VD patch on a visit to a leaf node. Instead, a primitive index and ray index are stored in a buffer for further processing. (Precisely, we also store the mesh index, which is necessary to get its transform.) An atomic operation is used to allocate space for a pair in the buffer. After the top- and middle-level hierarchy traversals, the computed hits are only those computed with triangles and quads. Thus, we need to determine if there are closer intersections with VD patches.

The primitive index and ray index are stored in random order. As we process patch by patch, these values are sorted by the primitive index using a radix sort [Harada and Howes 11], and the start and end indices of pairs for a primitive are computed. The buffer storing the start indices is used as a job queue.

(a) Bark   (b) Bark (base mesh)

(c) Barks   (d) Barks (base mesh)

(e) Pumpkin   (f) Pumpkin (base mesh)

Figure 16.7. Some of our test scenes with and without vector displacement mapping.

We then execute a kernel described in Section 16.4, which computes the intersection with VD patches. The minimum number of work groups filling the GPU is executed and each work group fetches an unprocessed VD patch from the queue and then processes one after another.

16.6   Results and Discussion

We created models with vector displacement maps in Mudbox for evaluating the method. Base meshes and vector displacement maps are exported in object space. We created four test scenes with these models and models without vector displacement maps (Figures 16.1 and 16.7). To stress the renderer, we intention-

Scene	Pretessellation	Direct Ray Tracing
Party	52 GB	16 MB
Bark	1.7 GB	0.47 MB
Barks	12 GB	3.3 MB
Pumpkin	380 MB	0.12 MB

Table 16.1. Memory usage for geometry and acceleration structure.

ally did not use instancing for these tests, although we could use it to improve the performance for a scene in which a same geometry has been placed several times. We used an AMD FirePro W9100 GPU for all the tests.

The biggest advantage of using vector displacement maps is their small memory footprints, as they create highly detailed geometry on the fly rather than preparing a high-resolution mesh. The memory usages with the proposed method and with pretessellation are shown in Table 16.1. The "Party" scene requires the most memory and does not fit into any existing GPU's memory with pretessellation. Even if we could store such a large scene in memory, it takes time to start the rendering because of the preprocess for rendering, such as IO and spatial acceleration structure build. This prevents a fast iteration of modeling and rendering. On the other hand, those overheads are low when direct ray tracing of vector displacement maps is used. The difference is noticeable, even for the simplest "Pumpkin" scene.

The advantage of the memory footprint is obvious, but the question is, "What is the cost at runtime, (i.e., the impact for the rendering speed)?" Despite its complexity in the ray-casting algorithm, direct ray tracing of vector displacement maps was faster for most of the experiments. We rendered direct illumination of the scene under an environment light (i.e., one primary ray cast and one shadow ray cast) and measured the breakdown of the rendering time, which is shown in Figure 16.8.[2] Pretessellation is faster only for the "Pumpkin" scene whose geometric complexity is the lowest among all tests. Pretessellation is slower for the "Bark" scene and it fails to render the other two larger scenes. This is interesting because direct ray tracing is doing more work than pretessellation. This performance came from less divergent computation of direct ray tracing (i.e.,the top- and middle-level hierarchies are relatively shallow, and we batch the rays intersecting with a VD patch).

To understand the ray-casting performance for direct ray tracing better, we analyzed the breakdown of each ray-cast operation for the scenes (Figure 16.9). These timings include kernel launch overhead, which is substantial especially for sorting that requires launching many kernels. Computation time for sorting is roughly proportional to the number of hit pairs, although it includes the overhead. Most of the time is spent on bottom-level BVH build and ray casting for

---

[2]The renderer is a progressive path tracer, and thus all screenshots are taken after it casts some samples per pixel.

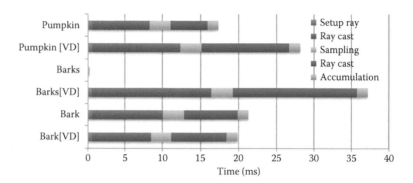

Figure 16.8. Breakdown of computational time for a frame. There are two graphs for each scene. One is with pretessellation and the other (VD) is with the proposed method. Barks cannot render without using instancing with VD patches.

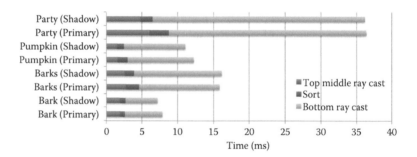

Figure 16.9. Time for top and middle ray casts, sort, and bottom ray cast.

VD patches. The time does not change much when we compare primary and shadow ray casts for the "Barks" scene, although the number of shadow rays is smaller than the number of primary rays. This indicates the weakness of the method, which is that the bottom-level BVH construction cost can be amortized when there are a large number of rays intersecting with a VD patch, but it cannot be amortized if this number is too low. This is why the ray casting for shadow rays in the "Pumpkin" scene is so slow compared to the time with pretessellation. The situation gets worse as the ray depth increases. We rendered indirect illumination with five ray bounces (depths) for the "Bark" scene (Figure 16.10). Figure 16.11 shows the ray casting time measured for each ray bounce. Although the number of active rays decreases as it goes deeper, the ray casting time did not decrease much. This can be improved by caching the generated bottom-level BVH, which is disposed and computed again for each ray casting operation. This is an opportunity for future research.

Figure 16.10. The "bark" scene rendered with five-bounce indirect illumination.

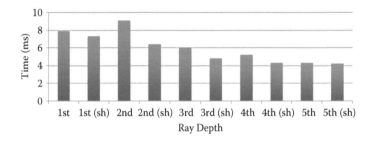

Figure 16.11. Ray casting time for each ray depth in indirect illumination computation. Those marked (sh) are ray casts for shadow rays.

16.7 Conclusion

In this chapter, we have presented a method to ray-trace vector displacement-mapped surfaces on the GPU. Our experiments show that direct ray tracing requires a small memory footprint only, and ray tracing performance is competitive or faster than ray tracing with pretessellation. The advantage gets stronger as there are more VD patches in the scene.

From the breakdown of the rendering time, we think that optimizing the BVH build for the scene and ray casting for simple geometries such as triangles and quads are not as important as optimizing the bottom-level hierarchy build and ray casting because the complexity of the bottom-level hierarchy easily becomes higher than the complexity of the top- and middle-level hierarchies once we start adding vector displacement to the scene.

Bibliography

[Hanika et al. 10] Johannes Hanika, Alexander Keller, and Hendrik P. A. Lensch. "Two-Level Ray Tracing with Reordering for Highly Complex Scenes." In *Proceedings of Graphics Interface 2010*, pp. 145–152. Toronto: Canadian Information Processing Society, 2010.

[Harada and Howes 11] T. Harada and L. Howes. "Introduction to GPU Radix Sort." Supplement to *Heterogeneous Computing with OpenCL*, edited by Benedict Gaster, Lee Howes, David R. Kaeli, Perhaad Mistry, and Dana Schaa. San Francisco: Morgan Kaufmann, 2011. Available at http://www. heterogeneouscompute.org/?page_id=7.

[Smits et al. 00] Brian E. Smits, Peter Shirley, and Michael M. Stark. "Direct Ray Tracing of Displacement Mapped Triangles." In *Proceedings of the Eurographics Workshop on Rendering Techniques*, pp. 307–318. Aire-la-Ville, Switzerland: Eurographics Association, 2000.

17

Smooth Probabilistic
Ambient Occlusion
for Volume Rendering
Thomas Kroes, Dirk Schut, and Elmar Eisemann

17.1 Introduction

Ambient occlusion [Zhukov et al. 98] is a compelling approach to improve depth
and shape perception [Lindemann and Ropinski 11, Langer and Bülthoff 99],
to give the illusion of global illumination, and to efficiently approximate low-
frequency outdoor lighting. In principle, ambient occlusion computes the light
accessibility of a point, i.e., it measures how much a point is exposed to its surrounding environment.

An efficient and often-used version of ambient occlusion is screen-space ambient occlusion [Kajalin 09]. It uses the depth buffer to compute an approximate
visibility. This method is very appealing because its computational overhead
is minimal. However, it cannot be applied to direct volume rendering (DVR)
because voxels are typically semitransparent (defined via a transfer function).
Consequently, a depth buffer would be ambiguous and is not useful in this context.

The first method to compute ambient occlusion in DVR, called *vicinity shading*, was developed by Steward [Stewart 03]. This method computes the ambient occlusion in each voxel by taking into account how much the neighboring
voxels obscure it. The resulting illumination is stored in an additional volume,
which needs to be recomputed after each scene modification. Similarly, Hernell
et al. [Hernell et al. 10] computed ambient occlusion by ray tracing inside a small
neighborhood around the voxel. Kroes et al. extended this method by taking the
entire volume into account [Kroes et al. 12].

Our approach tries to avoid costly ray tracing and casts the problem into a
filtering process. In this sense, it is similar in spirit to Penner and Mitchell's

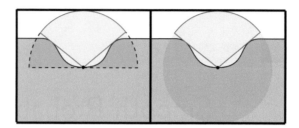

Figure 17.1. The hemisphere around a point that determines ambient occlusion (left). The blue part is unoccluded. Volumetric obscurance relies on a full sphere (right).

method [Penner and Mitchell 08], which uses statistical information about the neighborhood of the voxels to estimate ambient occlusion, as well as the method by Ropinski et al., which is similar and also adds color bleeding [Ropinski et al. 08]. Furthermore, our approach relates to Crassin et al.'s [Crassin et al. 10], which proposes the use of filtering for shadow and out-of-focus computations.

Our Smooth Probabilistic Ambient Occlusion (SPAO) is a novel and easy-to-implement solution for ambient occlusion in DVR. Instead of applying costly ray casting to determine the accessibility of a voxel, this technique employs a probabilistic heuristic in concert with 3D image filtering. In this way, ambient occlusion can be efficiently approximated and it is possible to interactively modify the transfer function, which is critical in many applications, such as medical and scientific DVR. Furthermore, our method offers various quality tradeoffs regarding memory, performance, and visual quality. Very few texture lookups are needed in comparison to ray-casting solutions, and the interpretation as a filtering process ensures a noise-free, smooth appearance.

17.2   Smooth Probabilistic Ambient Occlusion

There are various definitions for ambient occlusion. Here, we define it as the part of a point that is accessible from the outside world. A 2D example is given in Figure 17.1 and illustrates the ambient occlusion computation. More formally, the ambient-occlusion value $\mathcal{A}(p, n)$ is given by the integral of the visibility function over the hemisphere Ω centered around a point p in the direction of the normal n of that point:

$$\mathcal{A}(p, n) := \frac{1}{\pi} \int_{\Omega(n)} V(p, \omega) d\omega,$$

where V is the visibility function. In other words, V stems from the volume data itself after it was transformed by the transfer function. Note that $V(p, \omega)$ is 0 if the ray from point p in direction ω is blocked and 1 if it is unblocked; an intermediate value attenuates the ray. To simplify the description, we will use only the notion of blocked and unblocked rays in the following. Please notice that we can interpret intermediate values of V as a probability for a ray to be blocked. For example, if V returns a value of 0.5, there is a 50% chance for a ray to be blocked.

It is also possible to integrate the visibility function over the whole sphere around a point, making Ω a full sphere, instead of a hemisphere and making it independent of n. The result is called obscurance and denoted $\mathcal{A}(p)$, and it produces similar effects. Calculating obscurance instead of ambient occlusion has the advantage that it does not require a normal. However, this definition will lead to parts of the volume that are located behind the point to intervene in the computation. This property can be a disadvantage for standard scenes, as the result might become too dark, but in the context of DVR, it is sometimes even preferable, as it will unveil information below the surface, which is often desired.

Both ambient occlusion and obscurance only depend on the geometry of the volume. Therefore, they can be stored in an additional volume that is then used to modulate the original volume's illumination. The occlusion values can be calculated directly from the opacity of the original volume. Nonetheless, the values have to be recomputed when the original volume changes—for example, when the user changes the transfer function. This latter step can be very costly and makes it impossible to interact with transfer functions while maintaining a high visual fidelity. Our approach is fast to compute and enables a user to quickly apply such modifications without having to wait a long time for the result.

Initially, our solution will be explained in the context of obscurance, but in Section 17.3, we will extend our algorithm to approach ambient occlusion by making use of the normals to reduce the influence of the part of the volume below the surface.

17.2.1 Overview

To approximate obscurance at a certain point in the volume, we avoid ray casting. Instead, we introduce an approximation that is based on the probability of the rays being blocked by the volume. Instead of solving $\mathcal{A}(p)$ and its integral entirely, we consider a limited region around p, formed by volumes of increasing size. The volume between successive volumes forms a layer of voxels, a so-called shell (Figure 17.2). We will show how to derive the probability of a random ray to be blocked by a shell. From this result, we deduce an approximation of the integral $\mathcal{A}(p)$ assuming that the entire volume is represented by a single shell. Finally, the results for these various shells are combined heuristically to yield our occlusion approximation for the entire volume.

First, we consider shells being represented by a sphere with a one-voxel-wide boundary S. These shells are formed by a set of successive spheres, which each grow in radius by one voxel. In this situation, if we consider one independent shell, any random ray sent from its center will intersect exactly one voxel. If all

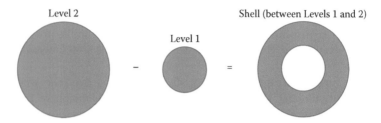

Figure 17.2. A shell is a layer of voxels formed by the difference between two differently sized volumes. By creating a cascade of these volumes, a set of shells is formed. For each shell, we approximate the probability of a ray to be blocked and combine these probabilities heuristically to form the final obscurance value.

directions are equally likely, the probability for a ray to be blocked then boils down to an average of all voxel values in the shell, $\text{average}_S(p)$. Looking carefully at this definition, it turns out that this probability is equivalent to solving for $\mathcal{A}$ in the presence of a single shell.

If we now decompose the volume into such a set of shells around a point, we can compute the probability of the rays to be blocked by each shell, but still need to combine all these blocking contributions together. In order to do so, we make use of a heuristic. We assume a statistical independence between the value distributions in the various shells. The probability of rays originating at p to be blocked by a set of n englobing shells $\{S_i\}_{i=1}^n$ ordered from small to large is then given by

$$\prod_{i=1}^n (1 - \text{average}_{S_i}(p)).$$

To understand this formula, it helps considering only two layers $\{S_1, S_2\}$. A random ray from p traverses S_1 with probability $(1 - \text{average}_{S_1}(p))$. If this ray passed S_1, it is again, potentially, stopped by S_2, this time with probability $(1 - \text{average}_{S_2}(p))$, yielding a total probability of $(1 - \text{average}_{S_1}(p))(1 - \text{average}_{S_2}(p))$. In the following, we will describe an efficient and GPU-friendly approach to compute an approximation of this solution.

17.2.2 Approximating Obscurance for Cube Shells

In practice, we will use box-shaped shells instead of spheres (Figure 17.3). We will show in the next section that this choice will allow us to benefit from GPU texture filtering to compute average_{S_i}, making the algorithm very efficient. The cubes are chosen to be of increasing size and centered at each point p of the volume. The shells are then defined by hollowing out these cubes by subtracting the next-smaller cube from its successor. In reality, these cubes will never have

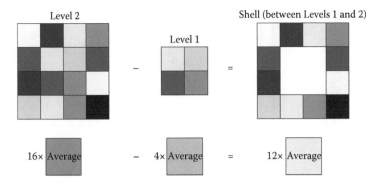

Figure 17.3. In this 2D illustration, the shell on the right is a one-voxel-thick hull that is formed by subtracting the average opacity from level 1 (in the middle) from level 2 (on the left).

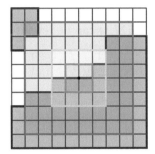

Figure 17.4. Cube shells used to approximate obscurance.

to be constructed explicitly, but it is helpful to think of them for illustrative purposes. The process is illustrated in Figure 17.4.

Following the previously described steps, we need to deduce average$_{S_i}$ for each of the shells, which in our new situation corresponds to the average of all voxel values between two successive cubes. If we assume for now that we have a quick way of determining the average inside of a complete cube, we can rapidly determine average$_{S_i}$. To illustrate this computation, we will assume that we want to determine average$_S$ of a shell S defined by two cubes C_1 and C_2, with voxel-value averages A_1 and A_2 and number of voxels S_1, S_2 ($S_1 < S_2$), respectively. The solution is then given by

$$\text{average}_S = \frac{S_2 A_2 - S_1 A_1}{S_2 - S_1}. \tag{17.1}$$

In other words, we can subtract from the total voxel sum of one cube $S_2 A_2$ the total voxel sum of the next-smaller one ($S_2 A_2$) and normalize the result by the number of voxels in the shell between both (Figure 17.3, lower row).

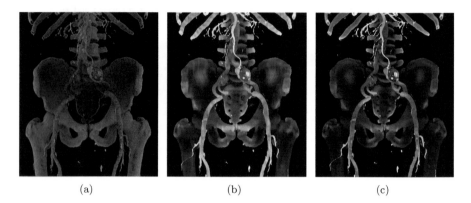

(a)   (b)   (c)

Figure 17.5. Volumetric obscurance using (a) ray tracing (256 rays/voxel), (b) mipmap filtering, and (c) N-buffer filtering.

Please note that Equation (17.1) can be rewritten as

$$\text{average}_S = \frac{1}{1 - \frac{S_1}{S_2}} \left(A_2 - \left(\frac{S_1}{S_2} \right) A_1 \right).$$

Consequently, only the average and the relative change in size (S_1/S_2) is needed to deduce average_S, which facilitates computations further. Imagine that each cube is obtained by doubling the length of each edge of the predecessor. Then, the ratio would be $1:8$, resulting in $\text{average}_S = \frac{8}{7}(A_2 - \frac{1}{8}A_1)$.

17.2.3 Fast Cube Averages

In the previous section, we assumed to have a quick method to determine the average inside of a cube. Here, we will propose two possible solutions to this problem. Our observation is that, for a given cube size, the averages are equivalent to a box filtering of the volume.

Determining averages of various kernel sizes is a common problem in computer graphics in the context of texture mapping. These techniques translate to corresponding operations in a 3D volume. The most common such approximation is mipmapping, but we will also present N-buffers [Décoret 05], which deliver higher-quality filtering at an additional cost.

As mipmaps are rather standard, we will only focus on N-buffers here. Like mipmaps, they consist of multiple levels l, each representing the average values of the original volume inside cubes of width 2^l. Unlike mipmaps, the resolution of an N-buffer is not reduced in each level. Consequently, it is possible to retrieve the exact filled part of a cube at every position in the volume, whereas for a mipmap linear interpolation can provide only an approximation based on the eight closest voxels, which reduces the quality (Figure 17.5).

```
                                                      0,0 0,0 0,0 0,0 0,0 0,0 0,0 0,0 0,0 0,0
                                                      0,0 0,1 0,1 0,1 0,1 0,0 0,0 0,0 0,0 0,0 0,0
                                 0,0 0,0 0,0 0,0 0,0 0,0 0,0 0,0 0,0 0,0 0,0   0,0 0,1 0,1 0,1 0,1 0,0 0,1 0,1 0,0 0,0 0,0
0,0 0,0 0,0 0,0 0,0 0,1 0,0 0,0 0,0 0,0    0,0 0,3 0,3 0,0 0,0 0,1 0,1 0,0 0,0 0,0 0,0   0,0 0,2 0,3 0,3 0,4 0,3 0,2 0,2 0,1 0,1 0,0
0,0 1,0 0,0 0,0 0,1 0,1 0,1 0,0 0,0 0,0    0,0 0,5 0,5 0,0 0,1 0,2 0,2 0,1 0,0 0,0 0,0   0,0 0,3 0,4 0,5 0,6 0,5 0,4 0,3 0,2 0,1 0,1
0,0 1,0 0,0 0,0 0,1 0,3 0,1 0,0 0,0 0,0    0,0 0,5 0,8 0,5 0,5 0,4 0,3 0,2 0,1 0,0 0,0   0,1 0,3 0,4 0,6 0,8 0,6 0,5 0,4 0,3 0,2 0,1
0,0 1,0 1,0 1,0 1,0 0,3 0,3 0,3 0,1 0,0    0,1 0,6 1,0 1,0 1,0 0,7 0,4 0,3 0,3 0,1 0,0   0,1 0,3 0,4 0,7 0,9 0,8 0,7 0,6 0,4 0,3 0,1
0,5 1,0 1,0 1,0 1,0 0,5 0,3 0,3 0,3 0,1    0,3 0,6 0,8 0,9 1,0 0,8 0,4 0,3 0,3 0,2 0,1   0,1 0,2 0,3 0,5 0,7 0,7 0,8 0,6 0,4 0,3 0,1
0,5 0,5 1,0 1,0 0,5 0,3 0,3 0,3 0,3 0,1    0,1 0,4 0,5 0,8 1,0 0,8 0,6 0,5 0,3 0,1 0,0   0,0 0,1 0,2 0,3 0,5 0,5 0,6 0,5 0,4 0,2 0,1
0,0 0,5 0,5 1,0 1,0 0,5 1,0 0,3 0,1 0,0    0,0 0,3 0,4 0,4 0,8 0,9 0,9 0,6 0,1 0,0 0,0   0,0 0,1 0,1 0,2 0,3 0,3 0,4 0,4 0,3 0,2 0,0
0,0 0,5 0,0 0,0 1,0 1,0 1,0 0,1 0,0 0,0    0,0 0,1 0,1 0,0 0,3 0,6 0,7 0,4 0,0 0,0 0,0   0,0 0,0 0,0 0,0 0,1 0,1 0,2 0,2 0,2 0,1 0,0
0,0 0,0 0,0 0,0 0,0 0,3 0,3 0,0 0,0 0,0    0,0 0,0 0,0 0,0 0,0 0,1 0,2 0,1 0,0 0,0 0,0   0,0 0,0 0,0 0,0 0,0 0,0 0,0 0,0 0,0 0,0 0,0
0,0 0,0 0,0 0,0 0,0 0,0 0,0 0,0 0,0 0,0    0,0 0,0 0,0 0,0 0,0 0,0 0,0 0,0 0,0 0,0 0,0   0,0 0,0 0,0 0,0 0,0 0,0 0,0 0,0 0,0 0,0 0,0
```

Figure 17.6. A 2D example of how N-buffers are calculated. A dataset is shown on the left, with the first two N-buffer levels next to it. In each level, the average of four values of the previous level is combined into one value.

The N-buffer construction is efficient, as each new level can be computed from the previous using only eight lookups. A 2D example of the calculation is shown in Figure 17.6. Nonetheless, N-buffers result in higher memory consumption, so it can be useful to apply a few mipmap levels before processing the rest using N-buffers.

17.3 Approximating Ambient Occlusion

In Section 17.2, we explained that ambient occlusion in comparison with obscurance can provide cues that are closer to realistic lighting because voxels behind the point of interest are not taken into account. To reduce this effect, we can offset the lookup operations in the direction of the normal. When choosing the offset carefully, the increase in size of the cubes and the offset can be correlated to obtain shells that correspond now to hemispheres. This goal can be achieved by multiplying the normal vector by half the size of the box. An example with a shorter vector is illustrated in Figure 17.7.

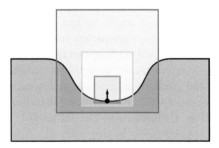

Figure 17.7. The lookups of the cubes from a point with a normal of length 0.75 in the upward direction.

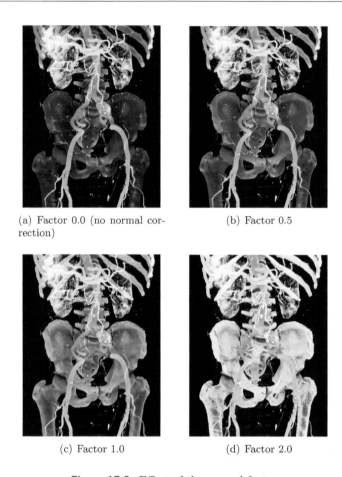

(a) Factor 0.0 (no normal correction)   (b) Factor 0.5

(c) Factor 1.0   (d) Factor 2.0

Figure 17.8. Effect of the normal factor.

However, in DVR, a normal is not always clearly defined, e.g., inside a homogeneous semitransparent volume like jelly pudding. Similarly, between two different semitransparent voxels, it might be less clear how to define a normal at the interface between opaque and transparent materials. Consequently, we propose to scale the cube offset based on how strong the gradient is. Interestingly, while most techniques derive normals from the normalized gradient via central differences, we can use the gradient magnitude to determine if a normal is clearly defined. Hence, we propose to remove the normalization operation and instead normalize the voxel values themselves to the range [0,1], which will lead to the gradient becoming an appropriately scaled normal. Additionally, we allow the user to specify a global scale to either pronounce or reduce the impact of this ambient-occlusion approximation (Figure 17.8).

	N-buffers	**Mipmaps**	**Ray trace, 512 rays**
Level 0	30.93 ms	33.00 ms	-
Level 1	33.99 ms	4.58 ms	-
Level 2	40.13 ms	0.66 ms	-
Level 3	41.16 ms	0.17 ms	-
Level 4	42.69 ms	0.14 ms	-
Level 5	38.09 ms	0.13 ms	-
Level 6	41.91 ms	0.12 ms	-
Levels Total	268.90 ms	38.8 ms	-
AO Computation	63.24 ms	110.39 ms	425.36 sec
Total	332.14 ms	149.19 ms	425.36 sec

Table 17.1. Performance measurements for the Macoessix data set ($512 \times 512 \times 512$) for N-buffers and mipmap-based SPAO. For each technique we show the time it takes to compute the individual levels and to combine them into an ambient occlusion volume.

17.4   Results

Our method has been implemented in a CUDA-based stand-alone software program for DVR. The program and its source code are available under the original BSD license. It is shipped with sample datasets. The transfer function and, thus, the visual representation can be changed on the fly. Also, the user can select from three different methods of ambient occlusion computation: mipmaps, N-buffers, and ray tracing. Our program makes use of CUDA 3.0 texture objects and will not support lower CUDA versions.

We tested the performance of our technique using the publicly available Macoessix dataset from the Osirix website[1] (see Table 17.1). All tests were peformed on an Intel Xeon W3530 (2.80 GHz) workstation with 12 GB RAM and a GeForce GTX TITAN Graphics Card with 4 GB of RAM. N-buffers are slightly more costly than mipmaps, but both are orders of magnitude faster than a volumetric ambient-occlusion ray tracer. The latter takes more than four minutes, see Table 17.1.

Figure 17.9 shows some results of our approach on the Backpack and Manix datasets.

17.5   Conclusion

This chapter presents a novel approach to compute ambient occlusion for DVR. We demonstrate that by considering the ambient-occlusion computation as a filtering process, we can significantly improve efficiency and make it usable in a real-time DVR application. Such an approach is useful for medical visualization applications, where transfer functions are very often subject to change.

---

[1] http://www.osirix-viewer.com/datasets/

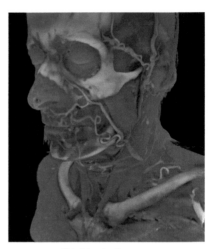

(a) Backpack data set   (b) Manix data set

Figure 17.9. SPAO applied to the Backpack ($512\times512\times461$) and Manix ($512\times512\times460$) data sets.

Our approach is efficient and simple to implement and leads to a very good quality/performance tradeoff. Nonetheless, we also experimented with more complex combinations of the shells, especially, as the assumption of independence of the occlusion probabilities is usually not true in most datasets. In practice, it turns out that our solution seems to be a good choice, and any increase in complexity also led to a significant performance impact. Nonetheless, this topic remains interesting for future work. Furthermore, we would like to investigate approximating physically plausible light transport, such as global illumination, with our filtering technique, which could further enhance the volume depiction.

Bibliography

[Crassin et al. 10] Cyril Crassin, Fabrice Neyret, Miguel Sainz, and Elmar Eisemann. "GPU Pro: Advanced Rendering Techniques." edited by Wolfgang Engel, Chapter Efficient Rendering of Highly Detailed Volumetric Scenes with GigaVoxels, pp. 643–676. Natick, MA: A K Peters, 2010.

[Décoret 05] Xavier Décoret. "N-Buffers for Efficient Depth Map Query." *Computer Graphics Forum* 24:3 (2005), 393–400.

[Hernell et al. 10] Frida Hernell, Patric Ljung, and Anders Ynnerman. "Local Ambient Occlusion in Direct Volume Rendering." *IEEE Transactions on Visualization and Computer Graphics* 16:4 (2010), 548–559.

[Kajalin 09] Vladimir Kajalin. "Screen Space Ambient Occlusion." In *ShaderX7*, edited by Wolfgang Engel, Chapter 6.1. Boston: Cengage Learning, 2009.

[Kroes et al. 12] Thomas Kroes, Frits H. Post, and Charl P. Botha. "Exposure Render: An Interactive Photo-realistic Volume Rendering Framework." *PLoS ONE* 7:7 (2012), e38586.

[Langer and Bülthoff 99] Michael S Langer and Heinrich H Bülthoff. "Depth Discrimination from Shading under DiffuseLighting." *Perception* 29:6 (1999), 649–660.

[Lindemann and Ropinski 11] Florian Lindemann and Timo Ropinski. "About the Influence of Illumination Models on Image Comprehension in Direct Volume Rendering." *IEEE Trans. Visualization and Computer Graphics: Vis Proceedings* 17:12 (2011), 1922–1931.

[Penner and Mitchell 08] Eric Penner and Ross Mitchell. "Isosurface Ambient Occlusion and Soft Shadows with Filterable Occlusion Maps." In *Proceedings of the Fifth Eurographics/IEEE VGTC Conference on Point-Based Graphics*, pp. 57–64. Aire-la-Ville, Switzerland: Eurographics Association, 2008.

[Ropinski et al. 08] Timo Ropinski, Jennis Meyer-Spradow, Stefan Diepenbrock, Jörg Mensmann, and Klaus Hinrichs. "Interactive Volume Rendering with Dynamic Ambient Occlusion and Color Bleeding." *Computer Graphics Forum* 27:2 (2008), 567–576.

[Stewart 03] A James Stewart. "Vicinity Shading for Enhanced Perception of Volumetric Data." In *Proceedings of the 14th IEEE Visualization 2003 (VIS'03)*, p. 47. Los Alamitos, CA: IEEE Computer Society, 2003.

[Zhukov et al. 98] Sergey Zhukov, Andrei Iones, and Grigorij Kronin. "An Ambient Light Illumination Model." In *Rendering Techniques 98*, pp. 45–55. New York: Springer, 1998.

18

Octree Mapping
from a Depth Camera
Dave Kotfis and Patrick Cozzi

18.1 Overview

To render artificial objects with consistent shading from arbitrary perspectives, a 3D scene needs to be constructed from the camera frames. Data parallel GPU computing allows for real-time 3D mapping of scenes from depth cameras such as the Kinect sensor. Noise in the camera's depth measurements can be filtered over multiple image frames by representing the scene as a voxel-based map rather than as a collection of raw point clouds. However, a dense voxel grid representation is not suitable for large scenes or live rendering for use in games.

In this chapter, we present our method that uses CUDA to reconstruct 3D scenes from depth cameras at near real-time speeds. A scene is represented by a *sparse voxel octree* (SVO) structure that scales to large volumes. We render these scenes with CUDA and OpenGL using methods that eliminate the slow process of generating meshes from point clouds or voxel grids. We will describe an SVO

Figure 18.1. Augmented reality: A kitchen scene rendered with voxel cone tracing (left); rendering a textured Stanford Bunny sitting behind a stool in the kitchen (center); and the augmented scene rendered from an alternative view (right).

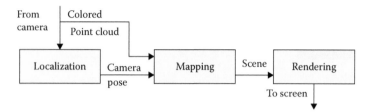

Figure 18.2. Top-level system view of an augmented reality system that simultaneously maps and renders a scene.

representation of a scene and data parallel methods to update and expand from incrementally received colored point clouds. While real-time 3D mapping has a variety of applications ranging from robotics to medical imaging, this chapter will focus on applications to augmented reality. (See Figure 18.1.)

18.1.1   Augmented Reality

In recent years, low-cost depth cameras using structured light or time of flight methods have become commonplace. These *RGB-D* (color + depth) cameras directly measure additional 3D information that previously could only be generated through sophisticated computer vision algorithms in software. These cameras are useful for creating models for 3D printing, computer vision for robotics, and creating immersive and interactive video game experiences.

Augmented reality (AR) is a field that lives on the boundary between computer graphics and vision to create experiences that blend artificial graphics with the real world. AR systems today typically render virtual objects in front of a raw depth camera frame. Future AR systems will seamlessly render virtual graphics blended with a live camera scene. Real scenes could be viewed with artificial lighting conditions and with virtual objects that cast shadows. (See Figure 18.2.)

There are many AR applications where raw color and depth data provides sufficient 3D data. This is generally the case where the application does not need to make use of information that is outside of the current physical camera view. A few example applications of mapping include object collisions with occluded surfaces and casting shadows from objects outside of view. Multiple nearby cameras could interact with the same AR application, by registering and merging their maps to establish a cohesive operating picture. Even without mapping, some AR applications may need at least a localized estimate of the camera's motion. This is required for a moving camera to maintain fixed virtual object locations. Many current AR systems use inertial sensing available on smartphones to track orientation changes. With this sensing, the absolute positioning will drift over time, but a more robust visual motion estimate can improve performance.

18.1.2 Localization

To reconstruct a scene, the movement of the camera between each frame must be determined so the points in each frame can be spatially correlated. GPU computing enables dense camera pose tracking techniques that match every pixel in 640 × 480 frames at 30 frames per second to track the motion of the camera without the need for a motion capture system. Previously, sparse techniques required detection of a smaller set of invariant features to track, which are not always available [Dryanovski et al. 13].

RGB-D cameras provide enough information to generate 3D positions and surface normals. The *iterative closest point* (ICP) algorithm attempts to align one frame to the previous by iteratively reducing the error between the points of each frame and the surfaces of the scene. Visual odometry with depth is a similar process that minimizes a photometric (color) error term rather than a geometric one [Steinbrucker et al. 11]. In different scenes, either geometric or photometric detail may be more prominent, so recent approaches use a combined error function that mixes the two [Whelan et al. 12].

The hard part is computing the error gradient fast enough to keep up with the camera's motion for the solution to converge. If that rate cannot be maintained and frames are skipped, the space of possible transformations that must be searched to align the frames grows. This increases the computational burden, slowing the computation down even further and creating a vicious cycle that makes the process fail. GPU computing that exploits the parallelism of the computation is critical to achieve the speeds required to avoid this downward spiral.

The methods presented in this chapter focus on mapping and rendering techniques. However, a localization method for tracking a camera's motion is a necessary part of any mapping application involving a moving camera. The ICP techniques described above offer real-time localization solutions using camera data, though alternative methods exist. An alternate approach requires the use of an external motion capture system, and many commercial *virtual reality* (VR) systems use this method for localization of a user's head pose.

18.1.3 Mapping

Reconstructing a scene requires a map representation to incrementally update and store data from each camera frame. There are many possible representations to do this, the simplest of which would be to concatenate each new point cloud by transforming all points according to the pose of the camera, assuming it is known. However, the size of this map would grow linearly with time, even when observing the same part of the scene, so it is not a suitable candidate for concurrent rendering. A standard RGB-D camera can generate several GB of raw data within only a minute. This data explosion could easily be avoided by fixing the map size to a maximum set of frames, though this can create undesirable effects when parts of the map become forgotten over time.

We will focus our discussion on mapping methods that accumulate information over the full life of a program rather than a fixed history of frames. If the camera used for mapping remains in a finite volume of space, the map size will be finite as long as spatially redundant information is never duplicated in the representation. To do this, 3D bins at a maximum resolution can be used to identify and filter duplicate points. However, this will result in loss of detail, and the map will contain any noise produced by the camera data. While the binning of the points is trivially data parallel, the removal of point duplicates requires parallel sorting and reduction.

18.2   Previous Work and Limitations

18.2.1   KinectFusion

KinectFusion is a 3D reconstruction technique that attempts to filter the noise of incoming depth data by representing the map as a 3D voxel grid with a truncated signed distance function (TSDF) data payload storing the distance from a surface [Newcombe et al. 11]. The values are truncated to avoid unnecessary computations in free space as well as reduce the amount of data required for surface representation. Building this grid is far more maintainable than storing a raw point cloud for each frame, as the redundancy enables the sensor noise to be smoothed. It also avoids storing significant amounts of duplicate data and is highly data parallel for GPU acceleration.

However, the memory footprint of a voxel grid approach scales poorly to large volumes. The dense representation requires voxel cells allocated in memory for the large amount of free space that will almost always be prominent in scenes. Also, while the voxel grid and TSDF are an appropriate representation for the surface function, it is inefficient for any color data. The rendering process either requires ray marching to directly render the grid, or a slow surface extraction and remeshing process, neither suitable for concurrent real-time rendering.

18.2.2   OctoMap

OctoMap is a probabilistic framework where the log-odds of occupancy are stored in an octree data structure [Hornung et al. 13]. Log-odds is a quantity directly related to the probability, though it is in a form that provides the convenience of an update rule that uses addition and subtraction to incorporate information from new observations. The sparse octree structure overcomes the scalability limitations of a dense voxel grid by leaving free space unallocated in memory. OctoMap also filters sensor noise by assigning probabilities of hit and miss that represent the noise of the sensor. Nodes in the tree are updated by logging each point from a point cloud as a hit. All points along the ray from the camera position to the end point are logged as a miss. This process takes place serially on a CPU, looping over each point in each frame.

The OctoMap is rendered by iterating through the leaves of the tree and extracting cells that have a probability greater than 0.5 of being occupied. These voxels are rendered as cubes with edge length determined by the depth of the corresponding node in the octree. This framework is most commonly used with LIDAR sensors, which have only a few points per scan, which has little benefit from parallelization. An RGB-D sensor would provide millions of points per frame that could be parallelized. However, the pointer-based octree structure used by OctoMap is less suitable for GPU parallelization than a stackless linear octree.

18.3   Octree Scene Representation

18.3.1   Data Format

We developed a sparse octree representation of a scene on a GPU, along with methods to efficiently update and expand it from incrementally received colored point clouds. The GPU data structure is based on the work of GigaVoxels [Crassin et al. 09] that uses a node pool in linear memory and a brick pool in texture memory. The nodes are composed of two 32-bit words. The first word has two 1-bit flags and 30 bits for the index of the first child node. The second word holds either an RGBA value or the location in the brick pool to be used when interpolating values within the node.

Although the sparse octree does not allocate every node of the tree in memory, we use Morton codes as keys for unique identification of voxels. Here is an example key: 1 001 010 111. The key starts with a leading 1 to identify the length of the code, and thus the depth in the tree. After that, the key is made up of a series of 3-bit tuples that indicate a high or low value on the binary split of the x-, y-, and z-dimensions, respectively.

Using a 32-bit integer, this can represent 10 levels of depth in the tree. However, this is insufficient for mapping with a Kinect camera. The Kinect has a range of 0.3–5.0 meters in depth resolution, and doing a back-of-the-envelope calculation for the horizontal resolution (480 pixels, 5-m range, 43 degree field of view) shows that the camera will typically provide sub-centimeter resolution. A 10-meter edge volume can only achieve 1-cm resolution using 10 levels of depth. Therefore, we have transitioned to representing these keys with long integers (64 bit), which could represent more than kilometers of volume at millimeter precision, if needed. Figure 18.3 and Listing 18.1 provide descriptions of our data format.

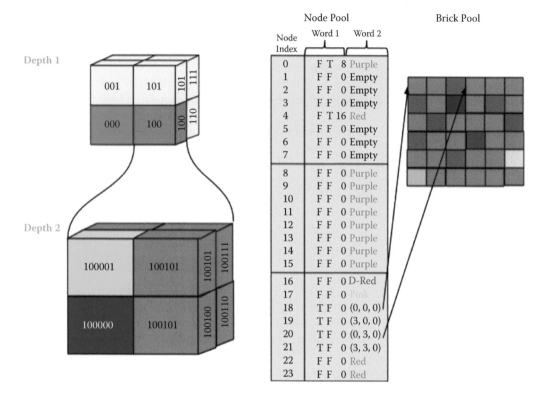

Figure 18.3. Sparse voxel octree data structure in linear GPU memory. It uses keys based on Morton codes to uniquely index nodes. The compact structure uses 64 bits per node. For hardware interpolation of values within the tree, node values can be backed by a brick in texture memory.

18.3.2 Updating the Map

Because our data structure is sparse, each new point cloud frame may contain points in parts of space that were previously unallocated in memory. For this reason, updating the map requires two steps: resizing the octree structure into newly observed space, and updating the color values within the tree with the new observations. Figure 18.4 shows the program flow for updating the map in more detail.

Update octree structure   To expand our scene into unallocated space, we first must determine which new points correspond to unallocated nodes. We do this by computing the key for each point to determine its location in the octree. Fortunately, we can do this with only the constant octree parameters, its size and center location, without the need for any data within the octree. This makes the calculation completely data parallel over the incoming point cloud positions. The process of computing keys is in Listing 18.2.

```
struct char4 {
  char x, y, z, w;
};

struct Octree {
//The node data in GPU memory.
//Each node is 2 unsigned int's long.
unsigned int* node_pool;
//The number of nodes allocated in the node pool.
int size;
//The half length of each edge of the root node of the octree.
float edge_length;
//The 3D position of the center of the root node of the octree.
glm::vec3 center;
//The brick pool data in CUDA texture memory.
//Note: Our examples are limited to use of the node pool only.
cudaArray* brick_pool;
};

struct PointCloud {
//The 3D position of each point in the point cloud.
glm::vec3* positions;
//The corresponding RGBA color of each corresponding point.
char4* colors;
//The number of points in the cloud.
int size;
};
```

Listing 18.1. Data structures representing a sparse linear octree and colored point cloud data in GPU memory.

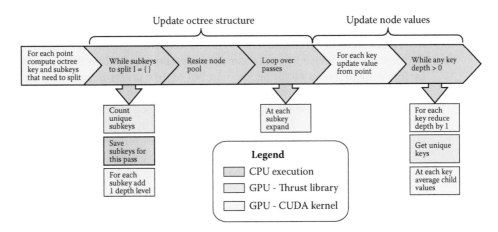

Figure 18.4. Program flow for updating the sparse octree from a point cloud frame. The process of updating the octree map from each incoming point cloud starts by counting how many new octree nodes must be created and resizing the node pool. Then, we can filter the updated color values through the tree.

```
typedef long long int octkey;

__device__ octkey computeKey(const glm::vec3& point,
  glm::vec3 center, const int tree_depth,
  float edge_length) {
  //Initialize the output value with a leading 1
  //to specify the depth.
  octkey key = 1;

  for (int i = 0; i < tree_depth; i++) {
    key = key << 3;

    //Determine in which octant the point lies.
    uint8_t x = point.x > center.x ? 1 : 0;
    uint8_t y = point.y > center.y ? 1 : 0;
    uint8_t z = point.z > center.z ? 1 : 0;

    //Update the code.
    key += (x + 2*y + 4*z);

    //Update the edge length.
    edge_length /= 2.0f;

    //Update the center.
    center.x += edge_length * (x ? 1 : -1);
    center.y += edge_length * (y ? 1 : -1);
    center.z += edge_length * (z ? 1 : -1);
  }
  return key;
}
```

Listing 18.2. CUDA device function to compute a key for a point. A kernel that parallelizes over points should call this.

The process of increasing the SVO size requires copying the data from GPU device to GPU device into a larger memory allocation. The SVO is represented by linear memory, so counting the number of new nodes is necessary to allocate sufficient continuous memory. Once we have the keys for all nodes that need to be accessed, we can use these keys to determine the subset that are not currently allocated in memory. This prepass loops through every tree depth, each time truncating all of the keys at the current depth and removing duplicate keys. We check the node for each key to determine whether its child nodes are allocated in memory. In each stage, keys that need to be allocated are stored in a list, and the length of this list ×8 is the number of new nodes that need to be allocated, one for each child node.

With the set of unallocated keys in hand, we allocate a new set of continuous memory large enough for the new nodes, and we copy the old octree into this new location. Now, for each depth we parallelize over the keys in our collected set to initialize the new nodes. If GPU memory is available, it is advantageous to preallocate a large volume of memory to avoid this costly resizing process.

Update node values We use the same model as OctoMap, giving the probability that leaf node n is occupied given a series of sensor measurements $z_{1:t}$:

$$P(n|z_{1:t}) = \left[1 + \frac{1 - P(n|z_t)}{P(n|z_t)} \frac{1 - P(n|z_{1:t-1})}{P(n|z_{1:t-1})} \frac{P(n)}{1 - P(n)}\right]^{-1}.$$

This model conveniently reduces to addition of individual measurements when stored as a log-odds value. For convenience, we choose to use symmetric probability models where the probabilities of hit and miss are both equivalent. This reduces our log-odds calculation into simply keeping a running count of hits and misses.

To update the node values, we use the alpha channel of RGBA to encode a pseudo-log-odds of occupancy for each cell. When allocated, we initialize our cells to alpha = 127, which we interpret as probability 0.5 because it is the midpoint for an 8-bit unsigned integer. For a Kinect sensor, we use a probability of hit such that each observation adds 2 to the alpha value. This is for convenience since alpha is stored as an unsigned integer, and it seems to work well for the Kinect sensor model, saturating after 64 consistent hits or misses. The more often a point is observed within a portion of space, the more confident we are that the node is occupied. This helps to filter sensor noise in depth measurements by ensuring that we consistently receive point returns from a location before considering it to be occupied.

We also filter the color values received by the camera by using a running average, using the alpha channel as a weight function. Listing 18.3 shows the update and filtering process for each node. After the values are updated in the leaves of the octree, we can trickle them into the inner limbs of the tree by having each parent assume a value that averages their children.

18.3.3 Dynamic Scenes

When building a scene where all objects are static, it would be sufficient to update the map in only an additive fashion as discussed earlier. However, when objects are moving, it becomes necessary to have an update process that can remove parts of the map when they are observed to be unoccupied. Similar to OctoMap, we do this by processing the free space between the camera origin and each point in our point cloud. In each update, these nodes are observed to be free. Rather than adding an additional registered hit to these nodes, we register them as misses. With enough misses, these nodes will eventually return to being unoccupied.

Once these nodes are completely unoccupied, the memory for them is released. Rather than the expensive process of shifting all of the data in memory to fill in these holes, maintaining a list of free memory slots allows future tree expansions to fill data into them first.

```
__device__ int getFirstValueAndShiftDown(octkey& key) {
  int depth = depthFromKey(key);
  int value = getValueFromKey(key, depth-1);
  key -= ((8 + value) << 3 * (depth - 1));
  key += (1 << 3 * (depth - 1));
  return value;
}

__global__ void fillNodes(const octkey* keys, int numKeys,
  const char4* values, unsigned int* octree_data) {

  int index = blockIdx.x * blockDim.x + threadIdx.x;

  //Don't do anything if out of bounds.
  if (index >= numKeys) {
    return;
  }

  //Get the key for this thread.
  octkey key = keys[index];

  //Check for invalid key.
  if (key == 1) {
    return;
  }

  int node_idx = 0;
  int child_idx = 0;
  while (key != 1) {
    //Get the child number from the first three bits of the
    //Morton code.
    node_idx = child_idx + getFirstValueAndShiftDown(key);

    if (!octree_data[2 * node_idx] & 0x40000000) {
      return;
    }

    //The lowest 30 bits are the address of the child nodes.
    child_idx = octree_data[2 * node_idx] & 0x3FFFFFFF;
  }

  char4 new_value = values[index];
  unsigned int current_value = octree_data[2 * node_idx + 1];

  char4 current;
  short current_alpha = current_value >> 24;
  current.r = current_value & 0xFF;
  current.g = (current_value >> 8) & 0xFF;
  current.b = (current_value >> 16) & 0xFF;

  //Implement a pseudo low-pass filter with Laplace smoothing.
  float f1 = (1 - ((float)current_alpha/256.0f));
  float f2 = (float)current_alpha / 256.0f;
  new_value.r = new_value.r * f1 + current.r * f2;
  new_value.g = new_value.g * f1 + current.g * f2;
  new_value.b = new_value.b * f1 + current.b * f2;
  octree_data[2 * node_idx + 1] = ((int)new_value.r) +
    ((int)new_value.g << 8) + ((int)new_value.b << 16) +
    (min(255, current_alpha + 2) << 24);
}
```

Listing 18.3. CUDA kernel for updating values stored in octree nodes based on newly observed colors.

18.3.4 Managing Memory

The sparse octree used to represent a reconstructed 3D map will quickly grow too large to fit entirely in GPU memory. Reconstructing a typical office room at 1 cm resolution will often take as much as 6–8 GB. Use of a GPU with more memory will allow for larger scenes at higher resolutions, but there will always be applications where a physical memory increase is not practical to meet the requirements.

To handle this, we developed an out-of-core memory management framework for the octree. At first glance, this framework is a standard stack-based octree on the CPU. However, each node in the tree has an additional boolean flag indicating whether the node is at the root of a subtree that is located in linear GPU memory. It also holds a pointer to its location on the GPU as well as its size.

Next, these nodes can push/pull the data to and from the GPU. The push method uses recursion to convert the stack-based data into a linear array in CPU memory, then copies the memory to the GPU. It avoids the need to over-allocate or reallocate the size of the linear memory by first recursing through the node's children to determine the size of the subtree. The pull method copies the linear memory back to the CPU, then uses it to recursively generate it as a stack-based structure.

We use a *least recently used* (LRU) approach where all methods operating on the tree must provide an associated bounding box of the area that they will affect. First, this allows us to make sure that the entire affected volume is currently on the GPU before attempting to perform the operation. The octree will also keep a history of the N most recently used bounding boxes. When space needs to be freed, it will take the union of these stored bounding boxes and pull data that lies outside of this region back to the CPU.

18.4 Rendering Techniques

18.4.1 Extracting and Instancing Voxel Cubes

The brute-force method for rendering the SVO map is to extract the color values and 3D positions of each occupied leaf node. With these values, we can render a cube at each center position with a scale based on the depth in the SVO. (See Figure 18.5.)

Extracting the voxels requires two steps. First, in a prepass where each CUDA thread is assigned a Morton code, each voxel traverses into the SVO to determine whether the node with the corresponding code is occupied. We start with a set of keys at the minimum depth, iteratively create the 8 child keys for the occupied nodes, and remove the unoccupied node keys. Once we have determined the valid keys, we allocate space for our resulting data and extract it from the SVO into the buffer. We decode the Morton codes back into the 3D positions for each voxel.

Figure 18.5. Octree scene constructed from a live Kinect camera stream using CUDA. (a) The original raw camera image. (b) Voxel extraction and instanced rendering of an SVO map. (c) Voxel cone tracing of an SVO map. (d) Voxel cone tracing from a virtual camera view that does not match the physical view.

Once we have the position and color for each occupied voxel, we map it to an OpenGL *texture buffer object* (TBO), which is used by our vertex shader that instances a colored cube to represent the voxels (Listing 18.4).

18.4.2   Voxel Cone Tracing

Voxel cone tracing (VCT) is a physically based rendering technique similar to ray tracing [Crassin et al. 11]. It exploits the SVO data structure to avoid Monte Carlo integration of multiple rays to approximate the integral of the rendering equation. Instead, it approximates a cone by sampling values at higher levels of the SVO as the cone becomes wider. If all of the needed lighting information is incorporated into the octree, mip-mapping the values into the inner tree branches and texture interpolation performs the integration step inherently. (See Figure 18.6.)

We used voxel cone tracing to render our scene with CUDA. For each pixel, a CUDA thread traverses along a ray and samples a value from the SVO. The

```
#version 420

uniform mat4 u_mvpMatrix;
uniform mat3 u_normMatrix;
uniform float u_scale;

out vec3 fs_position;
out vec3 fs_normal;
out vec3 fs_color;

layout (location = 0) in vec4 vox_cent;
layout (location = 1) in vec4 vox_color;

layout (binding = 0) uniform samplerBuffer voxel_centers;
layout (binding = 1) uniform samplerBuffer voxel_colors;

const vec3 cube_vert[8] = vec3[8](
  vec3(-1.0, -1.0, 1.0),
  vec3(1.0, -1.0, 1.0),
  vec3(1.0, 1.0, 1.0),
  vec3(-1.0, 1.0, 1.0),
  vec3(-1.0, -1.0, -1.0),
  vec3(1.0, -1.0, -1.0),
  vec3(1.0, 1.0, -1.0),
  vec3(-1.0, 1.0, -1.0)
);

const int cube_ind[36] = int[36] (
  0, 1, 2, 2, 3, 0,
  3, 2, 6, 6, 7, 3,
  7, 6, 5, 5, 4, 7,
  4, 0, 3, 3, 7, 4,
  0, 1, 5, 5, 4, 0,
  1, 5, 6, 6, 2, 1
);

void main (void){
  gl_Position = u_mvpMatrix *
    vec4(cube_vert[cube_ind[gl_VertexID]]*u_scale +
    vec3(texelFetch(voxel_centers, gl_InstanceID)), 1.0);
  fs_position = gl_Position.xyz;
  fs_normal = u_normMatrix *
    normalize(cube_vert[cube_ind[gl_VertexID]]);
  fs_color = vec3(texelFetch(voxel_colors, gl_InstanceID));
}
```

Listing 18.4. GLSL vertex shader for instancing of colored voxel cubes using a TBO bound from CUDA.

octree depth sampled, d, for a distance, r, along the ray with a camera field of view, θ, the number of pixels in the camera image, n, and with an octree root node size, o, is given by

$$d = \left\lceil \log_2 \frac{o * n}{r \tan \theta} \right\rceil. \tag{18.1}$$

Each pixel continues to integrate its total color value using the alpha channel until it reaches its maximum of 255, or until the ray reaches a maximum length (usually 10 m).

Figure 18.6. Multiple renders of the same scene, both with voxel cone tracing. On the left, the maximum resolution is 1 cm, while on the right, it is capped at 16 cm.

18.5 Results

We tested the time required to expand, update, and filter an SVO scene with an updated point cloud frame from a Kinect sensor. We found that the time increased logarithmically with the number of allocated nodes in the SVO (Figure 18.7). The kernels that update the SVO execute serially in tree depth, but parallel over the nodes in each depth. The octree structure divides the nodes

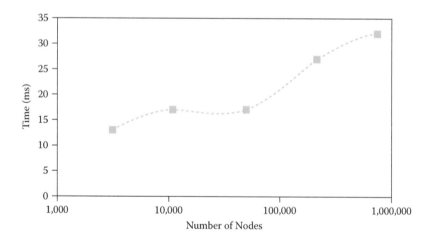

Figure 18.7. Evaluation of updating the SVO scene from a Kinect camera using an NVIDIA GTX 770 with 2 GB memory. The same scene is updated with multiple maximum depths. The edge length of the full SVO is 1.96 meters. We evaluate the update time and compare it with the change in the number of allocated nodes in the octree.

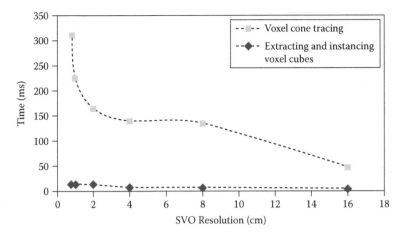

Figure 18.8. The SVO scene rendered with both voxel extraction and instancing and cone tracing (same scene as Figure 18.7). Voxel extraction and instancing achieves real-time performance at every resolution tested, but cone tracing slows down below real-time resolutions higher than 16 cm.

so that we can expect the depth to increase logarithmically with the number of nodes.

We compare the rendering time between both the voxel instancing and voxel cone tracing approaches with an identical scene at multiple levels of resolution. We found that the voxel instancing approach has steady real-time performance at all resolutions tested. Even at the lowest resolution, the voxel cone tracing technique was not real time. The runtime for VCT grows exponentially as the resolution increases (Figure 18.8).

18.6 Conclusion and Future Work

We have found that use of an SVO map allows for memory-efficient mapping. Camera noise is quickly filtered out within a few frames to create stable scenes. For debug views, voxel extraction and instanced rendering is useful for rendering values of the map at different levels of resolution. However, voxel cone tracing requires minimal additional computational cost and can render the scene at different views with similar quality to that of the original. (See Figure 18.9.)

There are similar mapping techniques implemented using conventional CPU computing, and we would like to benchmark the performance of our GPU mapping method against them on common data sets. We will also evaluate performance of complete AR pipelines (localization, mapping, rendering) with various hardware (GPUs, cameras) to determine the conditions where our techniques work best.

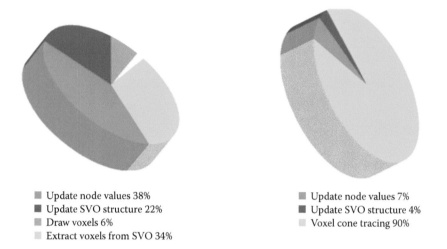

- ■ Update node values 38%   ■ Update node values 7%
- ■ Update SVO structure 22%   ■ Update SVO structure 4%
- ■ Draw voxels 6%   ░ Voxel cone tracing 90%
- ░ Extract voxels from SVO 34%

Figure 18.9. Using NVIDIA GeForce GTX 770 with 2 GB RAM, we measure the relative runtimes of mapping and rendering stages. In both cases, we map and render a $4 \times 4 \times 4$ meter volume at 2 cm resolution: Mapping and rendering with voxel instancing takes 32 ms (left) and with voxel cone tracing requires 184 ms (right).

We would like to explore use of intrinsic images in preprocessing the color values before adding them to the map. This would allow us to re-cast an artificial light into the scene without the rendering artifacts that we expect from improper shading. Rendering with a virtual light source would also blend virtual objects into the scene by casting shadows.

Also, today we are only able to add static virtual objects to our constructed scenes. It would be useful for dynamic virtual objects to move efficiently within the SVO.

18.7 Acknowledgment

We would like to thank Nick Armstrong-Crews for his valuable feedback in reviewing this chapter.

Bibliography

[Crassin et al. 09] Cyril Crassin, Fabrice Neyret, Sylvain Lefebvre, and Elmar Eisermann. "GigaVoxels: Ray-Guided Streaming for Efficient and Detailed Voxel Rendering." In *Proceedings of the 2009 Symposium on Interactive 3D Graphics and Games*, pp. 15–22. New York: ACM, 2009.

[Crassin et al. 11] Cyril Crassin, Fabrice Neyret, Miguel Sainz, Simon Green, and Elmar Eisemann. "Interactive Indirect Illumination Using Voxel Cone Tracing." *Computer Graphics Forum* 30:7 (2011), 1921–1930.

[Dryanovski et al. 13] Ivan Dryanovski, Roberto G. Valenti, and Jizhong Xiao. "Fast Visual Odometry and Mapping from RGB-D Data." In *IEEE International Conference on Robotics and Automation (ICRA)*, pp. 2305–2310. Washington, DC: IEEE Press, 2013.

[Hornung et al. 13] Armin Hornung, Kai M. Wurm, Maren Bennewitz, Cyril Stachniss, and Wolfram Burgard. "OctoMap: An Efficient Probabilistic 3D Mapping Framework Based on Octrees." *Autonomous Robots* 34:3 (2013), 189–206.

[Newcombe et al. 11] R.A. Newcombe, S. Izadi, O. Hilliges, D. Molyneaux, D. Kim, A. J. Davison, P. Kohli, J. Shotton, S. Hodges, and A. Fitzgibbon. "KinectFusion: Real-Time Dense Surface Mapping and Tracking." In *IEEE International Symposium on Mixed and Augmented Reality (ISMAR)*, pp. 127–136. Washington, DC: IEEE Press, 2011.

[Steinbrucker et al. 11] F. Steinbrucker, J. Sturm, and D. Cremers. "Real-Time Visual Odometry from Dense RGB-D Images." Paper presented at ICCV Workshop on Live Dense Reconstruction with Moving Cameras, Barcelona, Spain, November 12, 2011.

[Whelan et al. 12] T. Whelan, J. McDonald, M. Fallon M. Kaess, H. Johannsson, and J. Leonard. "Kintinuous: Spatially Extended KinectFusion." Paper presented at RSS Workshop on RGB-D: Advanced Reasoning with Depth Cameras, Sydney, Australia, July 9–13, 2012.

19

Interactive Sparse Eulerian Fluid
Alex Dunn

19.1 Overview

Real-time simulation of fluid dynamics has been around for a while now, but it has not made its way into many games because of its performance characteristics, which have never been at a level acceptable enough to be deemed "game-ready." In game development, there is this imaginary scale used to determine whether or not a piece of visual effects (VFX) will make it into a game: on one end of this scale is ultra-high visual quality—which is used to describe the purest of physically based effects—and at the other end is low-quality/performance. All real-time VFX are subject to this scale, and all lie somewhere around the middle of the two extremes; this can be thought of as the *performance/quality tradeoff*. When it is desirable to take an effect from the physically based perfection side over to the performance (game-ready) side, then some work has to be done in order to significantly reduce the cost of that effect while still maintaining as much quality as possible.

This chapter describes a method for computing and rendering smoke-like fluid in real time on the GPU using DirectX 11+ with a key focus on the advantages of simulating and storing these simulations in a sparse domain. Simulation is only half the battle; in order to view fluid in its full glory, advancement in rendering is also required. This chapter also presents an extension of common volume rendering techniques that dramatically reduces the cost associated with rendering volumetric fluid simulations.

19.2 Introduction

Fluid emulation in games is quite common—e.g., things like smoke and fire effects—and typically these effects are implemented as particle systems using a relatively simple equation of motion—compared to its real-world counterparts. It is these equations of motion that ultimately dictate how the overall effect looks. Real-time fluid simulation offers a physically based alternative to particle kinematics, where these effects can move and interact with the world in a much more realistic manner. Simulation of this complexity does not come without a cost, but using the technique outlined in this chapter, we can reduce this cost to the absolute minimum—a step up on other real-time techniques for simulating fluid.

The type of fluid simulation in question is the *Eulerian* simulation; this is a grid-based simulation in which quantitative fluid data such as velocity and pressure are calculated at fixed cell intervals across a Cartesian grid. On the GPU, it is fairly typical to represent this grid using volume textures.

The Eulerian method for simulating fluid is not to be confused with *Lagrangian* fluid simulation, like SPH (smoothed particle hydrodynamics) [Müller et al. 03], which does not use the fixed cell model, but instead uses free-moving particles to calculate this data.

Current Eulerian simulation implementations in use today tend to perform a simulation across the entire grid. This is not only computationally expensive, but it consumes a lot of memory in 3D—amongst other things. This chapter will be addressing these issues by proposing a method for simulating and storing these grids sparsely.

19.3   GPU Eulerian Fluid Simulation

A simplified motion of fluid can be expressed by the inviscid Euler equation for incompressible flow [Landau and Lifschitz 82, p. 3]:

$$\frac{\partial u}{\partial t} + u \cdot \Delta u = -\frac{\Delta P}{\rho}.$$

(The incompressibility constraint dictates that the volume of the fluid does not change over time, a perceptually subtle modification that allows for a significant reduction in mathematics.) Using this, we can fairly accurately approximate the motion of fluid.

Solving the above equation on the GPU requires us to break it down into smaller pieces and compute each piece individually, one after the other [Harris 04]. Breaking the equation down in this manner exploits the parallel nature of the GPU, in order to achieve the most optimal speed possible. Each equation section can be implemented using compute shaders in DirectX 11. (See Figure 19.1.)

Figure 19.1. Simulation flow diagram, with time traversal between the various stages of simulation.

```
Texture3D<float4> g_VelocityRO : register(t0);
RWTexture3D<float4> g_VelocityRW : register(u0);

[numthreads(8, 4, 4)]
void main(uint3 idx : SV_DispatchThreadID)
{
    float3 uvw = idx * g_invGridSize.xyz + g_halfVoxel.xyz;
    float3 relativePos = uvw - g_emitter.Position.xyz;

    // A simple falloff function.
    float invSqrMag = saturate(1 - dot(relativePos, relativePos) /
                      (g_emitter.Radius*g_emitter.Radius)); // [0-1]

    float strength = invSqrMag * invSqrMag * invSqrMag
                     * g_emitter.Force;

    float4 velocity = g_VelocityRO[idx];

    velocity.xyz += g_emitter.Direction.xyz * strength;

    g_VelocityRW[idx] = velocity;
}
```

Listing 19.1. A compute shader emitting fluid into the system using a sphere primitive. It is worth noting that this has been simplified to only update the velocity textures—in practise it will likely be favorable to also update the density/opacity textures.

19.4   Simulation Stages

19.4.1   Inject

The *inject* stage is not strictly speaking part of the equation, but it is a necessary step in the simulation process. It is here that fluid is "injected" into the simulation domain through various user-defined emitters; such emitters can be based on primitive shapes, like spheres or cubes (see Listing 19.1), or they can be more complex, such as emitting from a texture or mesh.

19.4.2   Advect

During the *advect* stage, fluid quantities (such as opacity—for rendering—or velocity) are moved through the grid with respect to velocity. The advection technique used in this chapter is backward advection, which is a first-order scheme and as such is subject to a degree of numerical diffusion due to interpolation artifacts between the fixed grid cell locations. See Listing 19.2.

19.4.3   Pressure

The *pressure* term of the equation must be solved, and for that there are many options; for simplicity's sake, this chapter will focus on the Jacobi method for

```
Texture3D<float4> g_VelocityRO : register(t0);
RWTexture3D<float4> g_VelocityRW : register(u0);

[numthreads(8, 4, 4)]
void main(uint3 idx: SV_DispatchThreadID)
{
    float3 velocity = g_VelocityRO[idx].xyz;

    float3 uvw = idx * g_invGridSize.xyz + g_halfVoxel.xyz;
    float3 sample = uvw - velocity;

    float3 newVelocity = g_VelocityRO.Sample(BilinearBorder, sample);

    g_VelocityRW[idx] = float4(newVelocity, 0);
}
```

Listing 19.2. A compute shader advection kernel—first-order backward advection is implemented. This shader has been simplified to only show the velocity advection—but other fluid quantities such as density/opacity should also be updated.

computing pressure in a localized system. The Jacobi method is an iterative solver, and though this method can yield very accurate results, the number of iterations required for satisfactory convergence is quite high. It can be too high, in fact, for real-time simulation. For this reason when using the Jacobi solver in real-time simulations, more often than not a small number of iterations is used—which leads to reduced quality—or a different method for calculating pressure is used—such as the multi-grid method [Chentanez and Müller 11], which converges much faster. For simplicities sake we are using a Jacobi solver with a reasonable number of iterations. See Listing 19.3.

```
Texture3D<float2> g_PressureRO : register(t0);
RWTexture3D<float2> g_PressureRW : register(u0);

[numthreads(8, 4, 4)]
void main(uint3 idx: SV_DispatchThreadID)
{
    float2 C = g_PressureRO[idx];

    float U = g_PressureRO[idx + int3(0, 1, 0)].x;
    float D = g_PressureRO[idx - int3(0, 1, 0)].x;
    float L = g_PressureRO[idx - int3(1, 0, 0)].x;
    float R = g_PressureRO[idx + int3(1, 0, 0)].x;
    float F = g_PressureRO[idx + int3(0, 0, 1)].x;
    float B = g_PressureRO[idx - int3(0, 0, 1)].x;

    float divergence = C.y;
    float pressure = (U + D + L + R + F + B - divergence) / 6;

    g_PressureRW[idx] = float2(pressure, divergence);
}
```

Listing 19.3. A compute shader that calculates pressure using the Jacobi method. This shader should be run for several iterations in order to achieve accurate results.

```
Texture3D<float4> g_VelocityRO : register(t0);
RWTexture3D<float4> g_VorticityRW : register(u0);

[numthreads(8, 4, 4)]
void main(uint3 idx : SV_DispatchThreadID)
{
  float3 U = g_VelocityRO[idx + int3(0, 1, 0)].xyz;
  float3 D = g_VelocityRO[idx - int3(0, 1, 0)].xyz;
  float3 L = g_VelocityRO[idx - int3(1, 0, 0)].xyz;
  float3 R = g_VelocityRO[idx + int3(1, 0, 0)].xyz;
  float3 F = g_VelocityRO[idx + int3(0, 0, 1)].xyz;
  float3 B = g_VelocityRO[idx - int3(0, 0, 1)].xyz;

  float3 dX = R - L;
  float3 dY = U - D;
  float3 dZ = F - B;

  float3 vorticity = float3((dY.z - dZ.y), (dZ.x - dX.z),
                            (dX.y - dY.x));
  g_VorticityRW[idx] = float4(length(vorticity), vorticity);
}
```

Listing 19.4. A compute shader calculating the curl gradient of the velocity field and storing that vector, along with its magnitude, in a separate vorticity field.

19.4.4 Vorticity Confinement

Vortices in fluid dynamics best describe the swirling or rotational motion of turbulent flow. Due to dissipation of fluid details caused by first-order advection schemes, it can be desirable to detect these vortices and increase motion around their center of rotation. Doing so in a GPU solver is a two-step process first introduced in [Fedkiw et al. 01] and is known as *vorticity confinement*.

First, vortices are determined by calculating the tangential gradient of the velocity grid and storing the magnitude along with the vector in a vorticity grid. See Listing 19.4. The vorticity grid is later used to apply a rotational force in the evolve stage, which adds the swirling motion back in.

19.4.5 Evolve

The *evolve* stage quantifies all forces in the system and ticks the simulation. See Listing 19.5. It is here that the vorticity force described in the pervious section is applied, but it is also what is typically referred to as the *project stage*—where the force coming from pressure is applied.

```
Texture3D<float4> g_VelocityRO : register(t0);
Texture3D<float4> g_PressureRO : register(t1);
Texture3D<float4> g_VorticityRO : register(t2);

RWTexture3D<float4> g_VelocityRW : register(u0);

[numthreads(8, 4, 4)]
void main(uint3 idx : SV_DispatchThreadID)
{
  float4 FC = g_VelocityRO[idx];

  // Apply the density force.
  {
    float U = g_PressureRO[idx + int3(0, 1, 0)].x;
    float D = g_PressureRO[idx - int3(0, 1, 0)].x;
    float L = g_PressureRO[idx - int3(1, 0, 0)].x;
    float R = g_PressureRO[idx + int3(1, 0, 0)].x;
    float F = g_PressureRO[idx + int3(0, 0, 1)].x;
    float B = g_PressureRO[idx - int3(0, 0, 1)].x;

    float dX = R - L;
    float dY = U - D;
    float dZ = F - B;

    FC.xyz -= float3(dX, dY, dZ) * 0.5f;
  }

  // Apply the vorticity force.
  {
    float4 C = g_VorticityRO[idx];

    float3 uvw = idx * g_invGridSize.xyz + g_halfVoxel.xyz;
    float U = g_VorticityRO.Sample(PointClamp, uvw + g_invSize.wyw).x;

    float D = g_VorticityRO.Sample(PointClamp, uvw - g_invSize.wyw).x;

    float R = g_VorticityRO.Sample(PointClamp, uvw - g_invSize.xww).x;

    float L = g_VorticityRO.Sample(PointClamp, uvw + g_invSize.xww).x;

    float F = g_VorticityRO.Sample(PointClamp, uvw + g_invSize.wwz).x;

    float B = g_VorticityRO.Sample(PointClamp, uvw - g_invSize.wwz).x;

    float dX = R - L;
    float dY = U - D;
    float dZ = F - B;

    float3 force = float3(dX, dY, dZ);

    // Do not normalize(0).
    if (dot(force, force) > 0.0f)
    {
    float3 vorticityForce = cross(normalize(force), C.yzw);
    FC.xyz += vorticityForce * g_VorticityForce;
    }
  }

  g_VelocityRW[idx] = FC;
}
```

Listing 19.5. A compute shader that sums up all the forces acting on the fluid and advances the simulation to the next frame.

Simulation (256³)

☐ Inject   ☐ Advect   ☐ Vorticity   ☐ Pressure   ■ Evolve

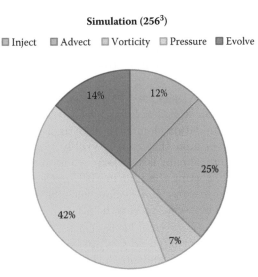

Figure 19.2. A chart showing the GPU cycle distribution of simulation stages across a number of modern GPUs.

19.5 Problems

19.5.1 Performance

Using the code above, a simple test application was devised. This test was run on a number of GPUs, and the chart in Figure 19.2 shows the average distribution of simulation work among the various stages of the simulation.

The top two hitters in terms of performance are the pressure and advect stages—and for similar reasons. Using GPU profiling, we can see that the amount of data the GPU is required to read is incredibly large. Doing some back-of-the-envelope calculations, we can see that the pressure stage (with 10 iterations on a 256^3 grid) reads around 2.5 GB per simulation cycle. Given that an NVIDIA GTX980 has a memory bandwidth of 224 GB/sec [NVIDIA n.d.], that would allow a speed-of-light FPS of 90—for the pressure stage alone. The advect stage suffers from a similar problem. Note how the advect stage accounts for 25% of the total simulation time (slightly more than half of that of pressure), but the amount of data read per simulation cycle (using the same conditions as we did for pressure) is only around 864 MB (around three times less than pressure). The additional problem with the advect stage is the relatively low cache hit rate caused by sampling voxels in a seemingly random sampled pattern—this is because we read from locations in the volume relative to the velocity at each cell.

19.5.2 Features

As well as the main performance concerns discussed above, there are some other flaws with this type of fluid simulation that we would like to address in the solution.

Fluid is not naturally box shaped! The Eulerian fluid simulation attempts to encapsulate fluid within a grid volume. This leads to one of two common problems: either the simulation domain is too tightly discretised around the flowing-fluid—resulting in fluid that can be visibly seen leaving the simulation space—or the simulation domain is too large—and there is a vast amount of empty simulation space, costing the user in GPU cycles and memory. Both are undesirable for separate reasons, and dealing with these issues consumes much time in authoring—time better spent elsewhere.

In a game scenario, it is more than likely that more than one fluid simulation volume will be required. (How often do you just see a single particle system in a game?) Doing this with current fluid simulation implementations would require placing and configuring many small simulation volumes around the game scene, or placing one large volume in some cases. The problem with this ("many volumes") approach is that each simulation is separate. Forgetting the fact that this means lots of time must be spent in authoring having to place all these volumes, try to reduce clipping/wastage, etc. But perhaps most importantly, *these simulation volumes are individual*; in other words, there is no volume-to-volume interaction. Sure, it is possible to implement such a thing, but it is nontrivial; would it not be better if this "just worked"?

The ideal approach would be to create a single large volume that would encompass the entire game scene, avoiding all the above mentioned problems. In order to maintain satisfactory visual fidelity for such a simulation volume, an extremely high grid density would be required—Figure 19.3 shows the memory consumed by a single volume texture across a range of grid densities.

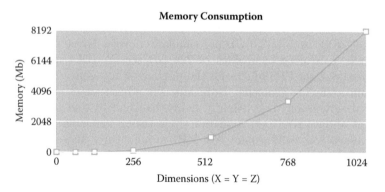

Figure 19.3. Graph showing the memory consumption of a 4-channel, 16-bit floating point volume texture across a variety of resolutions.

Figure 19.4. The brick discretization of the simulation domain.

Considering that (at the time of writing this chapter) the largest memory capacity on any consumer GPU is 12 GB—and that this graph only shows memory consumption for a single texture—running a simulation at higher than 256^3 resolution in a real game scenario is not practical yet. This is where the idea of sparse simulation comes in, which decouples (mostly) the cost of simulation—in terms of memory and computational complexity—from the grid resolution, which makes it possible to create highly detailed simulations that cover a large space (such as an entire game scene).

19.5.3 Sparse Simulation

Going back to a point touched on earlier, *wastage* is a problem born from creating largely empty simulation volumes in an attempt to encapsulate the entire fluid simulation within its bounded domain. It is quite likely that wastage occurs—to some degree—in every fluid volume. That is to say, there is likely a percentage of the volume that contains data that does not affect the result of the simulation—this is an assumption based on the likelihood that fluid is not necessarily box shaped. The first optimization presented here attempts to address this by calculating a sparse domain for a simulation to run within.

Bricking is not a new concept in computer graphics; in the context of fluid simulation, it is the process of dividing up the simulation volume at regular intervals of voxels, and each grouping of voxels is now furthermore known as a *brick*. (See Figure 19.4.) The idea is that each brick can be simulated independently of the others, making it possible to disable bricks that do not affect the simulation.

By creating an additional volume texture, it is possible to track which bricks are of interest to the simulation. This volume texture is called a *brick map* and should have dimensions equal to the number of bricks contained within the simulation on each axis. Storing either a 1 or a 0 in each voxel of the brick map—depending on whether the brick requires simulation, or if it should be ignored—is an effective method for tracking active simulation bricks.

Using an entire voxel to store either a 1 or 0 may seem wasteful; however, it does not require atomics unlike other methods [Gruen 15], which keeps it nice and fast. Constraining the algorithm to only allow for setting either the entire brick map to 0 at once (e.g., the clear at the start of the simulation frame) or

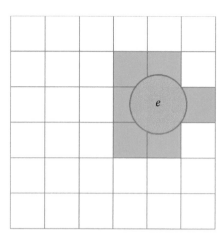

Figure 19.5. A 2D representation of a simulation grid—note the primitive emitter e and the overlapping simulation bricks denoted in red.

a particular voxel to 1 based on some condition, avoids the need for atomics without introducing any race conditions.

When the simulation first starts, a way of identifying which bricks should initially be part of the simulation domain is essential. Emitters specify where fluid gets injected into the simulation. This makes it possible to determine which bricks the emitter(s) occupy and to use this information to kick the simulation off. (See Figure 19.5.) It is also worth doing this calculation throughout the life of the simulation if the emitter moves from frame to frame so that any bricks it is overlapping continue to be part of the simulation domain.

Once the actual simulation is underway, a way of identifying which bricks should or should not continue to be part of the simulation is required. For this two new terms are introduced—*expansion* and *reduction*—and both are handled during the old evolve stage.

Expansion occurs when fluid moves from one brick to another; this can be calculated by checking if the axial velocity in a simulation cell is large enough to transverse the brick boundary. If so, the neighboring brick must be included in the next simulation frame.

Reduction, which is the opposite of expansion, occurs when fluid dissipates or completely moves out of a brick. In this algorithm, this is taken care of by clearing the brick map at the beginning of every simulation step and letting expansion do its work.

Figure 19.6 shows how the sparse simulation looks. Note the addition of the new steps (in blue) that were not in the basic algorithm initially put forward in Figure 19.1. The first is a *clear* step that sets all bricks to an "ignore" state in the brick map. This is done before each simulation frame. After the usual

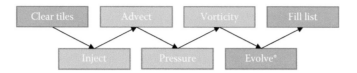

Figure 19.6. A chronological flow diagram showing the various stages of sparse simulation. Note the addition of new stages in blue—compare to Figure 19.1.

```
Texture3D<uint> g_BrickMapRO : register(t0);
AppendStructredBuffer<uint4> g_ListRW : register(u0);

[numthreads(8, 4, 4)]
void main(uint3 idx : SV_DispatchThreadID)
{
    if(g_BrickMapRO[idx] != 0)
    {
        g_ListRW.Append(idx);
    }
}
```

Listing 19.6. A compute shader to create a linear list of bricks to be included in the sparse simulation domain.

simulation steps, inject, advect, pressure, and vorticity—which have not changed significantly—the check for expansion is inserted in the evolve stage after the velocity of each cell has been calculated in preparation for the next frame. Lastly, in order to feed the following simulation frame, a list of bricks that are part of the next frame simulation needs to be populated. This is done using a compute shader, run at a granularity of one thread per brick; see Listing 19.6.

When using a list of brick indices like this, a subtle modification to the previous code listings for the various simulation stages is required, allowing the algorithm to handle the sparse simulation—that is, to dispatch enough thread groups (number of bricks × number of thread groups per brick)—and to check the index of the current brick from the list. See Listing 19.7.

```
StructredBuffer<uint4> g_ListRO : register(t0);

[numthreads(8, 4, 4)]
void main(uint3 threadIdx: SV_DispatchThreadID)
{
    uint3 idx = g_Sparse ? g_ListRO[GetBrickIdx(threadIdx)].xyz :
    threadIdx;
    ...
}
```

Listing 19.7. A code snippet demonstrating how to determine the current location of a simulation cell when simulating sparsely compared to non-sparsely. The variable g_Sparse should be set accordingly.

Physical memory

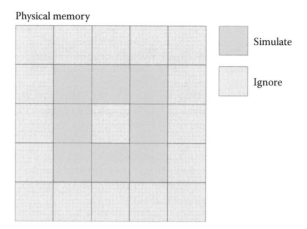

Simulate

Ignore

Figure 19.7. A 2D representation of the memory usage in a typical simulation. All memory is allocated but only regions pertinent to simulation are used.

All of this allows for sparsely simulating fluid but so far does not offer up anything in terms of memory savings. (See Figure 19.7.)

By only sparsely computing a fluid simulation in the above manner, there has not actually been a reduction in any memory used. This method for storing simulations is called *uncompressed storage*. Recalling back, part of the problem with using fluid simulations in games is the awful memory consumption. So, what are the options?

One solution is to use compressed storage. (See Figure 19.8.) A volume texture is used to store offsets for each brick into what can conceptually be thought of as a list of bricks (`vector<brick>`). This results in good memory consumption as it is only required to allocate memory for bricks that are pertinent to the simulation. The downside to this approach is that in order to reap the memory saving benefits, the list resource must be dynamically resized on the fly. The better the memory savings, the more aggressive the resizing strategy has to be; and resizing is not free! Along with the resizing issue, another problem here is that all cell lookups now require an indirection. This is called *software translation*, and it is particularly bad in the case of a bilinear filtering operation that happens to straddle a brick corner. In this case, each of the eight lookups that are part of the filtering kernel may end up reading from regions of memory very distant from one another, affecting cache performance. One option to mitigate this issue is to pad each brick with one extra cell on each side and to copy neighboring data into these padding cells before simulation.

As a representative example, take a four-cubed brick and add the padding cells, as in Figure 19.9. The number of cells per brick will more than triple in this example. Still an option, the memory savings on the whole might outweigh the extra cells required for padding; however, it is not ideal.

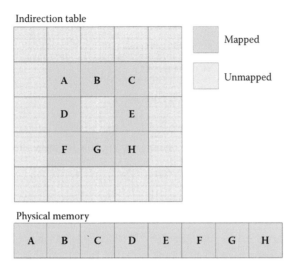

Figure 19.8. A diagram showing the memory usage pattern in a compressed simulation. Physical memory can be seen along the bottom while the 2D indirection table showing regions of simulation space mapped and unmapped above.

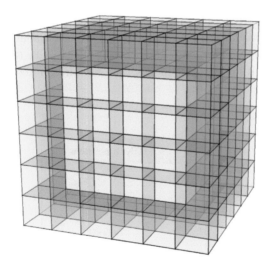

Figure 19.9. A simulation brick padded to include neighboring values. In this case the number of cells in the original brick is 64, and a further 152 cells are required for padding.

```
ID3D11Device3* pDevice3 = nullptr;
pDevice->QueryInterface(&pDevice3);

D3D11_FEATURE_DATA_D3D11_OPTIONS2 support;
pDevice3->CheckFeatureSupport(D3D11_FEATURE_D3D11_OPTIONS2,
                              &support,
                              sizeof(support));

m_UseVTR = support.TiledResourcesTier ==
D3D11_TILED_RESOURCES_TIER_3;
```

Listing 19.8. A snippet of C++ code demonstrating how to query the driver for volume tiled resources support in DirectX 11.3.

19.5.4   Enter DirectX 11.3

Tiled resources are not new; support for 2D tiled resources has been around since DirectX 11.2. In DirectX 11.3 it is now possible to extend this functionality into the third dimension, allowing for tiled resource operations on volume textures— this feature is called *Volume Tiled Resources* (VTRs).

With DirectX 11.3 cvomes the return of the caps system used in DirectX 9—in other words, it is once again no longer safe to assume as a developer that all GPUs that support DirectX 11.3 can support all its features; and one of those features is VTRs. Querying the device for VTR support is demonstrated in the code example in Listing 19.8. This means that as a developer a fall-back technique should be considered for the case where VTRs are not available.

Similar to DirectX 11.2 tiled resources, each tile must be 64 KB in size. With respect to volume resources, this means that tiles are limited to the dimensions shown in Table 19.1.

BPP	Tile Dimensions
8	64×32×32
16	32×32×32
32	32×32×16
64	32×16×16
128	16×16×16

Table 19.1. The various tile dimensions with respect to the number of bytes per voxel.

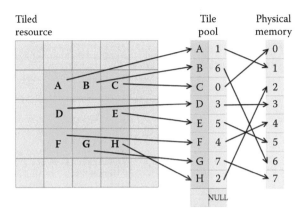

Figure 19.10. A 2D representation of a simulation grid using tiled resources.

Using tiled resources, it is possible to get the best features of the two previously mentioned memory storage techniques: compressed and uncompressed. This is partly because tiled resources appear and behave like regular volume resources (a trait from uncompressed storage) and partly because, in terms of physical memory, only a minimal set of tiles necessary to compute the simulation are allocated.

Tiled resources are a high-level abstraction of the paged memory model used in modern GPUs. Physical memory is allocated in pages, and virtual address tables (pointers in C++ terms) allow indexing of the hardware pages. Most modern memory architectures work in this fashion.

In the context of fluid simulation, tiled resources can be used to sparsely allocate the simulation grid (one brick per tile), and the virtual address table can be manipulated to represent our indirection volume. (See Figure 19.10.) This becomes a powerful tool because, like compressed storage, simulation memory is only allocated for select bricks and the indirect cell lookup can be handled in hardware—and becomes as simple as any paged memory read (which is any read on any resource on modern GPUs). All the tricky corner cases exposed by compressed storage are handled at the hardware level, which means speed-of-light memory access—something that is of high value in bandwidth-bound regimes.

Of course, there is a downside to using tiled resources, and that is that tile mappings must be updated from the CPU—the DirectX API does not allow for any other method at this present time.

Updating the tile mappings from the CPU is done using the DirectX API call `UpdateTileMappings`—which has not changed since DirectX 11.2. (See Listing 19.9.)

It is highly recommended when using this API that tile mapping deltas are calculated and used within the API—mappings can be one of three states: mapped,

```
HRESULT ID3D11DeviceContext2::UpdateTileMappings(
    ID3D11Resource                          *pTiledResource,
    UINT                                    NumTiledResourceRegions,
    const D3D11_TILED_RESOURCE_COORDINATE
                            *pTiledResourceRegionStartCoordinates,
    const D3D11_TILE_REGION_SIZE
                                    *pTiledResourceRegionSizes,

    ID3D11Buffer                            *pTilePool,
    UINT                                    NumRanges,
    const UINT                              *pRangeFlags,
    const UINT                              *pTilePoolStartOffsets,
    UINT                                    *pRangeTileCounts,
    UINT                                    Flags );
```

Listing 19.9. The function prototype for the `UpdateTiledMappings` method in C++ DirectX.

unchanged, and unmapped. Using the unchanged state to define which tiles have not changed since the last simulation frame has significant performance benefits. This can be done using the `pRangeFlags` parameter:

$$
\begin{array}{rcl}
\text{Mapped} & \rightarrow & \texttt{D3D11\_TILE\_RANGE\_REUSE\_SINGLE\_TILE} \\
\text{Unchanged} & \rightarrow & \texttt{D3D11\_TILE\_RANGE\_SKIP} \\
\text{Unmapped} & \rightarrow & \texttt{D3D11\_TILE\_RANGE\_NULL}
\end{array}
$$

It is worth reiterating the importance of the `D3D11_TILE_RANGE_SKIP` flag; without it the driver would not know which tiles can safely be skipped when updating paged memory access tables, and the performance of the `UpdateTileMappings` function would suffer *significantly* as a result.

What use is a CPU API that controls the domain bounds of a GPU simulation? Fortunately, this is a restriction that can be worked around using the (somewhat) predictable nature of fluids.

19.6   Latency Resistant Sparse Fluid Simulation

For a long time it has been possible to get data back from the GPU to the CPU, although the feature is something of a taboo in real-time graphics. The reason for which is the inherent risk of causing a CPU-GPU synchronization point. The CPU and GPU run out of sync with one another as they are two completely separate systems. The GPU is fed with commands from the CPU using the producer/consumer model of parallel systems—and reading the contents of GPU resident memory forces a synchronization of that process. The only efficient way of fetching data back from the GPU is to allow for two frames of latency in reading that data back—this ensures that the data requested has finished being processed by the GPU. (See Figure 19.11.)

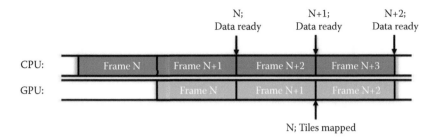

Figure 19.11. Accessing GPU resident data from the CPU without causing a synchronization point.

Reading the list of simulation bricks back on the CPU two frames after they have been calculated to feed information about which bricks should be resident in memory for the current frame would create artifacts because the resident memory would be two frames behind.

In the case of fluid simulation, this can be handled by predicting the course simulation ahead of time using simple Eulerian integration. A maximum velocity for each brick is calculated at the time of simulation, and this value is read back as part of the brick information contained within the simulation brick list. This maximum velocity is used for dead reckoning logic on the CPU, which determines the next two frames of *probable* simulation bricks and adds them to the list of *definite* bricks obtained from the GPU. This process is called the *prediction engine* in Figure 19.12.

In Figure 19.12 the flow of the overall algorithm can be seen. Again, the new stages discussed in this section are shown in blue (and, for simplicities sake, the previously covered stages for *sparse Eulerian simulation* have been combined into a single green block). Note how the simulation flow begins with a branch on the CPU. Is read-back data ready? This is a necessary step in dealing with the latency introduced by the CPU read-back. For the first two frames of the simulation or if any fluid emitter has changed, there would not be any (meaningful) data available for read-back. So, the algorithm must have a fall-back—which is to use the bricks overlapping any emitter.

19.7 Performance

A deterministic performance testing scene was constructed; a spherical emitter spins around the bottom of a simulation volume. The test was run for several minutes and the results were averaged during that time. The test was performed on a NVIDIA GTX980 using Windows 10. See the results in Table 19.2.

Clearly, the sparse grid simulation provides a significant speedup over the full grid method—however, admittedly, this amount will vary wildly on a case-by-case

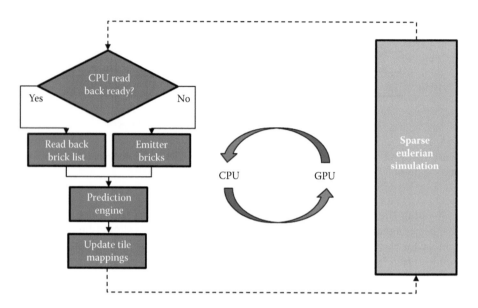

Figure 19.12. The flow diagram for latency-resistant fluid simulation. On the left (in blue) you can see the various CPU components, while on the right is the previous sparse fluid simulation algorithm presented in Figure 19.6.

	\multicolumn{5}{c}{**Grid Resolution**}				
	128^3	256^3	384^3	512^3	$1{,}024^3$
	\multicolumn{5}{c}{**Full Grid**}				
Num. Bricks	256	2048	6,912	16,384	131,072
Memory (MB)	80	640	2,160	5,120	40,960
Simulation	2.29 ms	19.04 ms	64.71 ms	NA	NA
	\multicolumn{5}{c}{**Sparse Grid**}				
Num. Bricks	36	146	183	266	443
Memory (MB)	11.25	45.63	57.19	83.13	138.44
Simulation	0.41 ms	1.78 ms	2.67 ms	2.94 ms	5.99 ms
Scaling Sim.	78.14%	76.46%	75.01%	NA	NA

Table 19.2. The performance statistics of the sparse simulation versus the regular simulation across a variety of grid resolutions. Note the significant reduction in time taken for the simulation. This is mostly down to the fact that the simulation volume contained lots of empty space. The "Num. Bricks" line shows how many bricks were actively involved in the simulation.

basis. The same can be said about memory consumption. Note how the 4-GB frame buffer of the GTX980 cannot run full grid simulations at a resolution of 512 or higher. This is because the simulation would not fit in memory at around 5 GB.

19.8 Sparse Volume Rendering

19.8.1 Introduction

Volumetric rendering is traditionally performed by blending a collection of samples taken from a data set at a fixed step along each screen pixel's view ray. This is usually done in real-time graphics by using a method called a ray marching [Pawasauskas 97]. The problem with the traditional approach to volume rendering with respect to fluid simulation is that many of the samples collected when traversing a screen pixels view ray would not contribute to the final color of the pixel, due to them coming from areas of the volume not containing any data—in other words, empty regions of memory. Using the information gathered from the simulation, it is possible to implement a mechanism to skip over the empty regions while performing the volume rendering, significantly reducing the number of samples collected and making the whole process faster.

19.8.2 Preprocess

Being with the list of simulation bricks calculated during simulation—this list of bricks should be available on the CPU (see Section 19.6). This list of bricks next needs to be sorted in front-to-back order before being ready for rendering.

An index/vertex buffer is constructed at start-up time. The contents will be a number of unit cubes placed at the origin, one cube for each brick—so that there are enough to cover the maximum expected number of bricks. With the number of bricks for rendering at hand, it is time to `DrawIndexed` on that index/vertex buffer, ensuring to set the correct parameters so that there is one unit cube rendered for each brick in the sorted simulation brick list.

19.8.3 Vertex Shading

During the vertex shader execution, a lookup into the simulation brick list is performed to determine the offset of the brick currently being rendered (there are a number of ways to do this, e.g., using the `SV_VertexID` semantic to index the buffer). Listing 19.10 is an example vertex shader; note how, rather than passing the texture space position `posTS` down to the pixel shader, a ray direction is calculated instead. This is to avoid any triangle order sorting artifacts that might occur during rendering. A direction is not order dependant because it has a lack of positional identity. In the pixel shader, `posTS` is recalculated for the front and back faces using a ray-box intersection test.

```
// List of brick indices to render.
StructuredBuffer<uint4> g_OccupiedTileListRO;

// Vertex shader.
v2f vsMain(float4 Pos : POSITION, uint idx : SV_VertexID)
{
  v2f o;

  // Div num verts in cube to get idx.
  uint brickIdx = idx / 8;

  // Get currently rendering brick UVW offset.
  float3 cellOffset = g_OccupiedTileListRO[ brickIdx ].xyz
                      * g_invGridSize;

  // Calculate brick size (actually uniform across grid).
  float3 brickSize = BRICK_SIZE_XYZ * g_invGridSize;

  // Bounding box for brick.
  o.boxmin = cellOffset;
  o.boxmax = cellOffset + brickSize;

  // NOTE: VB consists of a unit cube.
  float3 posTS = lerp(o.boxmin, o.boxmax, Pos.xyz);
  float3 posWS = mul(g_fluidToWorldMatrix, float4(posTS, 1)).xyz;

  o.posPS = mul(g_worldToProjectionMatrix, float4(posWS, 1));

  // Calculate ray direction in texture space.
  float3 relPosTS = posTS - g_eyePositionTS;
  o.rayDirTS = relPosTS / dot(relPosTS, g_eyeForwardTS);

  return o;
}
```

Listing 19.10. A vertex shader demonstrating how to calculate the necessary components for ray marching. A brick map index is determined from the vertex index, which is used to determine the brick offset in the simulation.

19.8.4   Pixel Shading

For each desired brick, ray marching is performed through its bounding box just as would be done for the bounding box of a regular (non-sparse) volume; this is done using a pixel shader. As ray direction is calculated and passed from the vertex shader, ray intersections must be calculated during the pixel shader stage. The code in Listing 19.11 efficiently calculates ray intersections with a box defined by its minimum and maximum bounds [Green 05].

With the pixel–view-ray intersection information, it is now possible to ray-march through each brick. Sampling from the volume tiled resource is exactly the same as sampling from a regular volume texture in HLSL. The only difference is on the memory transaction code happening behind the scenes in the driver and hardware, as discussed earlier.

```
float2 IntersectBox(Ray r, float3 boxmin, float3 boxmax)
{
    // Compute intersection of ray with all six bounding box planes.
    float3 invR = 1.0 / r.d;
    float3 tbot = invR * (boxmin.xyz - r.o);
    float3 ttop = invR * (boxmax.xyz - r.o);

    // Reorder intersections to find smallest and largest on
    // each axis.
    float3 tmin = min (ttop, tbot);
    float3 tmax = max (ttop, tbot);

    // Find the largest tmin and the smallest tmax.
    float2 t0 = max (tmin.xx, tmin.yz);
    tnear = max (t0.x, t0.y);
    t0 = min (tmax.xx, tmax.yz);

    tfar = min (t0.x, t0.y);

    return float2(tnear, tfar);
}
```

Listing 19.11. A vertex shader demonstrating how to calculate the necessary components for ray marching. A brick map index is determined from the vertex index, which is used to determine the brick offset in the simulation.

19.8.5   Bucketed Opacity Thresholding

Sparse volume rendering may provide a considerable performance boost over non-sparse techniques when rendering fluid, but the algorithm prevents handy rendering optimization typically used in regular volume rendering: early ray termination. This is because each brick is being ray-marched separately; early ray termination can (and should) be performed within the brick but cannot be extended to cover the whole volume because of this.

An alternative to early ray termination is to use *bucketed opacity thresholding* [Dunn and Bavoil 14]. Here, the depth testing hardware is repurposed to terminate rays early if their full opacity has been reached—in other words, if following samples would not contribute to the final outcome of the rendering. To do this, bricks must be presorted in a front-to-back order, and the under blend operator must be used. This is because the under blend operator stores alpha in the render target, a quantity which is required to be known. The following are the under blend mode equations for the color and alpha channel modes:

$$C_{\text{dst}} = A_{\text{dst}} \left(A_{\text{src}} C_{\text{src}} \right) + C_{\text{dst}},$$
$$A_{\text{dst}} = 0 + \left(1 - A_{\text{src}} \right) A_{\text{dst}}.$$

Bricks are grouped into view-Z buckets, each rendered in separate draw calls. Immediately following each bucket's draw call, a full screen pass must be run that checks every pixel in the render target used to render the bucket and determines

 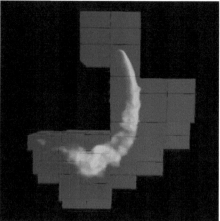

Figure 19.13. Sparse fluid simulation and rendering in action: a still of the test scene described in Section 19.5.1 (left) and an overlay of the bricking structure for the same image (right).

if there are any for which further blending operations (under operator) would have no effect. This is done by checking the alpha channel of each pixel (which holds the transmittance value when using under blending), and if it is 0 (or close to it), then this pixel can safely be discarded from all other operations.

Once these pixels have been determined, a 0 (or min-Z) value is written to the depth buffer at these locations—and with depth testing enabled when rendering the fluid volumes, this effectively implements early ray termination using the depth testing hardware present on GPUs. The stencil buffer could also have been used to perform this kind of thing; however, during testing, it became apparent that use of the depth buffer was far more performant across a wide range of hardware.

19.9 Results

Figures 19.13, 19.14, and 19.15 show the algorithm in action.

19.10 Conclusion

This chapter has described an effective method for computing and rendering smoke-based, Eulerian fluid simulations, in real-time, on the GPU using the DirectX 11+ APIs by leveraging the sparse nature of fluid, allowing the GPU to skip over areas of simulation that would not contribute to the final result. Several sparse simulation methods have been discussed—each with their own benefits and each applicable for use in modern games.

Figure 19.14. A still from the NVIDIA Mech Ti demo—using the sparse fluid simulation and rendering presented in this chapter.

Figure 19.15. A high-resolution still from the test scene mentioned in Section 19.5.1.

The recommended solution for computing fluid is described in Section 19.6; however, if platform-specific constraints prevent the use of VTRs, then a suitable fall-back can be found in Section 19.5.3. Using one of the memory storage solutions presented there—although they may yield slightly worse performance—the "uncompressed storage" method has worse memory consumption and the "compressed storage" method consumes more GPU cycles. When using one of these fall-back methods, quality reduction should be considered in order to make up for the benefits lost with VTRs.

A method for rendering the sparse grid information produced by the simulation has been demonstrated in Section 19.8. Using the list of simulation bricks from the simulation, it is possible to construct a rendering primitive to represent the sparse domain, which can then be used for volume rendering. By using this method, empty space within the simulation can be removed from the rendering process—significantly speeding up the technique.

Bibliography

[Chentanez and Müller 11] Nuttapong Chentanez and Matthias Müller. "Real-Time Eulerian Water Simulation Using a Restricted Tall Cell Grid." In *ACM SIGGRAPH 2011 Papers*, article no. 82. New York: ACM, 2011.

[Dunn and Bavoil 14] Alex Dunn and Louis Bavoil. "Transparency (or Translucency) Rendering." https://developer.nvidia.com/content/transparency-or-translucency-rendering, 2014.

[Fedkiw et al. 01] R. Fedkix, J. Stam, and H. W. Jensen. "Visual Simulation of Smoke." In *SIGGRAPH '01: Proceedings of the 28th Annual Conference on Computer Graphics and Interactive Techniques*, pp. 15–22. New York: ACM, 2001.

[Green 05] Simon Green. "Volume Rendering for Games." http://http.download.nvidia.com/developer/presentations/2005/GDC/Sponsored_Day/GDC_2005_VolumeRenderingForGames.pdf/, 2005.

[Gruen 15] Holger Gruen. "Block-Wise Linear Binary Grids for Fast Ray-Casting Operations." In *GPU Pro 6: Advanced Rendering Techniques*, edited by Wolfgang Engel, pp. 489–504. Boca Raton, FL: A K Peters/CRC Press, 2015.

[Harris 04] Mark Harris. "Fast Fluid Dynamics Simulation on the GPU." In *GPU Gems*, edited by Randima Fernando, pp. 637–665. Upper Saddle River, NJ: Addison-Wesley, 2004.

[Landau and Lifschitz 82] L. D. Landau and E. M. Lifschitz. *Fluid Mechanics*, Second Edition. Oxford, UK: Pergamon Press, 1982.

[Müller et al. 03] Matthias Müller, David Charypar, and Markus Gross. "Particle-Based Fluid Simulation for Interactive Applications." In *Proceedings of the 2003 ACM SIGGRAPH/Eurographics Symposium on Computer Animation*, pp. 154–159. Aire-la-Ville, Switzerland: Eurographics Association, 2003.

[NVIDIA n.d.] NVIDIA. "GeForce GTX 980 Specifications." http://www.geforce.co.uk/hardware/desktop-gpus/geforce-gtx-980/specifications, no date.

[Pawasauskas 97] John Pawasauskas. "Volume Visualization with Ray Casting." Course notes for CS563 Advanced Topics in Computer Graphics, http://web.cs.wpi.edu/~matt/courses/cs563/talks/powwie/p1/ray-cast.htm, 1997.

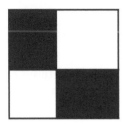

About the Contributors

Francisco Ávila is a research engineer at the King Abdullah University of Science and Technology (KAUST), Saudi Arabia, where he works on lightweight visualization techniques for the web. Before joining KAUST, he was a research intern at Intel working on ray-tracing techniques, data structures, and GPU programming. He received a BS in computer science from ITESM, Mexico, in 2011.

Pál Barta is pursuing a MS degree at the Technical University in Budapest, Hungary. Over the last two years, his main focus has been on computer graphics. His 2010 BSc thesis topic was order independent transparency, which later evolved into the volumetric transparency method described in this book.

Samuel Boivin is a research scientist at INRIA in leave of absence. He is now the head of Research and Development at SolidAnim, a company specializing in Visual Effects for movies and video games. He earned a PhD in computer graphics in 2001 from Ecole Polytechnique in Palaiseau (France). He has published several papers about computer graphics in many conferences, including SIGGRAPH. His research topics are photorealistic real-time rendering, real-time augmented reality, fluid dynamics, and inverse techniques for acquiring material properties (photometric, mechanical) from videos.

Fabrice Colin earned a PhD in mathematics from the University of Sherbrooke (Canada) in 2002, under the supervision of Dr. Kaczynski (University of Sherbrooke) and Dr. Willem (Université catholique de Louvain), with a thesis in the field of partial differential equations (PDE). In 2005 he was hired by the Mathematics and Computer Science Department at Laurentian University, where he is currently a professor. His primary research interests are the variational and topological methods in PDE. But besides his theoretical work, he started collaborating in 2003 with Professor Egli, from the Department of Computer Science (University of Sherbrooke), on the numerical simulations of PDE related, for instance, to fluid dynamics or computer graphics.

Patrick Cozzi is coauthor of *3D Engine Design for Virtual Globes* (2011), coeditor of *OpenGL Insights* (2012), and editor of *WebGL Insights* (2015). At Analytical Graphics, Inc., he leads the graphics development of Cesium, an open source

WebGL virtual globe. He teaches "GPU Programming and Architecture" at the University of Pennsylvania, where he received a master's degree in computer science.

Carsten Dachsbacher is a full professor at the Karlsruhe Institute of Technology. His research focuses on real-time computer graphics, global illumination, scientific visualization, and perceptual rendering, on which he published articles at various conferences and journals including SIGGRAPH, IEEE VIS, EG, and EGSR. He has been a tutorial speaker at SIGGRAPH, Eurographics, and the Game Developers Conference.

Paul Dufort earned BSc and MSc degrees from the Department of Physics at the University of Toronto and a PhD in computational biophysics from the U of T's Institute of Medical Science in 2000. He served as a computer graphics consultant to the U of T Institute for Aerospace Studies' Flight Simulation Laboratory from 1996 to 2009 and was a founding partner and Director of Research and Development at medical imaging start-up Tomographix IP from 2000 to 2009, before joining the University Health Network's Joint Department of Medical Imaging in Toronto as a Computational Imaging Scientist in 2009. He presently specializes in the development and application of high-performance image processing and computer vision algorithms to problems in medical imaging, with an emphasis on the application of machine learning algorithms and graphical models to problems in structural and functional neuroimaging.

Alex Dunn, as a developer technology engineer for NVIDIA, spends his days passionately working toward advancing real-time visual effects in games. A former graduate of Abertay University's Games Technology Course, Alex got his first taste of graphics programming on the consoles. Now working for NVIDIA, his time is spent working on developing cutting-edge programming techniques to ensure the highest quality and best player experience possible is achieved.

Jonathan Dupuy is a French PhD student working on high-quality rendering under the supervision of Victor Ostromoukhov and Jean-Claude Iehl from the Université Claude Bernard de Lyon I and Pierre Poulin from the Université de Montréal. His PhD focuses on deriving and exploiting linearly filterable object representations that can be rendered at constant cost with very little memory overhead and benefit from GPU acceleration. In contrast to sampling-based methods whose computational costs increase proportionally to sub-pixel detail, this approach promises images of comparable quality at much higher frame rates.

Richard Egli has been a professor in the Department of Computer Science at University of Sherbrooke since 2000. He received his BSc degree and his MSc degrees in computer science at the University of Sherbrooke (Québec, Canada). He received his PhD in computer science from the University of Montréal (Québec,

Canada) in 2000. He is the chair of the MOIVRE research center (Modélisation en Imagerie, Vision et Réseaux de neurones). His research interests include computer graphics, physical simulations, and artificial life.

Elmar Eisemann is a professor at Delft University of Technology (TU Delft), heading the Computer Graphics and Visualization Group. Before, he was an associated professor at Telecom ParisTech (until 2012) and a senior scientist heading a research group in the Cluster of Excellence (Saarland University / MPI Informatik) (until 2009). His interests include real-time and perceptual rendering, alternative representations, shadow algorithms, global illumination, and GPU acceleration techniques. He coauthored the book *Real-Time Shadows* and participated in various committees and editorial boards. He was local organizer of EGSR 2010, EGSR 2012, and HPG 2012, as well as co-paper chair for HPG2015, and he was honored with the Eurographics Young Researcher Award in 2011.

Anders Eklund earned a MSc degree in applied physics and electrical engineering and a PhD degree in medical informatics from Linköping University, Sweden, and is currently a postdoctoral associate at Virginia Tech. His research interests include using functional magnetic resonance imaging (fMRI) to study brain activity, medical imaging, machine learning, and non-parametric statistics. He especially likes to combine these research areas with high-performance computing.

Arturo García holds a BS degree in computer sciences from the University of Guadalajara. He received an MS degree in computer science from CINVESTAV and an MBA degree from ITESO. He is currently Engineering Manager at Intel.

Martin Guay completed a BSc in mathematics in 2007 and then Martin Guay joined Cyanide's Montreal-based studio, where he worked on the development of several game titles as a graphics programmer. In 2010 he joined the MOIVRE research centre, Université de Sherbrooke, as a graduate student in computer science, where he effectuated research in the fields of computational physics and physically based animation of fluids.

Dongsoo Han works as a researcher in AMD's GPU Tech Initiatives Group. At AMD, he focuses on developing physics simulations such as rigid body, fluid, cloth, hair, and grass for real-time applications. His research focuses on parallelizing physics simulation algorithms on GPUs. His hair simulation technique is a part of TressFX and has been used for several games and demos. He earned his master's degree in computer science at University of Pennsylvania, where he focused on various fluid simulation methods.

Takahiro Harada is a researcher and the architect of a GPU global illumination renderer called Firerender at AMD. He developed Forward+ and the GPU rigid body simulation solver that is used as a base of Bullet 3.0. Before joining AMD, he engaged in research and development on real-time physics simulation on PC and game consoles at Havok. Before coming to the industry, he was in academia as an assistant professor at the University of Tokyo, where he also earned his PhD in engineering.

Jean-Claude Iehl is an associate professor at the LIRIS laboratory of the Université Claude Bernard de Lyon I. He holds a PhD and MSc from the Université de Saint-Etienne, both in computer science. His research interests are focused on efficiently rendering complex scenes using graphics hardware and off-line Monte Carlo methods.

Dave Kotfis is a software engineer and is pursuing a master's degree in robotics at the University of Pennsylvania. He also competes in the DARPA Robotics Challenge. His research interests include augmented reality, artificial intelligence, and virtual worlds. He has a passion for tackling hard research problems.

Balázs Kovács is a BSc student at the Technical University in Budapest, Hungary. His research interests include interactive global illumination rendering techniques and tomographic reconstruction algorithms in CUDA.

Thomas Kroes is a PhD student in computer science at Delft University of Technology (TU Delft). He has a bachelor's degree in mechanical engineering and a master's in industrial design engineering. He is interested in medical visualization, in particular real-time photo-realistic volume visualization. He is the author of Exposure Render, an interactive photo-realistic volume rendering framework.

Olivier Le Maître is a member of the research staff at the French National Center for Research (CNRS), working in the Department of Mechanics and Energetics of the LIMSI lab. After receiving a PhD in computational fluid dynamics in 1998 he joined the University of Evry, where he taught scientific computing, numerical methods, and fluid mechanics. He joined CNRS in 2007 as a full-time researcher, where he directs research in complex flow simulations, uncertainty quantification techniques, and stochastic models.

Sergio Murguía received a BSc from the University of Guanajuato in 2005 and an MSc from the Center of Research in Mathematics (CIMAT) in Mexico. In 2009, he joined Intel to work on software validation of DirectX and OpenGL drivers. He is currently working as a software validation engineer for high performance products. His areas of interest include computer graphics and photorealistic rendering.

Sebastien Noury is a PhD student in computer science at Paris-Sud University in Orsay, France, where he received his MSc in software engineering in 2009. He also studied game development in Montreal and interned at independent game studios in Paris and Singapore before joining the VENISE team of the CNRS/LIMSI lab to work on real-time fluid dynamics for virtual reality. His research interests include GPU acceleration of dynamic simulations, real-time rendering, and human-computer interaction.

Stefan Petersson received a BSc and an MSc in computer science from Blekinge Institute of Technology (BTH), Sweden. He is currently a lecturer and PhD student in the School of Computing, where he is part of the GSIL Computer Graphics group. Stefan is also a program manager for the Master of Science in Game and Software Engineering program at BTH. His current research and teaching interests include computer graphics and GPGPU.

Pierre Poulin is a full professor in the Computer Science and Operations Research department of the Université de Montréal. He holds a PhD from the University of British Columbia and a MSc from the University of Toronto, both in computer science. He is associate editor for the journals *Computer Graphics Forum* and *Computer Animation and Virtual Worlds*; has been program co-chair of CASA 2014, Eurographics 2013, CGI 2011, EG Workshop on Natural Phenomena 2005, and GI 2000; and has served on program committees of more than 50 international conferences. His research interests cover a wide range of topics, including image synthesis, image-based modeling, procedural modeling, natural phenomena, scientific visualization, and computer animation.

Hauke Rehfeld received his diploma in computational visualistics (computer science) at the University of Koblenz-Landau in 2011. He is currently a scientific researcher with the computer graphics group at Karlsruhe Institute of Technology, working on his PhD. His research interests include real-time rendering, light transport, visibility, ray tracing, GPU computing, and game design.

Leo Reyes studied computer engineering at the University of Guadalajara, Mexico. He received his MS and PhD degrees in computer vision from the Center of Research and Advanced Studies (CINVESTAV). His research interests include computer vision, computer graphics, image processing, and artificial intelligence. He is currently working at Intel Labs in Guadalajara.

Philip Rideout works at Medical Simulation Corporation in Denver, where he develops novel rendering techniques for fluoroscopy and ultrasound simulation. Philip has written a book on 3D programming for the iPhone and maintains a blog for graphics tricks at http://prideout.net. In his spare time he can be found watching *Doctor Who* with Sreya, Pragati, and Arnav.

Dirk Schut is a student at Delft University of Technology. He worked on the chapter as part of the honors track of his bachelor's degree in computer science. Now he is doing a master's degree in computer science, focussing on computer graphics and signal processing. Before he started studying, he programmed computer graphics techniques for fun.

Michael Schwarz is currently a postdoc at Cornell University and holds an MS and a PhD, both in computer science, from the University of Erlangen-Nuremberg, Germany. His graphics-related research interests include real-time computer graphics, GPU techniques, global illumination, scalable approaches, procedural modeling, and perception-aware graphics.

Jason Stewart is a developer technology engineer at AMD. He studied computer science and computer graphics at the University of North Carolina at Chapel Hill. Prior to joining the developer technology team at AMD, he worked in the game industry for eight years, developing and optimizing graphics features for several major titles. He previously worked at Electronic Arts and Red Storm Entertainment, shipping games on original Xbox, Xbox 360, Playstation 2, Playstation 3, Wii, 3DS, and iOS. Prior to his game industry work, he worked as a hardware and real-time embedded software engineer. In his roll at AMD, he works with professional game developers to integrate technologies and optimize performance on AMD graphics hardware.

László Szécsi is an associate professor at the Technical University in Budapest, Hungary. He gives lectures in programming, computer graphics, and computer game development. His research revolves around global illumination, real-time rendering techniques, and the combination of the two. László has published numerous scientific papers and has been a regular contributor to the *ShaderX* book series.

Nicolas Thibieroz has spent all of his professional life working in developer relations for graphics hardware companies. He taught himself programming from an early age as a result of his fascination for the first wave of "real-time" 3D games such as *Ultima Underworld*. After living in Paris for 22 years, he decided to pursue his studies in England where he obtained a Bachelor of Electronic Engineering in 1996. Not put off by the English weather, Nicolas chose to stay and joined PowerVR Technologies to eventually lead the developer relations group, supporting game developers on a variety of platforms and contributing to SDK content. He then transitioned to ATI Technologies and AMD Corporation, where he is now managing the worldwide ISV Gaming Engineering group.

Tobias Zirr is a student research assistant at Karlsruhe Institute of Technology (KIT), where he is currently pursuing a master's degree in computer science. A long-time computer graphics enthusiast, he started working in visualization at the age of 16. In 2013, he received a research scholarship for outstanding students at KIT. His current work includes visualization of particle-based simulations as well as novel real-time global illumination and rendering solutions. He is also an ex-demoscener. More of his work can be found at http://alphanew.net.

T - #0755 - 101024 - C380 - 235/191/17 [19] - CB - 9781138484412 - Gloss Lamination